Lecture Notes in Computer Science 1577

Edited by G. Goos, J. Hartmanis and J. van Leeuwen

Springer

Berlin
Heidelberg
New York
Barcelona
Hong Kong
London
Milan
Paris
Singapore
Tokyo

Jean-Pierre Finance (Ed.)

Fundamental Approaches to Software Engineering

Second International Conference, FASE'99
Held as Part of the Joint European Conferences
on Theory and Practice of Software, ETAPS'99
Amsterdam, The Netherlands, March 22-28, 1999
Proceedings

 Springer

Series Editors

Gerhard Goos, Karlsruhe University, Germany
Juris Hartmanis, Cornell University, NY, USA
Jan van Leeuwen, Utrecht University, The Netherlands

Volume Editor

Jean-Pierre Finance
Université Henri Poincaré, Nancy 1
24-30, Rue Lionnois, B.P. 3069
F-54013 Nancy Cedex, France
E-mail: finance@loria.fr

Cataloging-in-Publication data applied for

Die Deutsche Bibliothek - CIP-Einheitsaufnahme

Fundamental approaches to software engineering : second
international conference ; proceedings / FASE '99, held as part of the
Joint European Conferences on Theory and Practice of Software,
ETAPS '99, Amsterdam, The Netherlands, March 22 - 28, 1999.
Jean-Pierre Finance (ed.). - Berlin ; Heidelberg ; New York ;
Barcelona ; Budapest ; Hong Kong ; London ; Milan ; Paris ;
Singapore ; Tokyo : Springer, 1999
   (Lecture notes in computer science ; Vol. 1577)
   ISBN 3-540-65718-5

CR Subject Classification (1998): D.2, D.3, F.3.4

ISSN 0302-9743
ISBN 3-540-65718-5 Springer-Verlag Berlin Heidelberg New York

Typesetting: Camera-ready by author
SPIN 10703090   06/3142 – 5 4 3 2 1 0   Printed on acid-free paper

Foreword

ETAPS'99 is the second instance of the European Joint Conferences on Theory and Practice of Software. ETAPS is an annual federated conference that was established in 1998 by combining a number of existing and new conferences. This year it comprises five conferences (FOSSACS, FASE, ESOP, CC, TACAS), four satellite workshops (CMCS, AS, WAGA, CoFI), seven invited lectures, two invited tutorials, and six contributed tutorials.

The events that comprise ETAPS address various aspects of the system development process, including specification, design, implementation, analysis and improvement. The languages, methodologies and tools which support these activities are all well within its scope. Different blends of theory and practice are represented, with an inclination towards theory with a practical motivation on one hand and soundly-based practice on the other. Many of the issues involved in software design apply to systems in general, including hardware systems, and the emphasis on software is not intended to be exclusive.

ETAPS is a loose confederation in which each event retains its own identity, with a separate programme committee and independent proceedings. Its format is open-ended, allowing it to grow and evolve as time goes by. Contributed talks and system demonstrations are in synchronized parallel sessions, with invited lectures in plenary sessions. Two of the invited lectures are reserved for "unifying" talks on topics of interest to the whole range of ETAPS attendees. As an experiment, ETAPS'99 also includes two invited tutorials on topics of special interest. The aim of cramming all this activity into a single one-week meeting is to create a strong magnet for academic and industrial researchers working on topics within its scope, giving them the opportunity to learn about research in related areas, and thereby to foster new and existing links between work in areas that have hitherto been addressed in separate meetings.

ETAPS'99 has been organized by Jan Bergstra of CWI and the University of Amsterdam together with Frans Snijders of CWI. Overall planning for ETAPS'99 was the responsibility of the ETAPS Steering Committee, whose current membership is:

André Arnold (Bordeaux), Egidio Astesiano (Genoa), Jan Bergstra (Amsterdam), Ed Brinksma (Enschede), Rance Cleaveland (Stony Brook), Pierpaolo Degano (Pisa), Hartmut Ehrig (Berlin), José Fiadeiro (Lisbon), Jean-Pierre Finance (Nancy), Marie-Claude Gaudel (Paris), Susanne Graf (Grenoble), Stefan Jähnichen (Berlin), Paul Klint (Amsterdam), Kai Koskimies (Tampere), Tom Maibaum (London), Ugo Montanari (Pisa), Hanne Riis Nielson (Aarhus), Fernando Orejas (Barcelona), Don Sannella (Edinburgh), Gert Smolka (Saarbrücken), Doaitse Swierstra (Utrecht), Wolfgang Thomas (Aachen), Jerzy Tiuryn (Warsaw), David Watt (Glasgow)

ETAPS'98 has received generous sponsorship from:

- KPN Research
- Philips Research
- The EU programme "Training and Mobility of Researchers"
- CWI
- The University of Amsterdam
- The European Association for Programming Languages and Systems
- The European Association for Theoretical Computer Science

I would like to express my sincere gratitude to all of these people and organizations, the programme committee members of the ETAPS conferences, the organizers of the satellite events, the speakers themselves, and finally Springer-Verlag for agreeing to publish the ETAPS proceedings.

Edinburgh, January 1999   Donald Sannella
                                          ETAPS Steering Committee Chairman

Preface

FASE'99, the Second International Conference on Fundamental Approaches to Software Engineering is one of the major events of ETAPS'99, aiming to bridge the gap between theory and practice.

FASE'99 is intended to provide a forum where fundamental approaches are presented, compared and discussed. Based on the principle that to enhance software quality, the software production process requires rigorous methods, firmly grounded on scientifically justified techniques, the conference addresses basic issues, especially in the integration of so-called formal and informal aspects as well as rigorous experimental studies of effectiveness and applicability of formal methods.

After a rigorous refereeing process, followed by a fifteen-days electronic selection meeting, 13 papers were selected for presentation and are included in this volume. It also includes two invited papers and two demos.

The FASE'99 Program Committee (PC) members are :
- ↦ Jean-Pierre Finance (Chair, Université Henri Poincaré, France)
- ↦ Egidio Astesiano (Universitá di Genova, Italy, former chair)
- ↦ Michel Bidoit (Ecole Normale Supérieure de Cachan, France)
- ↦ Dan Craigen (Canada)
- ↦ Carlo Ghezzi (Politecnico di Milano, Italy)
- ↦ Hartmut Ehrig (Technische Universität Berlin, Germany)
- ↦ René Jacquart (CERT DERI, Toulouse, France)
- ↦ Cliff Jones (UK)
- ↦ Tom Maibaum (Imperial College, London, UK)
- ↦ F. Orejas (Barcelona, Spain)
- ↦ Doug Smith (Kestrel Institute, Palo Alto, California, USA)
- ↦ Axel Van Lamsweerde (Université Catholique de Louvain, Belgium)
- ↦ Martin Wirsing (Universität München, München, Germany)

I thank the PC very much for its efficient cooperation during the refereeing and selection process, and my thanks also go to the other referees involved. The discussions were often lively, sometimes heated, but always fair and constructive.

I would like to express my sincere gratitude to Don Sannella, the coordinator of the ETAPS'99 Steering Committee, who helped us in a firm but always kindly way to respect the calendar and our deadlines.

In all interactions with authors and the publisher, I have been invaluably supported by Nadine Beurné and Jean-Michel Antoine : many thanks to them.

Nancy, January 1999   Jean-Pierre Finance
                                                      FASE'99 PC Chairman

Table of Contents

Demos

Research Issues in the Renovation of Legacy Systems

Arie van Deursen[1], Paul Klint[1,2], and Chris Verhoef[2]

[1] CWI, P.O. Box 94079, 1090 GB Amsterdam, The Netherlands
[2] University of Amsterdam, Programming Research Group
Kruislaan 403, 1098 SJ Amsterdam, The Netherlands

```
arie@cwi.nl,   http://www.cwi.nl/~arie
paulk@cwi.nl,  http://www.cwi.nl/~paulk
x@wins.uva.nl, http://adam.wins.uva.nl/~x
```

Abstract. The goals of this tutorial are to: (*i*) give the reader a quick introduction to the field of software renovation as a whole; (*ii*) show that many techniques from compiler technology and formal methods can be applied; (*iii*) demonstrate that research should be driven by real-life, industrial, case studies; and (*iv*) indicate that many challenging problems are still unsolved. During the presentation of this tutorial, demonstrations will be given of several of the case studies discussed here.

1 Introduction

Software renovation is using tomorrow's technology to bring yesterday's software to the level of today. In this paper, we provide an overview of this research area. We start (in this section) by exploring the need for software renovation. Moreover, we provide definitions of the basic terminology, and pointers to the most important literature. We then proceed to discuss two aspects of software renovation in more detail. In Section 2 we study how we can increase our understanding of a given legacy system, and how we can apply this knowledge for the purpose of migrating the legacy to object technology. Techniques like type inference and concept analysis play an essential role here. In Section 3 we deal with ways of building renovation factories that are capable of restructuring legacy systems of millions of lines of code in an entirely automatic manner. In Section 4 we conclude this tutorial and present some findings based on our experience in software renovation research.

Initially triggered by concerns regarding the renovation of our own software, we have since 1996 closely cooperated with several Dutch banks, and (inter)national software houses and telecommunications firms on the question how to prepare their software system assets for future flexibility. The work presented here is directly driven by their industrial needs.

1.1 Setting the stage

Is there enough legacy software in the world to justify investments in software renovation technology? It turns out that we are living on a software *volcano*: large numbers

Language	Statements/FP
Assembler	320
C	128
Fortran77	107
Cobol85	107
C++	64
Visual Basic	32
Perl	27
Smalltalk	21
SQL	13

(a)

Language	Used in % of total
COBOL	30
Assembler	10
C	10
C++	10
500 other languages	40

(b)

Table 1. (a) Function Points *versus* Lines of Code; (b) Distribution of languages

of new and old software systems control our lives. We admire the sheer bulk of the magnificent volcano, benefit from the fertile grounds surrounding it, yet at the same are suffering from frequent eruptions of lava, steam, and poisonous gas, uncertain what is going on within the volcano, and when the next large eruption will be.

The figures collected by Jones [31] provide insight in the size of the problem. He uses the *function point* (FP) as unit of measurement for software. It abstracts from specific programming languages and specific presentation styles of programs. The correlation between function points with the measurement in lines of code differs per programming language, and is summarized in Table 1(a). Another point of reference is that the size of Windows 95 is equal to 8.5×10^4 FP.

The *total volume of software* is estimated at 7×10^9 FP (7 *Giga-FP*). The distribution of the various programming languages used to implement all these function points is summarized in Table 1(b). Older languages dominate the scene: even today 30% of the 7 Giga-FP is written in COBOL. If we (hypothetically) assume that all software is written in COBOL we get an estimation (via 107 COBOL statements per FP) of 6.4×10^{11} COBOL statements for the total volume of software.

As measure of software quality (or rather, the lack of it), Jones has estimated that on average 5 errors occur per function point. This includes errors in requirements, design, coding, documentation and bad fixes. The result is a frightening figure of 35×10^9 programming errors (35 *Giga-bugs*) waiting for a chance to burst out sooner or later.

Developing better ways of developing *new* software will not solve this problem. When an industry approaches 50 years of age—as is the case with computer science— it takes more workers to perform maintenance than to build new products. Based on current data, Table 2 shows extrapolations for the number of programmers working on new projects, enhancements and repairs. In the current decade, four out of seven programmers are working on enhancement and repair projects. The forecasts predict that by 2020 only one third of all programmers will be working on projects involving the construction of new software.

Therefore, we must conclude that the importance of maintenance and gradual improvement of software is ever increasing and deserves more and more attention both in computer science education and research.

Year	New projects	Enhancements	Repairs	Total
1950	90	3	7	100
1960	8500	500	1000	10000
1970	65000	15000	20000	100000
1980	1200000	600000	200000	2000000
1990	**3000000**	**3000000**	**1000000**	**7000000**
2000	4000000	4500000	1500000	10000000
2010	5000000	7000000	2000000	14000000
2020	7000000	11000000	3000000	21000000

Table 2. Forecasts for numbers of programmers (worldwide) and distribution of their activities

1.2 Goals of this tutorial

The goals of this tutorial are to

- give the reader a quick introduction to the field of software renovation as a whole;
- show that many techniques from compiler technology and formal methods can be applied;
- demonstrate that research should be driven by real-life, industrial, case studies;
- indicate that many challenging problems are still unsolved.

We will present the approach we have taken in Amsterdam to solve a variety of problems in the area of system renovation. In the remainder of this introduction we will now first define what software renovation is (Section 1.3), sketch the technological infrastructure we use (Section 1.4), and give pointers for further reading (Section 1.5).

1.3 What is software renovation?

Chikofsky and Cross [17] have proposed a terminology for the field of re-engineering. The term *reverse engineering* has its origins in hardware technology and denotes the process of obtaining the specification of a complex hardware system. Today the notion of reverse engineering is also applied to software. While *forward engineering* goes from a high-level design to a low-level implementation, *reverse engineering* can be seen as the inverse process. It amounts to analyzing a software system to both identify the system's components and their interactions and to represent the system on a higher level of abstraction.

This higher level of abstraction can be achieved by filtering out irrelevant technical detail, or by combining legacy code elements in novel ways. Alternatively, it can be realized by recognizing instances of a library of higher level *plans* in the program code [44, 55, 23]. This latter technique is in particular applied to the problem of *program comprehension*, which aims at explaining pieces of source code to (maintenance) programmers. Techniques from the debugging and program analysis area, such as *slicing* [53], can be used for this purpose. The problem of explaining the overall *architecture* of a legacy system, indicating all the components and their interrelationships, is referred to as *system understanding*.

Adaptation of a system is the goal of *system renovation*. This can be done in one of two ways. The first is *system restructuring*, which amounts to transforming a system from one representation to another at the same level of abstraction. An essential aspect of restructuring is that the semantic behaviour of the original system and the new one remain the same; no modification of the functionality is involved. The alternative way is to perform the renovation via a reverse engineering step, which is called *re-engineering*: first a specification on a higher level of abstraction is constructed, then a transformation is applied on the design level, followed by a forward engineering step based on the improved design. A *renovation factory* is a collection of software tools that aim at the fully automatic renovation of legacy systems by organizing the renovation process as an assembly line of smaller, consecutive, renovation steps.

Last but not least, one can distinguish *methodology* and *technology* for system renovation. The former deals with process and management aspects of renovation and typically identifies phases like system inventory, strategy determination, impact analysis, detailed planning, and conversion. The latter provides the necessary techniques to implement the steps prescribed by the methodology. Although methodology and technology form a symbiosis, we will here mostly concentrate on the technological aspects of system renovation. In this tutorial, we will deal with system understanding (Section 2) as well as system renovation (Section 3).

1.4   ASF+SDF

The technical infrastructure we will use for renovation is primarily based on the ASF+SDF Meta-Environment. The specification formalism ASF+SDF [3, 29, 19] is a combination of the algebraic specification formalism ASF and the syntax definition formalism SDF. ASF+SDF specifications consist of modules, each module has an SDF-part (defining lexical and context-free syntax) and an ASF-part (defining equations). The SDF part corresponds to signatures in ordinary algebraic specification formalisms. However, syntax is not restricted to plain prefix notation since arbitrary context-free grammars can be defined. The syntax defined in the SDF-part of a module can be used immediately when defining equations, the syntax in equations is thus *user-defined*. The equations in an ASF+SDF specification have the following distinctive features:

- Conditional equations with positive and negative conditions.
- Non left-linear equations.
- List matching.
- Default equations.

It is possible to execute specifications by interpreting the equations as conditional rewrite rules. The semantics of ASF+SDF is based on innermost rewriting. Default equations are tried when all other applicable equations have failed, because either the arguments did not match or one of the conditions failed.

One of the powerful features of the ASF+SDF specification language is list matching. The implementation of list matching may involve backtracking to find a match that satisfies the left-hand side of the rewrite rule as well as all its conditions. There is only backtracking within the scope of a rewrite rule, so if the right-hand side of the rewrite rule is normalized and this normalization fails *no* backtracking is performed to find a new match.

The development of ASF+SDF specifications is supported by an interactive programming environment, the ASF+SDF Meta-Environment [32]. In this environment specifications can be developed and tested. It provides syntax-directed editors, a parser generator, a pretty printer generator, and a rewrite engine. Given this rewrite engine terms can be reduced by interpreting the equations as rewrite rules. An overview of industrial applications of the system can be found in [6, 10].

1.5 Further Reading

General introductions to renovation are books on data reverse engineering [1], the migration of legacy systems [14], the transition to object technology [49], and software maintenance [43]. An annotated bibliography of current renovation literature can be found in [9]. The following workshops and conferences are of interest:

- *Working Conferences on Reverse Engineering* [5].
- *European Conferences on Maintenance and Reengineering* [39].
- *International Workshops on Program Comprehension* [52].
- *International Conferences on Software Maintenance* [2].

Regularly, sessions on maintenance and renovation occur in general software engineering conferences. Another useful source is the *Journal of Software Maintenance*. Other relevant information includes:

- An on-line database of publications on renovation (including abstracts)[1].
- A CASE tool vendor list[2] (useful for tools that can be used in reverse engineering).
- The home page of the SEI Reengineering Centre [3].
- An overview[4] of the Georgia Tech reverse engineering group presenting papers, tools and pointers to other groups.
- A description[5] of the research activities related to program comprehension and reengineering performed at the CARE (Computer-Aided Reengineering) Laboratory in the Computer Science Department of Tennessee Technological University.

2 Object Identification

A key aspect of software renovation is *modernization*: letting a legacy system, developed using the technology of decades ago, benefit from current advancements in programming languages. In this section, we will look at techniques that can help when going from a system developed following the traditional, procedural methodology, towards a system set up according to the principles of object orientation.

---

[1] http://www.informatik.uni-stuttgart.de/ifi/ps/reengineering/

[2] http://www.qucis.queensu.ca/Software-Engineering/vendor.html

[3] http://www.sei.cmu.edu/reengineering/

[4] http://www.cc.gatech.edu/reverse/

[5] http://www.csc.tntech.edu/~linos/

2.1 Challenges

A transition from a traditional COBOL environment to an object oriented platform should enhance a system's correctness, robustness, extendibility, and reusability, the key factors affecting software quality[6]. Moreover, object technology is an enabler for *componentization*: splitting a large application into reusable components, such that they can be accessed independently, and possibly replaced incrementally by commercial off-the-shelf components. Sneed discusses several other, highly practical, reasons for renovation[7] [49]. In short, finding objects[8] in legacy systems is a key research area in software renovation.

The literature reports several systematic approaches to object identification, some of which can be partially automated, such as [42, 36, 18, 40, 26, 54]. These typically involve three steps: (1) identify legacy records as candidate classes; (2) identify legacy procedures or programs as candidate methods; (3) determine the best class for each method via some form of cluster analysis [34].

There are several problems, however, with the application of these approaches to actual systems.

1. Legacy systems greatly vary in source language, application domain, database system used, etc. It is not easy to select the identification approach best-suited for the legacy system at hand.
2. It is impossible to select a *single* object identification approach, since legacy systems typically are heterogeneous, using various languages, database systems, transaction monitors, and so on.
3. There is limited experience with actual object identification projects, making it likely that new migration projects will reveal problems not encountered before.

Thus, when embarking upon an object identification project, one will have to select and compose one's own blend of object identification techniques. Moreover, during the project, new problems will have to be solved.

In this section, we will look at three object identification issues in more detail: support for providing legacy system understanding (Section 2.2), ways to find types in a COBOL system (Section 2.3), and techniques for combining the types found with selected legacy functionality, thus arriving at candidate classes (Section 2.4).

2.2 System Understanding

Finding meaningful objects in a fully automatic way is impossible. The higher the level of automation, the stronger the components found will rely on the actual technical im-

---

[6] Of course, object-technology will create its own renovation problems since features like multiple inheritance, unwieldy class hierarchies, and polymorphism severely complicate program analysis. In this tutorial, we will not further explore this interesting topic.

[7] As an example, an additional reason is that it will become more and more difficult to find mainframe maintenance programmers, since young programmers coming from university are not willing to learn about old technology, but want to work using modern languages instead.

[8] Strictly speaking, we search for *classes*. The term *object identification*, however, is so commonly used that we stick to this terminology.

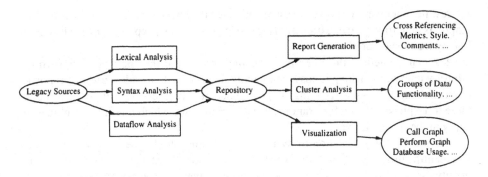

Fig. 1. Repository-based System Understanding

plementation of the legacy code. The purpose, however, is to find object that are close
to the application domain, not to the technical infrastructure.

Therefore, tool support for object identification must not aim at full automation, but
rather at providing interactive *system understanding*, i.e., at assisting the re-engineer
in understanding what components (modules, databases, screens, copybooks, ...) the
system consists of, and how these are related to each other.

Figure 1 shows the extractor–query–viewer approach used in most reverse engineering tool sets [37, 16, 20]. It can be used to extract all sorts of facts from the legacy
sources into a database. This database, in turn, can be queried, and relations of interest
can be visualized.

In the extractor phase, syntactic analysis will help to unravel the structure of the
legacy code. This requires the availability of a parser (or grammar) for the legacy language, which is not always the case. Issues pertaining to parser development are discussed in more detail in Section 3. If no parser is available, and if the required fact
extraction is sufficiently simple, lexical analysis methods may be used: these are less
accurate, but simpler, faster to develop and to run, and tolerant with respect to unknown
language constructs or errors in the source code [38, 20].

In the querying phase, operations on the repository include relational queries, restriction of relations to names matching regular expressions, taking transitive closures
of, for example call relations, lifting call relations from procedures to files, etc. A crucial
aspect of querying is *filtering*: restricting the relations to those items that are relevant
for the understanding task at hand, Such a task could be, e.g., finding variables and
programs representing *business* entities and rules. Several heuristics for filtering in the
COBOL domain, for example based on call graph metrics or the database usage, are
discussed in [20].

In the viewing phase, the derived relations can be shown to the re-engineer in various forms. One way is to use metrics for this purpose, pointing the re-engineer to,
for example, programs with a complexity measure higher than average. An alternative
technique is the use of *cluster analysis* in which a numeric distance between items is
used for the purpose of grouping them together. Of particular importance is system
visualization. Most common in the area of system understanding is the use of graph
visualization, to display, for example, call graphs, database usage, perform graphs, etc.

Interesting other ways of program visualization are discussed by Eick [24], who, for example, is able to visualize extremely large code portfolios by representing each source line by just one colored pixel.

The main benefit of this three-phase tooling approach is that the repository permits arbitrary querying, making it possible to apply the tool set to a wide variety of renovation problems. Generally speaking, a system understanding session will iterate through these three phases, using, for example, visualization to see which filtering techniques to apply in the next iteration.

Obviously, the application of system understanding tools goes beyond mere object identification: other possibilities include generation of (interactive) documentation, quality assessment, and introducing novice programmers to a legacy application.

2.3   Type Inference

Many object identification methods work by grouping procedures based on the type of the arguments they process [34]. Unfortunately, COBOL is an untyped language, blocking this route for object identification purposes. To remedy this problem, we propose to infer types for COBOL variables based on their actual usage [22]

At first sight COBOL may *appear* to be a typed language. Every variable occurring in the statements of the procedure division, must be declared in the data division first. A typical declaration may look as follows:

```
01 TAB100.
   05 TAB100-POS    PIC  X(01) OCCURS 40.
   05 TAB100-FILLED PIC S9(03) VALUE 0.
```

Here, three variables are declared. The first is TAB100, which is the name of a record consisting of two fields: TAB100-POS, which is a single character byte (picture "X") occurring 40 times, i.e., an array of length 40; and TAB100-FILLED, which is an integer (picture "9") comprising three bytes initialized with value zero.

Unfortunately, the variable declarations in the data division suffer from a number of problems, making them unsuitable to fulfill the role of types. First of all, since it is not possible to separate type definitions from variable declarations, when two variables for the same record structure are needed, the full record construction needs to be repeated. This violates the principle that the type hides the actual representation chosen.

Besides that, the absence of type definitions makes it difficult to group variables that represent the same kind of entities. Although it might well be possible that such variables have the same byte representation, the converse does not hold: One cannot conclude that whenever two variables share the same byte representation, they must represent the same kind of entity.

In addition to these important problems pertaining to type definitions, COBOL only has limited means to accurately indicate the allowed set of values for a variable (i.e., there are no ranges or enumeration types). Moreover, in COBOL, sections or paragraphs that are used as procedures are type-less, and have no explicit parameter declarations.

To solve these problems, we have proposed the use of *type inference* to find types for COBOL variables based on their actual *usage* [22]. We start with the situation that every variable is of a unique primitive type. We then generate equivalences between these types based on their usage: if variables are compared using some relational operator, we infer that they must belong to the same type; and if an expression is assigned to a variable, the type of the expression must be a subtype of that of the expression.

Primitive Types We distinguish three primitive types: (1) elementary types such as numeric values or strings; (2) arrays; and (3) records. Initially every declared variable gets a unique primitive type. Types are made unique by encoding a label into them: since variable occurrences must have unique names in a COBOL program (module), the variable names can be used for this. We qualify variable names with program names to obtain uniqueness at the system level. We use T_A to denote the primitive type of variable A.

Type Relations By looking at the *expressions* occurring in statements, an *equivalence relation* between primitive types can be inferred. The following cases are distinguished:

- For relational expressions such as $v = u$ or $v \leq u$, an equivalence between T_v and T_u is inferred.
- For arithmetic expression such as $v + u$ or $v * u$, an equivalence between T_u and T_v is inferred.
- For two different array accesses $a[v]$ and $a[u]$ an equivalence between T_v and T_u is inferred.
- From an assignment $v := u$ we infer that T_u is a *subtype* of T_v,

By *type*, we will generally mean an *equivalence class of primitive types*. Subtyping is important to avoid the problem of *pollution*, the derivation of counter-intuitive equivalences due to commutativity and transitivity of the equivalence relation [22].

System-Level Analysis In addition to inferring type relations within individual programs, we infer type relations at the system-wide level. Such relations ensure that if a variable is declared in a copybook (include file), its type is the same in all the different programs that copybook is included in. Furthermore, we infer that the types of the actual parameters of a program call at the module level (listed in the USING clause) are subtypes of the formal parameters (listed in the linkage section), and that variables read from or written to the same databases have equivalent types.

Related Work Type inference for COBOL is related to earlier work on type inference for C [41] and on various approaches for detecting and correcting year 2000 problems [28]. An approach for dealing with the year 2000 problem based on type theory is presented by [25]. A detailed overview of related work is given in [22].

Clearly, type inference for COBOL has applications beyond mere object identification: in [22] we explain how types can also be used to replace literal values by symbolic constants, year 2000 and Euro conversions, language migrations, and maintenance monitoring.

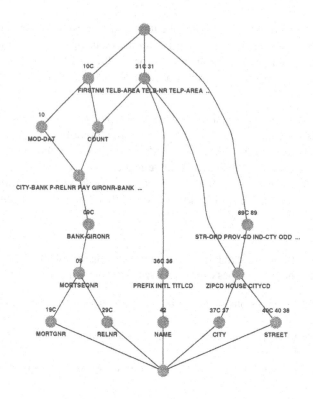

Fig. 2. Concept lattice combining data fields with programs

2.4 Concept Analysis

For many business applications written in COBOL, the data stored and processed represent the core of the system. For that reason, the data records used in COBOL programs are the starting point for many object identification approaches (such as [18, 40, 26]). These records are then in turn combined with procedures or programs, thus arriving at candidate classes. A common way of finding the desired combinations is to use *cluster analysis* [34].

Recently, the use of mathematical *concept analysis* has been proposed as an alternative to the use of cluster analysis for the purpose of legacy code analysis [35, 48, 50, 51]. As has been argued in [21], concept analysis avoids some of the problems encountered when using cluster analysis for the purpose of object identification.

Concept analysis starts with a table indicating the *features* of a given set of *items*. It then builds up so-called *concepts* which are maximal sets of items sharing certain features. All possible concepts can be grouped into a single lattice, the so-called *concept lattice*. The smallest concepts consist of few items having potentially many different features, the largest concepts consist of many different items that have only few features in common.

An example concept lattice is shown in Figure 2. This lattice was derived automatically from a 100,000 LOC COBOL case study. The *items* in this lattice are *fields* of records that are read from or written to file. They are shown as names below each concept in Figure 2. The *features* are based on the use of fields in *programs*: If a field (or in fact, the *type* inferred for that field) is used in a given program, this program becomes a feature of that field. The programs are written above each concept in Figure 2. Each concept in that figure corresponds to a combination of fields and the programs using them, as occurring in the legacy system. Each concept is a candidate class. Connections between classes correspond to aggregation, association, or inheritance.

To see how the lattice of Figure 2 can help to find objects, let us browse through some of the concepts. The row just above the bottom element consists of five separate concepts, each containing a single field. As an example, the leftmost concept deals with *mortgage numbers* stored in the field MORTGNR. With it is associated program 19C, which according to the comment lines at the beginning of this program performs certain checks on the validity of mortgage numbers. This program *only* uses the field MORTGNR, and no other ones. As another example, the concept STREET (at the bottom right) has three different programs directly associated with it. Of these, 40 and 40C compute a certain standardized extract from a street, while program 38 takes care of standardizing street names.

If we move up in the lattice, the concepts become larger, i.e., contain more items. The leftmost concept at the second row contains *three* different fields: the *mortgage sequence number* MORTSEQNR written directly at the node, as well as the two fields from the lower concepts connected to it, MORTGNR and RELNR. Program 09 uses all three fields to search for full mortgage and relation records.

Another concept of interest is the last one of the second row. It represents the combination of the fields ZIPCD (zip code), HOUSE (house number), and CITYCD (city code), together with STREET and CITY. This combination of five is a separate concept, because it actually occurs in four different programs (89C, 89, 31C, 31). However, there are no programs that *only* use these variables, and hence this concept has no program associated with it. It corresponds to a common superclass for both the 89C, 89 and the 31, 31C concepts.

In short, the lattice provides insight into the organization of the legacy system, and gives suggestions for grouping programs and fields into classes. The human re-engineer can use this information to select initial candidate classes based on the data and functionality available in the legacy.

The crucial step with both cluster and concept analysis is to apply the correct filtering criteria, in order to reduce the overwhelming number of variables, sections, programs, databases, and so on, to the relevant ones. Such selection criteria may differ from system to system, and can only be found by trying several alternatives on the system being investigated—this is exactly where the system understanding tool set discussed in Section 2.2 comes in. The selection criteria used to arrive at Figure 2 are based on persistent data and metrics derived from the call relation, as discussed in [20, 21].

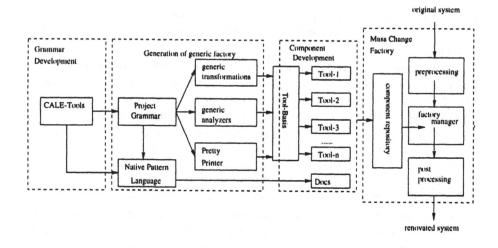

Fig. 3. Four phases in the creation and use of software renovation factories

3 Renovation Factories

As soon as the architecture of a legacy system has been recovered and the overall understanding of the system has been increased using the techniques described in the previous sections, we are in a position to determine what should be *done* with it. Should it be
abandoned or renovated? In reality, there is a close interplay between analysis and renovation since the analysis of well-structured code will yield more precise analysis results
than the analysis of badly structured code. It is not uncommon that analysis/renovation
is an iterative process. For simplicity we treat them in this section as sequential steps
and concentrate on a factory-like approach to renovation (Section 3.1). Next, we discuss
two examples (Section 3.2).

Unlike system understanding, which is inherently interactive, here the ultimate goal
is a completely automated renovation factory, which can process millions of lines of
code without human interaction.

3.1 Creation and use of renovation factories

In practice, there are many needs for program transformations and program restructuring like simple global changes in calling conventions, migrations to new language
dialects, goto elimination, and control flow restructuring. Since these transformations
will affect millions of lines of code, a factory-like approach, with minimal human in-
tervention, is desired to achieve a cost-effective, high-quality, solution. Recall from
Section 1.3, that we define a renovation factory as a collection of software tools that
aim at the fully automatic renovation of legacy systems by organizing the renovation
process as an assembly line of smaller, consecutive, renovation steps.

Legacy systems show a lot of variety regarding their overall architecture, programming languages used, database organization, error handling, calling conventions, and the like. Experience shows that each renovation project is unique and requires an extensively tailored approach. The generation and customization of renovation factories is therefore a major issue. In order to promote flexibility and reusability, renovation factories should be built-up from from individual tools that are as small and general as possible. Our approach is illustrated in Figure 3 and consists of four phases:

- Grammar development: determine the project grammar.
- Factory generation: generate a generic framework for the renovation factory. This amounts to automatically deriving generic tools (parser, pretty printer, frameworks for analysis and transformation) from the project grammar.
- Component development: develop dedicated tools for the factory that are specific for this project.
- Factory production environment: configure and run the factory.

We will now discuss these phases in turn.

Grammar development Grammars form the basis for our factory generation approach. However, in practice it is completely non-trivial to obtain and manage such grammars. The grammar may be included in an international standard, it may be contained in a manual for a proprietary language, or it may be embedded in the source code of existing tools such as compilers or pretty printers [46]. Another problem is that these grammars tend to be huge (several thousands of grammars rules) since they cover various language dialects as well as various local language extensions. From a grammar maintenance perspective, standard LR parsing techniques become unsuitable here. since they tend to generate too many shift/reduce conflicts after each modification to the grammar. We completely depend on the Generalized LR parsing method provided by the ASF+SDF Meta-Environment which is capable of handling arbitrary context-free grammars. It is a research issue how to obtain grammars for languages in a cost-effective manner. We have labeled this activity *Computer Aided Language Engineering* (CALE) and have a collection of tools for grammar extraction and manipulation.

Factory Generation Once the project grammar has been determined, we can focus on the automatic generation of components that are language parameterized such as frameworks for generic analysis, transformation, and pretty printing [13]. Since we are working in a first-order setting, we cannot use higher-order analysis and transformation functions. Instead, we generate from the grammar specific analysis and transformation functions which perform a default operation for each language construct. This default behaviour can be overruled by writing conditional equations that define the desired behaviour for specific language constructs.

This immediately raises the question, who should write these equations: a formal specification expert or a programmer knowledgeable in the legacy languages of the project? It is clearly necessary to be able to describe certain patterns in the code to facilitate analysis and automatic change. The approach we take is to automatically generate a *pattern language* [47] from the project grammar that resembles the language defined by the project grammar as much as possible. Thanks to the tight integration between abstract and concrete syntax in ASF+SDF, we can express patterns over the abstract syntax tree using the concrete syntax of the language being reengineered. In this way, a programmer knowledgeable in that language can specify search and replacement patterns in conditional equations without needing to know all the formal machinery that is used in the factory as a whole.

It is important to have complete control over what steps are taken during a (automated) renovation process and over how their intermediate results are handled. We automatically generate support for a form of "scaffolding" which is similar to the inclusion of pseudo-code or assertions in comments during traditional code development. In our case, we see a scaffolding as an extension to the project grammar that allows the representation of intermediate results of analysis or transformation as annotations of the program code.

Component prototyping As already mentioned, renovation factories should be built-up from individual tools that are as small and general as possible. This results not only in better flexibility and reuse, but also in increased control over and understanding of each tool. Apart from general tools for bringing program parts in certain standard forms and for performing program simplifications, we have developed tools for upgrading embedded SQL, for normalizing the control flow of embedded CICS, and for step by step restructuring of COBOL code [11, 45].

Factory Production Environment The final phase in our approach is actually building the renovation factory. The components that have been developed and prototyped need to be put into operation in an efficient production environment.

Given the size of legacy systems, issues like scalability and multi-processor execution of the factory are now also coming into play. Important supporting technologies are compilers that turn prototype specifications into efficient stand-alone C programs [7] and middleware that is optimized for the connection of language-oriented tools [4]. References [8, 33, 10, 15] give overall pictures and further discussions of renovation factories.

3.2 Two examples

We will now discuss two examples. The first example concerns the grammar extraction and factory generation for a proprietary language for switching systems. The second example illustrates the use of a COBOL factory for extracting business logic from programs by separating computation from coordination.

Grammar development for a switching system's language Most software and hardware for switching systems is proprietary. This includes central processing units, compilers and operating systems that have been developed in-house. For instance, Lucent Technologies, uses UNIX and C targeted towards their own proprietary processor. They have to maintain their own UNIX and their own C compiler. The same phenomenon occurs at Ericsson: they have developed their own central processor and their own operating systems, languages and compilers. The difference between the two situations is that Ericsson uses tools that are *not* widely used for other processors. As a result, software renovation tools are not available in large amounts for their software. The Ericsson case is therefore an ideal test case for our approach.

As described in the previous section, the first step in generating a renovation factory is the development of a relevant project grammar. In this case, it concerns the proprietary language SSL (Switching System Language). A program in SSL is in fact a collection of programs in 20 different languages that are combined into a single file.

The only complete and reliable source for the SSL grammar is the source code of the SSL compiler. Several steps are needed to extract this grammar. First, the compiler source code is reverse engineered so that the grammar part is identified. Then the essential grammar information is extracted from this part of the compiler. This resulted in the extraction of more than 3000 lexical and context-free production rules in Backus-Naur Form (BNF). Unfortunately, this grammar is not yet usable for reengineering since it is too heavily oriented towards compilation. For instance, the compilation-oriented grammar removes comments, whereas during renovation, the comments should be seen as part of the source since they have to be retained in the final result of the renovation.

As a preparatory step for the reengineering of this intermediate SSL grammar, we have generated a renovation factory for the language BNF itself and have added a number of components that are useful for the reengineering of grammars, such as a transformation of BNF into SDF (the syntax definition language of the ASF+SDF Meta-Environment). This BNF-factory has been used to retarget the extracted SSL grammars.

Using the BNF-factory, we could transform the grammar of one of the sublanguages of SSL in 7 minutes processing time (on a standard workstation) from its initial BNF version into an SDF version that is usable for renovation purposes. Next, we were able to parse about 1 MLOC in this sublanguage in about 70 minutes processing time. Finally, a complete renovation factory for this sublanguage could be generated. When completed with the desired renovation components, it can be used for the factory-like renovation of programs in this particular SSL subset.

Currently, the complete SSL grammar is being assembled by combining the 20 embedded subgrammars. As a next step, we will generate a complete SSL-factory. When that SSL-factory is ready, we have in fact generated from the compiler source code a production line for the rapid development of component-based tools that facilitate the automated solution of software reengineering problems.

Separating coordination and computation in COBOL A typical renovation problem is to migrate transaction systems from a mainframe to a networked PC environment. Such systems are strongly tied to mainframes by the use of embedded languages like CICS that deal with transaction monitors and the coordination of data. In order to migrate to a client/server architecture, it is therefore necessary to remove this embedded CICS code. Once that is done, the code needs to be made more maintainable by removing all traces of the platform migration from the source code.

In the example that we will now discuss, a German company (SES GmbH) had already eliminated some dangerous CICS code, and we have constructed a migration tool to separate coordination from computation so that all CICS code could be removed. One of the main problems was to eliminate jump instructions from the code. Figure 4

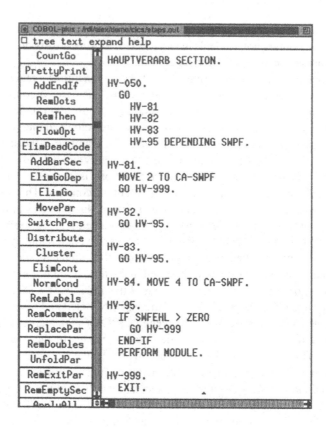

Fig. 4. Original COBOL code with GO statements

shows a strongly simplified version of the "spaghetti" code of the original program. The code fragment is representative of the overall quality of the code that can be found on mainframes. The first GO ... DEPENDING ... is actually a case statement, and contains four cases that are all GOs. So in fact in this small fragment we have 8 jump instructions.

Using a restructuring method based on a systolic algorithm we can remove the GOs in about 25 steps in such a way that the coordination and computation are separated, and the logic of the program becomes more clear. In Figure 5 the final output is shown. As can be seen, the code has been changed dramatically. Superfluous code is gone and coordination is separated from computation.

Paragraph HV-050 provides the coordination part of the program and resembles a main program in C. The EVALUATE ... END-EVALUATE statement is the result of migrating the original GO ... DEPENDING ... statement; the original four cases could be collapsed into two cases. In the HAUPTVERARB-SUBROUTINES section, we can see that two computations are present. They are only reachable via the coordination part, since the STOP RUN blocks other access. This is comparable to a preamble in say Pascal where procedures are declared.

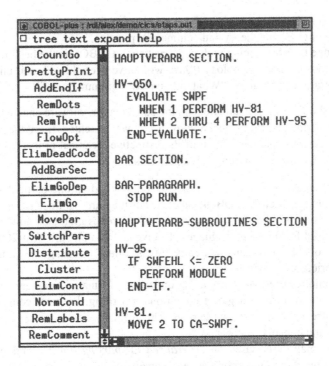

Fig. 5. Final COBOL code with all GO's removed

An original program and all intermediate steps that are carried out to remove the jump instructions and to separate computations from coordination are available on Internet.[9] We discuss this kind of restructuring in more detail in [45].

4 Conclusions

In this tutorial, we have covered a variety of issues in the area of system renovation. Starting with a discussion on the economic need for maintenance and renovation, we have presented our approaches to problems like object identification, system understanding, grammar reengineering, and the creation of renovation factories.

Several observations can be made about the field of software renovation as a whole. A most challenging aspect of software renovation research is the number of different areas in which proficiency is required. These include:

- Historic programming languages and systems, such as COBOL and the mainframe environment.
- Target new programming language technologies, such as CORBA or Java, and the current and future market standards.

---

[9] An on-line demonstration of all steps involved is available at `http://adam.wins.uva.nl/~x/systolic/systolic.html`.

- Migration technology, such as the ASF+SDF Meta-Environment.
- Software engineering theory and commercial practice.
- Knowledge transfer, coping with conservatism ("COBOL is the best"), unrealistic expectations of new technology ("Java will solve everything"), and unfamiliarity with migration technology ("What did you say a grammar was?").

Clearly, this should also have an effect on the curricula for software engineering.

Concerning the migration technology used, we benefited from the use of the ASF+SDF Meta-Environment. Three of its distinctive technical properties turned out to be of great significance for renovation purposes:

- The techniques used are *generic*: they do not depend on one particular programming language, such as COBOL or PL/I, but they are parameterized with a language definition. As a result, major parts of our renovation techniques can be directly reused for different languages. To give an example, the Year 2000 problem resides probably in systems written in 500 "standard" languages [31] plus another 200 proprietary languages [30].
- The techniques used are *formal*: the underlying formal notions are many-sorted signatures and positive/negative conditional rewriting. Program conversions are, for instance, expressed as rewrite rules. This formalization increases the quality of analyses and conversions [27].
- Syntactic analysis is based on *generalized LR parsing* (GLR). This enables the construction of modular grammars and parsers for languages with large grammars and many dialects (like COBOL) [12]. More traditional parsing techniques (e.g., LALR(1) as used in parser generators like Yacc and Bison) lead to increased maintenance problems for large grammars: the time needed to add language constructs needed for new dialects becomes prohibitive.

The driving force behind software renovation is the strong need to maintain and renovate parts of the software volcano. This implies that software renovation research has to be carried out in close cooperation with industrial partners that are in the possession of problems that *have* to be solved. Fortunately, we can be confident that progress in areas like compiler and programming language technology and formal methods, will continue to help to offer the right tools at the right time. At the same time, the analysis of legacy systems provides the empirical foundation for programming language research. It uncovers the effects, both positive and negative, of years of intensive use of a programming language in the real world.

As we have tried to show here, software renovation research also reveals new challenging problems. Techniques for analysis or code generation that were satisfactory from the perspective of a traditional compiler may no longer be satisfactory from the perspective of interactive program understanding. The gigantic scale of renovation projects presents implementation problems (and opportunities) that may inspire research for many years to come.

Finally, the largest challenge we see is to try to bridge the gap between research aimed at building *new* software and research aimed at maintaining or renovating old software. We strongly believe that an integrated approach to both is the best way to proceed. This implies introducing maintenance and renovation considerations much earlier in the software construction process than is usual today. This also implies designing new languages and programming environments that are more amenable to maintenance and renovation.

Acknowledgments

Although the three of us wrote this text, it represents the work of many colleagues with whom we have cooperated or are cooperating. We thank them all for their direct or indirect contributions to the current paper. Tobias Kuipers commented on initial drafts of this tutorial.

References

1. P.H. Aiken. *Data Reverse Engineering*. McGraw-Hill, 1996.
2. K. Bennett and T.M. Khoshgoftaar, editors. *Proceedings of the International Conference on Software Maintenance*. IEEE Computer Society, November 1998.
3. J.A. Bergstra, J. Heering, and P. Klint, editors. *Algebraic Specification*. ACM Press Frontier Series. The ACM Press in co-operation with Addison-Wesley, 1989.
4. J.A. Bergstra and P. Klint. The discrete time TOOLBUS—a software coordination architecture. *Science of Computer Programming*, 31:205–229, 1998.
5. M.H. Blaha, A. Quilici, and C. Verhoef, editors. *Proceedings of the Fifth Working Conference on Reverse Engineering*. IEEE Computer Society, October 1998.
6. M. G. J. van den Brand, A. van Deursen, P. Klint, S. Klusener, and E. van der Meulen. Industrial applications of ASF+SDF. In M. Wirsing and M. Nivat, editors, *Algebraic Methodology and Software Technology (AMAST '96)*, volume 1101 of *Lecture Notes in Computer Science*, pages 9–18. Springer-Verlag, 1996.
7. M.G.J. van den Brand, P. Klint, and P. Olivier. Compilation and memory management for ASF+SDF. In *Proceedings of the 8th International Conference on Compiler Construction, CC'99*, LNCS. Springer-Verlag, 1999. To appear.
8. M.G.J. van den Brand, P. Klint, and C. Verhoef. Core technologies for system renovation. In K.G. Jeffery, J. Král, and M. Bartošek, editors, *SOFSEM'96: Theory and Practice of Informatics*, volume 1175 of *LNCS*, pages 235–255. Springer-Verlag, 1996.
9. M.G.J. van den Brand, P. Klint, and C. Verhoef. Reverse engineering and system renovation – an annotated bibliography. *ACM Software Engineering Notes*, 22(1):57–68, 1997.
10. M.G.J. van den Brand, P. Klint, and C. Verhoef. Term rewriting for sale. In C. Kirchner and H. Kirchner, editors, *Second International Workshop on Rewriting Logic and its Applications*, Electronic Notes in Theoretical Computer Science. Springer-Verlag, 1998.
11. M.G.J. van den Brand, M.P.A. Sellink, and C. Verhoef. Control flow normalization for COBOL/CICS legacy systems. In P. Nesi and F. Lehner, editors, *Proc. 2nd Euromicro Conf. on Maintenance and Reengineering*, pages 11–19. IEEE Computer Society, 1998.
12. M.G.J. van den Brand, M.P.A. Sellink, and C. Verhoef. Current parsing techniques in software renovation considered harmful. In S. Tilley and G. Visaggio, editors, *Proc. Sixth International Workshop on Program Comprehension*, pages 108–117. IEEE Computer Society, 1998.
13. M.G.J. van den Brand and E. Visser. Generation of formatters for context-free languages. *ACM Transactions on Software Engineering and Methodology*, 5:1–41, 1996.
14. M. L. Brodie and M. Stonebraker. *Migrating Legacy Systems: Gateways, interfaces and the incremental approach*. Morgan Kaufman Publishers, 1995.

15. J. Brunekreef and B. Diertens. Towards a user-controlled software renovation factory. In P. Nesi and C. Verhoef, editors, *Proc. Third European Conference on Software Maintenance and Reengineering.* IEEE Computer Society, 1999. To Appear.

16. Y.-F. Chen, G. S. Fowler, E. Koutsofios, and R. S. Wallach. Ciao: A graphical navigator for software and document repositories. In G. Caldiera and K. Bennett, editors, *Int. Conf. on Software Maintenance; ICSM 95*, pages 66–75. IEEE Computer Society, 1995.

17. E.J. Chikofsky and J.H. Cross. Reverse engineering and design recovery: A taxonomy. *IEEE Software*, 7(1):13–17, 1990.

18. A. Cimitile, A. De Lucia, G. A. Di Lucca, and A. R. Fasolino. Identifying objects in legacy systems using design metrics. *Journal of Systems and Software*, 1998. To appear.

19. A. van Deursen, J. Heering, and P. Klint, editors. *Language Prototyping: An Algebraic Specification Approach*, volume 5 of *AMAST Series in Computing*. World Scientific Publishing Co., 1996.

20. A. van Deursen and T. Kuipers. Rapid system understanding: Two COBOL case studies. In S. Tilley and G. Visaggio, editors, *Sixth International Workshop on Program Comprehension; IWPC'98*, pages 90–98. IEEE Computer Society, 1998.

21. A. van Deursen and T. Kuipers. Finding objects using cluster and concept analysis. In *21st International Conference on Software Engineering, ICSE-21*. ACM, 1999. To appear.

22. A. van Deursen and L. Moonen. Type inference for COBOL systems. In I. Baxter, A. Quilici, and C. Verhoef, editors, *Proc. 5th Working Conf. on Reverse Engineering*, pages 220–230. IEEE Computer Society, 1998.

23. A. van Deursen, S. Woods, and A. Quilici. Program plan recognition for year 2000 tools. In *Proceedings 4th Working Conference on Reverse Engineering; WCRE'97*, pages 124–133. IEEE Computer Society, 1997.

24. S. G. Eick. A visualization tool for Y2K. *IEEE Computer*, 31(10):63–69, 1998.

25. P. H. Eidorff, F. Henglein, C. Mossin, H. Niss, M. H. Sorensen, and M. Tofte. Anno Domini: From type theory to Year 2000 conversion tool. In *26th Annual Symposium on Principles of Programming Languages, POPL'99*. ACM, 1999. To appear.

26. H. Fergen, P. Reichelt, and K. P. Schmidt. Bringing objects into COBOL: MOORE - a tool for migration from COBOL85 to object-oriented COBOL. In *Proc. Conf. on Technology of Object-Oriented Languages and Systems (TOOLS 14)*, pages 435–448. Prentice-Hall, 1994.

27. W.J. Fokkink and C. Verhoef. Conservative extension in positive/negative conditional term rewriting with applications to software renovation factories. In *Fundamental Approaches to Software Engineering*, LNCS, 1999. To Appear.

28. J. Hart and A. Pizzarello. A scaleable, automated process for year 2000 system correction. In *Proceedings of the 18th International Conference on Software Engineering ICSE-18*, pages 475–484. ACM, 1996.

29. J. Heering, P.R.H. Hendriks, P. Klint, and J. Rekers. The syntax definition formalism SDF — Reference manual. *SIGPLAN Notices*, 24(11):43–75, 1989.

30. C. Jones. *Estimating Software Costs*. McGraw-Hill, 1998.

31. Capers Jones. *The Year 2000 Software Problem – Quantifying the Costs and Assessing the Consequences*. Addison-Wesley, 1998.

32. P. Klint. A meta-environment for generating programming environments. *ACM Transactions on Software Engineering and Methodology*, 2:176–201, 1993.

33. P. Klint and C. Verhoef. Evolutionary software engineering: A component-based approach. In R.N. Horspool, editor, *IFIP WG 2.4 Working Conference: Systems Implementation 2000: Languages, Methods and Tools*, pages 1–18. Chapman & Hall, 1998.

34. A. Lakhotia. A unified framework for expressing software subsystem classification techniques. *Journal of Systems and Software*, pages 211–231, March 1997.

35. C. Lindig and G. Snelting. Assessing modular structure of legacy code based on mathematical concept analysis. In *19th International Conference on Software Engineering, ICSE-19*, pages 349–359. ACM, 1997.

36. S. S. Liu and N. Wilde. Identifying objects in a conventional procedural language: An example of data design recovery. In *International Conference on Software Maintenance; ICSM'90*, pages 266–271. IEEE Computer Society, 1990.

37. H. A. Müller, M. A. Orgun, S. R. Tilley, and J. S. Uhl. A reverse engineering approach to subsystem structure identification. *Journal of Software Maintenance*, 5(4):181–204, 1993.

38. G. C. Murphy and D. Notkin. Lightweight lexical source model extraction. *ACM Transactions on Software Engineering Methodology*, 5(3):262–292, 1996.

39. P. Nesi and C. Verhoef, editors. *Proceedings of the Third European Conference on Software Maintenance and Reengineering*. IEEE Computer Society, March 1999.

40. P. Newcomb and G. Kottik. Reengineering procedural into object-oriented systems. In *Second Working Conference on Reverse Engineering; WCRE'95*, pages 237–249. IEEE Computer Society, 1995.

41. R. O'Callahan and D. Jackson. Lackwit: A program understanding tool based on type inference. In *19th International Conference on Software Engeneering; ICSE-19*. ACM, 1997.

42. C. L. Ong and W. T. Tsai. Class and object extraction from imperative code. *Journal of Object-Oriented Programming*, pages 58–68, March–April 1993.

43. T. M. Pigoski. *Practical Software Maintenance – Best Practices for Managing Your Software Investment*. John Wiley and Sons, 1997.

44. C. Rich and R. Waters. *The Programmer's Apprentice*. Frontier Series. ACM Press, Addison-Wesley, 1990.

45. M.P.A. Sellink, H.M. Sneed, and C. Verhoef. Restructuring of COBOL/CICS legacy systems. In P. Nesi and C. Verhoef, editors, *Proc. Third European Confrence on Software Maintenance and Reengineering*. IEEE Computer Society, 1999. To appear.

46. M.P.A. Sellink and C. Verhoef. Development, assessment, and reengineering of language descriptions. In *Proceedings of the 13th International Automated Software Engineering Conference*, pages 314–317. IEEE Computer Society, 1998.

47. M.P.A. Sellink and C. Verhoef. Native patterns. In M. Blaha, A. Quilici, and C. Verhoef, editors, *Proceedings of the 5th Working Conference on Reverse Engineering*, pages 89–103. IEEE Computer Scociety, 1998.

48. M. Siff and T. Reps. Identifying modules via concept analysis. In *International Conference on Software Maintenance, ICSM97*. IEEE Computer Society, 1997.

49. H.M. Sneed. *Objectorientierte Softwaremigration*. Addison-Wesley, 1998. In German.

50. G. Snelting. Concept analysis — a new framework for program understanding. In *Proceedings of the ACM SIGPLAN/SIGSOFT Workshop on Program Analysis for Software Tools and Engineering (PASTE'98)*, 1998. SIGPLAN Notices 33(7).

51. G. Snelting and F. Tip. Reengineering class hierarchies using concept analysis. In *Foundations of Software Engineering, FSE-6*, pages 99–110. ACM, 1998. SIGSOFT Software Engineering Notes 23(6).

52. S. Tilley and G. Visaggio, editors. *Proceedings of the Sixth International Workshop on Program Comprehension*. IEEE Computer Society, June 1998.

53. F. Tip. A survey of program slicing techniques. *Journal of Programming Languages*, 3:121–189, 1995.

54. T. Wiggerts, H. Bosma, and E. Fielt. Scenarios for the identification of objects in legacy systems. In I.D. Baxter, A. Quilici, and C. Verhoef, editors, *4th Working Conference on Reverse Engineering*, pages 24–32. IEEE Computer Society, 1997.

55. S. Woods, A. Quilici, and Q. Yang. *Constraint-based Design Recovery for Software Reengineering: Theory and Experiments*. Kluwer Academic Publishers, 1997.

Continuous Engineering of Information and Communication Infrastructures Extended Abstract

Herbert Weber

Technische Universität Berlin
Fraunhofer-Institut für Software- und Systemtechnik Berlin

Abstract. Information and Communication Infrastructures (ICIs) are business, mission, project or product critical, long living and usually highly heterogeneous hardware/software systems. They represent a substantial investment and need to be adapted continuously to changing requirements for the protection of that investment. Their users critically depend on their permanent availability.

Continuous Engineering (CE) ensures an organized evolution of ICIs by providing guidelines, methods and tools for their construction and continuous change.

1 New Challenges

Radical changes are taking place throughout the economy. Efforts aimed at gaining a competitive edge in terms of price and quality are seldom limited to regional markets. Today's entrepreneurs face competition on a global scale, and this global change has put them under increasing pressure to review traditional products and organizational and work processes — including the underlying information technology.

Information has long since become a production factor. A smooth and steady flow of information, both within and between organisations, is now a strategic imperative. A competitive advantage will thus only be enjoyed by those who exploit to the full the potential benefits of modern information and communication technology.

Information highways, broadband communication, multimedia, video conferences, teleworking and telecooperation — these are just a few of the catchwords used to denote the possibilities seen in the years ahead. This development heralds the end of an era in which centralized company departments were made responsible to provide for the information technology requirements of all users.

The 1980s were characterized by dramatic advances in hardware development. Large mainframes were complemented by midrange computers which were in turn complemented by powerful personal computers and workstations.

Networked workstations have already brought about a decentralization of computer services in many corporations. These networks encourage the integration of independent data processing capabilities and isolated subsystems into larger configurations.

A further change in the structure of information technology has been taken place since the beginning of the 1990's. Individual information systems were being inter-connected to form coherent structures.

Such integrations lead to new configurations which — analogous to other basic structural forms — are referred to as Information and Communication Infrastructures.

Transforming independent information systems into integrated structures also changes their basic characteristics. Whereas previously such systems were developed to satisfy immediate needs, the principle aim pursued in the development of Information and Communication Infrastructures is to ensure that the systems' useful life can be prolonged indefinitely, in much the same way as this principle applies to comparable infrastructural entities, such as road networks and telephone systems.

2 New Applications

2.1 Business Applications

Private enterprises and public organizations continuously address themselves to the task of reorganization. Business concepts — such as lean management. lean production or business process reengineering — can only be put into practice successfully if supported by information technology. Companies with flat, customer-oriented management structures must be able to call upon high-performance communication systems that are readily adaptable to changing needs.

The organization of activities into work groups plays a key role in the decentralized management structures being adopted today. The effectiveness of such groups has a decisive influence on critical business performance factors such as costs, processing time, productivity, time to market and the quality of products and services.

Industry and public organizations are increasingly aware of the need to enhance the effectiveness of such work groups. They are now taking a critical look at their organizational structures and procedures, as well as at the corresponding business processes.

Computer supported process management provides organizations with far-reaching advantages:

- Explicit models enable cooperative processes to be more readily understood and critically examined.
- Teamwork is improved, and cooperation between team members is guided and comprehensively supported.
- Problems in communication, attributable to misunderstandings, misdirection etc., can be alleviated.

Changes in the business structures implemented in industry have intensified the demand for an effective exchange of information and improved efficiency in communication between collaborative work groups. The transitions from closed

DP "islands" to integrated distributed system solutions as well as the division of corporations into cooperative and flexible profit centers, the flattening of administrative hierarchies and the integration of outsourced external services have become an essential factor in responding to global markets.

2.2   Technical application

Information and communication technologies are paving the way towards intelligent products of many different kinds. Therefore they are developed as an integral part of many engineering systems like

- automobiles
- aircraft and space vehicles, and
- last but not least, many household goods.

The infrastructures in demand here are expected to conform to especially high quality standards which in turn lead to demands for "safety-critical" or even "zero-defect" software in information and communication infrastructures.

Many new products like telephone sets, consumer electronic products, microelectronic devices etc. are subject to permanent improvements and refinements and this demands for their continuous engineering. These improvements and refinements are wherever possible left to changes to software of the embedded information and communication infrastructures.

Manufacturing technologies undergo again dramatic changes. Early attempts to fully integrate different stages in the production of goods are reconsidered now and brought to a consolidation based on new integration technologies for information and communication infrastructures. As a consequence manufactured goods are brought to the market faster and global competition is largely based on "time-to-market" performance of corporations. By the same token the continuous improvement and refinement of goods demands for continuous adaptations of their manufacturing technologies. Once again many of these adaptions are meant to be achieved with changes in the supporting information and communication infrastructure.

Most visibly are at the moment dramatic changes in production technologies for the car manufacturing. These publicly debated revolutionary developments represent however just the tip of the iceberg. Both the production and disposal of almost all technical goods is being reconsidered, new production technologies based on new divisions of labor and on new information and communication technologies are implemented in almost all sectors of the industry.

Last but not least, information and communication technologies are replacing traditional technologies. The best known example is the replacement of hydrolic steering and control systems in aircrafts by "fly-by-wire" technologies, which are again based on highly complex information and communication infrastructures.

3   New Structures

Substantial productivity gains can be achieved in many domains with the amalgamation of previously autonomous computer applications. In this way, programs and software systems do not remain separate but become linked via different kinds of integration and communication platforms into compounds that become critically important to the application. As a consequence, many of the programs and software systems installed in recent years have evolved into assets of an unexpected durability. We therefore refer to such durable and evolving systems as Information and Communication Infrastructures.

Like other kinds of infrastructures, Information and Communication Infrastructures are developed for continuous use and to enable adaptations and extensions through partial renewal, partial extension and partial replacement. The establishment of Information and Communication Infrastructures thus demands a wide range of skills:

- the skill of the business consultant for the analysis of business structures and practices which the infrastructures are meant to support,
- the skill of the engineer for the analysis of the engineering problem and for the specification of the requirements for the needed infrastructure,
- the skill of the technology advisor for the choice of the right concepts and systems for the infrastructure,
- the skill of the technology developer for the adaptation of existing products to their use in an infrastructure,
- the skill of the technology and systems integrator for the amalgamation of individual technologies and systems into a coherent overall infrastructure.

Information and communication infrastructures are meant to provide numerous decisive advantages when compared with traditional systems:

- ICIs are built to be improved in an evolutionary manner based on a fundamental concept that has been carefully planned and established.
- ICIs are built to be altered and extended at any time, allowing entrepreneurs essential flexibility in responding to changing requirements.
- ICIs make it possible to utilize new and improved components in conjunction with older existing systems.
- This capacity to develop infrastructures gradually over an extended period of time safeguards investments.

ICIs present a substantial change to software and systems engineering. The logical relationships between the components in software and systems are highly complex, and this complexity increases as these systems themselves are combined into a larger whole. That demands for modern architectures that are

modular: Components are constructed as independent, reusable entities.
open: Systems can be used and adapted over long times
compatible: Structures have to be established that are compatible to acceptanced principles, and the use of standardized interfaces, components and invariant platforms.

4 New Characteristics

Information and Communication Infrastructures are in most cases product, mission or even business critical. They must guarantee maximum safety and reliability. This is particularly true for systems used in high-risk applications, such as nuclear power stations and aircraft piloting, traffic control, banking and telephone networks.

The infrastructures currently used often do not fulfil this prerequisite. In many cases there are substantial shortcomings in their quality:

- Systems are often faulty and unreliable. This can often be attributed to such factors as unsystematic engineering techniques, a lack of theory and formalization, inadequate quality assurance, and bad systems management, among others.
- The architecture and functions of legacy systems are often not known in detail. In the majority of cases this is attributable to inadequate maintenance techniques, and to incomplete or non-existent documentation.

If these factors are present simultaneously, systems can become an incalculable risk. This presents corporate users with new challenges, particularly in view of their exposure to competition in international markets.

5 New Technologies

5.1 Computer Technologies

Various developments in information technology are currently paving the way for the inter-connection of independent applications:

- Client/server systems based on PCs and workstations complement centralized mainframe architectures.
- Computers are being transformed into working environments capable of supporting complex work processes.
- Substantial progress has been made in establishing international standards for protocols, platforms, and interfaces, such as TCP/IP, http, HTML, X.400, X.500, SQL, EuroISDN.
- Manufacturer alliances are being formed to enforce industrial standards, for example OMG with CORBA, OSF with MOTIF and DCE.
- Simple alphanumeric terminals are being replaced by others equipped with graphic interface systems, window technology and multimedia capabilities.
- High-speed broadband networks are advancing rapidly to replace slower conventional telecommunications lines.
- Groupware and workflow systems enable the coordination of teamwork in offices and even the coordination of work in large organisations.
- Multimedia systems allow for the visualization of complex information.
- Virtual reality systems allow the simulation of activities in 3D spaces etc.

All these new concepts and technologies contribute to the "re-vitalization" or even "re-invention" of many applications like

- in the banking business
- in the insurance business
- in commerce
- in the publication business
- in the logistics business
- in tourism
- in the service and maintenance business

etc.

5.2 Network Technologies

Network technologies facilitate the construction of integrated Information and Communication Infrastructures, offering several substantial benefits:

- They support geographically distributed organizations.
- They protect investments made in independent systems and user-specific software.
- They reduce the high cost of new developments through the integration of existing systems.
- They improve and accelerate work practices by providing reliable collaboration support to users.

Network technologies allow now the deployment of:

- heterogeneous communication systems
- heterogeneous information management systems, comprising file systems, relational and object-oriented databases
- different hardware and software within the same Information and Communication Infrastructure.

5.3 Information Management Technologies

Development of Information Modelling and Management Techniques increasingly support the implementation of comprehensive information systems.
These information systems:

- offer a uniform, global view on information maintained in an enterprise, and
- enable the documentation of relationships between the data compiled in different parts of an organization

They facilitate:

- a better understanding of complex organizational structures
- the application integration into Information and Communication Infrastructures

– the systematic design of software

New information systems are applied to

– document the semantic content of data at various levels of abstraction
– check on their syntactic and semantic consistency
– enable the development of domain and customer specific view on models
– enable their implementation by means of different kind of data management systems like data bases, object bases etc.
– enable the coexistence of different models in heterogeneous Information and Communication Infrastructures
– enable the re-engineering and migration of information systems.

6 Continuous Engineering

Software and systems that make up Information and Communication Infrastructures are different in nature from those that serve as products of a limited lifetime. Their development and evolution require practises other than those of classical software and systems engineering.

Continuous Engineering aimes for a number of goals that are not yet in focus of software engineering. From a business perspectives ICIs are meant

– to be kept adequate with respect to their business function, up-to-date with respect to their technology base, reliable for their continuous functioning and robust against their unintended use
– to be continuously improved with respect to their functionality and user satisfaction, with respect to their cost, quality and performance
– to be continuously expanded to support new business functions as well as new and more users
– to be reorganized once in a while to mirror respective business reorganizations.

From a system perspective ICIs will need to have built-in provision for their later change. This in turn requires the denotation of the objects of interest of ICIs like

– material artefacts (i.e. computers, networks etc.)
– conceptual artefacts (i.e. programs, specifications, models etc.)
– data about material and conceptual artefacts
– information (i.e. date in context) about material and conceptual artefacts
– uncoded knowledge (i.e. interpreted information) about material and conceptual artefacts.

The change of ICIs will then be governed by a variety of dependencies existing between the different objects of interest and will be constrained by a number of chosen ICI invariants. It is argued here that ICIs should be built around four categories of invariants of different life times

– category 1 (indefinite life time) encompasses standards for formats of architectures and components
– category 2 (reduced life time) encompasses standard platforms, interfaces and protocols
– category 3 (further reduced life time) encompasses data and information structures maintained by an ICI as well as execution structures across components of an ICI (i.e. the intension of an ICI)
– category 4 (further reduced life time) encompasses data and operations themselves (i.e. the extension of an ICI).

Introducing and categorizing invariants gives raise to the development of continuous engineering processes for building, maintaining, changing and renovating ICIs.

Continuous Engineering of Information and Communication Infrastructures poses many questions and problems to software and systems engineers. Only vague ideas exist on how to tackle the involved technical problems like:

– the analysis of existing (legacy) software and to document its results
– the (re) integration of existing (legacy) systems into Information and Communication Infrastructures
– the conversion and transformation of existing (legacy) systems into renewed Information and Communication Infrastructure.

Everyone of these tasks can be performed only with a deep understanding of the meaning of the different appearances of ICIs as e.g. models, specifications, repositories, code, architectures etc. It would be hopeless to apply known semantic formalism to them. Instead a pragmatic semantics is sought that can help to pin-down some of the critical properties of ICIs and may be used to validate the changes made in the continuous engineering process.

A Formal Framework with Late Binding*

Davide Ancona, Maura Cerioli, and Elena Zucca

DISI - Università di Genova
Via Dodecaneso, 35, 16146 Genova (Italy)
fax: +39-10-3536699
email: {davide,cerioli,zucca}@disi.unige.it

Abstract. We define a specification formalism (formally, an institution) which provides a notion of *dynamic type* (the type which is associated to a term by a particular evaluation) and *late binding* (the fact that the function version to be invoked in a function application depends on the dynamic type of one or more arguments). Hence, it constitutes a natural formal framework for modeling object-oriented and other dynamically-typed languages and a basis for adding to them a specification level. In this respect, the main novelty is the capability of writing axioms related to a given type which are not required to hold for subtypes, hence can be "overridden" in further refinements, thus lifting at the specification level the possibility of reusing code which is offered by the object-oriented approach.

Introduction

After many years of research on the foundations of object-oriented programming, a point of view which has recently emerged [2] is to consider as its distinguishing feature the fact that in method calls the correct variant of the method to be invoked is determined at run-time (*late* or *dynamic binding*), in other words a policy of *dynamic resolution of overloading* is applied.

We clarify further this terminology, adapting more or less the presentation of [2]. A distinction extensively used in language theory for the last two decades is that between *parametric* (or *universal*) polymorphism and *ad hoc* polymorphism. Parametric polymorphism allows one to write a function whose code can work on arguments of different types, while by ad hoc polymorphism it is possible to write functions that execute different code for arguments of different types. The first kind of polymorphism has been widely investigated on and developed, while the second form, usually known as *overloading*, has had little theoretical attention. This is probably due to the fact that traditional programming languages offer a very limited form of overloading, where the correct variant of the function to be applied is always decided at compile time, i.e. the *overloading resolution* is static (*early* or *static binding*). Clearly this form of overloading can be reduced to a useful syntactic abbreviation which does not significantly affect the language.

The real gain of power of overloading occurs with languages where types are computed during the execution. Indeed, in this case, the correct variant of the function to be applied can be decided depending on the *dynamic type* of arguments, i.e. the type computed at run-time; hence there is *late binding* of the function name to the code to be executed, or, in other words, dynamic resolution of overloading. This happens typically in object-oriented languages. In most of them dynamic overloading resolution is adopted only for what concerns the "receiver" (i.e. the first, implicit, parameter) of a method call. Nevertheless, the same policy can be applied to all the arguments of a function, as it happens e.g. in *multimethods* [8,4].

---

* Partially supported by Murst 40% - Modelli della computazione e dei linguaggi di programmazione and CNR - Formalismi per la specifica e la descrizione di sistemi ad oggetti.

In this paper we define a specification formalism (formally, an institution in the sense of [6]) which provides dynamic resolution of overloading. The basic idea is to handle overloading at the *model* (semantic) level and not at the *signature* (syntactic) level. More precisely, we model a function $op: \bar{s} \to s$ which[1] has many different variants, as e.g. a method in the object-oriented case, by a unique function symbol in the signature, whose interpretation in a model is a *multifunction*, i.e. a family of functions $op_{\bar{u}}$, one for each existing subtype $\bar{u}$ of $\bar{s}$. In other words, the existence of different variants is seen as *redefinition*, and distinguished from static overloading.

We see two main motivations and directions of application for the approach we propose.

First, we provide a formal framework for modeling object-oriented languages or, more in general, languages which provide some form of dynamic overloading resolution. In particular, the term language of our formalism is, syntactically, a variant of the standard term language in, say, order-sorted frameworks [7], but we are able to define what is the *dynamic type* of a term (the type of the element obtained by its evaluation). Furthermore, in the evaluation of a function application the variant to be used is (possibly) determined using late binding. Hence, our term language with its semantic interpretation provides a unifying metalanguage allowing to express by immediate translation the semantics of languages with dynamic overloading resolution. Applications of this kind rely on just the model part (signatures and models) of our formalism.

Considering now the logical part (sentences and satisfaction relation), the main novelty is that we are able to express two different kinds of requirements over elements of a given type s:

- requirements which must hold for elements of any possible subtype of s, written $\forall x : s_{\leq}.\varphi$;
- requirements which must hold for elements which have s as most specific type, but not for elements of proper subtypes, written $\forall x : s.\varphi$.

Note that requirements of the second kind are not expressible by sentences of "usual" formalisms (without a notion of dynamic type).

This possibility is very interesting since it allows, in a sense, to lift at the specification level the possibility of reusing code which is the main advantage offered by the object-oriented approach (and more in general by late binding). Indeed, assume that we have a specification SP which describes a type s and its related functions. Later, we want to define a specialization s' of s which behaves "more or less" like s, but for instance one of the functions must be changed in a way that it does no longer satisfy some axiom, say $\forall x : s.\varphi$. In usual frameworks it is not possible to obtain a specification SP' of this specialization by reusing SP as it stands, i.e. by enrichment. Indeed, φ is required to hold for each element of (a subtype of) s. Hence, we have to give up either to reuse specifications or to write axioms which we are not sure should hold in all possible present or future refinements.

In our framework, since the sentence $\forall x : s.\varphi$ is not required to hold for subtypes, this axiom can coexist with other axioms for the subtype s' which specify a different behavior, even in contradiction. In other words, it is possible to have reuse of specifications possibly "overriding" some axioms, in analogy to what happens with programming languages. In our opinion this represents a true novelty, and makes our formalism a good starting point for adding a specification level to languages with late binding.

The paper is structured as follows. In Sect. 1 we provide an informal introduction to the formalism, showing how some simple Java classes can be semantically interpreted and how to write axioms specifying their expected behavior. In Sect. 2 we formally define

---

[1] Here and later let $\bar{x}$ denote the tuple $x_1 \ldots x_n$.

our formalism as an institution in the sense of [6] and prove that it also satisfies the amalgamation property. In Sect. 3 we discuss the interference between the redefinition (dynamically solved overloading) modeled in our framework and usual (statically solved) overloading. Finally, in the Conclusion we summarize the results of the paper and provide some comparison with related work.

Proofs are omitted here for reasons of space and can be found in [1].

1   An Informal Presentation

In this section, we will first show how our framework provides a semantic foundation for programming languages with late binding, typically object-oriented languages. Then, we will illustrate how it could be taken as starting point for adding a specification level to such languages.

We will consider a standard example written in a toy object-oriented language. We adopt a Java-like syntax for convenience, but consider in the following for simplicity a purely functional interpretation, where objects are records and a method with side effects on some object's components is seen instead as a function returning a record consisting of the updated components. Indeed, handling imperative aspects is orthogonal to the problems we aim at solving in this paper and there are standard techniques for that (see e.g. [11]), which could be applied to our framework as well.

Let us conside a software module consisting of two class definitions, describing points in the Cartesian plane (2D-points) and in the space (3D-points). We assume that, for some reason, moving a 3D-point has the side effect of incrementing by one its third coordinate.

```
class 2DPoint {
  private int x,y;
  int X () { return x;}
  int Y () { return y;}
  void move (int dx, int dy) { x = x + dx; y + dy;}
}

class 3DPoint extends 2DPoint {
  private int z;
  int Z () { return z;}
  void move (int dx, int dy) { x = x + dx; y = y + dy; z = z + 1;}
}
```

The semantic counterpart of this module is given, in our framework, by a signature Σ_P (P for "points") modeling the syntactic interface of the module to users and a model M_P over Σ_P providing an interpretation for symbols in the interface.

The definition of Σ_P is the following:

> **sig** $\Sigma_P =$
> > **sorts** $int, 3D \leq 2D$
> > **opns** ... standard functions on integers ...
> > > $X, Y: 2D \to int$
> > > $move: 2D, int, int \to 2D$
> > > $Z: 3D \to int$

Note that there is a unique function symbol corresponding to **move**; indeed, as we will see below, redefinition is handled at the semantic level.

The model M_P defines an interpretation for the sort and function symbols. Sort symbols are interpreted as sets, as usual.

$$int^{Mp} = \mathbb{Z}, 2D^{Mp} = \mathbb{Z} \times \mathbb{Z}, 3D^{Mp} = \mathbb{Z} \times \mathbb{Z} \times \mathbb{Z}$$

However, the intended meaning is different from the standard; in a model M, the interpretation s^M of a sort s defines the set of the elements which have s as most specific type, called the *proper carrier* of sort s (for instance, 2D-points for *2D*). The *(extended) carrier* of sort s, denoted $s_{\leq}^M$, is then defined to be the disjoint union of all the proper carriers of subtypes of s. In the example:

$$2D_{\leq}^{Mp} = \{p : 2D \mid p \in 2D^{Mp}\} \cup \{p : 3D \mid p \in 3D^{Mp}\},$$

while $3D_{\leq}^{Mp} = 3D^{Mp}$ since *3D* has no proper subtypes. Note that by definition $s_{\leq}^M \subseteq s'^M_{\leq}$ holds whenever $s \leq s'$.

We illustrate now the interpretation of function symbols. As said above, redefinition of a method in a heir class is modeled at the semantic level. Indeed, the interpretation of *move* consists of two different functions, called *variants*, as shown below.

$$move_{2D}^{Mp} : 2D_{\leq}^{Mp} \times int^{Mp} \times int^{Mp} \to 2D_{\leq}^{Mp}$$
$$move_{2D}^{Mp}(p, dx, dy) =$$
$$\langle x + dx, y + dy \rangle : 2D \text{ if } p = \langle x, y \rangle : 2D,$$
$$\langle x + dx, y + dy, z \rangle : 3D \text{ if } p = \langle x, y, z \rangle : 3D$$
$$move_{3D}^{Mp} : 3D^{Mp} \times int^{Mp} \times int^{Mp} \to 2D_{\leq}^{Mp}$$
$$move_{3D}^{Mp}(\langle x, y, z \rangle, dx, dy) = \langle x + dx, y + dy, z + 1 \rangle$$

The latter variant, acting on 3D-points only, corresponds to the new definition of the method in **3DPoint**; the former corresponds to the old definition, which can be invoked not only on 2D-points, but also on 3D-points (for instance in **Java** using the **super** keyword in the class **3DPoint**).

In general, the interpretation in a model M of a function symbol, say $op : \overline{s} \to s$, is a *multifunction*, i.e. a family of functions $op_{\overline{u}}^M : \overline{u}_{\leq}^M \to s_{\leq}^M$, one for each subtype $\overline{u}$ of $\overline{s}$. Of course in practice a function could be redefined only for some subtypes, but we assume that a model provides a variant for each possible subtype for sake of simplicity (no redefinition being simply obtained by having two variants which have the same behavior on arguments of the more specific type). Domain and codomain of each variant $op_{\overline{u}}^M$ are the extended carriers of $\overline{u}$ and s, reflecting the intuition that this variant could be applied to argument tuples of any subtype of $\overline{u}$ and, analogously, the result could be an element of any subtype of s. Note moreover that multiple inheritance can be modeled as well.

Assume now that we want to use the module consisting of the two classes **2DPoint** and **3DPoint** as an implementation for the following restricted interface Σ_{2D}.

sig $\Sigma_{2D} =$
    sorts *int, 2D*
    opns ... standard functions on integers ...
        $X, Y : 2D \to int$
        move : *2D, int, int* $\to$ *2D*

This is intuitively sensible since the module has a richer interface and is captured, in the algebraic formalisms, by the notion of *reduct*; that is, it should be possible to define, starting from M_P, a model $M_{P|\Sigma_{2D}}$ over Σ_{2D} which is the formal counterpart of the behavior of the module when accessed only through the restricted interface. Intuitively, $M_{P|\Sigma_{2D}}$ should be obtained from M_P "forgetting" the type *3D* and the function Z. However, this cannot be achieved by simply throwing away 3D-points, since 3D-points and the corresponding variant of *move* are still available because of late binding. Assume, to see this more clearly, that Σ_{2D} also offers a constant $myPoint : \to 2D$ whose implementation in M_P returns a 3D-point (this could correspond for instance in **Java** to a static method in the class 2DPoint with body return new 3DPoint()). Then, the evaluation of the term $move(myPoint, 1, 1)$ (2DPoint.myPoint.move(1,1) in Java syntax) in the model M_P involves the $move_{3D}$ variant even if the user has no knowledge of the existence of the type 3DPoint.

The technical solution we adopt is that of decoupling *syntactic types* (types which appear in the signature, and are used for static typing of terms) and *semantic types*, which are used as indexes in function variants. Hence a model M over a signature Σ with sorts S defines a set s^M for each s in a set of semantic types S^M and an (order-preserving) map $\iota : S \to S^M$ which specifies how syntactic types are mapped into semantic types. For instance, in the model $M_{P|\Sigma_{2D}}$ this map is just an inclusion, corresponding to the intuition that the type $3D$ is not visible at the syntactic level, but can be the dynamic type of some term.

In order to illustrate the logical part of our formalism, i.e. sentences expressing requirements over models, we first briefly present *terms*. Assume that $p2$ and $p3$ are two variables of (static) type $2D$ and $3D$, respectively. Terms are of three kinds: variables, function applications and casted terms.

A first form of function application is exemplified by $move(p2, 1, 1)$, $move(p3, 1, 1)$, $Z(p3)$. In this case, the syntactic form of terms is standard, but not the evaluation. Let us consider for instance the evaluation of $move(p2, 1, 1)$ w.r.t., say, M_P; reflecting what actually happens in languages with subtyping, the variable $p2$ can denote either a 2D-point or a 3D-point (formally, valuations of variables have as codomain extended carriers), and the variant used for interpreting $move$ (either $move_{2D}^{M_P}$ or $move_{3D}^{M_P}$) depends on the *dynamic type* of $p2$, that is the (most specific) type of the element denoted by $p2$.

Another form of function application is that where we force static binding, like e.g. in $move(p2 : 2D, 1, 1)$. In this second case, even if the dynamic type of $p2$ is $3D$, the variant which is invoked is that with index $2D$.

The combination of the first two forms where terms are of the general form $op(t_1[: s_1], \ldots, t_n[: s_n])$, where square brackets denote optionality, allows much more flexibility than in object-oriented languages, where the binding is always dynamic for the first (implicit) argument (apart the limited possibility offered by the super mechanism) and always static for the remaining arguments.

Finally, we allow casted terms, like e.g. $(3D)p2$. This feature is instead completely analogous to what offered e.g. in Java by *casting down* (type conversion from a supertype to a subtype) and is typically useful for using in a context of the subtype (hence through a richer interface) a term which we expect to have this subtype as dynamic type. For instance, if we write $Z((3D)p2)$, then we are able to get the third dimension of the point denoted by $p2$, if we have good reasons to suppose that this point is actually a 3D-point. If, on the other side, our supposition is wrong and $p2$ denotes a 2D-point, then we get a run time error (formally, the evaluation of the term is undefined). Note however that, as in Java, casting does not influence the dynamic type, hence in $move((3D)p2, 1, 1)$ the version which is invoked is still $move_{3D}^{M_P}$ if $p2$ denotes a 3D-point. Finally, we recall that this casting down is conceptually analogous to the so-called *retracts* in order-sorted frameworks [7], even if the technical treatment is different.

We do not consider casting up (type conversion from a subtype to a supertype) since it is not significant except than for static overloading resolution (see Sect. 3 for more details).

We can now show some sentences. Let us consider for instance the following axioms expressing requirements for the type $2D$.

1. $\forall p : 2D_\prec . \forall dx : int . \forall dy : int . X(move(p, dx, dy)) = X(p) + dx$
2. $\forall p : 2D_\prec . \forall dx : int . \forall dy : int . Y(move(p, dx, dy)) = Y(p) + dy$
3. $\forall p : 2D . move(p, 0, 0) = p$

4. $\forall p : 2D.\forall dx : int.\forall dy : int.move(move(p, dx, 0), 0, dy) = move(p, dx, dy)$

The first two axioms express, intuitively, requirements that we want to hold for 2D-points and to be also preserved in any possible specialized version of them. For instance, these axioms must be verified by 3D-points, too.

On the contrary, the last two axioms express perfectly reasonable requirements for the type $2D$, which could however not hold for all subtypes; for instance, these axioms do not hold for 3D-points, since the $move$ function is assumed to have an additional effect on them.

The difference between the two kinds of axioms is expressed by the two different quantifications, suggesting exactly the interpretation explained above.

The possibility of writing in a specification axioms of the two kinds is very important: for instance, we can write a specification SP_{2D} for 2D-points including the axioms above and then write a specification SP_{3D} for 3D-points as an enrichment of SP_{2D} by adding, e.g., the axiom[2]

$$\forall p : 3D.\forall dx : int.\forall dy : int.Z(move(p, dx, dy)) = Z(p) + 1.$$

In usual formalisms, this axiom and axiom (3) and (4) would be in contradiction, hence the specification SP_{3D} could not be obtained by reusing SP_{2D}, but should be rewritten from scratch.

From the methodological point of view, the designer should choose between the two forms of quantification depending on the intuition about the property expressed by the axiom (either a *conservative* property, expected to hold in all the possible future refinements of a type, or a *specific* property, required to hold for that type but not necessarily for subtypes). This allows to have in the specification any desired degree of control over inheritance.

2 An Institution for Late Binding

This section is devoted to the formal definition of our framework. The readers are encouraged to compare the notions presented here with the examples of application of the previous section.

2.1 Syntax

The subtyping relation is represented by a *preorder*; thus, our notion of signature is similar to that of order-sorted signatures [7]. But, for sake of simplicity, we do not allow static overloading: that is, we do not allow the same function symbol to have two different functionalities. This is somehow drastic, because many cases of overloading are harmless and helpful, but allows us to focus our attention on *redefinition* (or *dynamic overloading*). In Sect. 3 we will see how this requirement can be relaxed, following quite standard techniques, in order to get a more user-friendly language.

Definition 1. *A preorder* $(S, \leq)$ *consists of a set S and a reflexive and transitive binary relation $\leq$ on S. Given preorders $(S, \leq)$ and $(S', \lesssim)$, a morphism of preorders is a function $\sigma^S : S \to S'$ s.t. $s \leq s'$ implies $\sigma^S(s) \lesssim \sigma^S(s')$ for all $s, s' \in S$.*

Any preorder $\leq$ can be componentwise extended to sequences, that is $\bar{s} \leq \bar{u}$ holds iff $\bar{s}$ and $\bar{u}$ have the same length n and $s_i \leq u_i$ for all $i = 1 \ldots n$. We denote by $\mathbf{PreOrd}$ the category of preorders.

---

[2] We use the standard quantification for integers, since we consider them as a fixed predefined data type which cannot be furtherly specialized.

An order-sorted signature without overloading, *from now on simply signature*, $\Sigma = (S, \leq, O, \delta 0, \delta 1)$ *consists of a preorder* $(S, \leq)$ *of sorts, a set* O *of* function symbols *and two functions* $\delta 0: O \to S^*$ *and* $\delta 1: O \to S$ *returning the* arity *and the* result type *of each function symbol, respectively.*

For each $op \in O$, if $\delta 0(op) = \overline{s}$ and $\delta 1(op) = s$ then we will write $op: \overline{s} \to s$.

Definition 2. *Given signatures* $\Sigma = (S, \leq, O, \delta 0, \delta 1)$ *and* $\Sigma' = (S', \leq, O', \delta 0', \delta 1')$, *a* morphism $\sigma: \Sigma \to \Sigma'$ *consists of a morphism of preorders* $\sigma^S: S \to S'$ *and a renaming of functions symbols* $\sigma^F: O \to O'$ *that is consistent with the sort renaming, that is s.t. for all* $op: \overline{s} \to s$ *we have* $\sigma^F(op): \sigma^S(\overline{s}) \to \sigma^S(s)$, *where* σ^S *is componentwise extended to sequences of sorts.*

The category of signatures, where identities and compositions are defined in the obvious way, will be denoted by **OSign**.

Notation 1 *From now on, let* Σ *denote the signature* $(S, \leq, O, \delta 0, \delta 1)$, Σ' *the signature* $(S', \leq O', \delta 0', \delta 1')$ *and* σ *the morphism* $\sigma: \Sigma \to \Sigma'$ *with components* (σ^S, σ^F). *In the following we will simply denote* σ^S *and* σ^F *by* σ, *provided that no ambiguity arises.*

2.2 Semantics

As shown in Sect. 1, the models of a signature Σ in our framework are quite different from usual order-sorted algebras. Indeed, first of all the elements of a model are classified by a set of *semantic types*. This captures the intuition that we are using modules with a possibly larger collection of types through a restricted interface, described by the signature. Then, the interpretation of each semantic type (the *proper carrier*) consists only of the elements having that sort as most specific type. Thus, we have no subsumption among the proper carriers, though this property is recovered at the level of *extended carriers*. Finally, each function symbol $op: \overline{s} \to s$ of the signature is interpreted in a model M as a *multifunction*, that is a family of functions $op_{\overline{u}}^M: \iota(\overline{u})_{\leq}^M \to \iota(s)_{\leq}^M$ for each possible specialization $\overline{u} \leq \overline{s}$.

Definition 3. *A* Σ-model M *consists of*

- *a preorder* $(S^M, \preceq)$ *and a morphism of preorders* $\iota: (S, \leq) \to (S^M, \preceq)$; *if* ι *is an inclusion (as in most concrete cases), we will omit it;*
- *for each* $s \in S^M$, *a set* s^M, *called the* proper carrier *of sort* s *in* M. *We will denote by* $s_{\leq}^M$ *the disjoint union of* s'^M *for all* $s' \preceq s$, *i.e. for all* $s \in S^M$:

$$s_{\leq}^M = \{a : s' \mid a \in s'^M, s' \preceq s\}$$

The set $s_{\leq}^M$ *is called the* (extended) carrier *of sort* s. *Moreover, for each sequence* $\overline{s}$ *of sorts in* S^M *with length* n, *we will denote by* $\overline{s}_{\leq}^M$ *the Cartesian product* $s_{1\leq}^M \times \ldots \times s_{n\leq}^M$.
- *for each* $op: \overline{s} \to s$ *and each* $\overline{u} \preceq \iota(\overline{s})$, *a partial function* $op_{\overline{u}}^M: \iota(\overline{u})_{\leq}^M \to \iota(s)_{\leq}^M$.

We will denote by **OMod**(Σ) *the set of all* Σ-models.

We allow the interpretation of function symbols to be *partial* in order to be able to give an immediate semantics to programming languages, where partiality is inherent, due to non-termination.

Notation 2 *Here and later let* M *denote the* Σ-model *with components* $(S^M, \preceq)$, ι, s^M *and* $op_{\overline{u}}^M$ *and, analogously,* M' *denote the* Σ'-model *with components* $(S^{M'}, \preceq)$, ι', $s^{M'}$ *and* $op_{\overline{s}}^{M'}$.

We are not interested here in features related with model morphisms, like initiality. We plan to study the nature of the *category* of models in an extended forthcoming version of the paper.

Lemma 1 (Subsumption). *Let M be a model of Σ. Then, $s \preceq s'$ implies $s_{\preceq}^{M} \subseteq s'_{\preceq}^{M}$.*

As usual in algebraic approaches, we have to say how models can be translated along signature morphisms, in order to support structured specifications.

Definition 4. *Let the reduct M of M' along σ, denoted $M'|_{\sigma}$, be defined by*

- *$(S^M, \preceq) = (S^{M'}, \precsim)$ and ι is the composition of ι' and σ.*
- *for each $s \in S^M$, $s^M = s^{M'}$;*
- *for each function symbol $op: \overline{s} \to s$ and each $\overline{u} \preceq \iota(\overline{s})$ we define $op_{\overline{u}}^{M} = \sigma(op)_{\overline{u}}^{M'}$.*

Moreover, let $OMod(\sigma): OMod(\Sigma') \to OMod(\Sigma)$ be the function defined by $OMod(\sigma)(M') = M'|_{\sigma}$.

Proposition 1. *Using the notation of Def. 3 and 4, $OMod: OSign \to Set^{op}$ is a functor.*

Here we allow resolution of dynamic overloading on all the parameters, like in *multimethods*, while in most object-oriented languages it is solved only w.r.t. the first (implicit) parameter, the receiver. Thus, if we want to use our formalism only to give semantics to such languages, then we can simplify the models, requiring that for each $op: \overline{s} \to s$ the interpretation of op consists of a partial function $op_{\overline{u}}^{M}: \iota(\overline{u})_{\preceq}^{M} \to \iota(s)_{\preceq}^{M}$, for each $\overline{u}$ s.t. $u_1 \preceq s_1$ and $u_i = s_i$ for all $i = 2 \dots n$. In this way, models are "smaller", because multifunctions have less variants. The theory developed for this less general case is, hence, a trivial simplification of the theory presented here.

2.3 Amalgamated Sum

Even though not crucial for any kind of institution, it is widely recognized that the amalgamation property [5] makes institutions particularly suitable for dealing in an elegant way with modular software systems and specifications. Indeed, as already stated in the Introduction, two main motivations for this work are the definition of an algebraic framework for modeling languages with late binding and the possibility to lift at the specification level the reuse of code typical of the object-oriented approach. This implies that we have to face the problem of modularization at the level both of models (indeed, object-oriented programs are usually structured) and specifications (since, for reusing specifications, we necessarily deal with some modularization mechanism). However, we need to prove the amalgamation property only for models, since the corresponding property for axiomatic presentations comes for free from the former (see [13]).

We first show that **OSign** is finitely cocomplete, so that signatures can be combined together; then, we state the amalgamation property in its most general formulation, that is, by considering any kind of pushouts. Proofs are given in the Appendix.

The proof of finite cocompleteness is based on the fact that both **Set** and **PreOrd** are (finitely) cocomplete and shows that every colimit in **OSign** can be defined by simply putting together the two colimits in **PreOrd** and **Set** obtained by forgetting function and sort symbols, respectively. More formally, let $U^S: OSign \to PreOrd$, $U^F: OSign \to Set$ be the two forgetful functors defined by $U^S(S, \leq, O, \delta0, \delta1) = (S, \leq)$, $U^S(\sigma^S, \sigma^F) = \sigma^S$ and $U^F(S, \leq, O, \delta0, \delta1) = O$, $U^F(\sigma^S, \sigma^F) = \sigma^F$. Then U^S and U^F turn out to be finitely cocontinuous. This property allows the proof for the amalgamation property to be simpler, since we are able to reason at the level of the underlying categories **Set** and **PreOrd** rather than **OSign**.

Proposition 2. *The category **OSign** is finitely cocomplete. Furthermore, the two forget-ful functors U^S and U^F are finitely cocontinuous.*

Proposition 3 (Amalgamation). *For any pushout diagram in **OSign***

$$
\begin{array}{ccc}
\Sigma_1 = (S_1, \leq_1, O_1, \delta 0_1, \delta 1_1) & \xrightarrow{\ \sigma'_1\ } & \Sigma = (S, \leq, O, \delta 0, \delta 1) \\[2mm]
\sigma_1 \big\uparrow & & \big\uparrow \sigma'_2 \\[2mm]
\Sigma_0 = (S_0, \leq_0, O_0, \delta 0_0, \delta 1_0) & \xrightarrow[\ \sigma_2\ ]{} & \Sigma_2 = (S_2, \leq_2, O_2, \delta 0_2, \delta 1_2)
\end{array}
$$

and for any Σ_1-model M_1 and any Σ_2-model M_2, if $M_{1|\sigma_1} = M_{2|\sigma_2}$, there exists a unique Σ-model M s.t. $M_{|\sigma'_i} = M_i$, $i = 1, 2$.

2.4 Language

As shown in Sect. 1, terms are of three kinds: variables, function applications and casted terms. In function applications, we allow, but not require, arguments to be explicitly typed, to direct the choice of which variant of the multifunction has to be used (static binding). If no type is provided, then the dynamic type of the argument is used as a default (late binding).

A casted term is of the form $(s')t$, where t is a term of some supersort of s' and denotes the value of t seen as an element of type s', if possible (i.e. if the dynamic type of t is a subtype of s'); it is undefined otherwise.

Finally, note that we do not have an explicit subsumption rule. Hence any term has a unique (static) type, due to the absence of static overloading. But a term can be used as argument for a function application whenever its type is smaller than the expected type.

Definition 5. *Given a set S, an S-indexed family of variables X is any family $\{X_s\}_{s \in S}$ of pairwise disjoint (sub)sets X_s (of some fixed universe). In the following we will denote by X the (necessarily disjoint) union of the X_s's, too.*

For each S-indexed family of variables X, the S-indexed family $T_\Sigma(X)$ of terms over Σ and X is inductively defined by

- $X_s \subseteq T_\Sigma(X)_s$
- $t \in T_\Sigma(X)_s$ *and $s' \leq s$ implies $(s')t \in T_\Sigma(X)_{s'}$ (casting)*
- *if $t_i \in T_\Sigma(X)_{s''_i}$ and $s''_i \leq s'_i \leq s_i$ for all $i = 1 \ldots n$, then $op(\bar{\tau}) \in T_\Sigma(X)_s$ for each function symbol $op : \bar{s} \to s$ and each $\bar{\tau}$ of length n s.t. τ_i is t_i or $t_i : s'_i$.*

The free variables of a term are inductively defined by

- $FV(x) = \{x\}$ *for all $x \in X_s$;*
- $FV((s')t) = FV(t)$;
- $FV(op(\bar{\tau})) = \cup_{i=1 \ldots n} FV(t_i)$ *if τ_i is either t_i or $t_i : s'_i$.*

For each $t \in T_\Sigma(X)_s$ we say that s is the static type of t.

Notice that we are able to give semantics to the casting construct only because we have adopted *partial* models. Indeed, the evaluation of such construct cannot yield any value if applied to a value outside the carrier of the sort on which we are casting.

Definition 6. *Given an S-indexed family of variables $X = \{X_s\}_{s \in S}$, a valuation of X into M, denoted by $V: X \to M$, is a function from X into the disjoint union of all the proper carriers of M s.t. if $x \in X_s$, then $V(x) \in \iota(s)_{\leq}^M$. Moreover, we will denote $[V: X \to M]$ the set of all valuations of X in M.*

For each valuation $V: X \to M$, the evaluation $t^{M,V}$ of a term t in M w.r.t. V is inductively defined by:

- $x^{M,V} = V(x)$ *for all* $x \in X$
- *if* $t^{M,V} \in \iota(s')_{\leq}^M$, *then* $(s')t^{M,V} = t^{M,V}$, *else* $(s')t^{M,V}$ *is undefined*
- *if* $t_i^{M,V} = a_i : s''_i$ *and* $u_i = \begin{cases} \iota(s'_i) & \text{if } \tau_i = t_i : s'_i \\ s''_i & \text{if } \tau_i = t_i \end{cases}$ *for all* $i = 1 \ldots n$, *then* $op(\overline{\tau})^{M,V} = op_{\overline{u}}^M(t_1^{M,V}, \ldots, t_n^{M,V})$.

If $t^{M,V} = a : s$, then s is the dynamic type *of t.*

Note that the evaluation of a term may be undefined not only because the term contains a casting, but also because the interpretation of function symbols are *partial* functions. However, if the evaluation of a term $t \in T_\Sigma(X)_s$ yields a value, then that value belongs to $\iota(s)_{\leq}^M$.

Expressions of an object-oriented language where dynamic binding is applied only to the receiver have to be transformed in our formalism in terms where each function call has all the arguments, but the first, explicitly typed by the types expected by the function. So, for instance, if we have R.f(A1...An) for some method f declared with argument types $s_1 \ldots s_n$, then we translate this call into $f(r, a : s_1, \ldots, a : s_n)$ (where the translation is recursively applied to the subterms as well). In this way we choose the variant to be used in term evaluation independently from the dynamic type of the arguments.

An alternative approach is to use simplified models where the variants of multifunction are indexed only by the subtypes of the receiver type, as sketched at the end of Sect. 2.2. In this case explicitly typing arguments but the first has no effect on the semantics and hence it is not needed.

Finally note that the **super** construct should be transformed into the explicit typing of the receiver by the parent class of its static type.

Terms are translated along signature morphisms replacing sort and function symbols by their translation, while variables are unaffected.

Definition 7. *For each S-indexed family X of variables, let $\sigma(X)$ be the S'-indexed family of variables defined by $\sigma(X)_{s'} = \cup_{\sigma(s)=s'} X_s$ for all $s' \in S'$.*

Moreover, let the translation of Σ-terms along σ be inductively defined by

- $\sigma(x) = x$ *for all variables x;*
- $\sigma((s')t) = (\sigma(s'))\sigma(t)$
- $\sigma(op(\overline{\tau})) = \sigma(op)(\overline{\tau'})$ *where $\overline{\tau}$ and $\overline{\tau'}$ are of the same length n and if $\tau_i = t_i$, then $\tau'_i = \sigma(t_i)$ else $\tau_i = t_i : s'_i$ and $\tau'_i = \sigma(t_i) : \sigma(s'_i)$.*

Lemma 2. *Using the notation of Def. 7, if $t \in T_\Sigma(X)_s$, then $\sigma(t) \in T_{\Sigma'}(\sigma(X))_{\sigma(s)}$.*

As expected, term evaluation in the reduct of a model coincides with the evaluation of translated terms in the source model.

Lemma 3. *Given an S-indexed family X of variables, let us denote by M the reduct $M'|_\sigma$. Then:*

- *the function χ from $[V: X \to M]$ into $[U: \sigma(X) \to M']$ associating each valuation V with the valuation $\sigma(V)$, defined by $\sigma(V)(y) = V(y)$ for all variables y, is an isomorphism.*
- *for each term $t \in T_\Sigma(X)$ and each valuation V, $t^{M,V} = \sigma(t)^{M',\sigma(V)}$.*

2.5 Logic

The main novelty of our approach is the definition of two different kinds of quantification, where variables range over elements of the proper and extended carrier, respectively, of a given sort. In the latter case we state properties holding for all possible realizations of the type, while in the former we impose conditions that can be overridden in further refinements. We illustrate the two kinds of quantification in the case of the Horn-Clauses on equality, but the approach extends naturally to existential quantification and first-order logic as well, adding predicates to signatures and their interpretation to models, following the same intuition as for function symbols and allowing variants.

Definition 8. *Given an S-indexed family of variables X, the atoms over Σ and X consists of (here and in the following t, possibly decorated, is a term over Σ and X):*

– *definedness assertions of the form $D(t)$;*
– *(strong) equalities of the form $t = t'$, with t and t' of static types having a common supersort;*

Then, Horn Clauses have the form $\epsilon_1 \wedge \ldots \wedge \epsilon_n \supset \epsilon_{n+1}$, where each ϵ_i is an atom for $i = 1 \ldots n+1$. The ϵ_i for $i = 1 \ldots n$ are called premises and ϵ_{n+1} is called consequence. The set of all Horn Clauses over Σ and X will be denoted by $HC(\Sigma, X)$. We will write a Horn Clause with an empty set of premises simply as the atom that is its consequence. The free variables of a Horn Clause φ are the union of the free variables of its subterms, that is

– $FV(D(t)) = FV(t)$;
– $FV(t = t') = FV(t) \cup FV(t')$;
– $FV(\epsilon_1 \wedge \ldots \wedge \epsilon_n \supset \epsilon_{n+1}) = \cup_{i=1\ldots n+1} FV(\epsilon_i)$;

Finally, conditional sentences *have the form*

$$\forall x_1 : s_{1_{\leqslant}} \ldots \forall x_k : s_{k_{\leqslant}} . \forall y_1 : s'_1 \ldots \forall y_n : s'_n . \varphi$$

for each $\varphi \in HC(\Sigma, X)$ with the quantified variables pairwise distinct, where $x_i \in X_s$, for all $i = 1 \ldots k$, $y_j \in X_{s'_j}$ for all $j = 1 \ldots n$ and $FV(\varphi) \subseteq \{x_1, \ldots, x_k, y_1, \ldots, y_n\}$.
The set of all conditional sentences over a signature Σ will be denoted by $OSen(\Sigma)$.

Satisfaction is defined, as usual, on the basis of validity w.r.t. *total* variables valuations, that is each variable denotes a value, following the intuition that the variables quantified as the x_i's above can be instantiated on any value in the carrier, while the variables quantified as the y_j's above have to be instantiated on values in the *proper* carrier of their sort.

Definition 9. *Given an S-indexed family of variables X, the validity of Horn Clauses over Σ and X w.r.t. a valuation $V: X \to M$ is defined as follows.*

– $M \models_V D(t)$ iff $t^{M,V}$ is defined;
– $M \models_V t = t'$, iff either $t^{M,V} = \alpha = t'^{M,V}$ for some $\alpha \in s_{\leqslant}^M$ or both $t^{M,V}$ and $t'^{M,V}$ are undefined;
– $M \models_V \epsilon_1 \wedge \ldots \wedge \epsilon_n \supset \epsilon_{n+1}$ iff $M \not\models_V \epsilon_i$ for some $i = 1 \ldots n$ or $M \models_V \epsilon_{n+1}$.

Then

$$M \models \forall x_1 : s_{1_{\leqslant}} \ldots \forall x_k : s_{k_{\leqslant}} . \forall y_1 : s'_1 \ldots \forall y_n : s'_n . \varphi$$

iff $M \models_V \varphi$ for all valuations $V: \{x_1, \ldots, x_k, y_1, \ldots, y_n\} \to M$, s.t. $V(y_j) = a_j : \iota(s'_j)$ for some $a_j \in \iota(s'_j)^M$.

Sentence translation immediately follows from term translation.

Definition 10. *The translation of Σ-formulae along σ is inductively defined by*

- $\sigma(D(t)) = D(\sigma(t))$;
- $\sigma(t = t') = \sigma(t) = \sigma(t')$;
- $\sigma(\epsilon_1 \wedge \ldots \wedge \epsilon_n \supset \epsilon_{n+1}) = \sigma(\epsilon_1) \wedge \ldots \wedge \sigma(\epsilon_n) \supset \sigma(\epsilon_{n+1})$;

and the translation $OSen(\sigma): OSen(\Sigma) \rightarrow OSen(\Sigma')$ of Σ-sentences along σ is defined by

$$OSen(\sigma)(\forall x_1 : s_{1_<}.\ldots.\forall x_k : s_{k_<}.\forall y_1 : s'_1.\ldots.\forall y_n : s'_n.\varphi) = \forall x_1 : \sigma(s_1)_<.\ldots.\forall x_k : \sigma(s_k)_<.\forall y_1 : \sigma(s'_1).\ldots.\forall y_n : \sigma(s'_n).\sigma(\varphi).$$

It is immediate to see that $OSen(\sigma)$ is a well-defined function.

Proposition 4. *Using the notation of Def. 8 and 10, $OSen$: $\textbf{OSign} \rightarrow \textbf{Set}$ is a functor.*

Proposition 5. *Using the notation of Lemma 3, $M \models_V \phi$ iff $M' \models_{\sigma(V)} \sigma(\phi)$ for any Horn Clause ϕ.*

Proposition 6. *For each Σ-sentence ϕ and each Σ'-model M'*

$$M' \models OSen(\sigma)(\phi) \qquad \Longleftrightarrow \qquad OMod(\sigma)(M') \models \phi$$

The technical results presented in this section can be summarized by saying that we have defined an institution (see e.g. [6]). Besides guaranteeing some degree of internal coherence, the fact that our framework is an institution makes directly available all the *institution independent* constructions, like structured specification languages, the notion of implementation, the capability of importing entailment systems through (suitable) coding in richer framework and so on.

Theorem 3. *The tuple $(OSign, OSen, OMod, \models)$ is an institution.*

3 Static Overloading

In concretely used languages, it may be convenient to allow the same function symbol to be used to declare functions of different types, all visible at the same level of nesting. The difference between this static overloading and the dynamic overloading modeled by our formalism is that in the latter case, the decision of which variant of the multifunction has to be invoked can be made only at run time and, hence, depends on the particular execution. On the contrary, the former kind of overloading can be solved, once and for all, at compile time. More precisely, a distinct internal name is associated with each declaration; then each function call is coded by substituting the user-defined name by the corresponding internal one, if it is possible to select, following some language-dependent rule, one definition among all those fitting that call, otherwise it is rejected as statically incorrect.

The same strategy can be adopted within algebraic frameworks (see e.g. [3]), distinguishing the level of the language for the end-users from the actual signature of the corresponding semantics.

Let us consider for instance how the static overloading allowed in the Java language could be solved in our framework.

In Java, a method name of a parent class can be redeclared in a heir class provided that either the number or the type of at least one argument is different (i.e., double declarations cannot be distinguished by the result type). For instance, let us modify the examples in Sect. 1, adding the following methods to the classes **2DPoint** and **3DPoint**:

```
class 2DPoint {
  ...
  bool equals (2DPoint P)              { ... }
  ...
}

class 3DPoint extends 2DPoint {
  ...
  bool equals (2DPoint P)              { ... }
  bool equals (3DPoint P)              { ... }
  bool inLine(2DPoint P1, 3DPoint P2) { ... }
  bool inLine(3DPoint P1, 2DPoint P2) { ... }
  ...
}
```

We can translate this interface into a signature where static overloading has been solved by renaming function names (a canonical way is using $f^{\overline{s},s}$ for each $f: \overline{s} \to s$, but for sake of simplicity in the example below we use an ad hoc, even though equivalent, renaming). In the case of our running example (omitting all the functions but equals and inLine)

$$\text{sig } \Sigma_P = \ldots$$
$$\text{sorts } int, 3D \le 2D$$
$$\text{opns}$$
$$equals^2 : 2D, 2D \to bool$$
$$equals^3 : 3D, 3D \to bool$$
$$inLine^{2,3} : 3D, 2D, 3D \to bool$$
$$inLine^{3,2} : 3D, 3D, 2D \to bool$$

Note that in Java the first equals in class 3DPoint is interpreted as a redefinition of equals in class 2DPoint, since the argument type is the same. On the contrary, the second is interpreted as a *new* method with the same name but different argument type. Correspondingly, in the signature we have two function symbols for the two methods with the same name, while there is no different function symbol corresponding to the redefinition.

Now, every method invocation in Java can be translated into a function application (a term over Σ_P) where all the actual parameters but the first (i.e. the receiver, for which the binding is dynamic) are explicitly typed; the name of the function and the types for the explicit typing of the parameters are determined by the algorithm for resolving static overloading in Java. For instance, assuming that P2 and P3 have (static) type 2DPoint and 3DPoint, respectively, the expression P2.equals(P3) is translated into $equals^2(p2, p3 : 2D)$, whereas the expression P3.equals(P3) is translated into $equals^3(p3, p3 : 3D)$. Note that there is no translation for the expression P3.inLine(P3,P3), since it is rejected by the Java compiler as statically incorrect.

It is interesting to note that there exists another possible solution for dealing with static overloading in our framework, besides the canonical one sketched above. This second solution, however, can be applied only when a set of overloaded methods $M(op)$ (i.e. all the methods having the same name op) has the following property[3]:

$$\exists \overline{s} \in S^*, s \in S \text{ s.t. } \forall op' : \overline{u} \to s' \in M(op) \;\; \overline{u} \le \overline{s}, s' = s$$

where S ranges over all types defined in the Java program. If this property holds, then we can simply associate to the program a signature with a unique function symbol op with functionality $\overline{s} \to s$.

---

[3] We could relax the condition by requiring $s' \le s$ instead of $s' = s$, but in this way we should use casting for having a correct translation.

For instance, in the example above, this property is satisfied both for $op =$ **equals** and for $op =$ **inLine**, with functionalities $2D, 2D \rightarrow bool$ and $3D, 3D, 3D \rightarrow bool$, respectively. Considering e.g. **equals**, we will have in the signature a function symbol $equals: 2D, 2D \rightarrow bool$ which expands in any model M_P to the variants

$$
\begin{aligned}
equals^{M_P}_{2D\,2D} &: \rightarrow 2D^{M_P}_{<} \times 2D^{M_P}_{<} bool^{M_P}_{<} \\
equals^{M_P}_{3D\,2D} &: \rightarrow 3D^{M_P}_{<} \times 2D^{M_P}_{<} bool^{M_P}_{<} \\
equals^{M_P}_{2D\,3D} &: \rightarrow 2D^{M_P}_{<} \times 3D^{M_P}_{<} bool^{M_P}_{<} \\
equals^{M_P}_{3D\,3D} &: \rightarrow 3D^{M_P}_{<} \times 3D^{M_P}_{<} bool^{M_P}_{<}
\end{aligned}
$$

which can be used for defining the semantics of the several versions of **equals**, either redefined or overloaded; in our example, $equals^{M_P}_{2D\,2D}$ represents the unique definition of **equals** in the class **2DPoint**, $equals^{M_P}_{3D\,2D}$ its redefinition in the class **3DPoint** and $equals^{M_P}_{3D\,3D}$ the overloaded version added in **3DPoint**. In this case, the version $equals^{M_P}_{2D\,3D}$ is of no use.

Of course, as happens for the first approach, also here we have to explicitly type all the arguments but the receiver; now the expression **P2.equals(P3)** is translated into $equals(p2, p3 : 2D)$, whereas the expression **P3.equals(P3)** is translated into $equals(p3, p3 : 3D)$.

Conclusion

We have presented a formal framework suitable to deal with functions with late binding, a crucial feature of the object-oriented approach. We have proved this formal framework to be an institution, so that our approach provides both a clean way for modeling object-oriented languages (including languages with multimethods like CLOS) and a logic appropriate for reasoning about object-oriented programs and for dealing with the problems that code redefinition via method overriding raises at the level of modular specifications. Furthermore, this institution verifies the amalgamation property, hence it is well-suited also for handling modularization, an important issue for object-oriented systems.

Since our emphasis is on dynamic overloading, in the model we have not taken into account static overloading; however, we have shown that, as happens in many other algebraic frameworks, static overloading can be reduced to a useful syntactic abbreviation, by means of an appropriate renaming and corresponding translation of terms. On the contrary, this simple solution cannot be adopted for dealing with dynamic overloading.

The source of inspiration of this work has been with no doubts [2]. We are in debt with this book for the central idea motivating this paper, i.e. recognizing dynamic overloading resolution as, on one side, the most important distinguishing feature of the object-oriented approach, on the other an extremely powerful mechanism of programming languages which hence deserves a deep theoretical investigation. However, the work presented in this paper faces the problem in a completely different formal framework (a specification formalism rather than a calculus) and with different technical solutions.

In the field of algebraic specification, the formalisms most closely related to ours are the many variants of *order-sorted algebras* [7, 3], since they too handle subtyping and overloading. We have already pointed out in the paper the technical differences. From a more substantial point of view, order-sorted algebras only allow overloading which is *static* (there is no notion of dynamic type in terms) and *conservative* (two function symbols with the same name and type related by the subtyping relation must behave in the same way on elements of the subtype; in few words, no redefinition). These two restrictions are too strong to model "real" inheritance in object-oriented languages.

The possibility of writing axioms which are not required to hold in subtypes presents some similarity with the use of *defaults* in specifications (see e.g. [10]). However, the approach presented there is based on temporal logic and non-monotonic reasoning, whereas we use classical first-order logic.

Finally, a research direction which has some contact points with our work is that studying the use of assertions in case of inheritance (see e.g. [9,12]). Anyway, a more precise comparison with the two last mentioned approaches is matter of further analysis.

References

1. D. Ancona, M. Cerioli, and E. Zucca. A formal framework with late binding. Technical Report DISI-TR-98-16, Dipartimento di Informatica e Scienze dell'Informazione, Università di Genova, 1998.
2. G. Castagna. *Object-Oriented Programming: A Unified Foundation.* Progress in Theoretical Computer Science. Birkhäuser, 1997.
3. M. Cerioli, A. Haxthausen, B. Krieg-Brückner, and T. Mossakowski. Permissive subsorted partial logic in CASL. In *Recent Trends in Algebraic Development Techniques (12th Intl. Workshop, WADT'97 - Selected Papers)*, number 1349 in Lecture Notes in Computer Science, pages 91–107, Berlin, 1997. Springer Verlag.
4. C. Chambers. Object-oriented multi-methods in Cecil. In *ECOOP '92*, number 615 in Lecture Notes in Computer Science, Berlin, 1992. Springer Verlag.
5. H. Ehrig and B. Mahr. *Fundamentals of Algebraic Specification 1. Equations and Initial Semantics*, volume 6 of *EATCS Monograph in Computer Science*. Springer Verlag, 1985.
6. J.A. Goguen and R.M. Burstall. Institutions: Abstract model theory for computer science. *Journ. ACM*, 39:95–146, 1992.
7. J.A. Goguen and J. Meseguer. Order-sorted algebra I: Equational deduction for multiple inheritance, overloading, exceptions and partial equations. *Theoretical Computer Science*, (105):217–273, 1992.
8. S.C. Keene. *Object Oriented Programming in Common Lisp: A Programming Guide in CLOS.* Addison-Wesley, 1989.
9. K. Lano and H. Haughton. Reasoning and refinement in object-oriented specification languages. In O. Lehrmann Madsen, editor, *ECOOP '92*, number 615 in Lecture Notes in Computer Science, pages 78–97, Berlin, June 1992. Springer Verlag.
10. U.W. Lipeck and S. Brass. Object-oriented system specification using defaults. In K. v. Luck and H. Marburger, editors, *Management and Processing Complex Data Structures, Proc. 3rd Workshop on Information Systems and Artificial Intelligence*, number 777 in Lecture Notes in Computer Science, pages 22–43, Berlin, 1994. Springer Verlag.
11. D. Sannella and A. Tarlecki. Towards formal development of programs from algebraic specifications: Implementations revisited. *Acta Informatica*, 25:233–281, 1988.
12. R. Stata and J.V. Guttag. Modular reasoning in the presence of subclassing. In *ACM Symp. on Object-Oriented Programming: Systems, Languages and Applications 1995*, pages 200–214. ACM Press, October 1995. SIGPLAN Notices, volume 30, number 10.
13. A. Tarlecki. Institutions: An abstract framework for formal specification. In *Algebraic Foundation of Information Systems Specification*. Chapman and Hall, 1999. To appear.

Yet Another Real-Time Specification for the Steam Boiler: Local Clocks to Statically Measure Systems Performance[*]

Candida Attanasio, Flavio Corradini, and Paola Inverardi

Dipartimento di Matematica Pura ed Applicata
Università dell'Aquila
Via Vetoio, Loc. Coppito, L'Aquila, Italy
fax +390862433180
{flavio,inverard}@univaq.it

Abstract. In this paper we apply a new real-time modeling to the well-known Steam Boiler case study. The novelty of our approach is in explicitly representing the various system components, i. e. hardware sensors, software controllers and so on, with separate local clocks. The aim of our approach is to be able to statically analyze the global system specification taking into account the relative speed of each system components. For example, we can statically verify if, and how changing the local speed of a component can affect the global performance of the system. Component behaviors are specified by means of a simple process algebra. Local clocks are modeled as higher order terms in a given signature, and *unification* is used to define the common clock. Then an operational semantics defines which transitions a process can perform and which transitions let time to elapse.

1 Introduction

In this paper we apply a new real-time modeling to the well-known "The Steam Boiler" case study taken from [2]. The novelty of our approach is in explicitly representing the various system components, i. e. hardware sensors, software controllers, etc with separate local clocks. The aim of our framework is to be able to statically analyze the global system specification taking into account the relative speed of each system components. For example, we can verify if, and how changing the local speed of a component can affect the global performance of the system. Component behaviors are specified by means of a simple process algebra [20, 15, 18]. Local clocks are modeled as higher order terms in a given signature, and *unification* is used to define the common clock [16]. Then an operational semantics defines which transitions a process can perform and which transitions let time to elapse similarly to [7, 14, 21, 10].

---

[*] This work has been partially funded by CNR, Progetto: Metodologie e strumenti di analisi, verifica e validazione per sistemi software affidabili

In particular we specify the architecture of a system as a network of (parallel) components, each one with its own local clock. This means that, from the behavioral point of view, we put the components in parallel and let them communicate upon synchronization, similarly to [18]. The global clock of the resulting system is obtained from the local clocks which are modeled as higher order terms in a given signature, through a *unification* process [16]. If there exists a unifier, all the local clocks will be expressed as suitable linear functions of the global one. Due to the properties of the unification process, i.e. the existence of a unique most general unifier, this clock configuration step represents the best way to relate the local clocks so that the maximum number of synchronizations in the system can happen. The ability of modeling this clock configuration step allows us, besides the usual behavioral and timing analysis, to statically analyze the systems with respect to different properties. For example, we can verify if, and how, changing the local speed (i.e. the local clock) of a component can affect the global performance of the system. That is the amount of synchronizations in the system increases or decreases.

The paper is organized as follows: Section 2, introduces the language of components, and its operational semantics. The language is CCS-like [20] and discusses the use of higher order terms to represent local clocks. Section 3, presents the steam boiler case study. This is a well known and studied example in the literature of which several different specifications exist [19]. Our interest in it is due to the possibility of performing a kind of *quantitative* analysis which has never been addressed in the previous specifications. Section 4 shows how we can statically reason on the system, that is how we can compare the behavior of different system specifications obtained by considering the same components but with different speed. Section 5 presents conclusions and future works.

1.1 Related Works

As far as related works are concerned, in a companion paper, [3] we have extensively motivated this approach in the emerging field of *component* programming. In fact, besides the traditional field of *control systems* [12, 2, 19], the need of assembling together heterogeneous components is more and more frequent due to the widespread diffusion of information technology in any application field, from multimedia applications to telecommunication systems.

The system description language we consider implements several ideas from classic timed process description languages. The idea of using local clocks is taken from [7, 14, 10], the view of system activities as instantaneous events is taken from [21] (and related works, see references therein). The rational for this choice is that since we are concerned with the static analysis of behavioral aspects of systems obtained by assembling together components running at (possibly) different speed we prefer to abstract from events duration while concentrating on the relative speed of the system components. The relative speed between components, indeed, directly influence the interaction capabilities of the system components which, in turn, may influence the system performance.

The main difference with these works is that we can model different speed for different system components. This is not possible neither in [21], where the existence of a unique global clock is made explicit (and based upon the fact that all system components must synchronize), nor in [7, 14, 10], where the local clocks are assumed to elapse in the same way (by making the system components running at the same speed).

The notion of local clocks and a calculus for synchronizing local clocks, is also presented in the language SIGNAL [1, 11]. There, a clock is associated with a signal and clocks can be of different frequencies. Although the notion of local clocks and of their calculus might resemble our approach, the use of these notions in the two approaches is different.

2 The Language and Its Transitional Semantics

We adopted a two-level syntax which distinguishes between regular processes and interactive processes. Intuitively, a regular process corresponds to a collection of threads of computation which must be performed at a single site. An interactive process corresponds to a (parallel) composition of regular processes which may evolve independently or communicate each other. The language of interactive processes is close to the language presented in [18].

Following [20], we assume a set of actions A (ranged over by α) from which we obtain the set of co-actions $\bar{A} = \{\bar{\alpha} \mid \alpha \in A\}$ useful to model process synchronizations. We use Act (ranged over by $a, b, \ldots$) to denote $A \cup \bar{A}$, the set of visible actions. The invisible action, useful to model internal activities of process executions, is denoted by $\tau \notin Act$ and we use Act_τ (ranged over by μ) to denote the set of all actions $Act \cup \{\tau\}$. V (ranged over by x), is the set of process *variables* used for recursive definitions.

We first define regular processes or $\mathcal{RP}$ [20] which specify finite, nondeterministic automata familiar from the theory of regular languages. The set of regular processes, $\mathcal{RP}$ (ranged over by p, q, ...), over Act_τ and V, is the set of closed (i.e., without free variables) generated by the following grammar:

$$p ::= nil \mid \mu.p \mid p + p \mid x \mid \text{rec } x.\, p\,.$$

Process nil denotes a terminated process. By prefixing a term p with an action μ, we get a process term $\mu.p$ which can perform an action μ and then behaves like p. $p_1 + p_2$ denotes the non deterministic composition of p_1 and p_2, while rec $x.\, p$ is used for recursive definitions. The standard operational semantics of regular processes is omitted. We just recall few standard notational conventions that will be used in the following. The notation $p[q/x]$, where p and q are terms of the syntax of $\mathcal{RP}$ terms and x is a process variable, is used to denote the term obtained from p by simultaneously replacing each free occurrence of x by q. A transition $p \overset{\mu}{\mapsto} p'$ says that process p evolves into process p' by performing an action μ (see [20] for its formal definition).

A distributed, interacting process, or $\mathcal{IP}$ term, is a (finite) parallel combination of regular processes equipped with their own local clocks, or a term restricted by an action, or a term relabeled according to a function $\Phi : Act_\tau \longrightarrow Act_\tau$ that preserves co-actions and leaves τ fixed.

Definition 1. (*Interacting Processes*) The set $\mathcal{IP}$ (ranged over by P, Q, ...) of interacting processes is the least one satisfying the following grammar:

$$P ::= \; < p, \lambda^N x.t^M(x) > \; \Big| \; P|Q \; \Big| \; P\backslash\{a\} \; \Big| \; P[\Phi]$$

where $p \in \mathcal{RP}$, $a \in Act$, N is called degree variable, and $M \in \mathbf{N}$.[1]

Let us spend some words explaining the local clocks and the role they play in analyzing the behavior of concurrent systems. In this paper we model local clocks with a restricted form of the so called "iterative terms" defined in [16]. Iterative terms are higher order terms that finitely represent infinite sequences of first order terms. Thus they seem natural candidates to model time in a discrete way (it can be thought as an infinite sequence of finite objects) and time passing.

Here we make use of a subclass of iterative terms of the form $\lambda^N x.t^m(x)$, where m is a natural number and N ranges over natural numbers. The intuitive meaning of this term is that by ranging N over natural numbers, we can obtain for each n a term by unfolding the context t^m n-times at the subterm x. Where, by convention, we denote a term $t(t(t(x)))$ with $t^3(x)$. For instance, a term like $\lambda^N x.t^2(x)$ denotes the infinite sequence $\{x, t^2(x), t^4(x), t^6(x), ...\}$. This sequence can be thought as the time instants (ticks) where a process is active and hence can perform an action. It is obtained by letting $N \in \{1, 2, ..., \omega\}$; $N = 0$ generates x, $N = 1$ generates $t^2(x)$, $N = 2$ generates $t^4(x)$, We can think of x as the starting time and of $t^i(x)$ as the i-th tic of the local clock (t is a first order term on a certain signature Σ). By varying on the degree variable and assuming different expressions in the body of λ iterative terms, we can have a different scale of the time and hence different local clocks (different speeds). For instance term $\lambda^L x.t^3(x)$ denotes $\{x, t^3(x), t^6(x), t^9(x), ...\}$ and is always obtained by letting $L \in \{1, 2, ..., \omega\}$.

$\lambda^N x.t^2(x)$ and $\lambda^L x.t^3(x)$ with N and L different variables denote the temporal scales of two systems evolving independently according to their own relative speed. The intuition here is that each λ iterative term represents an infinite sequence of elements, thus modeling the time sequence.

In this way, we can analyze how a global system behaves when a component is scheduled to be executed on a slower or faster architecture. This amounts at comparing two different systems where the same component has a slower, respectively faster, local clock. For instance a system with local clock $\lambda^N x.t^2(x)$ is faster than the one with local clock $\lambda^L x.t^3(x)$ because from the starting time (x) to a common time ($t^6(x)$) the former local clock has four ticks ($\{x, t^2(x), t^4(x), t^6(x)\}$) and hence the system is able to perform four actions, while the latter has only three ($\{x, t^3(x), t^6(x)\}$). Common times are particularly interesting to study possible system synchronizations. Two processes can synchronize if they can perform

---

[1] Note that in the syntax of interactive processes, parallelism can only appear at the top level. This ensures us that their standard operational semantics can be described by a finite state transition system.

communicating actions at the same time. Thus, according to the above example, two processes running with speed detected by $\lambda^N x.t^2(x)$ and $\lambda^L x.t^3(x)$ respectively, may synchronize (if they can perform communicating actions) at times ($\{t^6(x), t^{12}(x), t^{18}(x), ...\}$).

Thus common times represent times where process components possibly synchronize. Due to the way we have modeled clocks, the existence of common times depends on the existence of a unifier among all local clocks. The theory of iterative terms states that the problem of determining whether for any pair of iterative terms there exists an (infinite) sequence of common terms or not is decidable. In case it exists a theorem also gives the maximum sequence of common terms (which, intuitively, correspond to the maximum sequence of times where processes can synchronize). In the class of iterative terms we are considering it is always possible to find the maximum sequence of common terms. The theorem gives the most general unifier among terms. The most general unifier relates the degree variables of the iterative terms with a fresh variable degree which generate the maximum sequence of common terms. For instance, the two terms $\lambda^N x.t^2(x)$ and $\lambda^L x.t^3(x)$ initially independent unify for $L = 2Q$ and $N = 3Q$ with Q a fresh name. Thus we could also consider iterative terms $\lambda^{3Q} x.t^2(x)$ and $\lambda^{2Q} x.t^3(x)$ to generate the sequence $\{x, t^6(x), t^{12}(x), t^{18}(x), ...\}$

The notion of most general unifier is exploited in this paper to detect the least common time (after the starting one) of a given set of iterative terms representing local clocks of parallel processes. This time is the least time where all processes in the net can perform something. The iterative terms then behaves "periodically" with respect to this least time. In the period between the starting time, i.e. the degree variable is $= 0$, and the least time, each iterative term can generate different terms. For instance $\lambda^N x.t^2(x)$ generates $\{x, t^2(x), t^4(x), t^6(x)\}$ while $\lambda^L x.t^3(x)$ generates $\{x, t^3(x), t^6(x)\}$, where $t^6(x)$ is the least time . These terms can be ordered in a standard way: $x < t^2(x) < t^3(x) < t^4(x) < t^6(x)$. This ordered sequence gives the finest discrete representation of the time for the two components. At each time of the sequence one of them can perform an action. Being finite, this sequence can be put in bijection with a finite segment of the natural numbers. We can build a matrix of n entries and m columns where n corresponds to the length of the finest sequence from the starting time to the one preceding the least common time and m is the number of parallel regular processes in an interactive term. In our example we have four entries, one for each element of set $\{x, t^2(x), t^3(x), t^4(x)\}$ and two columns, one for each component.

This matrix indicates which processes are active at a given time, and hence also which processes may engage in a synchronization. To build the matrix, consider the finest (ordered) sequence of terms until the common one and take a term t. We put an X at the entry corresponding to t and column corresponding to the process p if the local clock associated with p has term t in its sequence. Clearly we denote with p also every p-derivative, that is every state p reaches during a computation. For this reason we will write $M(i,p) = X$ also when p is not exactly the process p, denoting a column of the matrix, but a p-derivative.

The matrix corresponding to interactive process

$$P = \; < p_1, \lambda^N x.t^2(x) > \; | \; < p_2, \lambda^M x.t^3(x) >$$

with p_1 and p_2 two regular processes is given in Fig. 1.

Table 1. A Matrix for P

	p_1	p_2
x	X	X
$t^2(x)$	X	
$t^3(x)$		X
$t^4(x)$	X	

With abuse of notation, in the rest of this paper, we identify the entries of the matrix (and hence times) with indexes of the matrix itself, i.e. the natural numbers from 0 to $n - 1$. We will also say "at time i" to mean the time corresponding to the natural number i in the finest sequence of local times.

Once matrix M is defined, the next step is to show how an interactive process evolves. We can now forget local clocks (they are memorized in the matrix) within interactive processes. To every regular process p we associate a natural number t. During the execution of a process which contain p as a component, t says whether p has been active or not at a certain time i. In particular, if p has not performed any action at time i then $t = i$, otherwise $t = i + 1$. Since, in our setting, time features as relative (not as absolute; i.e., relative to the starting time of the process execution), t will be called a "relative" local clock.

Definition 2. (*Processes with Relative Local clocks*) The set S (ranged over by d, d', ...) of processes with relative local clocks is the least one satisfying the following rules:

$$d ::= (p, t) \; | \; d|d \; | \; d\backslash\{a\} \; | \; d[\Phi]$$

where $p \in \mathcal{RP}$, $t \in \mathbf{N}$ and $a \in \text{Act}$. Clearly, we are only interested in the sublanguage of states d such that every relative local clock appearing within d is in $\{i, i + 1\}$ for some $i \in \mathbf{N}$.

We now define the transitional semantics of our $\mathcal{IP}$ processes. This is done by first defining which transitions a process can perform at a given (relative) time t (corresponding to an entry of the matrix) and then defining which transitions let time to elapse. The former transitions are given by defining a family of transition relations, one for each entry of the matrix M. Let i be an entry of M, then a transition, according to the transition relation indexed by i, is of the form $d \xrightarrow[M]{\mu}_i d'$. The inference rules defining this family of transition relations are given in Table 2, where we require for $d \xrightarrow[M]{\mu}_i d'$ be derivable that every relative local clock within d is in $\{i, i+1\}$.

Table 2. Transitional "at Time" t

$$\mathbf{Act)}\frac{p \xrightarrow{\mu} p' \text{ and } M(t,p) = X}{(p,t) \xrightarrow[M]{\mu}_t (p', t+1)}$$

$$\mathbf{Par_1)}\frac{d_1 \xrightarrow[M]{\mu}_t d_1'}{d_1|d_2 \xrightarrow[M]{\mu}_t d_1'|d_2} \qquad \mathbf{Par_2)}\frac{d_2 \xrightarrow[M]{\mu}_t d_2'}{d_1|d_2 \xrightarrow[M]{\mu}_t d_1|d_2'}$$

$$\mathbf{Synch)}\frac{d_1 \xrightarrow[M]{a}_t d_1', \; d_2 \xrightarrow[M]{\bar{a}}_t d_2'}{d_1|d_2 \xrightarrow[M]{\tau}_t d_1'|d_2'}$$

$$\mathbf{Res)}\frac{d \xrightarrow[M]{\mu}_t d', \; \mu, \bar{\mu} \neq a}{d\backslash\{a\} \xrightarrow[M]{\mu}_t d'\backslash\{a\}} \qquad \mathbf{Rel)}\frac{d \xrightarrow[M]{\mu}_t d'}{d[\Phi] \xrightarrow[M]{\Phi(\mu)}_t d'[\Phi]}$$

Let us comment the rules in Table 2. The rule for action prefixing **Act)** states that a regular process p can perform an action μ at time t leading to a regular process p', only if p is active ($M(t,p) = X$) and p has not already performed any action (its relative local clock t, not $t + 1$) at that time. The relative local clock is set to $t+1$ to remember that it cannot perform any other action at time t. Rule **Par$_1$)** (**Par$_2$)**) for the asynchronous execution of an action μ from the left (right) subprocess is almost standard. It says that if d_1 performs an action μ at time t, then the parallel composition $d_1|d_2$ can perform the same action at the same time. Rule **Synch)** deals with synchronization; two processes can synchronize if and only if they can perform complementary actions at the same time. Rules **Res)** and **Rel)** for restriction and relabeling are as usual.

Transitions which let time to elapse are of the form $d \xRightarrow[M]{\mu}_i d'$. It is worth of note that two subsequent transitions, such as $d \xRightarrow[M]{\mu}_i d'$ and $d' \xRightarrow[M]{\gamma}_j d''$ may occur at different times (time elapses), while regarding the transition relation $\xrightarrow[M]{\mu}_i$ we always have $i = j$.

The inference rules defining the elapsing of time are given in Table 3. There, up is a function which given a process d and a natural number n updates to n every relative local clock appearing within d (e.g., $up((a.p, 2)|(b.q, 3), 5) = (a.p, 5)|(b.q, 5)$).

When we write $d \not\xrightarrow[M]{\mu}_t$ (instead of $d \xrightarrow[M]{\mu}_t d'$) we mean that each relative local clock within d is in $\{t, t+1\}$ but there is no d' such that $d \xrightarrow[M]{\mu}_t d'$.

Table 3. Modelling the Elapsing of Time

$$
\textbf{TheSame)} \quad \frac{d \xrightarrow[M]{\mu}_t d'}{d \xRightarrow[M]{\mu}_t d'}
$$

$$
d \not\xrightarrow[M]{\tau}_t ,
$$

$$
\textbf{Time)} \quad \frac{up(d, (t+1) \bmod n) \xRightarrow[M]{\mu}_{t'} d'}{d \xRightarrow[M]{\mu}_{t'} d'}
$$

Only rule **Time)** needs explanation. Assume that process d cannot perform any τ action at time t while $up(d, t')$, where $t' = (t+1) \bmod n$ (we set every local clock within d to t' in order to figure out which transitions are possible at that time), can perform an action μ at t' leading to d'. Then also d can perform an action μ at time t' leading to d'.

The basic idea behind this rule is that synchronizations cannot be delayed. They must be performed as soon as they can. In other words, two processes can synchronize when they perform complementary actions at the same time; if one of the two is able to execute such an action before the other, then a form of *busy waiting* is allowed. This permits one to model a situation in which a faster process can wait for a slower partner. However, when both partners are ready to synchronize, the handshaking immediately occurs. On the other hand visible actions can be delayed arbitrarily long before firing. This treatment between visible and invisible actions is only apparently different. Invisible actions denote synchronizations between two parallel components of the same process ("internal" synchronizations), while visible actions model synchronizations with the external environment ("external" synchronizations). Thus delayed executions of visible actions models a situation in which the process responsible for their execution is slower (faster) with respect to an hypothetic external faster (slower) partner.

While Section 4 entirely concentrates on the analysis of the systems performance we now show, via a simple example, how the interaction capabilities of the system may influence also its functionality. This is because parallel components can only synchronize at given time instances (detected by the local clocks). Hence, some synchronizations might not happen. Consider, for instance, a simple system described by:

$$S = (< p_1, \lambda^N x.t^2(x) > \ | \ < p_2, \lambda^M x.t^4(x) >)\backslash\{b\}$$

where $p_1 = \text{rec } x.\tau.(b.x + \tau.x)$ and $p_2 = \text{rec } x.\bar{b}.x$.

The matrix associated with M is given in Table 4. It is not difficult to see that

Table 4. A Matrix for System S

p_1	p_2
X	X
X	

the synchronization on channel b never fires when the local clocks associated with the parallel components p_1 and p_2 are $\lambda^N x.t^2(x)$ and $\lambda^M x.t^4(x)$, respectively. This phenomenon does not arise if p_1 and p_2 are associated, instead, with local clocks generating the same temporal scale. Clearly, as will also be noted in Section 4, this phenomenon does not happen in the class of concurrent but not communicating actions. All actions will eventually be performed.

3　The Steam Boiler

The level of water in a boiler, that is heated to generate high-pressure steam, has to be controlled to guarantee certain minimal and maximal water level values (whose violation would damage the steam boiler).

The steam boiler consists of two sensors, $MeasS$ and $MeasW$, a pump, $Pump$, a valve, $Valve$ and two controllers, $PContr$ and $VContr$. The sensor $MeasS$ measures the steam pressure level value within the boiler while the sensor $MeasW$ measures the water level value. The $Pump$ is used to pump water in the boiler to replace the steam released, and $Valve$ is used to release steam when the pressure within the boiler becomes dangerous. The pump controller $PContr$ switches the pump off when the water reaches the high water level and on when it goes below the low water level. An operator must be informed of any level of the water becoming critical (below the low level water and over the high level water). The valve controller $VContr$ switches the valve on when the steam has to be released and off when the pressure steam level value becomes acceptable. As in the case of the pump controller, an operator must be informed of any level of the steam becoming critical (over the high level steam). See Figure 1 for the software architecture of the steam boiler.

Let us describe the intended behavior of the sensors. $MeasW$ performs an internal action τ when the level of water is between the low and high water

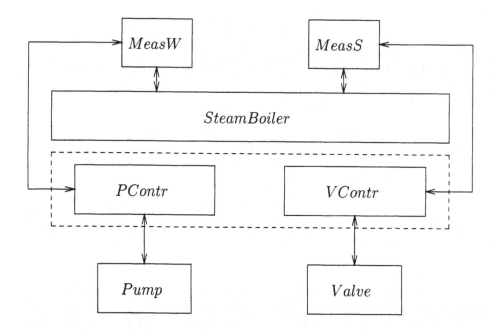

Fig. 1. The Steam Boiler Software Architecture

level. It performs an action LowWater (lw) when the water must be pumped in the boiler and action HighWater (hw) when the actual level of water sufficiently replaces the steam released. When the level of the water is too high or too low $MeasW$ performs an action DangerWater (dw). $MeasS$ has a similar behavior. It performs an action τ when the level value of the steam is between the low level and the high level, an action hs when the $Valve$ must be opened (because the level value of the steam is too high), an action ls when the $Valve$ has to be closed and an action ds when the level value of the steam becomes critical (higher than the maximum value allowed).

$$MeasW \equiv rec\ x.\ (\tau.x\ +\ hw.x\ +\ lw.x\ +\ dw.x)$$
$$MeasS \equiv rec\ x.\ (\tau.x\ +\ hs.x\ +\ ls.x\ +\ ds.x)$$

The pump receives *pon* or *poff* commands from the pump controller when the water must be pumped in or not respectively.

$$Pump \equiv rec\ x.\ (\overline{pon}.x\ +\ \overline{poff}.x)$$

The valve must be opened (closed) when it receives *von* (*voff*) commands from the valve controller.

$$Valve \equiv rec\ x.\ (\overline{von}.x\ +\ \overline{voff}.x)$$

The steam controller is the parallel composition of the pump controller and the valve controller: $PContr$ and $VContr$. $PContr$ receives signals by $MeasW$ and $VContrE$ by $MeasS$.

$$SContr \equiv PContr \mid VContr.$$

When $PContr$ receives a LowWater (it communicates with $MeasW$ by performing an action $\overline{lw}$) it switches on the pump and when it receives a HighWater (it communicates with $MeasW$ by performing an action $\overline{hw}$) it switches off the pump. Finally, if $PContr$ receives a DangerWater level (it communicates with $MeasW$ by performing an action $\overline{dw}$) the operator is informed through the execution of an action $Emergency$. $VContr$ behaves similarly.

$$
\begin{aligned}
PContr \equiv\ &rec\ x.\ \overline{dw}.Emergency.x\ + \\
&rec\ x.\ \overline{hw}.poff.x\ + \\
&rec\ x.\ \overline{lw}.pon.x \\
VContr \equiv\ &rec\ x.\ \overline{ds}.Emergency.x\ + \\
&rec\ x.\ \overline{hs}.von.x\ + \\
&rec\ x.\ \overline{ls}.voff.x
\end{aligned}
$$

The whole system is the parallel composition of the sensors, the pump, the pump controller, the valve and the valve controller. In our initial configuration, $System_1$, we assume that the $Valve$ and the $Pump$ are the faster devices. The sensors $MeasW$ and $MeasS$ are slower than the previous components but faster than the two controllers.

$$
\begin{aligned}
System_1 \equiv\ (&< MeasW, \lambda^N x.t^3(x) >\ | \\
&< MeasS, \lambda^S x.t^3(x) >\ | \\
&< PContr, \lambda^R x.t^4(x) >\ | \\
&< VContr, \lambda^M x.t^4(x) >\ | \\
&< Pump, \lambda^P x.t^2(x) >\ | \\
&< Valve, \lambda^Q x.t^2(x) >)\backslash\{dw, ds, lw, ls, hw, hs, pon, poff, von, voff\}
\end{aligned}
$$

The matrix associated with $System_1$ is shown in Table 5. The least common time is t^{12} (remember that it is the first time, after the starting time x, in the sequence generated by the most general unifier, that is the first time at which *all* components can perform an action). The finest sequence is

$$\{x, t^2(x), t^3(x), t^4(x), t^6(x), t^8(x), t^9(x), t^{10}(x)\}.$$

These times are denoted by the fragment of natural numbers $\{0, 1, 2, 3, 4, 5, 6, 7\}$. We recall that these are all the (local) times at which some component can perform an action.

4 Analyzing the Steam Boiler Behaviors

In this section we show how our model can be used to analyze system properties. We are particularly interested in proving properties related to the interaction capabilities of the system components. These may influence the system

Table 5. A Matrix for $System_1$

$MeasW$	$MeasS$	$PContr$	$VContr$	$Pump$	$Valve$
X	X	X	X	X	X
				X	X
X	X				
		X	X	X	X
X	X			X	X
		X	X	X	X
X	X				
				X	X

performance, as we will see in this section, besides the system functionality, as already seen in Section 2. Indeed, the parallel components can only synchronize at given time instances (detected by the local clocks). Hence, some synchronizations might be delayed for a while if not discarded at all.

We can give examples of systems where increasing the speed of a system component always means increasing the performance of the system as a whole.[2] Consider, for instance, $MeasW$ and $MeasS$ running in parallel:

$$< MeasW, \lambda^R x.t^4(x) > \; | \; < MeasS, \lambda^R x.t^4(x) > .$$

If we make the temporal scale finer, then the performance of such system always increases. In the case of sensors, this means that more checks are made in the same interval of time. Hence, also means that the danger level water/steam and the high level water/steam are detected sooner.

The slogan "increasing the speed of a system component always means increasing the performance of the system as a whole", however, on one hand is not always desirable, on the other is not always guaranteed. To see that it is not always desirable just think of $MeasW$ and $MeasS$ as video presentation device and sound presentation device in a multimedia system. In this case the two components must proceed together (at the same speed) because it is critical that a sound stream is played out within a reasonable interval of time after/before

---

[2] This is typical in the class of concurrent but non communicating systems.

the video stream is played out. Making a component faster than another one might imply making the presentation of the video and sound streams not "well-synchronized". In presence of synchronization, moreover, it is not always the case that faster components imply faster systems. Consider, for instance,

$$((MeasW, 0) \mid (MeasS, 0) \mid (PContr, 0) \mid (VContr, 0) \mid (Pump, 0) \mid (Valve, 0))$$
$$\backslash \{dw, ds, , hw, hs, lw, ls, pon, poff, von, voff\}$$

the initial state of $System_1$.

The earlier time the Valve (Pump) is opened in $System_1$, due to a HighSteam (LowWater) level, is $t^4(x)$ ($t^4(x)$). This is a case in which the Valve (Pump) runs faster than the Controllers.

As one would expect, if the Valve (Pump) runs slower than the Controllers (replace local clocks $\lambda^P x.t^2(x)$ and $\lambda^Q x.t^2(x)$ with $\lambda^P x.t^5(x)$ and $\lambda^Q x.t^5(x)$ in $System_1$) then we would have a worse performance: the Valve (Pump) would be opened at $t^{20}(x)$.

Nevertheless, in some cases, faster components imply worse performances. Consider the following assignment of speeds to the components of our steam boiler system:

$$
\begin{aligned}
System_2 \equiv (&< MeasW, \lambda^N x.t^3(x) > \mid \\
&< MeasS, \lambda^S x.t^3(x) > \mid \\
&< PContr, \lambda^R x.t^3(x) > \mid \\
&< VContr, \lambda^M x.t^3(x) > \mid \\
&< Pump, \lambda^P x.t^2(x) > \mid \\
&< Valve, \lambda^Q x.t^2(x) >) \backslash \{dw, ds, lw, ls, hw, hs, pon, poff, von, voff\}
\end{aligned}
$$

where the controllers are faster than the corresponding ones in $System_1$ while the other components are untouched. We get a matrix with only 4 entries but the least time the Valve (Pump) can be opened, due to a HighSteam (LowWater) level, is time $t^6(x)$ (against the $t^4(x)$ of $System_1$).

Other interesting properties related to our systems can be analyzed by mapping our abstract interpretation of time and time passing into the common notion of time. This can be done by associating the first order t term, appearing within local clocks, with an interval of real time. Then, every $t^N(x)$ (for $N \in \mathbf{N}$) denotes a real instant of time for an external observer. If n denotes the number of entries of the actual matrix, the real time associated with $t^N(x)$ can be calculated by $N \bmod n$ (the actual entry of the matrix or, in other words, the relative time) and by $N \operatorname{div} n$ (how many times the entry of the matrix reaches n and, hence, a new slot of observation is taken into account). Then, always regarding to the steam boiler system, we can answer to safety requirements such as:

- Can the pump be switched on in one hour?
- After how many time units $PContr$ switches on the pump after receiving a LowWater command by $MeansW$?
- Can the external environment be informed in one hour if the steam boiler gets an emergency state?
- When the controllers receive a DangerWater/DangerSteam which is the least time the environment is informed that the steam boiler gets an emergency state?

- Are there actions which will never be performed?
- Is our system deadlock-free? And, eventually, which is the least time it will reach a deadlock state?

These questions may have different answers depending on the local clocks chosen to specify the speed of the parallel components, that is depending on the considered configuration.

Moreover, we can prove that the labeled transition system associated with a configuration d is a finite state transition system. This is due to the fact that our systems are interactive processes (which are finite states according to the standard operational semantics [20]) and to the fact that the matrix we are dealing with are finite. Hence, we could use standard tools to generate and to verify the transition systems [8].

5 Conclusions and Future Work

In this paper we have applied our approach to model configurations of real-time components to the Steam Boiler case study. Our approach allows a more faithful modelling of systems obtained by assembling together heterogeneous components. The key feature of the approach is the possibility of statically analyze the interaction capabilities of the system components in terms of the possible global system synchronizations. This allows the designer to suitably *tune* the local speeds of the components, in order to achieve the best performance potentiality of the system. The kind of temporal analysis we have performed on the Steam Boiler example, is completely new with respect to what presented in previous specifications [2] and it is representative of a common need when designing this kind of systems. Very often, in the design of complex systems arises the need of setting the frequency with which a certain component, in our case a sensor but in general any kind of controller, has to exhibit a given event. Associated with the event, there can be a cost (e.g. a transmission cost), thus it is mandatory for the designer to choose the right local timing which maximizes the global performance while minimizing costs.

The λ iterative terms we used in this paper were very simple and did not show the λ iterative terms potentiality. We expect to better exploit the λ iterative terms expressive power in modeling, besides time, other quality parameters of heterogeneous system components, like for example frequency or capacity. Future works are in the direction of applying our approach to different kind of systems for which some kind of tuning of quality parameters should be done.

References

1. Amagbegnon,T.P., Besnard,L., Le Guernic,P.: Implementation of the data-flow Synchronous Language Signal. Proc. ACM Symposium on Programming Languages design and ImplementationACM (1995) 163-173.
2. *Formal Methods for Industrial Applications.* Abrial,J-R., Börger,e., Landmaack,H. Eds., Springer Verlag (1996).

3. Attanasio,C., Corradini,F., Inverardi,P.: Static Analysis of Real-Time Component-based Systems Configurations, Internal Report 11/98, Universita' dell'Aquila (1998).

4. Allen,R., Garlan,D.: A Formal Basis for Architectural Connection. ACM Transactions on Software Engineering and Methodology, 6(3) (1997) 213-249.

5. Blair,G.S., Blair,L., Bowman,H., Chetwynd,A.: Formal Specification in Distributed Multimedia Systems. University College London Press (1997).

6. Bowman,H., Faconti,G., Katoen,J-P., Latella,D., Massink,M.: automatic Verification of a Lip Synchronization Algorithm Using UPPAAL. In FMICS'98 (1998).

7. Aceto,L., Murphy,D.: Timing and Causality in Process Algebra. Acta Informatica 33(4) (1996), 317-350.

8. Cleaveland,R., Parrow,J., Steffen,B.: The concurrency workbench: A semantics-based tool for the verification of concurrent systems. In ACM Transaction on Programming Languages and Systems 15 (1993).

9. Coen-Porisini,A., Ghezzi,C., Kemmere,R.A.: Specification of Realtime Systems Using ASTRAL. In IEEE Transaction on Software Engineering 23 (9) (1997).

10. Corradini,F.,: On Performance Congruences for Process Algebras. Information and Computation 145 (1998), 191-230.

11. Project EP-ATR. Rapport d'activite' scientifique 1997. IRISA, INRIA-Rennes (1997).

12. Friesen,V., Jähnichen,S., Weber,M.: Specification of Software Controlling a Discrete-Continuos Environment. ACM Proceedings ICSE97 (1997), 315-325.

13. Ghezzi,C., Mandrioli,D., Morzenti,A.: TRIO: A Logic Language for Executable Specifications of Real-Time Systems. Journal Systems and Software, 25 (2) (1994).

14. Gorrieri,R., Roccetti,M., Stancampiano,E.: A Theory of Processes with Durational Actions. *Theoretical Computer Science* 140(1) (1995), 73-94.

15. Hoare,C.A.R.: *Communicating Sequential Processes*. Prentice-Hall, Englewood Cliffs, New Jersey (1985).

16. Intrigila,B., Inverardi,P., Venturini Zilli,M.: A Comprehensive Setting for Matching and Unification over Iterative Terms. submitted to *Fundamenta Informaticae*.

17. Inverardi,P., Wolf,A.L.: Formal Specification and Analysis of Software Architectures using the Chemical Abstract Machine Model. *IEEE Transactions on Software Engineering*, 21(4) (1995), 373-386.

18. Kramer,J., MageeJ.: Exposing the skeleton in the coordination closet. Proc. of Coordination'97, LNCS 1282, Springer-Verlag (1997), 18-31.

19. *Real-Time Systems Specification, Verification and Analysis*. Mathai,J. Ed., Prentice Hall Internation Series in Computer Science (1996).

20. Milner,R.: *Communication and concurrency*. International series on computer science, Prentice Hall International (1989).

21. Moller,F., Tofts,C.: A Temporal Calculus of Communicating Systems. Proc. of CONCUR'90, LNCS 459, Springer-Verlag (1990), 401-415.

Executable Tile Specifications
for Process Calculi*

Roberto Bruni[1], José Meseguer[2] and Ugo Montanari[1]

[1] Dipartimento di Informatica, Università di Pisa, Italia.
[2] Computer Science Laboratory, SRI International, Menlo Park, CA, U.S.A.
bruni@di.unipi.it, meseguer@csl.sri.com, ugo@di.unipi.it

Abstract. *Tile logic* extends *rewriting logic* by taking into account side-effects and rewriting synchronization. These aspects are very important when we model *process calculi*, because they allow us to express the dynamic interaction between processes and "the rest of the world". Since rewriting logic is the semantic basis of several language implementation efforts, we can define an executable specification of tile systems by mapping tile logic back into rewriting logic. In particular, this implementation requires the development of a metalayer to control rewritings, i.e., to discard computations that do not correspond to any deduction in tile logic. Our methodology is applied to *term tile systems* that cover and extend a wide-class of SOS formats for the specification of process calculi. The case study of full CCS, where the term tile format is needed to deal with recursion (in the form of the replicator operator), is discussed in detail.

1 Introduction

This paper reports on the application of tile logic to the specification and execution of process calculi. For the specification part, we take advantage of the synchronization mechanism of tile logic that extends well-known SOS formats. The execution is based on a general translation of tile logic into rewriting logic.

In *rewriting logic* [26], a logic theory is associated to a term rewriting system, in such a way that each computation represents a *sequent* entailed by the theory. The *entailment* relation is then specified by simple inference rules and deduction in the logic is equivalent to computing in the system. Given this correspondence, a sentence $t \Rightarrow t'$ has two readings: *computationally*, it means that when the system is in a state s, any instance of the pattern t in s can evolve to the corresponding instance of t', possibly in parallel with other changes; *logically*, it means that we can derive the *formula* t' from t. Moreover, the notion of state is entirely user-definable as an algebraic data type satisfying certain equational

---

* Research partially supported by MURST project Tecniche Formali per Sistemi Software, and by Esprit WG CONFER2. Also partially supported by DARPA through Rome Laboratories Contract F30602-97-C-0312 and NASA Contract NAS2-98073, by Office of Naval Research Contract N00014-96-C-0114, and by National Science Foundation Grants CCR-9505960 and CCR-9633363.

properties. Therefore, rewriting logic has good properties as a *semantic framework* where many different languages, systems and models of computation (e.g., labelled transition systems, grammars, Petri nets and algebraic nets, chemical abstract machine, concurrent objects, actors, graph rewriting, data flow, neural networks, real time systems, and many others) can be nicely expressed by natural encodings. For example, specifications of programming languages given in terms of rewrite theories become *de facto* interpreters for the languages in question. On the other hand, rewriting logic has also very good properties as a *logical framework* where many other logics can be naturally represented (several examples can be found in [25, 24]). Rewriting logic has also been used as a semantic framework for software architectures, providing a formal semantics for *architecture description languages* and their interoperation [31]. Further examples regards *theorem provers* and other formal methods tools, based on *inference systems* that can be specified and prototyped in rewriting logic. Also *communication protocols*, including *secure* ones, are another promising area [13]. Moreover, there exist several languages based on rewriting logic (e.g., Maude, ELAN, CafeObj), developed in different countries, and this growing community has recently organized two workshops to discuss all the aspects of rewriting logic [28, 23]. A progress report on the multiple activities connected to rewriting logic has been the topic of an invited talk at CONCUR'96 [27].

The semantics of process calculi for reactive systems and protocol prototyping are usually presented in the SOS form [35]. Such representation naturally yields a *conditional* rewriting system [25], where the basic rule of the rewrite theory can have the more general form: $t \Rightarrow t'$ if $s_1 \Rightarrow s_1' \wedge \cdots \wedge s_n \Rightarrow s_n'$.

Unfortunately, the implementation of conditional rules increases the expressive power of rewrite theories as much as the complexity of the underlying rewrite machine. Indeed, conditional rules are not supported by languages based on rewriting logic for efficency reasons. Hence, specifications must be adapted before becoming executable. Of course, such modification can be pursued in an ad hoc fashion for each model, but a better approach consists of having a *methodology* that automatically performs the translation for an entire class of problems.

The *tile model* [17, 19] is a formalism for modular descriptions of the dynamic evolution of concurrent systems. Basically, a set of rules defines the behaviour of certain *open* (e.g., partially specified) *configurations*, which may interact through their *interfaces*. Then, the behaviour of a system as a whole consists of a coordinated evolution of its sub-systems. The name "tile" is due to the graphical representation of such rules, which have the form

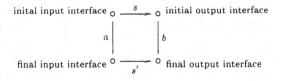

also written $s \xrightarrow[b]{a} s'$, stating that the *initial configuration* s of the system evolves to the *final configuration* s' producing the *effect* b, which can be observed by the rest of the system. However, such a step is allowed only if the subcomponents of s (which is in general an open configuration) evolve to the subcomponents of s', producing the *trigger* a. Triggers and effects are called *observations*. The vertices of each tile are called *interfaces*.

Tiles can be composed horizontally (synchronizing an effect with a trigger), vertically (computational evolutions of a certain component), and in parallel (concurrent steps) to generate larger steps. By analogy with rewriting logic, the tile model also comes equipped with a purely logical presentation [19], where tiles are just considered as (decorated) sequents subject to certain inference rules. Given a tile system, the associated tile logic is obtained by adding some "auxiliary" tiles and then freely composing in all possible ways (i.e., horizontally, vertically and in parallel) both auxiliary and basic tiles. As an example, auxiliary tiles may be necessary to represent consistent horizontal and vertical rearrangements of interfaces.

It is clear that tile logic extends (unconditional) rewriting logic, taking into account rewriting with side effects and rewriting synchronization, whereas, in rewriting systems, both triggers and effects are just identities (i.e., rewriting steps may be applied freely). This feature of tile logic has been at the basis of several successful application as a model of computation for reactive systems: varying the algebraic structures of configurations and observations many different aspects can be modelled, ranging from synchronization of net transitions [7], to causal dependencies for located calculi [16], to finitely branching approaches for name-passing calculi [15], to actor systems [34]. Moreover, tile logic allows one to reason about open configurations, in the style of *context systems* [21], whilst ordinary SOS formats work for ground terms only (e.g., *bisimulation* can be generalized to *tile bisimulation* that operates over contexts rather than just over terms).

A main question has concerned how to give an implementation to tile logic. Systems based on rewriting logic are a natural choice, due to the great similarity with the more general framework of tiles. This topic has been extensively investigated in [30], and successively in [4], where the results of [30] have been extended to the cases of *process* and *term tile logic*, where both configurations and effects rely on common auxiliary structures (e.g., for tupling, projecting or permuting interfaces). As a result, the mapping becomes effective provided that "the rewriting engine is able to filter computations". To achieve this, in [5] we make use of the *reflective* capabilities [11,8] of the Maude language [9] to define suitable *internal strategies* [10,12], which allow the user to control the computation and to collect the possible results.

In this paper we give a survey of some basic internal strategies, and we show how they can be applied to obtain executable specifications for a rich class of process calculi. To give an example of the implementation mechanism, we instantiate the general idea to the well-known case study of full CCS [32] whose presentation requires the term tile format. While a process calculus (located CCS) that needs *process* tile logic (rather than the simpler *monoidal tile logic* of [30]) has been modelled in [6], this is the first time that *term* tile logic is shown to be indispensable for certain features of process calculi.

Related Works. This work is part of our ongoing research aimed at developing general mechanisms for a uniform implementation of several tile formats. In recent papers, different mathematical structures have been employed to model configurations and observations. Basically, we can distinguish two approaches.

The first approach, proposed in [19], considers models arising from internal constructions in suitable categories with structure. Such "structure", usually determined by the algebra of configurations, is then lifted to tiles (in the horizontal dimension only), whilst the observations just yield a monoid over the sequences of basic actions. Within this class we recall a net model equipped with a synchronization mechanism between transitions, called *zero-safe nets* [7]. This is probably the simplest tile model one can imagine, because its configurations and its observations are just commutative monoids (the monoidal operation models both parallel and sequential compositions). Other examples consist of the monoidal tile system for finite CCS of [30], where discharged choices of nondeterministic sums are managed with explicit garbaging, and the algebraic tile system for finite CCS [19], where configurations have a cartesian structure (corresponding to the term algebra of processes), and free discharging of choices is allowed. Finally, we mention the simple coordination model based on graph rewriting and synchronization of [33] whose configurations, called *open graphs*, have an algebraic characterization as suitable *gs-graphs* (a structure with explicit subterm sharing and garbaging, offering a partial algebraic semantic for modelling graphs with subsets of sharable nodes), used to recast the hard computational problem of tile synchronization into a distributed version of constraint solving.

The second approach considers a richer class of models, where both configurations and observations have similar algebraic structures. Rather than based on internal constructions, such models rely on the notion of *hypertransformation*, which is able to characterize the analogies between the mathematical structures employed in the two dimensions. Within this class we recall the tile model for located CCS, which can take into account causal relationships between the performed actions, by looking at the *locations* where they take place. This model requires some auxiliary tiles for consistent permutations of the elements in the interfaces. Such tiles have been naïvely introduced in [16], and then characterized as suitable hypertransformations in [4, 6]. We also want to mention the tile models sketched in [34] to emphasize the similarities between *actor systems* and calculi with mobility (e.g., π-calculus).

The tile model for full CCS we propose in this paper is based on term structures on both dimensions and clearly belongs to the second class of systems.

The idea of translating tile models based on the first approach above into rewriting logic has been discussed for the first time by two of the authors in [30]. Then, it has been extended to the more general framework (based on hypertransformations) in [4]. Further directions of research have focused on control mechanisms over rewritings that are necessary to support the theoretical results at the implementation level of Maude. To this aim, the definition of a kernel of internal strategies in the language Maude has been fully discussed in [5].

An extensive presentation of the translation of tiles into ordinary rewrite rules can be found in the Technical Report [4] and in the forthcoming PhD Thesis of one of the authors [3]. In particular, we have investigated the similarities between rewriting logic and tile logic from the point of view of their categorical models[1].

Structure of the paper. In Section 2 we give a survey of tile logic and of its translation into rewriting logic. We also propose a brief comparison between several specification formats. In Section 3 we describe some useful internal strategies, written in a self-explanatory Maude-like notation, and in Section 4 we show their application to the field of process calculi. The case study presented in Section 4 consists of a full version of CCS, where the replicator is considered.

2 Mapping Tile Logic into Rewriting Logic

2.1 Tile Logic Specifications

The notions of configuration, observation and interface are the basic ingredients of tile logic, and all of them come naturally equipped with the operation of parallel composition. Moreover, the input (output) interface of the parallel composition of two configurations h and g is just the parallel composition of the two input (output) interfaces of h and g. Similarly for the interfaces of the parallel composition of two observations. To simplify the notation, in this presentation we assume that the parallel composition is associative and has the empty interface (configuration, observation) as neutral element, i.e., we assume that interfaces (configurations, observations) yield a *strict monoid*.

Informally, the interfaces represents connection points between different configurations of the system, and also between consecutive observations of the same component. Therefore, configurations (observations) also have sequential composition as a natural operation. In particular we can assume that configurations and observations form two *strict monoidal categories*, having the same class of objects (i.e., the interfaces). We denote the operators of parallel and of sequential composition by $\_ \otimes \_$ and by $\_;\_$ respectively.

Within tile logic, the basic methodology to specify the model of computation for a concrete system consists of the following steps: (1) define the set of basic configurations of the system; (2) define what the interfaces of each basic configuration are; (3) define the basic events that we want to observe and their interfaces according to the previous steps (if necessary, we can repeatedly apply

---

[1] A rewriting theory $\mathcal{R}$ yields a *cartesian 2-category* $\mathcal{L}_{\mathcal{R}}$, which does for $\mathcal{R}$ what a Lawvere theory does for a signature. Gadducci and Montanari pointed out in [18], that if also side-effects are introduced, then *double categories* (DC) [14] should be considered as a natural model: tiles are double cells, configurations are horizontal arrows, observations are vertical arrows, and objects model connections between the somehow static horizontal category and the dynamic vertical evolution. Depending on the structures under consideration, either monoidal DC [19], or symmetric DC, or cartesian DC must be considered (the last two notions being introduced in [4]).

these three steps, until the basic structures are chosen); (4) define the set of tiles that describe the basic behaviours of the system accordingly to the framework chosen in the first three steps (again, it could be necessary to iterate all the four steps to obtain a consistent definition of the tile system). The steps (1) and (3) must take into account the fact that the mathematical structures employed to represent configurations and observations are strict monoidal categories. Most of the times, it is convenient to assume that configurations and observations are just the categories freely generated from the basic configurations and from the basic observable actions that the system can perform.

For example, an obvious choice in the definition of tile models for many process algebras is to take the term algebra of processes as the category of configurations, and the free monoid over action strings as the category of observations (e.g., see [19]). This is correct because the tuple of terms can be seen as arrows of a suitable strict monoidal category (namely a cartesian category), where the parallel composition corresponds to tupling of terms and the sequential composition is term substitution. In this case, the structure employed for configurations is richer than the one requested by the framework. Indeed it allows free duplication and projection of terms. We refer to such operators as *auxiliary structures*, because they do not depend on the signature, and instead belong to any term algebra under consideration.

The tile model for full CCS introduced in Section 4 requires a term structure for both configurations and observations. Hence, similar auxiliary structures are necessary on both dimensions and a certain number of auxiliary tiles (for consistent rearrangements of interfaces on both dimensions) must be introduced in the model. We have investigated such kind of tile structures in [4], under the terminology *term tile systems* (tTS).

2.2   Term Tile Systems

In what follows we consider one-sorted signature only. The many-sorted case can be handled very easily in a similar way, but requires a more complex notation that is not necessary for our case study and therefore avoided.

An *algebraic theory* [22] is just a cartesian category having underlined natural numbers as objects. The free algebraic theory associated to a signature Σ is called the *Lawvere theory* for Σ, and is denoted by $\mathbf{Th}[\Sigma]$: the arrows from $\underline{m}$ to $\underline{n}$ are in a one-to-one correspondence with n-tuples of terms of the free Σ-algebra with (at most) m variables, and composition of arrows is term substitution. As a matter of notation, we assume a standard naming of the $\underline{m}$ input variables, namely $x_1, ..., x_m$. When composing two arrows $s : \underline{m} \longrightarrow \underline{k}$ and $t : \underline{k} \longrightarrow \underline{n}$, the resulting term $s; t$ is obtained by replacing each occurrence of x_i in t by the i-th term of the tuple s, for $i = 1, ..., k$. For example, constants a, b in Σ are arrows from $\underline{0}$ to $\underline{1}$, a binary operator $w(x_1, x_2)$ define an arrow from $\underline{2}$ to $\underline{1}$, and the composition $\langle a, b \rangle; \langle w(x_1, x_2), x_1 \rangle; \langle w(x_2, x_1) \rangle$ yields the term $w(a, w(a, b))$, which is an arrow from $\underline{0}$ to $\underline{1}$, in fact:

$$\langle a, b \rangle; \langle w(x_1, x_2), x_1 \rangle; \langle w(x_2, x_1) \rangle = \langle w(a, b), a \rangle; \langle w(x_2, x_1) \rangle = \langle w(a, w(a, b)) \rangle$$

When no confusion can arise, we avoid the use of angle brackets to denote term vectors. When configurations and observations are terms over two distinct signatures Σ_H and Σ_V, we can assume that each basic tile has the form:

$$
\begin{array}{ccc}
\underline{n} & \xrightarrow{\;h\;} & \underline{m} \\[4pt]
{\scriptstyle v}\downarrow & & \downarrow{\scriptstyle u} \\[4pt]
\underline{k} & \xrightarrow[\;g\;]{} & \underline{1}
\end{array}
$$

with $h \in T_{\Sigma_H}(X_n)^m$, $g \in T_{\Sigma_H}(X_k)$, $v \in T_{\Sigma_V}(X_n)^k$, and $u \in T_{\Sigma_V}(X_m)$, where $X_i = \{x_1, ..., x_i\}$ is a chosen set of variables, totally ordered by $x_{j_1} < x_{j_2}$ if $j_1 < j_2$, and $T_\Sigma(X)^n$ denotes the n-tuples of terms over the signature Σ and variables in X. Due to space limitation, we present tiles more concisely as logic sequents $n \vartriangleleft h \xrightarrow[u]{v} g$, where also the number of variables in the "upper-left" corner of the tile is made explicit (the values m and k can be easily recovered from the lengths of h and v). The idea is that each interface represents an ordered sequence (i.e., a tuple) of variables; therefore each variable is completely identified by its position in the tuple, and a standard naming $x_1, ..., x_n$ of the variables can be assumed. For example, if the variable x_i appears in the effect u of the above rule, then this means that the effect u depends on the i-th component h_i of the initial configuration. Analogously for the remaining connections. Notice that the same variable x_i, denotes the i-th element of different interfaces when used in each of the four border-arrows of the tile (in particular, only the occurrences of x_i in h and in v denote the same element of the initial input interface $\underline{n}$).

The format of term tiles is very general. In particular, it extends the *positive GSOS* format [1], where multiple testing of the same argument are allowed in the premises, and tested arguments can appear in the target of the transition in the conclusion, i.e., rules can have the more general form

$$
\frac{\{x_i \xrightarrow{a_{ij}} y_{ij} \mid 1 \le i \le k, 1 \le n_i\}}{f(x_1, ..., x_k) \xrightarrow{a} C[x_1, y_{11}, ..., y_{1n_1}, ..., x_k, y_{k1}, ..., y_{kn_k}]}
$$

where the variables are all distinct, f is a k-ary operator, $n_i \ge 0$, a_{ij} and a are actions and $C[_{-1}, ..., _{-N}]$ is a context that takes $N = \sum_{i=1}^k (n_i + 1)$ arguments. The corresponding tiles have the form $k \vartriangleleft f(x_1, ..., x_k) \xrightarrow[a(x_1)]{a} C[x_1 ... x_N]$, where $a = \langle x_1, a_{11}(x_1), .., a_{1n_1}(x_1), ..., x_k, a_{k1}(x_k), .., a_{kn_k}(x_k) \rangle$ is the vector of triggers (for each argument of f, a contains the idle trigger plus all the actions that are tested in the premises of the GSOS rule for that argument). We remark that the positive GSOS format cannot be handled by tile systems defined using the internal construction approach (see [19]). Term tile logic can also handle rules with *lookahead* as the one defined in [20]:

$$
\frac{x \xrightarrow{a^+} y, \; y \xrightarrow{a^-} z}{\mathit{combine}(x) \xrightarrow{a} \mathit{combine}(z)} \quad \text{becomes} \quad 1 \vartriangleleft \mathit{combine}(x_1) \xrightarrow[a(x_1)]{a^-(a^+(x_1))} \mathit{combine}(x_1) .
$$

Therefore, term tile format appears very expressive and this motivate us to provide an executable framework for it. However, an extensive comparison of existing formats is out of the scope of this paper and is left for future works.

2.3 From Tiles to Rewrite Rules

The comparison between tile logic and rewriting logic takes place by embedding their categorical models in a recently developed, specification framework, called *partial membership equational logic* (PMEqtl) [29]. PMEqtl is particularly suitable for the embedding of categorical structures, first because the sequential composition of arrows is a partial operation, and secondly because membership predicates over a poset of sorts allow the objects to be modelled as a subset of the arrows and arrows as a subset of cells. Moreover, the *tensor product construction* illustrated in [30] can be easily formulated in PMEqtl, providing a convenient definition of the theory of monoidal double categories as the tensor product of the theory of categories (twice) with the theory of monoids.

The advantage of modelling process algebras in tile logic (using the trigger/effect synchronization mechanism of rewritings) should be evident just considering the usual *action prefix* operation, denoted by $\mu.\_$. When applied to a certain process P it returns a process $\mu.P$ which can perform an action μ and then behaves like P. The corresponding tile is represented below (horizontal arrows are process contexts and vertical arrows denote computations). Notice that the horizontal operator $\mu.\_$ and the vertical operator $\mu(\_)$ are very different: the former represents the μ prefix context, which is a syntactic operator, and the latter denotes the execution of the observable action μ. Such tile can be composed horizontally with the identity tile of any process P to model the computation step associated to the action prefix.

$$
\begin{array}{ccc}
1 \xrightarrow{\mu.x_1} 1 & \quad 0 \xrightarrow{P} 1 \xrightarrow{\mu.x_1} 1 & \quad 0 \xrightarrow{\mu.P} 1 \\
\downarrow{\scriptstyle id} \quad \downarrow{\scriptstyle \mu(x_1)} & \downarrow{\scriptstyle id} \quad \downarrow{\scriptstyle id} \quad \downarrow{\scriptstyle \mu(x_1)} \; = & \downarrow{\scriptstyle id} \quad \downarrow{\scriptstyle \mu(x_1)} \\
1 \xrightarrow{id} 1 & \quad 0 \xrightarrow{P} 1 \xrightarrow{id} 1 & \quad 0 \xrightarrow{P} 1
\end{array}
$$

Now, let *nil* be the inactive process, and consider the process $Q = \mu_1.\mu_2.nil$. If the process Q tries to execute the action μ_2 before executing μ_1 it gets stuck, because there is no tile having $\mu_2(\_)$ as trigger and $\mu_1.\_$ as initial configuration.

$$
\begin{array}{c}
0 \xrightarrow{nil} 1 \xrightarrow{\mu_2.x_1} 1 \xrightarrow{\mu_1.x_1} 1 \\
\downarrow{\scriptstyle id} \quad \downarrow{\scriptstyle id} \quad \downarrow{\scriptstyle \mu_2(x_1)} \\
0 \xrightarrow{nil} 1 \xrightarrow{id} 1 \qquad ?
\end{array}
$$

In unconditional rewriting systems, this is not necessarily true, because rewriting steps can be freely contextualized (and instantiated). This problem is well-known in rewriting logic, and some partial solutions have been already proposed in the literature [25, 36]. However, our methodology seems to offer a unifying view for a wide class of related problems. The basic idea is to "stretch" tiles into ordinary rewriting cells as pictured below, maintaining the capability to distinguish between configurations and observations.

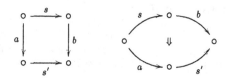

As a main result, given a tile system $\mathcal{R}$, a sequent $s \xrightarrow[b]{a} s'$ is entailed by $\mathcal{R}$ in tile logic if and only if a sequent $s; b \Rightarrow a; s'$ is entailed by the stretched version of $\mathcal{R}$ in rewriting logic and its proof satisfies some additional constraints (see [30, 4]). Indeed, the forgetful functor from the category of models of the stretched logic (where also the distinction between configuration and observations can be made) to the category of models of the tile logic has a left adjoint. Moreover, for a large class of tile systems (called *uniform*) the additional constraints reduce to check that the border of the sequent can be correctly partitioned into configurations and observations[2] (the source of the sequent must be a configuration followed by an observation, and the target must be an observation followed by a configuration).

It follows that a typical query in a tile system could be: "derive all (some of) the tiles with initial configuration s and effect b" (this corresponds to start with the state $s; b$ and apply the rewritings that simulate a tile computation with vertical source s and horizontal target b). Hence, we need to define some rewriting strategies for exploring the tree of nondeterministic rewritings until a successful configuration is reached. For instance, a general notion of success for uniform tile systems consists of VH configurations (i.e., an arrow of the vertical category followed by an arrow of the horizontal category) as we will see in Section 3.3.

3 Internal Strategies in Rewriting Logic

A rewrite theory T consists of a signature Σ of operators, a set E of equations, and a set of labelled rewrite rules. The deductions of T are rewrites modulo E using such rules, and the meaningful sentences are rewrite sequents $t \Rightarrow t'$, where t and t' are Σ-terms. We call *strategy* any computational way of looking for certain proofs of some theorems of T. An *internal strategy language* is a function S that sends each theory T to another theory $S(T)$ *in the same logic*, whose deductions simulate controlled deductions of T. The class of finitely presentable rewrite theories has universal theories, making rewriting logic reflective [10, 8].

---

[2] If the tile system is not uniform, then also the actual proof term decorating the derivation has to be taken into account. However, since at present we do not have any meaningful example of non uniform systems we are not really interested in having such an implementation.

This means that there exists a finitely representable rewrite theory U able to simulate deductions in all the other rewrite theories, i.e., there is a representation function $\overline{(\_ \vdash \_)}$ that encodes a pair consisting of a rewrite theory T and a sentence $t \Rightarrow t'$ in T as a sentence $\langle \overline{T}, \overline{t} \rangle \Rightarrow \langle \overline{T}, \overline{t'} \rangle$ in U, in such a way that

$$T \vdash t \Rightarrow t' \iff U \vdash \langle \overline{T}, \overline{t} \rangle \Rightarrow \langle \overline{T}, \overline{t'} \rangle,$$

where the function $\overline{(\_)}$ recursively defines the representation of rules, terms, etc. as terms in U. Hence, strategies in $S(U)$ are particularly important, since they represent, at the object level, strategies for computing in the universal theory.

3.1 A Strategy Kernel Language in Maude

Maude [9] is a logical language based on rewriting logic. For our present purposes the key point is that the Maude implementation supports an arbitrary number of levels of reflection and gives the user access to important reflective capabilities, including the possibility of defining and using internal strategy languages, their implementation and proof of correctness relying on the notion of a basic *reflective kernel*, that is some basic functionality provided by the universal theory U. The Maude implementation supports metaprogramming of strategies via a module-transforming operation which maps a module T to another module META-LEVEL[T] that is a definitional extension of U [12]. For simplicity, we adopt here a simpler version of the metalevel. In particular, the following operations are defined: meta-reduce($\overline{t}$) and meta-apply($\overline{t}, \overline{l}, n$).

meta-reduce($\overline{t}$) takes the metarepresentation $\overline{t}$ of a term t and evaluates as follows: (a) $\overline{t}$ is converted to the term it represents; (b) this term is fully reduced using the equations in T; (c) the resulting term t_r is converted to a metaterm which is returned as a result.

meta-apply($\overline{t}, \overline{l}, n$) takes the metarepresentations of a term t and of a rule label l, and a natural number and evaluates as follows: (a) $\overline{t}$ is converted to the term it represents; (b) this term is fully reduced using the equations in T; (c) the resulting term t_r is matched against all rules with label l; (d) the first n successful matches are discarded; (e) if there is a $(n+1)$-th match, its rule is applied using that match; otherwise {error*,empty} is returned; (f) if a rule is applied, the resulting term t' is fully reduced using the equations in T; (g) the reduced term t'_r is converted to a metaterm and returned as a result, paired with the match used in the reduction (the operator {_,_} constructs the pair, and the operator extTerm can be used to extract the metaterm from the result).

3.2 Strategies for Nondeterministic Rewritings

We need good ways of controlling the rewriting process – which in principle could go in many undesired directions – using adequate strategies. The importance of similar mechanisms is well-known, and other languages (e.g., ELAN [2]), have built-in functionalities that deal with general forms of nondeterminism. However, the approach based on the definition of suitable internal strategies in Maude is rather general (it is parametric w.r.t. a user-definable success predicate), can be integrated with the built-in membership predicates of Maude (very important for the implementation of uniform tile system based on term structures, as shown in Section 3.3), and allows the customization of the policy adopted.

In [5] we have specified a basic internal strategy language which is able to support nondeterministic specifications, extending the strategy kernel META-LEVEL. Such layer provides several kinds of visit mechanisms for the trees of nondeterministic rewritings in T (e.g., breadth-first, depth-first, etc.). A strategy expression has either the form rewWith($\bar{t}, S$) where S is the rewriting strategy that we wish to compute, or failure which means that something goes wrong. As the computation of a given strategy proceeds, $\bar{t}$ is rewritten according to S (and S is reduced into the remaining strategy to be computed). In case of termination, S becomes the trivial strategy idle. In doing so, we assume the existence of a user-definable predicate ok(_), defined over the collection of states, such that ok(st) = true if st is successful and ok(st) = false if st is failing.

As an example, we sketch here the depth-first visit with backtracking mechanism. The (meta)expression rewWith($\bar{t}$,depthBT($\bar{l}$)) means that the user wants to rewrite a term t in T using rules with label l, until a solution is found. This corresponds to the evaluation of the expression rewWithBT([($\bar{t}$,0)],$\emptyset$,$\bar{l}$). The function rewWithBT takes as arguments a sequence PL of pairs of the form ($\bar{t}, i$), where t is a term and i is a natural number, a set of (metarepresentations of) terms TS and the metarepresentation $\bar{l}$ of a label l. The set TS represents the set of visited terms. The sequence PL contains the terms that have to be "checked". If the first argument is the empty sequence, then the function evaluates to *failure*, which means that no solution is reachable. If there is at least one pair ($\bar{t}, i$) in the sequence, such that $\bar{t} \notin TS$ and ok(t) $\neq$ false, then only the first $i - 1$ rewritings of t have been already inspected and the i-th rewriting t_i of t (if any) should be the next. If ok(t) = true then t is a solution: the evaluation returns rewWith($\bar{t}$,idle) and the computation ends. The formal definition of such evaluation strategy is given in the Appendix, but we refer to [5] for more details and for the definition of other evaluation strategies.

3.3   Uniform Term Tile Systems

Let Σ_H and Σ_V be two (unsorted) disjoint signatures for configurations and observations. We call *term tile system* (tTS) over Σ_H and Σ_V any tile system whose configuration and observations are terms over Σ_H and Σ_V respectively. Term tile systems are quite close to the ordinary term rewriting framework, and the membership assertions and subsorting mechanism of Maude can be used (to-

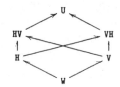

Fig. 1. The sorts of $\widehat{\mathcal{R}}$.

gether with the internal strategies presented in Section 3.2) to model any uniform tTS $\mathcal{R}$. The idea is to define a rewrite theory $\widehat{\mathcal{R}}$, that simulates $\mathcal{R}$ as described in Section 2, exploiting the membership mechanism of Maude to distinguish the correct computations. The theory $\widehat{\mathcal{R}}$ has the poset of sorts illustrated in Fig. 1.

We briefly comment on their meaning: the sort W informally contains the variables of the system as constants; the sort H contains the terms over the signature Σ_H and variables in W (similarly for the sort V); the sort HV contains those terms over the signature $\Sigma_{H\cup V}$ and variables in W such that they are decomposable as terms over signature Σ_V applied to terms over Σ_H (similarly for VH); and the sort U contains terms over the signature $\Sigma_{H\cup V}$. As summarized above, we introduce the following operations and membership assertions, for each $h \in \Sigma_H$ and $v \in \Sigma_V$ (with h of arity n and v of arity m):

```
op h : U^n -> U . op v : U^m -> U .
vars x_1 ... x_max : U .
cmb h(x_1,...,x_n) : H iff x_1 ... x_n : H .
cmb v(x_1,...,x_m) : V iff x_1 ... x_m : V .
cmb h(x_1,...,x_n) : VH iff x_1 ... x_n : VH .
cmb v(x_1,...,x_m) : HV iff x_1 ... x_m : HV .
```

The rewriting rules of $\widehat{\mathcal{R}}$ are the stretched versions of tiles $h\xrightarrow[u]{v}g$ in $\mathcal{R}$.

```
rl [tile] : u(h) => g(v) .
```

The following result characterizes the correctness of our implementation.

Theorem 1. *Given a uniform tTS $\mathcal{R}$, then $\mathcal{R} \vdash h\xrightarrow[u]{v}g \Longrightarrow \widehat{\mathcal{R}} \vdash u(h) \Rightarrow g(v)$. Moreover, if $\widehat{\mathcal{R}} \vdash u(h) \Rightarrow t$ and t : VH, then $\exists g$: H, $\exists v$: V such that $t = g(v)$ and $\mathcal{R} \vdash h\xrightarrow[u]{v}g$.*

4 Rewriting CCS Processes via Tiles

Milner's *Calculus for Communicating Systems* (CCS) [32] is among the better well-known and studied concurrency models. In the recent literature, several ways in which CCS can be conservatively represented in rewriting logic have been proposed [25, 36]. We present the executable implementation defined through the translation into Maude of the tile system for full CCS. This work extends the translation given in [19, 30] for a finitary version of CCS (i.e., without replicator).

4.1 CCS and its Operational Semantics

Let Δ (ranged over by α) be the set of *basic actions*, and $\bar{\Delta}$ the set of *complementary actions* (where $(\bar{\ })$ is an involutive function such that $\Delta = \bar{\bar{\Delta}}$ and $\Delta \cap \bar{\Delta} = \emptyset$). We denote by Λ (ranged over by λ) the set $\Delta \cup \bar{\Delta}$. Let $\tau \notin \Lambda$ be a *distinguished* action, and let $Act = \Lambda \cup \{\tau\}$ (ranged over by μ) be the set of CCS actions. Then, a *CCS process* is a term generated by the following grammar:

$$P ::= nil \mid \mu.P \mid P\backslash\alpha \mid P + P \mid P|P \mid !P.$$

We let P, Q, R, ...range over the set *Proc* of CCS processes. Assuming the reader familiar with the notation, we give just an informal description of CCS algebra operators: the constant *nil* yields the *inactive* process; $\mu.P$ behaves like P but only after the execution of action μ; $P\backslash\alpha$ is the process P with actions α and $\bar{\alpha}$ inhibited by the *restriction* $\_\backslash\alpha$; $P + Q$ is the *nondeterministic sum* of processes P and Q; $P|Q$ is the parallel composition of processes P and Q; finally, $!P$ is the *replicator* of process P. The dynamic behaviour of CCS processes is usually described by a transition system, presented in the SOS style.

Remark 1. To avoid dealing with the metalevel operation of substitution, we have chosen to use the replicator $!P$ instead of the ordinary recursive operator $\mathbf{rec}\,x.P$ of CCS. Our choice does not affect the expressivenes of the calculus, because it is well known that for each agent $\mathbf{rec}\,x.P$ there exists a weak equivalent agent that can simulate it, namely $(\alpha_x.nil\|!\bar{\alpha}_x.P')\backslash\alpha_x$, where α_x is a new channel name (i.e., not used by P) and P' is the process obtained by replacing each occurrence of the variable x in P by $\alpha_x.nil$.

Definition 1 (Operational Semantics). *The CCS transition system is given by the relation $T \subseteq Proc \times Act \times Proc$ inductively generated from the following set of axioms and inference rules (here and in the following we will omit the obvious symmetric rules for nondeterministic choice and asynchronous communication):*

$$\frac{}{\mu.P \xrightarrow{\mu} P} \qquad \frac{P \xrightarrow{\mu} Q}{P+R \xrightarrow{\mu} Q} \qquad \frac{P \xrightarrow{\mu} Q}{P\backslash\alpha \xrightarrow{\mu} Q\backslash\alpha}\; \mu \notin \{\alpha,\bar{\alpha}\}$$

$$\frac{P \xrightarrow{\mu} Q}{!P \xrightarrow{\mu} Q|!P} \qquad \frac{P \xrightarrow{\mu} Q}{P|R \xrightarrow{\mu} Q|R} \qquad \frac{P \xrightarrow{\lambda} Q,\; P' \xrightarrow{\bar{\lambda}} Q'}{P|P' \xrightarrow{\tau} Q|Q'}$$

where $P \xrightarrow{\mu} Q$ *stands for* $(P,\mu,Q) \in T$.

The operational meaning is that a process P may perform an action μ becoming Q if it is possible to inductively construct a sequence of rule applications to conclude that $P \xrightarrow{\mu} Q$. More generally, a process P_0 may evolve to process P_n if there exists a *computation* $P_0 \xrightarrow{\mu_1} P_1 \ldots P_{n-1} \xrightarrow{\mu_n} P_n$.

4.2 A Term Tile System for CCS

In [19] it is shown how to associate a tile system to finite CCS. We adapt their definition to settle the following tTS for the full version of the calculus.

Definition 2 (tTS for CCS). *The tTS $\mathcal{R}_{CCS}$ has the signature Σ_P of CCS processes as horizontal signature, the action signature $\Sigma_A = \{\mu(\_) : 1 \longrightarrow 1 \mid \mu \in Act\}$ as vertical signature, and the following basic tiles:*

$$1 \triangleleft \mu.x_1 \xrightarrow[\mu(x_1)]{x_1} x_1 \qquad 2 \triangleleft x_1 + x_2 \xrightarrow[\mu(x_1)]{\mu(x_1),x_2} x_1 \qquad 1 \triangleleft x_1\backslash\alpha \xrightarrow[\mu(x_1)]{\mu(x_1)} x_1\backslash\alpha \;\; (if\ \mu \notin \{\alpha,\bar{\alpha}\})$$

$$1 \triangleleft !x_1 \xrightarrow[\mu(x_1)]{\mu(x_1),x_1} x_1\|x_2 \qquad 2 \triangleleft x_1|x_2 \xrightarrow[\mu(x_1)]{\mu(x_1),x_2} x_1|x_2 \qquad 2 \triangleleft x_1|x_2 \xrightarrow[\tau(x_1)]{\lambda(x_1),\bar{\lambda}(x_2)} x_1|x_2$$

The tile for the action prefix has been already discussed in Section 2. As additional examples, we briefly comment the tile for left nondeterministic choice, and the tile for the replicator, also depicted below.

$$
\begin{array}{ccc}
2 \xrightarrow{\ x_1+x_2\ } 1 & \qquad & 1 \xrightarrow{\ !x_1\ } 1 \\
\;\;\downarrow{\scriptstyle \mu(x_1),x_2} \qquad \downarrow{\scriptstyle \mu(x_1)} & & \;\;\downarrow{\scriptstyle \mu(x_1),x_1} \qquad \downarrow{\scriptstyle \mu(x_1)} \\
2 \xrightarrow[\ x_1\ ]{} 1 & & 2 \xrightarrow[\ x_1|!x_2\ ]{} 1
\end{array}
$$

The meaning of the first tile is that the action μ (i.e., the effect $\mu(x_1)$) can be executed by the sum of two subprocesses (i.e., from the initial configuration) if the left subprocess (i.e., the variable x_1 in the initial input interface) can perform the action μ (i.e., the trigger $\mu(x_1)$), evolving to the same subprocess (i.e., the variable x_1 in the final input interface) that will be reached by the nondeterministic sum after such rewriting (i.e., the final configuration x_1). Notice that we can handle the garbaging of the discarded process in the easiest way, using a discharger to throw it away (thanks to auxiliary structure and tile that were not present in [30]). In our notation, this corresponds to not to mention a variable of the input interface (i.e., variable x_2 of the final input interface).

The second tile can be read in a similar way. The relevant thing is that its trigger refers to the same variable twice. This is not allowed in the model proposed by Gadducci and Montanari, where the structure of observations is just a freely generated strict monoidal category (i.e., it is not cartesian). Such duplication is necessary because in the final configuration we must refer both the process P linked to the variable of the initial input interface and the process Q reached by P after the firing of action μ, which acts as trigger for the rewriting. Hence, tTS can deal with more general format than those considered in [19], and in particular, can embed all the expressive power of full CCS.

Analogously to [19], the following result establishes the correspondence between the ordinary SOS semantics for CCS, and the sequents entailed by $\mathcal{R}_{CCS}$.

Proposition 1. *The tTS $\mathcal{R}_{CCS}$ is uniform, and for any CCS agents P and Q, and action $\mu\colon P \xrightarrow{\ \mu\ } Q \in T \iff \mathcal{R}_{CCS} \vdash 0 \triangleleft P \xrightarrow[\mu(x_1)]{} Q$.*

4.3 From Tiles for CCS to Rewrite Rules for CCS

By Proposition 1, it follows immediately that a suitable implementation of $\mathcal{R}_{CCS}$ can be obtained by taking the rewriting theory $\hat{\mathcal{R}}_{CCS}$ defined in Section 3.3, and by defining a suitable success predicate for the metastrategies of Section 3.1. Therefore the rules of $\hat{\mathcal{R}}_{CCS}$ (all labelled by `tile`) are:

$$\mu(\mu.x_1) \Rightarrow x_1 \qquad \mu(x_1 + x_2) \Rightarrow \mu(x_1) \qquad \mu(x_1\backslash\alpha) \Rightarrow \mu(x_1)\backslash\alpha \ (\text{if } \mu \neq \alpha, \bar{\alpha})$$

$$\mu(!x_1) \Rightarrow \mu(x_1)|!x_1 \qquad \mu(x_1|x_2) \Rightarrow \mu(x_1)|x_2 \qquad \tau(x_1|x_2) \Rightarrow \lambda(x_1)|\bar{\lambda}(x_2)$$

and the success predicate is defined by `ceq ok(t) = true if t : VH` .

Corollary 1. *For any CCS processes P and Q, and action μ:*

$$P \xrightarrow{\mu} Q \Longleftrightarrow \hat{\mathcal{R}}_{CCS} \vdash \mu(P) \Rightarrow Q.$$

A typical (meta)query is `rewWith(`$\overline{\mu(P)}$`,depthBT(`$\overline{\texttt{tile}}$`))`, where $\overline{\mu(P)}$ is the metarepresentation of the test $\mu(P)$ that can be used to see if the CCS process P can perform a transition labelled by μ. Then, the system tries to rewrite $\overline{\mu(P)}$ in all possible ways, until a solution of type `VH` is found (if it exists).

Example 1. Let us consider the CCS process $(\alpha.nil + \beta.nil)\backslash \alpha$. If the rules are applied without any metacontrol, then a possible computation for the test $\beta((\alpha.nil + \beta.nil)\backslash \alpha)$ is: $\beta((\alpha.nil + \beta.nil)\backslash \alpha) \Rightarrow \beta(\alpha.nil + \beta.nil)\backslash \alpha \Rightarrow \beta(\alpha.nil)\backslash \alpha$. Such computation ends in a state that is not a solution (in fact it is the composition of the horizontal arrow $\alpha.nil$, followed by the vertical arrow $\beta(x_1)$, followed by the horizontal arrow $x_1\backslash \alpha$) and that cannot be further rewritten. Therefore, it is discarded in the meta-controlled computation, and the only possible result `rewWith(Q,idle)`, where `Q` is the metarepresentation of $nil\backslash \alpha$, is returned.

5 Concluding Remarks

This work presents a general methodology for the specification and execution of process calculi via term tile systems, which is part of our ongoing research on the relations between tile logic and rewriting logic. We have defined some general metastrategies for simulating tile system specifications on a rewriting machinery equipped with reflective capabilities. We have implemented such strategies in Maude, and have experimented their application to the case study of full CCS (but more complex systems can be represented as well in our format).

Our general methodology for modelling process calculi (and more generally, reactive systems), can be summarized by the following steps: (1) define a tile model of computation of the given system, employing adequate mathematical structures to represent configurations and observations in such a way that the intrinsic modularity and synchronization mechanism of tiles are fully exploited; (2) translate the tiles into rewrite rules; (3) define, if necessary, a notion of successful computation (if the system is uniform, this can be done by just looking at the actual term reached); (4) compute at the metalevel, using the internal strategies that discard wrong computations, until a successful answer is reached. This procedure has been fully illustrated for process tile logic in [6] by the example of located CCS, and for term tile logic in the present paper by the example of full CCS. For each model, we have tested the computations of simple processes. Our experiments are encouraging, because Maude seems to offer a good trade-off between rewriting kernel efficiency and layer-swapping management (from terms to their metarepresentations and viceversa).

Acknowledgements We would like to thank Paolo Baldan and the anonymous referees for useful comments.

References

1. B. Bloom, S. Istrail, and A.R. Meyer, Bisimulation can't be Traced, *Journal of the ACM* **42**(1), 232–268 (1995).
2. P. Borovanský, C. Kirchner, H. Kirchner, P.-E. Moreau, and M. Vittek, ELAN: A logical framework based on computational systems, in [28].
3. R. Bruni, Tile Logic for Synchronized Rewriting of Concurrent Systems, PhD Thesis, Department of Computer Science, University of Pisa, forthcoming.
4. R. Bruni, J. Meseguer, and U. Montanari, Process and Term Tile Logic, Technical Report SRI-CSL-98-06, SRI International (1998).
5. R. Bruni, J. Meseguer, and U. Montanari, Internal Strategies in a Rewriting Implementation of Tile Systems, in [23].
6. R. Bruni, J. Meseguer, and U. Montanari, Implementing Tile Systems: some Examples from Process Calculi, in *Proc. ICTCS'98*, World Scientific, 168–179 (1998).
7. R. Bruni and U. Montanari, Zero-Safe Nets: Comparing the Collective and the Individual Token Approaches, *Information and Computation*, to appear.
8. M. Clavel, *Reflection in General Logics and in Rewriting Logic with Applications to the Maude Language*, PhD Thesis, Universidad de Navarra (1998).
9. M.G. Clavel, F. Duran, S. Eker, P. Lincoln, and J. Meseguer, An Introduction to Maude (Beta Version), SRI International (1998).
10. M. Clavel and J. Meseguer, Reflection and Strategies in Rewriting Logic, in [28].
11. M. Clavel and J. Meseguer, Axiomatizing Reflective Logics and Languages, in *Proceedings Reflection'96*, San Francisco, USA, 263–288 (1996).
12. M. Clavel and J. Meseguer, Internal Strategies in a Reflective Logic, in *Proc. of the CADE-14 Workshop on Strategies in Automated Deduction*, 1–12 (1997).
13. G. Denker, J. Meseguer, and C. Talcott, Protocol Specification and Analysis in Maude, in *Proc. Workshop on Formal Methods and Security Protocols* (1998).
14. C. Ehresmann, *Catégories Structurées*: I and II, Ann. Éc. Norm. Sup. 80, Paris (1963), 349–426; III, Topo. et Géo. diff. V, Paris (1963).
15. G.L. Ferrari and U. Montanari, A Tile-Based Coordination View of Asynchronous Pi-Calculus, in *Proc. MFCS'97*, Springer *LNCS* **1295**, 52–70 (1997),
16. G.L. Ferrari and U. Montanari, Tiles for Concurrent and Located Calculi, in *Proceedings of EXPRESS'97, ENTCS* **7** (1997).
17. F. Gadducci, *On the Algebraic Approach to Concurrent Term Rewriting*, PhD Thesis TD-96-02, Department of Computer Science, University of Pisa (1996).
18. F. Gadducci and U. Montanari, Enriched Categories as Models of Computations, in *Proc. ITCS'95*, World Scientific, 1–24 (1996).
19. F. Gadducci and U. Montanari, The Tile Model, in *Proof, Language and Interaction: Essays in Honour of Robin Milner*, MIT Press, to appear.
20. J.F. Groote, and F. Vaandrager, Structured Operational Semantics and Bisimulation as a Congruence, *Information and Computation* **100**, 202–260 (1992).
21. K.G. Larsen, and L. Xinxin, Compositionality Through an Operational Semantics of Contexts, in *Proc. ICALP'90, LNCS* **443**, 526–539 (1990).
22. F.W. Lawvere, Functorial Semantics of Algebraic Theories, in *Proc. National Academy of Science* **50**, 869–872 (1963).
23. C. Kirchner, H. Kirchner, Ed., *Proc. 2nd WRLA'98, ENTCS* **15** (1998).
24. N. Martí-Oliet and J. Meseguer, General Logics and Logical Frameworks, in: D. Gabbay, Ed., *What is a logical system?*, Oxford University Press (1994).
25. N. Martí-Oliet and J. Meseguer, *Rewriting Logic as a Logical and Semantic Framework*, SRI Technical Report, CSL-93-05 (1993). To appear in D. Gabbay, Ed., *Handbook of Philosophical Logic*, Kluwer Academic Publishers.

26. J. Meseguer, Conditional Rewriting Logic as a Unified Model of Concurrency, *TCS* **96**, 73–155 (1992).

27. J. Meseguer, Rewriting Logic as a Semantic Framework for Concurrency: A Progress Report, in *Proc. CONCUR'96*, Springer *LNCS* **1119**, 331-372 (1996).

28. J. Meseguer, Ed., *Proc. 1st International Workshop on Rewriting Logic and Applications*, *ENTCS* **4** (1996).

29. J. Meseguer, Membership Equational Logic as a Logical Framework for Equational Specification, in *Proc. 12th WADT'97*. Springer *LNCS* **1376**, 18–61 (1998).

30. J. Meseguer and U. Montanari, Mapping Tile Logic into Rewriting Logic, in *Proc. 12th WADT'97*, Springer *LNCS* **1376**, 62–91 (1998).

31. J. Meseguer and C. Talcott, Using Rewriting Logic to Interoperate Architectural Description Languages (I and II), Lectures at the Santa Fe and Seattle DARPA-EDCS Workshops (1997).

32. R. Milner, *Communication and Concurrency*, Prentice-Hall (1989).

33. U. Montanari and F. Rossi, Graph Rewriting, Constraint Solving and Tiles for Coordinating Distributed Systems, *Applied Categorical Structures*, to appear.

34. U. Montanari and C. Talcott, Can Actors and pi-Agents Live Together?, in *Proceedings HOOTS'97*, *ENTCS* **10** (1998).

35. G. Plotkin, A Structural Approach to Operational Semantics, Technical Report DAIMI FN-19, Computer Science Department, Aarhus University (1981).

36. P. Viry, *Rewriting Modulo a Rewrite System*, Technical Report TR-95-20, Department of Computer Science, University of Pisa (1995).

Appendix. Depth-First Visit with Backtracking

The depth-first strategy with backtracking is defined below in a self-explanatory notation: the Maude-like syntax has been extended by using some ordinary symbols (e.g., [], {}, ∪, ∈, 0, succ) to deal with lists, sets, natural numbers, etc.

```
var t̄ : Term .  var l̄ : Label .  var n : Nat .
var TS : TermSet .  var PL : TermList .
eq rewWith(t̄,depthBT(l̄)) = rewWithBT([(t̄,0)],∅,l̄) .
eq rewWithBT([],TS,l̄) = failure .
eq rewWithBT([(t̄,n)],TS,l̄) = if t̄∈TS then failure
   else if meta-reduce('ok[t̄]) == 'true then rewWith(t̄,idle)
        else if meta-reduce('ok[t̄]) == 'false then failure
             else if meta-apply(t̄,l̄,n) == error* then failure
                  else rewWithBT([(extTerm(meta-apply(t̄,l̄,n)),0),
                       (t̄,succ(n))],{t̄}∪TS,l̄) fi fi fi fi .
eq rewWithBT([(t̄,n),PL],TS,l̄) = if t̄∈TS then rewWithBT(TL,TS,l̄)
   else if meta-reduce('ok[t̄]) == 'true then rewWith(t̄,idle)
        else if meta-reduce('ok[t̄]) == 'false
             then rewWithBT(PL,{t̄}∪TS,l̄)
             else if meta-apply(t̄,l̄,n) == error*
                  then rewWithBT(PL,{t̄}∪TS,l̄)
                  else rewWithBT([(extTerm(meta-apply(t̄,l̄,n)),0),
                       (t̄,succ(n)),PL],{t̄}∪TS,l̄) fi fi fi fi .
```

JTN: A Java-Targeted Graphic Formal Notation for Reactive and Concurrent Systems *

Eva Coscia and Gianna Reggio

DISI, Università di Genova – ITALY
e-mail: {coscia,reggio}@disi.unige.it – fax: 39-010-3536699

Abstract. JTN is a formal graphic notation for Java-targeted design specifications, that are specifications of systems that will be implemented using Java.

JTN is aimed to be a part of a more articulated project for the production of a development method for reactive/concurrent/distributed systems. The starting point of this project is an existing general method that however does not cover the coding phase of the development process. Such approach provides formal graphic specifications for the system design that are too abstract to be transformed into Java code in just one step, or at least, the transformation is really hard and complex.

We introduce in the development process an intermediate step that transforms the above abstract specifications into JTN specifications, for which the transformation into a Java program is almost automatic and can be guaranteed correct. In this paper we present JTN on a simple toy example.

Introduction

In this paper we present a part of a more articulated project we are currently working on: a development method for reactive/concurrent/distributed systems (shortly systems from now on) that are finally implemented in Java. Such development process should be supported by formal tools and techniques, whenever possible, and by a set of user guidelines that describe in detail how to perform the various tasks. The formal bases and the main ideas come from previous work of one of the authors about the use of formal techniques in the development of systems that, however, did not ever considered the final coding step, see, e.g., [1, 2, 10, 11]. We chose Java as the implementation language since it is OO, widely accepted for its simplicity and, at the same time, for its richness. It is considered a language for the net, for its portability, but also a language for concurrency and distribution. Moreover, there exists a precise, even if informal, reference [4] for the semantics of the core language.

[11] presents a general method for giving formal graphic design specifications of systems, but such specifications are too abstract to be transformed into Java code in just one step, or at least, the transformation is really hard and complex.

---

* Partially funded by the MURST project: Sistemi formali per la specifica, l'analisi, la verifica, la sintesi e la trasformazione di sistemi software.

For example, following [11] you can specify systems with n-ary synchronous communications, where the components can exhibit any kind of non-determinism and can be coordinated by complex scheduling policies, which cannot have a direct implementation into Java.

Moreover, the complexity of this transformation into Java does not allow to check the correctness of the generated code, and there is no way to automatize it. Furthermore, [11] does not take into account the relevant, good characteristics of Java, as the OO features.

We think that it is useful to introduce an intermediate step in the development process that transforms an abstract design specification into a Java-targeted one, whose transformation into a Java program is really easy.

Abstract design specification $\xrightarrow[\text{(1)}]{\text{GUIDELINES}}$ JAVA targeted design specification $\xrightarrow[\text{(2)}]{\text{(AUTOMATIC) TRANSLATION}}$ JAVA code

Step (2) can be automatized and guaranteed correct whereas step (1) cannot be automatized, but we are working to give a rich set of guidelines for helping the user in such task.

Here we present JTN, a graphic formal notation for the Java targeted design specifications, obtained by targeting [11] to Java, that is by modifying the specification language to take into account the features and the limitations of Java.

JTN is graphic because every aspect of system (e.g., components, global architecture and behaviour) is described only by diagrams. But it is formal, because the diagrams composing the specifications are just an alternative notation for logic specifications as in [11] (the formal semantics of JTN is presented in [3]).

We think that JTN, with the associated method and software support tools, could help the development of reliable systems implemented in Java.

- We can describe the system design graphically, and that is helpful to grasp the system characteristics. However, the JTN graphic specifications are structured and that avoids one of the possible drawbacks of graphic notations: to handle very large diagrams that could be not understood.
- The level of the JTN descriptions is not too low: the designer avoids to specify too much details and the drawings are simple enough; for example, in JTN there are user defined data-types and abstract communication mechanisms, as synchronous and asynchronous channels.
- JTN specifications are formal, with the usual advantages to use formal methods without bothering the specifiers with too much formalities.
- The automatizable translation to Java reduces the time to a working system and also gives a prototyper for such specifications.

There are neither theoretical nor practical problems to realize a full tool-set for supporting the use of JTN using the current technology (e.g., interactive editor, static checker, hyper-textual browser, translator to Java, debugger); it is possible to realize them within a reasonable amount of time, we just need some human resources.

Here, for lack of room, we consider only a rich subset of JTN applied on a toy running example and give some ideas about its translation into Java; a detailed presentation of JTN and further examples are in [3]. In Sect. 6 we present the relations with other works as well as some hints on our future work.

The running example We specify the design of a Java program simulating a pocket calculator that computes and interacts with a keyboard, a display and a printer; think, for example, of a small application simulating a calculator on the desktop of a computer. The functionalities of the calculator are quite obvious: it can receive, by the keyboard, numbers and simple commands for performing operations (addition and multiplication) and for printing the display content.

1 JTN

In this section we first describe the main features of the abstract design specification technique of [11]; then we describe how to target it to Java and give an overall presentation of the JTN notation.

1.1 Abstract design specifications

The specification technique of [11] distinguishes among the data-types, the passive and the active components of a system, because these components have a different conceptual nature and play a different role within the systems.

The *data-types* are static structures used by the other components, with no idea of an internal state changing over time. The *passive* components have an internal state that can be modified by the actions of other active components. The *active* components have an internal state, but they are also able to act on their own (possibly by interacting among them and with the passive components).

We can completely describe a data-type by giving its values and the operations over them, whereas we describe the passive components by giving their states and the actions that can be performed over them, which obviously can change such states. We want to remark this difference. Data-types define stateless elements (essentially, values) that are used by (active and passive) components. Instead, the passive components are actual components of the system, having an internal state that can be updated by the active components. Finally we describe the active components by giving the relevant intermediate states of their lives and their behaviours, which are the possible transitions leading from one state to another one. Every transition is decorated by a label abstractly describing the information exchanged with the external, w.r.t. to the component, world. Notice that many transitions can have the same source, and that allows to handle nondeterminism.

Let us consider, for simplicity, a system having a database inside. The database is a passive component whose internal state is modified by the operations it supplies outside; the data managed and exchanged by the database are data-types; and the processes using the database are the active components of the system.

The activity of a system results by describing how its components *cooperate*, i.e., to say which transitions of the active components and which operations over the passive components have to be performed together, and which is the exchange of information with the external (w.r.t. the whole system) world.

A system, in turn, can be seen as an active component of another system, and so we can specify systems with a multi-level architecture.

The underling formal model for an active component (and thus for a system) is a labelled transition system (LTS), that is triple consisting of a set S of elements (intermediate states), a set L of the labels (interactions with the external world) and a ternary transition relation, a subset of $S \times L \times S$ (transitions). The passive components and the data-types are modelled by first-order structures.

The graphic specifications of [11] follow the system structure; thus they consist of diagrams for the data-types, for the components (the behaviour of the active components is represented as a kind of finite automata) and for the cooperation among them. Formally, these diagrams correspond to an algebraic/logic specification having LTS's as models, see [11]. Note that the specification language of [11] has neither concepts nor mechanisms related to OO, nor features of some particular programming language, as handshake communications and asynchronous channels; instead it allows the specifier to directly define any feature of the system by describing the corresponding behaviours and cooperation.

1.2 Java-Targeting

We designed JTN by adapting the technique presented in Sect. 1.1 to the features and to the limitations of Java.

We want to keep distinct, at this more concrete level too, the concepts of data-types, passive and active components of a system. In our opinion, it is useful to have this distinction to avoid confusion and to make the specification more readable.

Then, we introduce the new OO concepts of class and instance and provide an explicit representation of the relevant relationships among them, as inheritance and use; but in JTN we have three kinds of classes, one for each kind of entities that we consider: data-types, passive and active components.

The data-types are described at an abstract level by giving their constructors and by defining the associated operations, without considering an OO perspective; however it is easy to transform them into Java classes.

The passive components are seen as objects, whose state is given by a set of typed fields and the operations to modify them are methods. The transformation of such object specifications into Java classes is immediate.

The active components are seen as processes, with a state, an independent activity and communication channels to interact with other active components and with the external world. In this case, the natural implementation is given by Java threads. We chose to use communication among processes via channels, rather than via method calls. In this way, a process does not offer methods outside and we do not have to manage method calls while the process is performing its activity (in Java, there is no built-in mechanism to disable method calls).

As Java objects and threads communicate by method calls and streams, the main typologies of cooperation are: between a process and an object, by means of a call to an object method, and among a set of processes by communication along asynchronous and synchronous channels. The asynchronous channels are rendered by streams, and the synchronous ones are implemented by particular additional objects.

Java supports only system architectures of at most two levels. The first level corresponds to multi-threaded Java programs, and the second corresponds to distributed Java applications consisting of programs possibly running on different machines. For lack of room, in this paper we do not consider the second level.

For the same reason, here we consider simple objects and processes, i.e., without sub-objects and sub-processes, so calls to methods of other objects cannot appear in a method body. Moreover, we do not consider the dynamic creation of process and objects: we assume to start with an initial configuration of the system where all the components have been already created in the initial state.

Using the JTN concepts we model the running example as follows. The calculator has four active components: the keyboard driver reading keys from the keyboard, the computing unit performing the computations, the display driver echoing inputs and results to the display, and the print driver printing the display content. All such processes use an object, which records the content of the display, and three different types of data: digits, lists of digits and commands.

The keyboard driver receives the keys by an asynchronous channel from the keyboard (the external world); the display driver and the print driver send their outputs to, respectively, the display and the printer by two other asynchronous channels. The communications and the synchronizations among the active components are realized by some synchronous channels.

1.3 Overall structure of the JTN specifications

We factorize a system specification into several diagrams showing different aspects or parts of the system. Thus the diagrams are not too large and complicated, and so really useful. For example, some diagrams focus on the behaviour of the components and other focus on the architectural structure of the system.

Class Diagram The *class diagram* captures the classes of the system components and their relationships. We consider three different kinds of classes: *data-types, object classes* (for passive components) and *process classes* (for active components), graphically represented by different icons.

All the information about a class is given by two complementary diagrams: *interface* and *body*. The first one describes which are the services (different for each kind of class) that the class offers outside. The latter defines such services and can be given apart from the class diagram. The forms of the two diagrams depend on the class kind and are described in deeper details in Sect. 2.

In an OO perspective, stand-alone classes are not so meaningful; most of them are related to accomplish more complex functionalities. Thus, we complete the class descriptions with the relevant relationships among them.

Inheritance between classes of the same kind, it states that a class is a specialization or an extension of another one.

Usage states that a class (of any kind) uses the data defined by a data-type.

Clientship states that a process class assumes the existence of an object class, as it can use its methods.

JTN defines the operations, the methods and the process behaviours inside the body diagrams by ordered lists of conditional rules, with a uniform presentation, just a general form of "guarded commands". The alternatives of a command are evaluated in order and the first one having a satisfied guard is chosen. The guards are partly realized by a boolean condition and partly by pattern matching (as in ML [6]) over the parameters of the operation, of the method call and over the state of the process respectively. The use of pattern matching is useful to make shorter and more readable the whole definitions. Let us remark that we avoid problems with overlapping patterns and conditions by explicitly ordering the guards.

Architecture Diagram The architecture diagram describes which are the components of the system, and how they interact (by which communication channels and by which method calls).

Sequence Diagram A sequence diagram is a particular form of message sequence chart (see [8]) that describes a sequence of actions occurring in a (possibly partial) execution of the system and involving some components. The represented actions are communications over channels and method calls. We introduced these diagrams because they are used in the most widely accepted specification techniques in the field of Software Engineering, such as UML.

The class diagram (with the possibly separated body diagrams) and the architecture diagram fully describe a system. The sequence diagrams are an additional way to present information on the system that is very intuitive and easy to be understood.

2 Class Diagram

There is one global class diagram for the whole system, representing the classes of all its constituents. It is a graph, where the nodes represent classes and the arcs class relationships. The icons for a data-type, an object class and a process class are, respectively, ⬜ ⬜ ⬜.

For each class there are two diagrams, *interface* and *body*, both with a slot with the name of the class, i.e., the type of its elements. The interface diagrams are always in the class diagram, whereas the body ones can be given separately.

The contents of the interface and of the body diagrams vary with the kind of the class and in the following subsections we present them and the relationships among classes. In fig. 1 we report the class diagram for the calculator example.

Data-type We chose to describe a data-type by giving its constructors and defining the associated operations by means of conditional rules with pattern matching a la ML (see [6]).

The interface diagram for a data-type contains the list of its visible constructors and operations, and the body diagram contains the the private constructors and the definition of the visible and private operations. The body diagram is divided into many slots, separated by dashed lines, each one containing the definition of an operation, by conditional rules.

The most common data-types, either basic (e.g., NAT) or parametric (e.g., LIST), are predefined and implicitly used by all the classes, so we do not report them in the class diagram. Moreover, data-types defined by combinations of predefined ones can be renamed and grouped together. In fig. 1 DIGIT is a renamed subrange of CHAR and KEY is the union of DIGIT and COMMAND.

The APPLY data-type, defined in fig. 1 by inheriting from the others, contains some operation definitions, one public, Apply, and two private, Code and Decode. It implicitly uses NAT. Decode is defined by using the pattern matching: given an actual parameter a, if a matches the pattern Empty (i.e., $a=$ Empty, Empty is a constant constructor), then it returns 0; if a matches d::dl (i.e., $a = e :: l$, :: is the list constructor adding an element to a list), then it returns $(\text{Ord}(e)\text{-Ord}('0')) + 10 * \text{Decode}(l)$.

Object Class An object is a passive component of the system, which has an internal state but it does not perform an independent activity. Objects cooperate with other components by offering services (i.e., methods) that the processes can call to complete complex functionalities.

Here, for lack of room, we do not present the complete version of the object classes with sub-objects and local methods.

Interface Diagram The interface diagram of an object class contains the list of the public methods with their names, the types of their parameters and of the returned values (if any). The DISPLAY class (fig. 1) has two methods, Write and Add, with one parameter of type DIGIT_LIST, and Read, with no parameter, that returns a DIGIT_LIST value.
Body Diagram The object body diagram is divided into two slots, containing:

- the *fields*; in JTN there are only private fields that can be accessed only by methods. For each field we give the name and the type plus its initial value (see field Cont in fig. 2);
- the definition of *public* and *private* methods.

Using JTN, we define the methods by conditional rules with pattern matching.

A method $M(IT_1, \ldots, IT_k)$: OT is defined by an ordered list of conditional rules whose form is

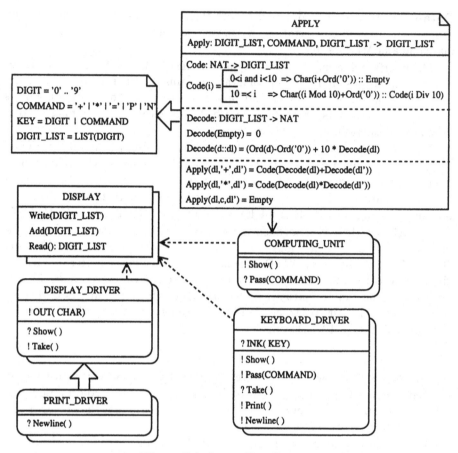

Fig. 1. Calculator: Class Diagram

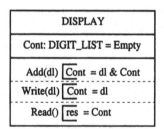

Fig. 2. Calculator: DISPLAY body diagram

$$
M(i_1,...,i_k) \begin{array}{|l|} \hline \text{if cond}_1 \{ \text{ assignement\_list}_1 \} \\ \hline \cdots \\ \hline \text{if cond}_n \{ \text{ assignement\_list}_n \} \\ \hline \end{array}
$$

where: for each h $(1 \leq h \leq k)$ i_h is a pattern, i.e., an expression of type IT_h built only by constructors and variables; for each j $(1 \leq j \leq n)$ $cond_j$ is a boolean expression over the variables in $i_1,...,i_k$ and the object fields; assignment_list$_j$ is a list of assignments of form either "f = e" or "res = e", with e an expression over the variables in $i_1,...,i_k$ and the object fields, f a field name and res a special variable of type OT denoting the result returned by the method.

A method call is executed as follows. We find the first, w.r.t. the ordering, rule whose pattern matches with the parameters of the call and with a condition that holds. If none matches, then we have an error. Then, the corresponding assignments are performed. The value returned by the method (if any) is the final value of the variable res. Trivial examples of method definitions are in the body of the class DISPLAY in fig. 2 (& is the operation for appending lists).

Process Class In our approach, processes are different from objects and their description cannot be given in the same way. First note that processes are *active* components that behave independently and do not offer methods outside. Their behaviours are not sequential, instead they run concurrently and cooperate by message exchange with those of the other processes. So, the process interface diagram does not contain methods, but the communication channels, synchronous and asynchronous.

The body diagram describes the behaviour of the process, by presenting its interesting intermediate states, each one characterized by a name and typed parameters, and its transitions, precisely from every intermediate state, some conditional rules define all the states it can reach by interacting with the external world (i.e., the labelled transitions of [11]). In the general method of [11], there is no restriction on the form of the external interactions, which are just described by labels. In JTN, a process can communicate with the external world only by calling the object methods or by using the communication channels.

We give a graphic presentation of the behaviour that naturally depicts what a process does, by showing all the possible transitions starting from any state.

Interface diagram JTN processes use two kinds of channels: synchronous and asynchronous; both kinds of channels are distinguished into input and output ones. Thus the interface diagram for a process class has two slots containing the *asynchronous* and the *synchronous* channels, respectively, with their names, their directions (described by ! and ?) and the types of exchanged values (if any).

For example, the DISPLAY_DRIVER interface diagram in fig. 1 declares two synchronous channels Show and Take used only for a synchronization purpose (no value exchanged), and an asynchronous one, OUT, on which an instance of DISPLAY_DRIVER sends a char outside.

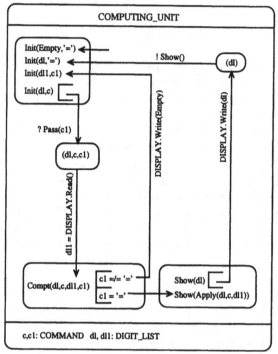

Fig. 3. Calculator: Computing Unit behaviour graph

Behaviour Graph [1] *(process body diagram)*
The *behaviour* of a process of a class is described by a graph, whose arcs represent "generic" labelled transitions, whose form is

$$S(pt_1,...,pt_n) \left\lceil cond(pt_1,...,pt_n) \xrightarrow{\quad l \quad} S'(e_1,...,e_k) \right.$$

where S, S' are state constructors, $pt_1, ...,pt_n$ are patterns for the state parameters, l is a pattern for the external interaction and $e_1,..,e_k$ are expressions over the variables in l and $pt_1,...,pt_n$.

The label l can have six different forms, depending on the kind of interaction that is performed with the external world:

- ?ACH(x), !ACH(e): input from/output to an asynchronous channel;
- $r = oe.m(x_1, ..., x_n)$ (or $oe.m(x_1, ..., x_n)$ if m has no return type): object method invocation;
- ?sch($x_1,...,x_k$),!sch($e_1,...,e_k$): input from/output to a synchronous channel;
- τ: internal activity, usually omitted.

---

[1] The behaviour graphs of JTN play the same role of the UML state diagrams.

All the sources and targets of transition representing state patterns of the same kind are grouped together into a node of the behaviour graph, avoiding repetitions. Thus each state pattern is written once, and the conditions are listed aside the corresponding state pattern to form an *alternative*, as below

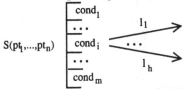

The arrows leaving a condition are ordered. Thus, inside a node of the graph we have an ordered list of alternatives plus state patterns that are only targets of transitions.

The interpretation of the behaviour graph is as follows. When a process is in a state K(args), we consider in order all the alternatives inside the node for the K states, until we find one whose pattern matches args. Then, inside the chosen alternative, we look for the first true condition. Finally we consider the labels on the arrows leaving the condition, trying to determine the first one that can be executed (recall they are ordered). If no matching pattern with a true condition is found, then the process is definitively stopped.

Not all choices of labels $(l_1,...,l_h)$ are meaningful; the admissible cases are as follows, and for each of them we explain how to select the one to execute:

1. $h = 1$ and l_1 is a method call or an output on an asynchronous channel or an internal transition; the corresponding transition can be executed.
2. $h \geq 1$ and for each i $(1 \leq i \leq h)$ $l_i = !sch_i(...)$ or $l_i = ?sch_i(...)$: all synchronous channels sch_i are checked in the order; if the communication on sch_i cannot be executed, then the following one is checked. If no communication can be executed, the process is suspended until the last communication completes.
3. $h \geq 1$ and for each i $(1 \leq i \leq h)$ $l_i = ?ACH_i(...)$: the asynchronous channels ACH_i are continuously tested in the order, until an available message is found.

In cases 2 and 3 we can add an arrow labelled with "else" with the meaning that whenever no other transition can be executed, such escape will be performed as an internal action, leading to another state from which the activity continues. An else label can be used in case 2 when no communication is immediately available, to return to the same state and start again the polling procedure. See e.g., the state Taking in fig. 4, where KEYBOARD_DRIVER can perform a synchronous communication on channel Take; otherwise KEYBOARD_DRIVER moves to another state (by else transition) in which it tries to read a character from the asynchronous input channel INK, and, if nothing is available, by another else transition, then it will come back to the state Taking.

Instead of explicitly declaring in a behaviour graph each state constructor with the type of its parameters, we add a slot for declaring the types of the used variables; obviously each state constructor must be typed consistently.

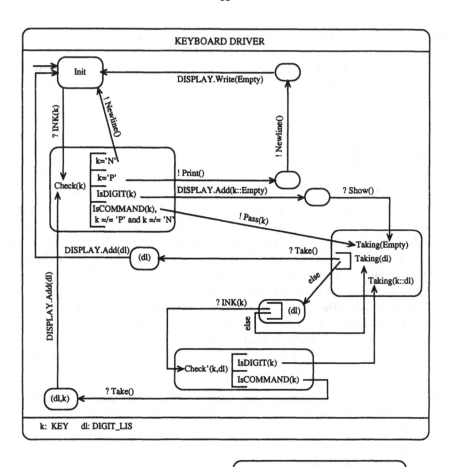

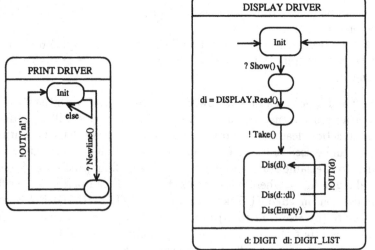

Fig. 4. Behaviour graphs

In fig. 3 and 4 we omit the name of a state every time it is not relevant; in such a case, the icon is empty, or just contains the list of the arguments.

An arrow with neither starting state nor label enters in the initial state of the system (see the upper left arrow in fig. 3)

Class Relationships Here we briefly illustrate the relationships among classes that we can put in the class diagram.

Inheritance ($\Leftarrow$) states that a class extends another one. It is restricted to classes of the same kind. What really the word "extends" does mean, depends on the particular kind of class. With regard to data-types, inheritance is used to add new operations. An example is APPLY, that adds the operation Apply. When considering an object class, inheritance is a mechanism for adding new methods and fields; finally, when considering a process class, inheritance adds transitions (i.e., behaviour) and new communication channels.

In our example, the PRINT_DRIVER class inherits from DISPLAY_DRIVER: its interface diagram is the one of DISPLAY_DRIVER with a new synchronous channel Newline; the behaviour graph of class PRINT_DRIVER depicts only the new transitions (see fig. 4), implicitly assuming those described in the behaviour graph of DISPLAY_DRIVER. More precisely, the transitions starting from states of the same kind are merged together; the new alternatives for a given state, as well as new transitions associated with an existing condition, are added at the end of the list, as they represent alternatives to be considered after the existing ones (we are currently studying more suitable mechanisms to describe how to re-order these alternatives).

The three different inheritance relations define three hierarchies over, respectively, data, object and process types (i.e., classes).

Usage ($\leftarrow$) states that a data-type is used by another class. It is represented by an arrow from the used data-type class to the using class. If all the system components use a data-type, then the usage relation is omitted.

Clientship ($\leftarrow$) states that a class assume the existence of another one, because it calls its methods. In our example, the process of all classes call the methods of the DISPLAY class.

In this paper we do not consider structured objects, calling other object methods, so clientship relates only process classes with the classes of the objects whose methods they call.

3 Architecture diagram

The architecture diagram describes the structure of the system showing its components and how they cooperate. The icons for the process and the object instances are slightly different from the corresponding ones for the classes; they are single boxes or single boxes with rounded corners: ⬜ ⬜.

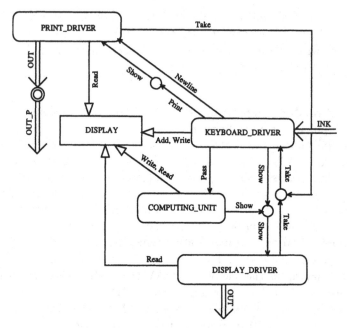

Fig. 5. Calculator: Architecture diagram

An instance icon contains only the instance identifier with the name of the corresponding class, separated by colons; the identifier is omitted if there is only one instance for such class, as in fig. 5.

The architecture diagram is a hyper-graph whose nodes are class instances that represent the components, and whose hyper-arcs represent how they cooperate. Let us remark that in this work we consider neither creation/deletion of components nor architectures having a generic number of components.

We can distinguish three kinds of hyper-arcs, representing:

method call: a process calls a method of an object; the icons of the two instances are linked by an arrow decorated with the method name; the arrow is oriented from the caller process to the called object.

asynchronous communication: fig. 6a) describes the connection of some asynchronous channels; OAC_i are output channels and IAC_i are input channels of the processes attached to the hyper-arc. The type of the exchanged message is the same for all the channels. Moreover, the channel types and versus must be in accord with the interfaces of the classes of the connected processes.

We can distinguish some cases. If $n = 1, m = 0$ or $n = 0, m = 1$, then the icon describes a channel for a process that communicates with the external world (e.g., the OUT channel associated with the DISPLAY_DRIVER in fig. 4). If $n > 0, m > 0$, a message sent on a generic OAC_i will be replied on all $IAC_1, .., IAC_m$. If $n = 1, m = 1$ the channel connects two processes or it is used to rename a channel, as we can see in fig. 5, where channel OUT of PRINT_DRIVER is renamed as OUT_P to avoid name clash with the same channel of DISPLAY_DRIVER.

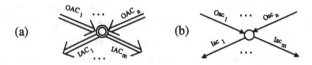

Fig. 6. Connectors for asynchronous and synchronous channels

synchronous communication: fig. 6b) describes the connection of some synchronous channels. We always have $n > 0, m > 0$, because synchronous channels cannot be used for communication with the external world. Again, the channel types and versus must be in accord with the interfaces of the classes of the connected processes.

The synchronous communication always involves two processes at a time: one process connected on a generic Osc_i acting as a sender, and one connected on a generic Isc_i acting as a receiver. Thus, the drawing can be interpreted as a shortcut for a set of channels connecting pairwise all sending to all receiving processes. An example is channel Show in fig. 5 that connects KEYBOARD_DRIVER, COMPUTING_UNIT (senders) and DISPLAY_DRIVER (receiver).

4   Sequence Diagram

A sequence[2] diagram is a kind of Message Sequence Chart [8] that gives a (possibly partial) description of a (possibly partial) execution of the system. Sequence diagrams are of particular interest because introduce in a specification formalism a technique that is used in the most widely accepted methods and notations in the Software Engineering field (such as UML).

A sequence diagram graphically represents some components taking part in a partial system execution and the ordered sequence of interactions among them and with the external world performed during such execution. The considered interactions are communications over channels and calls to object methods. The graphic presentation enlightens relevant aspects of the temporal ordering among interaction occurrences. Moreover, the diagram can be annotated with information about the state of the components, so it is possible to represent effects or conditions of action occurrences on single components.

The class and the architecture diagram supply complementary information about the system, whereas the sequence diagrams are just a different way to visualize information that has been already specified by the other diagrams. Several sequence diagrams may be presented for the same specification, to cover, e.g., the description of some interesting use cases of the system.

Sequence diagrams are not valuable for their information content (because it is already present in the other diagrams) but mainly from a methodological point of view and can be used for different purposes, for instance:

---

[2] In this case we use the same terminology of UML, since our sequences and the UML ones are rather similar; we can analogously define a form of collaboration diagram.

– to give a more natural and clear representation of the developed system to a client (e.g., to show how the calculator performs the addition);

– to show that the behaviour of the system specified by the class and the architecture diagrams is, in particular circumstances, the expected one. For example, by a sequence diagram we can show that if the user does not digit an "=" at the end of the operation, then the calculator does not return the result. From our experience, the construction of sequence diagrams, also if "by hand", helps to control the quality of the proposed design and allows to detect errors and omissions in the specification.

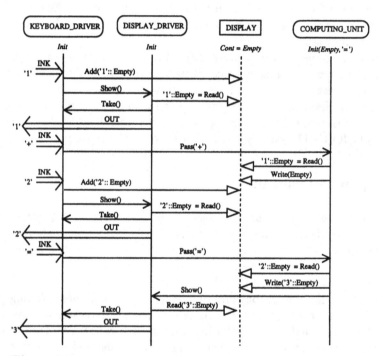

Fig. 7. Calculator: a sequence diagram for the computation of 1 + 2

Sequences diagrams are forms of message sequence charts, thus there are *vertical lines* representing the lives of the components involved in the execution. We use a dashed line to represent objects and a continuous line to represent processes. The *horizontal lines* describe the interactions occurring among the components or with the external world (i.e., communications on a channel, and method calls). Lines are put from top to bottom with respect to the temporal ordering of happening.

We use different icons for asynchronous communication (a double arrow), synchronous communication (a single arrow) and method call (a single arrow with outlined head) as we can see in fig. 7.

An asynchronous communication with the external world is just an incoming or outcoming double arrow, labelled by the channel name and by the exchanged data. An asynchronous communication between two processes is represented by two broken arrows. The part representing the start of the communication (send) is over the other one. They are separated by vertical dots and the data exchanged is annotated over both the two parts. Other actions may occur between the two phases of the asynchronous communications. A synchronous communication is decorated by the name of the channel and by the exchanged message. A method call is decorated by the name of the method and the parameters.

At any point of the vertical lines it is possible to put conditions on the value of the fields, for an object, and on the state and its arguments, for a process. The starting state of the execution may be described by such annotations, on the top of the corresponding vertical lines (see fig. 7).

Note that the elimination of a component and of its interactions returns another sequence diagram. If we drop DISPLAY_DRIVER in fig. 7, then we have a sequence diagram concerning only the updating of DISPLAY.

As sequence diagrams can erroneously depict executions that are not coherent with the rest of the specification, we must define when a sequence diagram is consistent with the information supplied by the class and the architecture diagrams.

Once we fixed the starting state of each instance, we can easily trace out how the system evolves. The object body diagrams describe how a method execution changes the state of an object. The behaviour graphs describe which communications or which method calls a process can perform from a given state and thus is the corresponding new state. The architecture diagram presents the topology of both the external as well as the inter-process communications. Thus, when we know which are the values arriving on the input asynchronous channels from the external world, we can find which actions the system components can perform and consequently which states the system can reach.

So, given a sequence diagram, we can determine the starting state of the system and then whether the depicted interactions can happen in the depicted order.

This consistency idea can be precisely defined, remembering that JTN is a formal specification language (the semantics of class plus architecture diagrams is an LTS) and that each sequence diagram corresponds to a formula in a branching time temporal logic saying that, from the starting state there exists a sequence of transitions where the depicted communications happened in the depicted order.

5   Implementation of main mechanisms

Here we briefly sketch out the implementation in Java of some of the JTN mechanisms. Obviously, the resulting Java program manages the classes and the instances shown in the diagrams, and also some auxiliary ones that are the standard implementation for synchronous and asynchronous channels and predefined data-types.

The predefined data-types are mostly obtained by combining Java primitive data (e.g., integer) and by extending some Java standard classes (e.g., Vector). The user-defined data-types have a standard translation: the constructors and their arguments are implemented as instance private fields; the component extractors operating on the data are trivial methods returning the value of the corresponding fields. The operations are translated into methods, whose code implements the guarded commands and the pattern matching used to define them.

The object classes are implemented as Java classes. The private fields implement the fields, initialized to the value represented in the body diagram; the methods are the direct encoding of the corresponding methods specified in the body diagram.

The process classes are implemented as Java thread classes and the intermediate states, described by constructors in the behaviour graph, are implemented by the fields of the class; the unique method is run, whose code is determined by the behaviour graph of the class.

```
class DisplayDriver extends Thread{
  private String state = "Init"; // state constructor implementation
  private List_Digit the_dl; // digit list;
  private Display the_d; // the display;

  private Synch_Sign Show; // synchronous communication channels
  private Synch_Sign Take;
  private FileOutputStream Out;   // asynchronous communication channel

  DisplayDriver(Synch_Sign s, Synch_Sign t, Display d){
   super();
   Show = s;
     ... // initialization part continues
  }
  public void run(){
   while(true){
    Show.get(); // receives a signal
    Take.put(); // sends a signal
    the_dl= the_d.Read(); // reads the Display content
    state = "Dis"; // changes its state
     while (!the_dl.isEmpty()){
      Out.println(the_dl.Head());
      the_dl = the_dl.Tail();
     }}}
}
```

Fig. 8. Java implementation of DISPLAY_DRIVER

The communication channels of a process are fields referencing particular objects. A synchronous channel is implemented by using a special object that act as a "synchronizer". When a process P1 tries to synchronize with P2, it accesses the synchronizer to check whether P2 is ready for the synchronization. If P2 is not ready, then P1 is suspended. When P2 is ready, P1 is resumed and reads or writes the exchanged data. To ensure that only one process at a time gains the access to a channel method, as well as to suspend-resume processes we use the **synchronized** and the **wait-notify** mechanisms of Java.

The asynchronous channels are trivially implemented by Java streams. In the particular case of asynchronous communication among process, we use the specialized stream classes for pipeline communication. Moreover, if the communication among processes involves m writers and n readers, a particular object implements the connector in fig. 6(a) that continuously reads a data from anyone among the input channels and replicate it on each one of the output ones.

6 Conclusions and Related Works

We think that JTN could help to design complex systems using Java, even if in this paper we have used it on a really toy example, for the following reasons:

- it is strongly visual; we have tried to visually render the process behaviours, the system architecture, the way the components cooperate, as well as the definition of data operations and of object methods;
- the complexity and the intricacies of the systems is mastered by keeping separated data-types, objects and processes, and allowing to design such entities at the most abstract level compatible with a direct implementation in Java; for example, data-types are not objects and the user can define her data with the constructors of her choice to represent them. For example, if we want to concatenate two lists L1 and L2, we do not have to create two objects realizing L1 and L2 respectively, and then call the concatenation method on L1 (or L2); instead, we just apply the concatenation operation to terms representing L1 and L2 respectively.
- there is a direct correct encoding of the specification into a Java program that it is possible to make automatic by the use of some tool.

JTN is not purely OO, as it only includes some OO concepts, precisely those that are useful to model the features of the considered systems. We use classes and instances, plus inheritance and other relationships, to model the three kinds of constituents of the systems (data-types, passive and active components). The interactions among processes via shared memory is modelled by objects and method calls; encapsulation allows to control how processes access the objects in the shared memory.

Although JTN is Java-targeted, it is not useful only to produce Java code; indeed it can also be fruitfully used to model and design systems implemented by using another programming language, as ADA.

Note that JTN is not addressed to real-time systems, because the abstract specification method of [11] and the features of Java do not adequately support real-time programming.

It is possible to produce a full set of software tools to support the use of JTN: from interactive graphic editors to a static checker including the consistency check of the sequence diagrams with respect to the other diagrams, to browsers enhancing the hyper-textual aspects of the diagrams composing the specifications, to the translator into Java. We are considering also a form of debugger obtained by using a variant of the translation into Java. The execution of the modified program produces an output that can be transformed in a sequence diagram and so we can have a graphic presentation of the execution. The underlined required technology for the realization of such tools is easily available. At the moment we are looking for human resources to realize them.

Our future work will consider how to complete JTN; we want to investigate the structuring of processes and objects by introducing sub-components, a mechanism for the packaging of classes when one global class diagram is too large, other communication mechanisms, the notation for the description of the distribution level of the architecture and so on. The notion of inheritance for the process class requires further investigations too, with the determination of an associated type hierarchy.

To fully take advantage of JTN we need to propose a method for passing from the abstract specifications of [11] to the more detailed JTN ones, that is guidelines and hints that help the user to perform this task.

We are not aware of other "Java targeted" specification languages/notations for systems in the literature, even if there exit tools for generating Java code from generic object-oriented specifications (e.g., ROSE for UML).

To relate our proposal to other approaches we must first recall that JTN is not an OO specification language, but it is intended for reactive/concurrent/ distributed systems; this is the reason why it uses ingredients as processes strongly different from objects, system architecture and channels. However JTN encompasses a few OO concepts, for example, "object" as a way to encapsulate shared memory and "class" (for objects and processes) with inheritance as a way to modularly define "types" of objects and processes.

The JTN specifications are both graphic and formal, and in this respect JTN is similar to SDL [7] and Statecharts [5]; the differences with these two notations lay in the way the processes cooperate and in the paradigm followed for representing the process behaviour.

What said above shows also the differences/relationships with UML [9]: UML is OO, JTN is concurrency oriented; UML is a notation that can be used by many different development processes at different points, JTN is for Java targeted design of systems (companion formal/graphic notations for abstract design and requirement specifications have been developed, see [11, 10]); UML is semi-formal (precise syntax including well-formed conditions, semantics by English text), JTN is fully formal (it has a complete formal semantics because it can be easily transformed into a graphic-formal specification of [11], see [3]).

The use of data-types with constructors and of pattern matching in guarded commands come from ML [6], because we think that in many case that could be a compact and clear way to represent the data-types and their operations.

References

1. E. Astesiano and G. Reggio. Formally-Driven Friendly Specifications of Concurrent Systems: A Two-Rail Approach. Technical Report DISI–TR–94–20, DISI – Università di Genova, Italy, 1994. Presented at ICSE'17-Workshop on Formal Methods, Seattle April 1995.
2. E. Astesiano and G. Reggio. A Dynamic Specification of the RPC-Memory Problem. In *Formal System Specification: The RPC-Memory Specification Case Study*, number 1169 in LNCS. Springer Verlag, 1996.
3. E.Coscia and G.Reggio. JTN: the Reference Manual. Technical report, DISI – Università di Genova, Italy, 1999.
4. Gosling, Joy, and Steele. *The Java Language Specification*. Addison Wesley, 1996.
5. D. Harel. Statecharts: A Visual Formalism for Complex Systems. *Science of Computer Programming*, 8, 1987.
6. R. Harper, D. MacQueen, and R. Milner. Standard ML. Technical Report ECS-LFCS-86-2, LFCS-University of Edinburgh, 1986.
7. ITU. Z.100 ITU Specification and Description Language (SDL). Technical report, ITU, Geneva, 1993.
8. ITU. Z.120: Message Sequence Chart (MSC). Technical report, ITU, Geneva, 1993.
9. RATIONAL. UML Notation Guide Version 1.1. Available at http://www.rational.com/uml/html/notation/, 1997.
10. G. Reggio. A Method to Capture Formal Requirements: the INVOICE Case Study. In *Int. Workshop Comparing Specification Techniques*. Universite de Nantes, 1998.
11. G. Reggio and M. Larosa. A Graphic Notation for Formal Specifications of Dynamic Systems. In *Proc. FME 97*, number 1313 in LNCS. Springer Verlag, 1997.

Conservative Extension in Positive/Negative Conditional Term Rewriting with Applications to Software Renovation Factories

Wan Fokkink[*1] and Chris Verhoef[2]

[1] University of Wales Swansea, Department of Computer Science, Singleton Park,
Swansea SA2 8PP, UK,
w.j.fokkink@swan.ac.uk, fax: +44 1792 295708
[2] University of Amsterdam, Department of Computer Science, Programming
Research Group, Kruislaan 403, 1098 SJ Amsterdam, The Netherlands,
x@wins.uva.nl, fax: +31 20 5257490

Abstract. We transpose a conservative extension theorem from structural operational semantics to conditional term rewriting. The result is useful for the development of software renovation factories, and for modular specification of abstract data types.

1 Introduction

There is a strong link between the worlds of conditional term rewriting [30, 8] and of structural operational semantics (SOS) [35]. In fact, from a conceptual level they can be seen as identical. In both fields, terms are built from a set of function symbols. The binary relations on terms, rewrite steps and transitions, both are defined inductively by means of proof rules, called conditional rewrite rules or transition rules, respectively. Those rules, together with the validity, or non-validity, of a number of relations between terms, may imply the validity of another relation between terms.

There is one small distinction between both worlds. For a conditional term rewriting system (CTRS), provability is closed under context, in other words, if $s \to t$ is provable, then $Con[s] \to Con[t]$ is provable for every context $Con[]$. The set of transitions provable from a Transition System Specification (TSS) does not have to satisfy this characteristic, so in general a TSS cannot be expressed as a CTRS. However, the reverse transposition is possible, that is, for each CTRS there is an equivalent TSS. This transformation is obtained by adding context rules for all function symbols.

This correspondence was noted, but not exploited, by Groote and Vaandrager [28, Example 3.5]. They refrain from transposing their congruence format from TSSs to CTRSs, because it would not serve any practical purpose. Namely, although term rewriting and SOS theory are rooted on the same basis, their

---

* Supported by a grant from The Nuffield Foundation

aims are fundamentally different. Term rewriting seeks for termination and confluence of reductions, while in SOS theory in general behaviour is infinite and non-confluent. Usually, TSSs need to define a congruence relation with respect to a certain semantics, i.e., if two terms s and t are semantically equivalent, then $Con[s]$ and $Con[t]$ are semantically equivalent for all contexts $Con[]$. Several formats for TSSs have been developed which guarantee that they define a congruence relation for bisimulation semantics [28, 9, 3, 44, 17]. Most CTRSs from the literature do not fit these formats.

When a TSS is extended with new transition rules, the question arises whether or not such an extension influences the transitions of terms in the original domain. Usually, it is desirable that an extension is conservative, in the sense that the transitions for an original term are the same both in the original and in the extended TSS. Several formats have been developed which imply that an extended TSS is conservative over the original TSS [28, 9, 43, 20, 14]. Groote and Vaandrager [28, Theorem 7.6] proposed the first syntactic restrictions for an original TSS and its extension. Bol and Groote [9] adapted this conservativity format to the setting with negative conditions. Verhoef [43] proposed more general syntactic criteria, which were later on extended to a setting with inequalities [14]. In [20], Verhoef's format was transposed to higher-order languages.

This SOS notion of conservative extension is also useful in the realm of conditional term rewriting. Namely, if a CTRS $R_0 \oplus R_1$ is both confluent and an operational conservative extension of the CTRS R_0, then this extension is conservative in the classic sense. That is, then the CTRSs $R_0 \oplus R_1$ and R_0 induce exactly the same initial model for original terms. In this paper we exploit the link between TSSs and CTRSs to transpose the conservative extension theorem from the world of SOS to CTRSs. The conservativity result formulates syntactic requirements on the form of conditional rewrite rules in CTRSs R_0 and R_1, to ensure that the rewrite relation induced by R_0 on original terms is not affected by rewrite rules in R_1. It requires that each conditional rewrite rule in R_0 is *deterministic* [21]. Furthermore, each rewrite rule in R_1 should contain a fresh function symbol in its left-hand side.

The current paper arose from the final section in [18], where a simplified version of the conservativity format is transposed to the setting of conditional term rewriting. Simplifications are that we only treat first-order terms and that we do not allow the possibility that the left-hand side of a rewrite rule in the extension is an original term. We refrain from transposing the conservativity format to CTRSs in full generality for the sake of presentation, and to leave space to indulge in relevant applications. We refer to [19] where the SOS result has been transposed to higher-order CTRSs.

The conservativity format is applicable in the field of abstract data types, where there is a long tradition in specifying by means of modules of CTRSs. In abstract data types, modular specification means conservative extension, in our terminology. Namely, original modules fix the semantics of original terms, which should not be changed thereafter; new modules give meaning to fresh terms, which did not have a semantics before; see [5]. Our result is also applicable in the area of automated software engineering. In this paper we give a formal definition of a software renovation factory that may consist of numerous CTRSs. In order to build such a factory those CTRSs are combined, and then our result comes into play: it gives sufficient conditions so that the functionality of each separate component is not influenced in the presence of other components. This enables reuse of components and a component-based development of such factories. Of course, it cannot be demanded of an operator in a software renovation factory that she remembers our conservativity result upon adding a module to another component. It is, however, possible to implement this check; an automated check on determinism in the SOS world has been incorporated in the tool LATOS [29]. To demonstrate the use of our result, we provide examples from the literature, concerning term rewriting, abstract data types, and software renovation factories.

We study positive/negative CTRSs [31], which may contain negative conditions of the form $s\neg Dt$ for relations D, to express that there does not exist a relation sDt. We give meaning to such negative conditions using three-valued stable models [37, 22] from logic programming. Van de Pol [36] used instances of this semantic notion to provide negative answers to three open questions in term rewriting with priorities [4].

2   A Conservative Extension Theorem

2.1   Conditional Rewrite Rules

Definition 1. *A (single-sorted) signature Σ consists of a countably infinite set $\mathcal{V}$ of variables, and a non-empty set of function symbols f with fixed arities.*

A function symbol of arity zero is called a *constant*.

Definition 2. *Let Σ be a signature. The collection of* (open) terms $s, t, \ldots$ *over Σ is defined as the least set satisfying:*

- *each variable from $\mathcal{V}$ is a term;*
- *if function symbol f has arity n, and $t_1, \ldots, t_n$ are terms over Σ, then $f(t_1, \ldots, t_n)$ is a term over Σ.*

A term is called *closed* if it does not contain any occurrences of variables.

We assume a signature Σ, and a set $\mathcal{D}$ of relation symbols. The symbols in $\mathcal{D}$ represent binary rewrite relations between closed terms over Σ. Following Kaplan [31] we study positive/negative CTRSs, which may contain negative conditions of the form $s\neg Dt$, meaning that the relation sDt is not valid.

Definition 3. *For closed terms s, t over Σ, and $D \in \mathcal{D}$, sDt is called a positive rewrite step, and $s\neg Dt$ is called a negative rewrite step.*

The standard rewrite relation is the one-step relation $\rightarrow$. But we will also encounter its transitive-reflexive closure $\twoheadrightarrow$, the join $\downarrow$, and the equality sign $=$.

Definition 4. *A* (positive/negative) conditional rewrite rule *is of the form* $p \Leftarrow C$, *where.*

- *the* conclusion p *is of the form* sDt;
- *C is a (possibly empty) set of* conditions *of the form* sDt *or* $s\neg Dt$;

with s and t open terms. A (positive/negative) conditional term rewriting system *(CTRS) is a set of positive/negative conditional rewrite rules.*

We extend the notion of a *deterministic* conditional rewrite rule [21] to the setting with negative conditions.

Definition 5. *For a conditional rewrite rule* $p \Leftarrow C$, *the deterministic variables in this rule are defined inductively as follows.*

- *All variables in the left-hand side of* p *are deterministic.*
- *If* sDt *is a positive condition in* C, *and all variables in* s *are deterministic, then all variables in* t *are also deterministic.*

A conditional rewrite rule is called deterministic *if all its variables are so.*

Definition 6. *A* proof *from a CTRS* R *for a closed rewrite rule* $p \Leftarrow C$ *(which contains only closed terms) consists of an upwardly branching tree in which all upward paths are finite, where the nodes of the tree are labelled by positive and negative rewrite steps, such that:*

- *the root has label* p,
- *if some node has label* q, *and* K *is the set of labels of nodes directly above this node, then*
  1. *either* $K = \emptyset$, *and* $q \in C$,
  2. *or* $q \Leftarrow K$ *is a closed substitution instance of a rewrite rule in* R.

2.2 Conservative Extension

We define a notion of (operational) conservative extension for CTRSs, which is related to an equivalence notion for TSSs in [24, 17]: two TSSs are equivalent if they prove exactly the same rewrite rules N/τ where N contains only negative transitions.

Definition 7. *Let* Σ_0 *and* Σ_1 *be signatures. Their sum (or union)* $\Sigma_0 \oplus \Sigma_1$ *is well-defined if each function symbol and each variable in* $\Sigma_0 \cap \Sigma_1$ *has the same functionality in both signatures.*

We assume two CTRSs R_0 and R_1 over $(\Sigma_0, \mathcal{D}_0)$ and $(\Sigma_1, \mathcal{D}_1)$ respectively, where $\Sigma_0 \oplus \Sigma_1$ is well-defined. Their sum (or union) is denoted by $R_0 \oplus R_1$.

Definition 8. $R_0 \oplus R_1$ *is a conservative extension of* R_0 *if for each closed rewrite rule* $p \Leftarrow C$ *with*

- *C contains only negative conditions;*

- *the left-hand side of p is a term over Σ_0;*
- *there exists a proof from $R_0 \oplus R_1$ for $p \Leftarrow C$;*

then there exists a proof from R_0 for $p \Leftarrow C$.

We give an example of an extension that is *not* conservative.

Example 1. Σ_0 consists of the constant a, and R_0 of the rewrite rule $a \to x \Leftarrow x \to x$. Furthermore, Σ_1 consists of the constant b, and R_1 of the rewrite rule $b \to b$. Clearly the rewrite step $a \to b$ is valid in $R_0 \oplus R_1$, but not in R_0. Since a is an original term, $R_0 \oplus R_1$ is not a conservative extension of R_0.

Note that the CTRS R_0 in Example 1 is not deterministic, because the variable x in the rewrite rule in R_0 is not deterministic (see Definition 5).

Theorem 1. *Assume two CTRSs R_0 and R_1 over $(\Sigma_0, \mathcal{D}_0)$ and $(\Sigma_1, \mathcal{D}_1)$ respectively, where $\Sigma_0 \oplus \Sigma_1$ is well-defined. Under the following conditions, $R_0 \oplus R_1$ is a conservative extension of R_0.*

1. *R_0 is deterministic.*
2. *For each rewrite rule in R_1, the left-hand side of its conclusion contains a function symbol from $\Sigma_1 \backslash \Sigma_0$.*

Proof. This result follows almost directly from a similar result for TSSs; see [20, Theo. 3.20]. We only need to resolve the distinction in the notion of provability for TSSs and CTRSs. For this reason we introduce for each function symbol f of arity n, and for each argument $i \in \{1, ..., n\}$ of f, a so-called context rule

$$f(x_1, ..., x_{i-1}, x_i, x_{i+1}, ..., x_n) \to f(x_1, ..., x_{i-1}, y, x_{i+1}, ..., x_n) \Leftarrow x_i \to y.$$

We make two observations.

1. For each original function symbol f, the context rules for its arguments are all deterministic. Namely, since $x_1, ..., x_n$ occur in the left-hand side of the conclusion it is deterministic. Moreover, since the variable x_i is deterministic, the condition $x_i \to y$ makes that y is also deterministic.
2. For each fresh function symbol f, the context rules for its arguments all contain the fresh function symbol f in their source.

So if we add the context rules for original function symbols to R_0, and the context rules for fresh function symbols to R_1, then R_0 and R_1 still comply with the syntactic requirements that were formulated in the theorem.

Owing to the extra context rules, we can use the provability notion from the SOS world, where closure under context is not taken for granted. hence, we can apply the conservative extension result for TSSs [20, Theo. 3.20] to conclude that $R_0 \oplus R_1$ is a conservative extension of R_0.

2.3 Three-Valued Stable Models

When there are negative conditions around, it is no longer straightforward to define a sensible rewrite relation. We consider some well-established notions from logic programming [37, 22]. See [24] for a thorough overview of possibilities to give meaning to negative conditions.

The notion of a three-valued stable model was introduced by Przymusinski [37] in logic programming. It consists of two disjoint collections of positive rewrite steps: intuitively, T contains the *true* rewrite steps, while U contains the rewrite steps of which it is *unknown* whether or not they are true. All positive rewrite steps outside $T \cup U$ are considered to be *false*. These intuitions are made precise in the definition of a three-valued stable model.

Definition 9. *The collections* (T, U) *of positive rewrite steps are a* three-valued stable model *for a CTRS R, if the following two requirements hold.*

1. *The elements of* T *are exactly those positive rewrite steps* sDs' *for which there exists a closed rewrite rule* $tDt' \Leftarrow C$ *such that:*
   - $s = Con[t]$ *and* $s' = Con[t']$ *for some context* $Con[]$,
   - *there exists a proof from R for* $tDt' \Leftarrow C$,
   - C *contains only negative rewrite steps,*
   - *for each* $s\neg Dt \in C$ *we have* $sDt \notin T \cup U$.
2. *The elements of* $T \cup U$ *are exactly those positive rewrite steps* sDs' *for which there exists a closed rewrite rule* $tDt' \Leftarrow C$ *such that:*
   - $s = Con[t]$ *and* $s' = Con[t']$ *for some context* $Con[]$,
   - *there exists a proof from R for* $tDt' \Leftarrow C$,
   - C *contains only negative rewrite steps,*
   - *for each* $s\neg Dt \in C$ *we have* $sDt \notin T$.

Example 2. The CTRS that consists of the rewrite rules $a \to b \Leftarrow a \not\to c$ and $a \to c \Leftarrow a \not\to b$ allows several three-valued stable models: $(\{a \to b\}, \emptyset)$ and $(\{a \to c\}, \emptyset)$ and $(\emptyset, \{a \to b, a \to c\})$.

If $R_0 \oplus R_1$ is a conservative extension of R_0, then each three-valued stable model for R_0 can be obtained by restricting a three-valued stable model for $R_0 \oplus R_1$ to the positive rewrite steps that have a closed original term as left-hand side. This theorem follows immediately from similar results for TSSs, Theorems 3.24 and 3.25 in [20], by the introduction of context rules.

Theorem 2. *Let* R_0 *be a CTRS over* Σ_0. *For three-valued stable models* (T, U) *for* $R_0 \oplus R_1$, *we define*

$$T|\Sigma_0 = \{sDt \in T \mid s \text{ a closed term over } \Sigma_0\}$$
$$U|\Sigma_0 = \{sDt \in U \mid s \text{ a closed term over } \Sigma_0\}.$$

If $R_0 \oplus R_1$ *is a conservative extension of* R_0, *then:*

1. *if* (T, U) *is a three-valued stable model for* $R_0 \oplus R_1$, *then* $(T|\Sigma_0, U|\Sigma_0)$ *is a three-valued stable model for* R_0;

2. *each three-valued stable model for R_0 is of the form $(T|\Sigma_0, U|\Sigma_0)$, with (T, U) a three-valued stable model for $R_0 \oplus R_1$.*

According to Przymusinski [37], each CTRS allows a unique three-valued stable model (T, U) for which the set U of unknown positive rewrite steps is maximal. Furthermore, Przymusinski showed that this model coincides with the *well-founded* model of Van Gelder, Ross and Schlipf [22]. The next corollary follows from Theorem 2.

Corollary 1. *Let R_0 be a CTRS over Σ_0. If $R_0 \oplus R_1$ is a conservative extension of R_0, and (T, U) is the well-founded model for $R_0 \oplus R_1$, then $(T|\Sigma_0, U|\Sigma_0)$ is the well-founded model for R_0.*

Two other semantic notions are related to three-valued stable models:

- A *stable model* [23] is a three-valued stable model $(T, \emptyset)$.
- A CTRS is *complete* [24] if its well-founded model is a stable model.

Suppose that the CTRS $R_0 \oplus R_1$ is complete; i.e., it has a well-founded model of the form $(T, \emptyset)$. Furthermore, let $R_0 \oplus R_1$ be a conservative extension of R_0; item 1 in Theorem 2 implies that $(T|\Sigma_0, \emptyset)$ is the well-founded model for R_0. If $R_0 \oplus R_1$ is confluent, then it follows that $R_0 \oplus R_1$ is conservative over R_0 in the classic sense from logic. That is, if the rewrite rules in $R_0 \oplus R_1$ and R_0 are taken to be equations, then both systems induce the same equations between original terms.

Remark 1. A positive CTRS induces a unique initial model of rewrite steps, which together constitute a minimal model for the CTRS. A rewrite step is in the initial model of a CTRS if and only if there exists a constructive proof for it. This is also the case for the rewrite steps in a three-valued stable model.

For a positive/negative CTRS, a *quasi-initial model* [31] of equations (instead of rewrite steps) is also required to constitute a minimal model for the CTRS. A quasi-initial model is not necessarily unique: the positive/negative CTRS R_0 that consists of the single rule $a \to c \Leftarrow a \neq b$ allows two quasi-initial models, $\{a = c\}$ and $\{a = b\}$. There does not exist a constructive proof for $a = b$; this contrasts with the semantics for positive CTRSs.

Theorem 2 does not hold if we replace "three-valued stable" by "quasi-initial". A counter-example is the extension of R_0 with the constant d and the CTRS R_1 that consists of the rewrite rules $d \to b$ and $d \to c$; this yields a unique quasi-initial model $\{a = b = c = d\}$. However, according to Theorem 1, $R_0 \oplus R_1$ is a conservative extension of R_0. The CTRS R_0 allows a unique three-valued stable model $(\{a \to c\}, \emptyset)$, and $R_0 \oplus R_1$ allows a unique three-valued stable model $(\{a \to c, d \to b, d \to c\}, \emptyset)$.

3 Application to CTRSs of Type III

A *CTRS of type III* consists of conditional rewrite rules of the form

$$s \to t \Leftarrow s_1 \twoheadrightarrow t_1, \ldots, s_n \twoheadrightarrow t_n.$$

$\twoheadrightarrow$ denotes the transitive-reflexive closure of the one-step relation $\rightarrow$. It is defined by two rewrite rules, which we add explicitly to each CTRS of type III:

$$x \twoheadrightarrow x \quad \text{and} \quad x \twoheadrightarrow z \Leftarrow x \rightarrow y, \, y \twoheadrightarrow z.$$

The first rule is clearly deterministic. In the second rule, x occurs in the left-hand side of the conclusion, so it is deterministic. Then y is deterministic by condition $x \rightarrow y$, so z is deterministic by condition $y \twoheadrightarrow z$.

On a rewrite rule $p \Leftarrow C$ we often see the following three requirements.

A. The left-hand side of p is not a single variable.
B. Variables in the right-hand side of p also occur in the left-hand side of p.
C. Variables in C also occur in p.

Criteria A and B are natural in the unconditional case, because then they are essential in order to obtain termination. According to Middeldorp [33, page 114], criterion C is often imposed "due to severe technical complications". We left out these criteria, because our results do not require to impose them. Criteria A and B would even be a hindrance, because the two rewrite rules that define the relation $\twoheadrightarrow$ do not satisfy these criteria.

We give an example of an extension of a CTRS of type III, taken from [15], to demonstrate the use of our conservativity result.

Example 3. The CTRS N_0 implements addition on natural numbers. It assumes the constant 0, the unary successor function S, and the binary addition function A. Its standard rules are

$$A(0, x) \rightarrow x$$
$$A(S(x), y) \rightarrow S(A(x, y))$$

The two rules in the CTRS N_0 are clearly deterministic, because they do not have conditions, and they satisfy criterion B.

The CTRS N_1 implements the Fibonacci numbers. It assumes 0 and S and A, together with the unary Fibonacci function Fib. The rules of N_1 are

$$Fib(0) \rightarrow (0, S(0))$$
$$Fib(S(x)) \rightarrow (z, A(y, z)) \Leftarrow Fib(x) \twoheadrightarrow (y, z)$$

The second rule in N_1 is considered difficult, because it does not satisfy criterion B: the variables y and z do not occur in the left-hand side of its conclusion. Nevertheless, since the left-hand sides of the conclusions of the two rules in N_1 contain the fresh function symbol Fib, and since N_0 is deterministic, Theorem 1 yields that $N_0 \oplus N_1$ is a conservative extension of N_0. The first rule in N_1 is clearly deterministic. In the second rule, x occurs in the left-hand side of the conclusion of the rule, so it is deterministic. Then condition $Fib(x) \twoheadrightarrow (y, z)$ makes that y and z are deterministic. So the second rule in N_1 is also deterministic.

We extend $N_0 \oplus N_1$ with the following two standard module N_2 for a binary equality function eq, which decides whether or not two natural numbers are syntactically equal.

$$eq(x, x) \rightarrow true$$
$$eq(x, y) \rightarrow false \Leftarrow eq(x, y) \not\twoheadrightarrow true$$

Since the left-hand side of the conclusions of both rules contain the fresh function symbol eq, and since $N_0 \oplus N_1$ is deterministic, it follows from Theorem 1 that $N_0 \oplus N_1 \oplus N_2$ is conservative over $N_0 \oplus N_1$.

In a *CTRSs of type III$_n$* (also called 'normal'), conditions are conjuncts of expressions $s \twoheadrightarrow t$ where t is a closed normal form. In particular, terms at the right-hand sides of conditions are closed, so it follows that the only deterministic variables in a type III$_n$ rule are the ones that occur in the left-hand side of its conclusion. Hence, a rule of type III$_n$ is deterministic if all its variables occur in the left-hand side of its conclusion, that is, if it satisfies criteria B and C.

In a *CTRSs of type II* (also called 'join'), conditions are conjuncts of expressions $s \downarrow t$, which denote that s and t reduce to the same term. This can be formulated in type III style: $s \twoheadrightarrow y$ and $t \twoheadrightarrow y$, where y is a fresh variable. Since the y is fresh, again the only deterministic variables in a type II rule are the variables that occur in the left-hand side of its conclusion. Hence, a rule of type II is deterministic if it satisfies criteria B and C.

Finally, in a *CTRSs of type I* (also called 'semi-equational'), conditions are conjuncts of expressions $s = t$, which denote that s rewrites to t if the rewrite rules may be applied both from left to right and from right to left. The following example shows that the syntactic criteria from Theorem 1 are not sufficient to ensure that an extension of a CTRS of type I is conservative.

Example 4. Let $\Sigma_0 = \{a, b\}$ and $\Sigma_1 = \{a, b, c\}$, where a, b, c are constants. Let R_0 consist of the single rule $a \rightarrow b \Leftarrow a = b$. Furthermore, let R_1 consist of the two rules $c \rightarrow a$ and $c \rightarrow b$.

R_0 is deterministic, and even satisfies criteria A, B, and C. Also, the left-hand side of the conclusions of the rules in R_1 contain the fresh function symbol c. However, $a \rightarrow b$ is provable from $R_0 \oplus R_1$, but not from R_0. Since a is an original term, $R_0 \oplus R_1$ is not a conservative extension of R_0.

4 Application to Software Renovation Factories

One way of looking at renovating a software system is to consider it as an annotated abstract syntax tree (AST) that needs to be manipulated. This manipulation can be rewriting. This idea underlies the following definition of a software renovation factory (this definition is implicitly assumed in [11] where it is shown how to generate useful rewrite systems from a context-free grammar).

Definition 10. *A software renovation factory is a set of software renovation assembly lines. A software renovation assembly line is an ordered set of (renovation) components. A (renovation) component is a positive/negative CTRS.*

We explain what our theorem and software renovation factories have in common (the reader is referred to [10, 16] for a quick introduction to the field of reverse engineering and system renovation). Code that needs to be renovated is first parsed, resulting in an abstract syntax tree (AST). Renovation of code amounts to conditionally rewriting the AST to a desired normal form. Then the AST is unparsed, resulting in renovated code. To renovate code, it is customary to combine existing renovation components. This can be done sequentially in an assembly line by applying components in a fixed order, or simultaneously by taking the sum of components, or as a combination of these two. Our theorem is important for the simultaneous combination of components, which amounts to taking the sum of positive/negative CTRSs. The question that arises is whether the sum is conservative over the separate components, i.e., is the functionality of an extended component the same as before?

We give an example, and apply our theorem to it, to ensure that the combination of components does not influence the behaviour of the separate components. The example uses COBOL (Common Business Oriented Language) [1]. It focuses on a many-sorted TRS; the conservative extension theorem in this paper generalizes to a many-sorted setting without any complications; see [18, 20].

In the example below we follow [39] in departing from the standard prefix notation for terms (see Definition 2). For example, a function symbol with three arguments can be defined as IF Boolean THEN Statement ELSE Statement END-IF -> Statement; this notations resembles Backus Naur Forms [2]. The name of the function symbol IF _ THEN _ ELSE _ END-IF is interspersed with its domain that would be Boolean × Statement × Statement in the standard notation. The form that we used here is known as distributed fix operators, distfix operators, or mixfix operators; these names are due to Mosses and Goguen [25]. The terms over a signature of distfix operators are constructed as usual. In [32, p. 202] an elegant correspondence between many-sorted terms and Backus Naur Forms is made, illustrating the natural connection of universal algebra and formal language definitions. In [32, p. 210] the syntax of while programs is discussed where the connection between distributed fix operations and terms in prefix notation is elegantly illustrated.

Example 5. Suppose that a company moves to Japan and that they wish to migrate their mission-critical business software from MicroFocus COBOL to Fujitsu COBOL, since the local programmers are familiar with the latter dialect. One of the components that we introduce migrates MicroFocus specific 78 level constant definitions to the SYMBOLIC CONSTANT clause (a Fujitsu COBOL specific feature) of the SPECIAL-NAMES paragraph. In fact, in the first dialect, the declaration of constants is done in a certain subtree of the AST, and we need to move this information from this subtree to another subtree (the word 'move' is loosely phrased since we also have to modify the syntax of the declarations). An extra problem with the other subtree is that we may need to create it, since it may not yet be present in the original code. The move is implemented in the CTRS R_0 below. It contains five hand crafted rewrite rules that represent the above requirements, plus hundreds of rewrite rules that take care of traversal of the AST, which are generated automatically from the grammar. For detailed information on this generative technology we refer to [11].

Before explaining the rewrite rules, first we focus on notations. The function symbols f_1-f_4 are generated automatically from the COBOL grammar (we renamed them for explanatory reasons). All other expressions that contain numerals are variables; the remaining expressions are terminals (or constant symbols in CTRS terminology). For example, Ident-div1 is a variable that matches a complete IDENTIFICATION DIVISION of a COBOL program; COMMENT2* stands for zero or more COBOL comments; Special-name1+ stands for one or more symbolic constants in a SPECIAL-NAMES section; and VALUE is a terminal representing the COBOL keyword VALUE. The five rewrite rules are:

```
[1] f_1(
    COMMENT1*
    Ident-div1
    Env-div1
    DATA DIVISION. COMMENT2*
      File-sec1
      WORKING-STORAGE SECTION. COMMENT3*
      Data-desc1*
      78 Id1 Dd-item1* VALUE Id2 Dd-item2*. COMMENT4*
        Dd-body1*
      Data-desc2*
      Link-sec1
    Proc-div1
    )^{ } =
    COMMENT1*
    Ident-div1
    f_2(Env-div1)^{ Id1 Id2 }
    DATA DIVISION. COMMENT2*
      File-sec1
      WORKING-STORAGE SECTION. COMMENT3*
      Data-desc1*
      Data-desc2*
      Link-sec1
    Proc-div1
[2] f_2( )^{ Id1 Id2 } = ENVIRONMENT DIVISION.  f_3( )^{ Id1 Id2 }
[3] f_3( )^{ Id1 Id2 } = CONFIGURATION SECTION.  f_4( )^{ Id1 Id2 }
[4] f_4( )^{ Id1 Id2 } = SPECIAL-NAMES. Id1 IS Id2.
[5] f_4(Special-name1+)^{ Id1 Id2 } = Special-name1+ Id1 IS Id2
```

First notice that R_0 is unconditional: for explanatory reasons we did not impose any conditions on the term rewriting rules of this example. From a software renovation point of view this is unrealistic. However, since we wish to illustrate our conservativity result rather than develop a software renovation factory in this paper, we keep the renovation components as simple as possible.

We explain the above rewrite rules in detail. Function symbol f_1 takes as input a MicroFocus COBOL program and has as output the desired Fujitsu

COBOL program; see the end of this section for a typical example of an original and a rewritten COBOL program. Rule [1] defines f_1. The argument of f_1 is a textual representation of an AST containing a pattern that matches a complete COBOL program. It can start with comments, then an IDENTIFICATION DIVISION (matched by Ident-div1), an ENVIRONMENT DIVISION (matched by Env-div1), a DATA DIVISION (specified in such detail that it matches the 78 level constant definitions that we wish to move to another subtree), and a PROCEDURE DEFINITION (matched by the variable Proc-div1). The output of f_1 shows that the first and last divisions are not modified: the parts COMMENT1* Ident-div1 and Proc-div1 are invariant. In the DATA DIVISION the 78 level constants are removed. The essential information, residing in variables Id1 and Id2, is stored in memory. This memory is simply a second argument of the function symbols f_1 – f_4, which we call an attribute, denoted using curly braces. The function f_2 that appears in the output of f_1 takes care of addition of the constants in the Fujitsu dialect. This is implemented in the rules [2]–[5]. If there is no ENVIRONMENT DIVISION in the COBOL program, then the variable Env-div1 matches an empty subtree, so that rule [2] creates a subtree with top-node ENVIRONMENT DIVISION and an empty subtree, which is handled by f_3. Rule [2] passes on the attributes to f_3. If the ENVIRONMENT DIVISION already exists, then rule [2] does not apply; in this case one of the generated rules for f_2 renames f_2 into f_3, and passes on the attributes to f_3 as well. We emphasize that whatever the initial situation was, we always end up in the situation that the next function is f_3. Rule [3] is similar to rule [2]; it creates a CONFIGURATION SECTION if it is not present. If the CONFIGURATION SECTION already exists, then rule [3] does not apply; in this case one of the generated rules for f_3 renames f_3 into f_4, and passes on the attributes to f_4 as well. Rule [4] is also similar to [2] and [3] in that it creates the SPECIAL-NAMES paragraph if it is not present. It also adds the Fujitsu specific SYMBOLIC CONSTANT clause and uses the removed variables that reside in the attributes. In the case that there was already such a paragraph, rule [5] matches those in the variable Special-name1+, copies them to the output, and adds the SYMBOLIC CONSTANT clause.

Since COBOL was intended to look like written English, sentences ending with separator periods were introduced. Such a separator period terminates the scope of *all* still open IF statements. Later on, in 1985, an explicit END-IF for IF statements in COBOL was introduced. Suppose that MicroFocus COBOL code is written by a programmer before 1985, and that we want to change the implicit separator periods in such programs into END-IF statements. This can be implemented by means of a CTRS R_1 with four handwritten rewrite rules (plus hundreds of generated ones). The first three rewrite rules handle the three possible ways to implicitly terminate a COBOL IF phrase (see [1]), respectively:

- by an END-IF phrase at the same level of nesting;
- by a separator period;
- if nested, by an ELSE phrase associated with an IF statement at a higher level of nesting.

An additional fourth rewrite rule removes separator periods. See [11, p. 150] for an elaborate discussion, explanation and implementation of the four rewrite rules constituting R_1, and [12] for more background on COBOL grammars.

```
[1] g_1(Bad-cond)^{Attr*} = g_4(Bad-cond)^{Attr*} END-IF
[2] g_2(IF L-exp Sent)^{Attr*} = IF L-exp g_3(g_2(Sent)^{Attr*}) END-IF.
[3] g_2(IF L-exp Cond-body ELSE Sent)^{Attr*} =
    IF L-exp g_1(Cond-body)^{Attr*}
    ELSE g_3(g_2(Sent)^{Attr*}) END-IF.
[4] g_3(Stat.) = Stat
```

Both R_0 and R_1 serve the purpose of uniformizing the code. It is useful to uniformize code before restructuring, since it decreases the number of possibilities in rewriting the AST in a later phase. For performance reasons we combine both uniformizing components R_0 and R_1. The question arises whether we can do this safely. This is the case indeed, since R_0 is deterministic, and each rewrite rule in R_1 contains a fresh function symbol from g_1-g_3 at the left-hand side of its conclusion. Such uniformization techniques are common practice in software renovation factories; see [13, 38] for a factory approach where an elimination assembly line for an important class of legacy systems is implemented.

Below we provide an original COBOL program and its rewritten code, which both print the word HAIKU. We explain the code fragments, and show where the rewrite rules changed the original code at the left-hand side. The 78 level constant CON and its value 1 are moved from the DATA DIVISION to the ENVIRONMENT DIVISION. They appear in the SYMBOLIC CONSTANT clause of the paragraph called SPECIAL-NAMES. Indeed, the appropriate paragraph, section and division have been created. The syntax of constants in MicroFocus COBOL and Fujitsu COBOL differs; of course, the rewrite rules take care of that. The IF is terminated by the separator period after the first print statement DISPLAY 'HAI'. The rewrite system adds an explicit scope terminator END-IF in the rewritten code.

```
IDENTIFICATION DIVISION.            IDENTIFICATION DIVISION.
PROGRAM-ID. HAIKU.                  PROGRAM-ID. HAIKU.
DATA DIVISION.                      ENVIRONMENT DIVISION.
WORKING-STORAGE SECTION.            CONFIGURATION SECTION.
01 VAR-1.                          SPECIAL-NAMES.
  02 SUB-1 PIC X COMP-X.             SYMBOLIC CONSTANT
78 CON VALUE 1.                        CON IS 1.
  02 SUB-2 PIC X COMP-X VALUE CON.  DATA DIVISION.
PROCEDURE DIVISION.                 WORKING-STORAGE SECTION.
  IF SUB-2 = 1                      01 VAR-1.
    DISPLAY 'HAI'.                    02 SUB-1 PIC X COMP-X.
  DISPLAY  'KU'.                      02 SUB-2 PIC X COMP-X VALUE CON.
                                    PROCEDURE DIVISION.
                                      IF SUB-2 = 1
                                        DISPLAY 'HAI'
                                      END-IF.
                                      DISPLAY  'KU'.
```

This transformation can be obtained automatically, using the implementation of the CTRSs R_0 and R_1. The CTRS R_1 has been implemented in [11]; the CTRS R_0 has been defined for the sake of this example, and has been implemented using the same technology.

Our theorem has also been applied in [38], where incrementally an algorithm was developed for eliminating very difficult GO TO statements from COBOL/CICS programs from a Swiss Bank. The use of the theorem was that already developed patterns for eliminating GO TOs could safely be extended with new patterns without distroying the original functionality. This important consequence of our theorem gives therefore rise to incremental development of software renovation factories. This is important since then we can heavily reuse already developed components which is cost-effective.

5 Related Work

The conservativity format for structural operational semantics has a direct application to term rewriting, as was noticed in [43]. It can help, for example, to obtain a simple completeness proof for the process algebra ACP [7]. In that paper, completeness of the equations for ACP is derived by means of a term rewriting analysis. The confluence proof of the TRS consists of about 400 cases. Completeness of the equations for ACP could also be obtained by the combination of a much simpler completeness result, a conservative extension result for the operational semantics, and an elimination result; see [43].

In general, studies on modular properties of term rewriting systems deal with the following question: given two (mostly unconditional) TRSs with a certain desirable property, such as confluence or termination, does the combination of these TRSs also satisfy this property? It is often assumed that the signatures of the two rewrite systems are disjoint, and that the variables in a rewrite rule all occur in its left-hand side. CTRSs that satisfy these requirements are automatically within our conservativity format. In this paper it is investigated whether the *full* rewriting relation is preserved for terms over only *one* of the signatures. The signatures of the original CTRS and its extension need not be disjoint. Toyama [40] showed that confluence is a modular property for TRSs [40], but that in general termination is not [41]. Klop and Barendregt gave a counter-example which shows that completeness is not modular, but Toyama, Klop and Barendregt [42] proved that completeness in combination with left-linearity is modular for TRSs. Ohlebusch [34] showed that if a combination of two TRSs does not terminate, then one of the TRSs is not $C_\mathcal{E}$-terminating, while the other TRS is collapsing. (This generalizes a similar result for finitely branching TRSs of Gramlich [27]). Middeldorp [33] presented a panorama of positive and negative results on modular properties of CTRSs. For example, he showed that confluence constitutes a modular property for CTRSs. Gramlich [26] showed that his main results in [27] extend to CTRSs.

References

1. ANSI X3.23–1985. Programming Language – COBOL. American National Standards Institute, Inc, 1985.
2. J.W. Backus. The syntax and semantics of the proposed international algebraic language of the Zurich ACM-GAMM conference. In *Proceedings ICIP*, pp. 125–131. Unesco, Paris, 1960.
3. J. Baeten and C. Verhoef. A congruence theorem for structured operational semantics with predicates. In *Proc. CONCUR'93*, LNCS 715, pp. 477–492. Springer, 1993.
4. J. Baeten, J. Bergstra, J.W. Klop, and P. Weijland. Term-rewriting systems with rule priorities. *Theoretical Computer Science*, 67(2/3):283–301, 1989.
5. J. Bergstra, J. Heering, and P. Klint, editors. *Algebraic Specification*. ACM Press/Addison Wesley, 1989.
6. J. Bergstra, J. Heering, and P. Klint. Module algebra. *Journal of the ACM*, 37(2):335–372, 1990.
7. J. Bergstra and J.W. Klop. Process algebra for synchronous communication. *Information and Control*, 60(1/3), 1984.
8. J. Bergstra and J.W. Klop. Conditional rewrite rules: confluence and termination. *Journal of Computer and System Sciences*, 32(3):323–362, 1986.
9. R. Bol and J.F. Groote. The meaning of negative premises in transition system specifications. *Journal of the ACM*, 43(5):863–914, 1996.
10. M. van den Brand, P. Klint, and C. Verhoef. Reverse engineering and system renovation – an annotated bibliography. *ACM SEN*, 22(1):57–68, 1997.
11. M. van den Brand, A. Sellink, and C. Verhoef. Generation of components for software renovation factories from context-free grammars. In *Proc. 4th Working Conference on Reverse Engineering*, pp. 144–155, 1997.
12. M. van den Brand, A. Sellink, and C. Verhoef. Obtaining a COBOL grammar from legacy code for reengineering purposes. In *Proc. 2nd Workshop on the Theory and Practice of Algebraic Specifications, 1997. Workshops in Computing*, Springer, Available at http://www.springer.co.uk/ewic/workshops/.
13. M. van den Brand, A. Sellink, and C. Verhoef. Control flow normalization for COBOL/CICS legacy systems. In *Proc. 2nd Euromicro Conference on Software Maintenance and Reengineering*, pp. 11–19. IEEE Computer Society Press, 1998.
14. P. D'Argenio and C. Verhoef. A general conservative extension theorem in process algebras with inequalities. *Theoretical Computer Science*, 177:351–380, 1997.
15. N. Dershowitz, M. Okada, and G. Shivkumar. Confluence of conditional rewrite systems. In *Proc. CTRS'87*, LNCS 308, pp. 31–44. Springer, 1987.
16. A. van Deursen, P. Klint, and C. Verhoef. Research issues in renovation of legacy software. In this volume, 1999.
17. W. Fokkink and R. van Glabbeek. Ntyft/ntyxt rules reduce to ntree rules. *Information and Computation*, 126(1):1–10, 1996.
18. W. Fokkink and C. Verhoef. A conservative look at term deduction systems with variable binding. Report 95-28, Eindhoven University of Technology, 1995.
19. W. Fokkink and C. Verhoef. An SOS message: conservative extension for higher-order positive/negative conditional term rewriting. Report P9715, University of Amsterdam, 1997.
20. W. Fokkink and C. Verhoef. A conservative look at operational semantics with variable binding. *Information and Computation*, 146(1):24–54, 1998.

21. H. Ganzinger and U. Waldmann. Termination proofs of well-moded logic programs via conditional rewrite systems. In *Proc. CTRS'92*, LNCS 656, pp. 430–437. Springer, 1993.

22. A. van Gelder, K. Ross, and J.S. Schlipf. The well-founded semantics for general logic programs. *Journal of the ACM*, 38(3):620–650, 1991.

23. M. Gelfond and V. Lifschitz. The stable model semantics for logic programming. In *Proc. Logic Programming Conference*, pp. 1070–1080. MIT Press, 1988.

24. R. van Glabbeek. The meaning of negative premises in transition system specifications II. In *Proc. ICALP'96*, LNCS 1099, pp. 502–513. Springer, 1996.

25. J. Goguen. Personal Communication, January 1993.

26. B. Gramlich. Sufficient conditions for modular termination of conditional term rewriting systems. In *Proc. CTRS'93*, LNCS 656, pp. 128–142. Springer, 1993.

27. B. Gramlich. Generalized sufficient conditions for modular termination of rewriting. *Applicable Algebra in Engin., Communic. and Comput.*, 5:131–158, 1994.

28. J.F. Groote and F. Vaandrager. Structured operational semantics and bisimulation as a congruence. *Information and Computation*, 100(2):202–260, 1992.

29. P. Hartel. LATOS – a lightweight animation tool for operational semantics. Report DSSE-TR-97-1, University of Southampton, 1997.

30. S. Kaplan. Conditional rewrite rules. *TCS*, 33(2):175–193, 1984.

31. S. Kaplan. Positive/negative conditional rewriting. In *Proc. CTRS'87*, LNCS 308, pp. 129–143. Springer, 1987.

32. K. Meinke and J. Tucker. Universal algebra. In *Handbook of Logic for Computer Science*, Volume I, pp. 189–411. Oxford University Press, 1993.

33. A. Middeldorp. Modular properties of conditional term rewriting systems. *Information and Computation*, 104(1):110–158, 1993.

34. E. Ohlebusch. On the modularity of termination of term rewriting systems. *Theoretical Computer Science*, 136(2):333–360, 1994.

35. G. Plotkin. A structural approach to operational semantics. Report DAIMI FN-19, Aarhus University, 1981.

36. J. van de Pol. Operational semantics of rewriting with priorities. *Theoretical Computer Science*, 200(1/2):289–312, 1998.

37. T. Przymusinski. The well-founded semantics coincides with the three-valued stable semantics. *Fundamenta Informaticae*, 13(4):445–463, 1990.

38. A. Sellink, H. Sneed, and C. Verhoef. Restructuring of COBOL/CICS legacy systems. In *Proceedings 3rd European Conference on Maintenance and Reengineering*. IEEE Computer Society Press, 1999.

39. A. Sellink and C. Verhoef. Native patterns. In *Proc. 5th Working Conference on Reverse Engineering*, pp. 89–103. IEEE Computer Society Press, 1998.

40. Y. Toyama. On the Church-Rosser property for the direct sum of term rewriting systems. *Journal of the ACM*, 34(1):128–143, 1987.

41. Y. Toyama. Counterexamples to termination for the direct sum of term rewriting systems. *Information Processing Letters*, 25(3):141–143, 1987.

42. Y. Toyama, J.W. Klop, and H. Barendregt. Termination for direct sums of left-linear complete term rewriting systems. *Journal of the ACM*, 34(1):128–143, 1987.

43. C. Verhoef. A general conservative extension theorem in process algebra. In *Proc. PROCOMET'94*, IFIP Transactions A-56, pp. 149–168. Elsevier, 1994.

44. C. Verhoef. A congruence theorem for structured operational semantics with predicates and negative premises. *Nordic Journal of Computing*, 2(2):274–302, 1995.

Dynamic Systems with Implicit State

Marie-Claude Gaudel[1], Carole Khoury[1], Alexandre Zamulin[2]

[1]L.R.I., URA CNRS 410
Université de Paris-Sud et CNRS, Bât. 490
91405 Orsay-cedex, France
{mcg, khoury}@lri.fr, fax 33 1 69 15 65 86
[2]Institute of Informatics Systems
Siberian Division of Russian Academy of Sciences
Novosibirsk 630090
zam@iis.nsk.su

Abstract. This paper presents a formalism of algebraic specifications with implicit state based on the concept of dynamic system. This is a synthesis of two approaches: algebraic specifications with implicit state, and abstract typed machines, developed previously by the authors. Our proposal aims at combining the advantages of these works, with a strong motivation to keep the specifications as abstract and non algorithmic as possible. In this approach a dynamic system is defined as some algebras representing the system's state, a set of access functions permitting to observe the state and a set of modifiers permitting to change the state. This formalism makes it possible to describe behaviors of systems where an internal memory evolves, without deciding at the specification level what will be stored or computed by the implementation, and without providing an algorithmic description of global changes.

1 Introduction

This paper presents a formalism of algebraic specifications with implicit state based on the concept of dynamic system. The purpose is to make easier the specification of systems with changing internal states. Such systems are not conveniently specified by classical algebraic specifications.

The version of the formalism presented here is a synthesis of two approaches:

- The one described in [18], which is an extension of the former proposals [2] and [3], motivated by the experience in writing a complex specification ([8]);
- and the one presented in [25] which is an extension of the former proposal [24], [23] attempting to combine algebraic specifications with evolving algebras [14].

The main feature of the approach presented is the definition of a dynamic system as some algebras, representing the system's states, with some access functions permitting to observe this state, and a set of modifiers permitting to change the state in a predetermined way. The second important feature of the approach is the definition of a formal specification method for such systems which is just a layer above classical algebraic specifications.

2 Dynamic Systems

The formalism being defined is based on the concept of implicit state à la Z ([22]) or VDM ([17]) and algebraic specifications. It is a convergence of two previous approaches known under the names AS-IS (as Algebraic Specifications with Implicit State) [18] and Typed Gurevich Machines [25]. The formalism serves for the specification of *dynamic systems* possessing a state and a number of operations for accessing and updating the state.

The signature of a system defined by AS-IS includes a part Σ which corresponds to some data types which are used for the specification of system's states and the description of possible state updates.

The system's states are defined by *elementary access functions*. The names and profiles of these functions, Σ_{eac}, are introduced in the second part of the system's signature which uses the sorts of Σ. An elementary access function is an operation, with or without arguments, which may be different in different states.

For instance in Figure 1, *counter* and *max* are elementary access functions which yield some information on the state of the system CLOCK. NAT is a used data type.

Definition A state is a Σ'-algebra where $\Sigma' = \Sigma \cup \Sigma_{eac}$.

Moreover, *dependent access functions* can be defined using the elementary access functions and the operations in Σ. The values produced by these functions depend both on the system's state and on the values of their arguments, if any. The names and profiles of these functions, Σ_{ac}, are introduced in the third part of the system's signature with the use of sorts of Σ.

In Figure 1 *delay* is a dependent access function.

A state update modifies the elementary access functions. Possible state updates are specified by *modifiers* defined in the fourth part of the system's signature, Σ_{mod}.

An update is the invocation of a modifier. It transforms a Σ'-algebra into another Σ'-algebra. An update can change the variable part of the state of a system, namely the access functions, but it must leave unchanged the data types. For this reason, we divide the class of possible states (Σ'-algebras) into subclasses called $state_A(\Sigma, \Sigma_{eac})$ which share the same (static) Σ-algebra A. Such a subclass is called the *carrier of a dynamic system*.

Definition
$$\forall A \in Alg(\Sigma), \ state_A(\Sigma, \Sigma_{eac}) = \{A' \in Alg(\Sigma \cup \Sigma_{eac}) \mid A'|_\Sigma = A\}$$

Definition
A dynamic system, $D(A)$, of signature $< \Sigma, \Sigma_{eac}, \Sigma_{ac}, \Sigma_{mod} >$, where A is a Σ-algebra, is a 3-uple with:
- some carrier $|D(A)| = state_A(\Sigma, \Sigma_{eac})$,
- some set of dependent access functions with names and profiles defined in Σ_{ac},
- some set of defined modifiers with names and profiles defined in Σ_{mod}.

Example :

     System CLOCK

     use NAT   ** $< \Sigma, Ax >$

     **specification of the elementary access functions*

     elementary accesses   ** Σ_{eac}

          $counter :\rightarrow Nat$

          $max :\rightarrow Nat$

     ** *In the initial state, counter is set to 0 and max is set to 100*

     Init

          $counter = 0$

          $max = 100$

     **specification of the dependent access functions*

     accesses   ** Σ_{ac}

          $delay :\rightarrow Nat$

     accesses axioms   ** Ax_{ac}

          $delay = max - counter$

     **specification of defined modifiers*

     modifiers   ** Σ_{mod}

          $RAZ : Nat$

          $Increment :$

     modifiers definitions   ** Def_{mod}

          $RAZ(x) = counter := 0$ **and** $max := x$

          $Increment =$

               begin

                    $delay > 0$ **then** $counter := counter + 1|$

                    $delay = 0$ **then** $RAZ(max)$

               end

     end system

Fig. 1. Example of a Specification of a Dynamic System

A dependent access function name $ac : s_1, ..., s_n \rightarrow s$ is interpreted in a dynamic system $D(A)$ by a map $ac^{D(A)}$ associating with each $D(A)$-algebra A' (i.e., an algebra belonging to the carrier of $D(A)$) a function $ac^{D(A)}(A')$: $A'_{s_1} \times ... \times A'_{s_n} \rightarrow A'_s$.

The operation associated with a defined modifier of Σ_{mod} is a transformation of a $D(A)$-algebra into another $D(A)$-algebra. In the example of the clock, possible updates are the updates of the value of the counter and of the max bound. It is clear that an update of these entities should not cause any change of the data type NAT.

3   Specification of a Dynamic System

Let $DS =< (\Sigma, Ax), (\Sigma_{eac}, Ax_{Init}), (\Sigma_{ac}, Ax_{ac}, \Sigma_{mod}, Def_{mod}) >$ be a dynamic system specification. It has three levels:

- The first level is a classical algebraic specification $< \Sigma, Ax >$ (cf. [5], [7]) which defines the data types used in the system. Semantics of this specification is given by the specification language used.
  The approach is relatively independent of a particular specification language. It is only required that the semantics of a specification is a class of algebras.
- The second level defines those aspects of the system's state which are likely to change, and the initial states. It includes:
  1. A signature, Σ_{eac}, which does not introduce new sorts. It defines the names and profiles of *elementary access functions*. A model of the $< \Sigma \cup \Sigma_{eac}, Ax >$ specification is a state. In the sequel we note $\Sigma' = \Sigma \cup \Sigma_{eac}$.
  2. A set of axioms, Ax_{Init}, characterizing the admissible initial states, i. e. stating the initial properties of the system.
- The third level defines some other, dependent, access functions, and the possible evolutions of the system's states in two parts :
  1. A specification of the *dependent access functions* $< \Sigma_{ac}, Ax_{ac} >$. It does not introduce new sorts and uses the elementary access functions and the operations of Σ. The specification $< \Sigma_{ac}, Ax_{ac} >$ must be hierarchically consistent with respect to $< \Sigma', Ax >$ and sufficiently complete. This last point reflects the fact that a state is completely defined (characterized) by its elementary access functions.
     A $D(A)$-algebra A' can be extended into an algebra A'', called its *extended state*, of signature $\Sigma'' = \Sigma' \cup \Sigma_{ac}$ satisfying Ax_{ac}. We denote by $Ext_{\Sigma''}(A')$ the extended state corresponding to the state A'. Any ground term of $T_{\Sigma''}$ corresponds to a value of A' since the specification of A'' does not introduce new sorts and is sufficiently complete with respect to the specification of A'. Thus, in the sequel, we use the notion of the value of a ground Σ''-term in a $D(A)$-algebra A'.
  2. A definition of the *defined modifiers*, $< \Sigma_{mod}, Def_{mod} >$. With each elementary access function ac, an *elementary modifier* "$ac :=$" is associated. Defined modifiers are defined as compositions of these elementary modifiers. The form of this definition is presented in Section 4.1.
     As sketched in the previous part, a modifier name $mod : s_1, ..., s_n$ from Σ_{mod} is interpreted in a dynamic system $D(A)$ by a map $mod^{D(A)}$ associating a $D(A)$-algebra B with each pair $< A', < v_1, ..., v_n >>$, where A' is a $D(A)$-algebra and v_i is an element of A'_{s_i}; this map must satisfy the definition of mod in Def_{mod}. We write $mod^{D(A)}(< A', < v_1, ..., v_n >>)$ for the application of $mod^{D(A)}$ to $< A', < v_1, ..., v_n >>$.

Note. To guarantee some encapsulation of the system, elementary modifiers are only usable for the definition of defined modifiers.

4 Update Expressions

4.1 Defined Modifiers

These modifiers specify the possible changes of states. In a system specification, the definition of a modifier in Def_{mod} is given in the following way:

$$mod(x_1, ..., x_n) = Em$$

In this definition, mod is the name of the modifier being defined, $x_1, ..., x_n$ are parameters, and Em is an update expression using $x_1, ..., x_n$.

For instance, in Figure 1 we have an unconditional definition of the modifier "RAZ" where $counter := 0$ is an elementary modifier which sets $counter$ to zero, and a conditional definition of the modifier "Increment" which increments the counter if $delay > 0$ and sets it to zero if $delay = 0$.

The invocation of a defined modifier corresponds to an atomic change of the system's state and must be done with constant arguments:

$$mod(t_i, ..., t_n) \text{ where } t_i \in T_{\Sigma''} \text{ (ground terms constructed on } \Sigma'').$$

However, when using a defined modifier (for example, M1) in the definition of another modifier (for example, M2) some variables may occur:

$$M2(x_1, \ldots, x_n) = \textbf{begin} \ldots M1(y_1 \ldots y_m) \ldots \textbf{end}$$

Here, the x_i are the parameters of $M2$ and the terms y_j are either ground terms or terms with variables belonging to the set $\{x_1, \ldots, x_n\}$. It is the same when using an elementary modifier in the definition of another modifier.

Update expressions used for the definition of modifiers are constructed using other defined modifiers, elementary modifiers, conditional elementary modifiers, different forms of update expression composition, and the inoperant modifier **nil** which lets the state unchanged. A precise syntax is given in [9].

4.2 Elementary Modifiers

As said above, an elementary modifier "$ac :=$" is associated with each elementary access function ac. If ac has the profile $s_1, ..., s_n \rightarrow s$, then "$ac :=$" has the profile $s_1, ..., s_n, s$ and can be used to construct update expressions of the form $ac(exp_1, ..., exp_n) := exp$ where the exp_i are terms of sort s_i and exp is a term of sort s.

To provide a possibility of global updates of access functions, one can use variables in the exp_i. In this case, they play a role similar to that of patterns in functional programming.

The modifier "$ac :=$" is used for the definition of a change of state in the following way:

$$\forall y_1, \ldots, y_p \ [ac(\pi_1, \ldots, \pi_n) := R]$$

where the variables of π_i, for $i \in [1..n]$, and those of R belong to $\{y_1, \ldots, y_n, x_1, \ldots, x_q\}$, where $(x_1, \ldots, x_q)$ are the parameters of the modifier being defined.

It is possible to have no quantification. In this case, π_i and R are ground terms. Then the expression

$$ac(\pi_1, ..., \pi_n) := R$$

indicates that ac should be updated at the point $< \pi_1, ..., \pi_n >$ by assigning to it the value of R (i.e., after the update of A into B, $ac^B(\pi_1^A, ..., \pi_n^A) = R^A$ must hold).

Example: the update $ac(3) := 1$ gives the value 1 to $ac(3)$; the value of ac is not changed elsewhere.

In the general case, the arguments π_i define a set of points where the function ac is updated: these points are computed by assigning all possible values to the variables in π_i. For the other values of the ac arguments, the result is not changed (it is the classical *frame assumption*).

Examples

- The update $\forall y \; [ac(y) := 0]$ forces ac to yield 0 for any argument.
- The update $\forall y \; [ac(succ(y)) := 1]$ assigns the value 1 to $ac(y)$ for all $y \neq 0$ and let the value of $ac(0)$ unchanged.

The right-hand side argument, R, of an elementary modifier is a term of sort s composed over the π_i, and defining the new results of ac at the update points. This ensures that an assignment of the variables in π_i uniquely defines the value of R. Counter-examples justifying this restriction are given in [9].

Example: the update $\forall y \; [ac(s(y)) := s(s(y))]$ assigns the value $y + 1$ to $ac(y)$ for all $y \neq 0$ and leaves the value of $ac(0)$ unchanged.

4.3 Conditional Elementary Modifiers

A conditional elementary modifier has the following form:

$\forall y_1, \ldots, y_p$ **cases**
ϕ_1 **then** $ac(\pi_1^1, \ldots, \pi_n^1) := R^1 | \ldots | \phi_m$ **then** $ac(\pi_1^m, \ldots, \pi_n^m) := R^m$
end cases

It describes a modification of the same elementary access function, ac, which is different depending on the different validity domains of the ϕ_i. In case of conflicts, i.e., if several ϕ_i are simultaneously valid, the update corresponding to the smallest index takes place.

Example: Let us have the access functions $ac_1, ac_2 : Nat \rightarrow Nat$ and the following operations:

$f_1, f_2 : Nat \rightarrow Nat$
$null : Nat \rightarrow Bool$.

The following conditional elementary modifier:

$\forall n$ **cases**
$null(ac_1(n)) = true$ **then** $ac_2(n) := f_1(n) \;|$
$null(ac_1(n)) = false$ **then** $ac_2(n) := f_2(n)$
end cases

assigns to ac_2 the value $f_2(n)$, for all n, when the corresponding value of $ac_1(n)$ does not satisfy the condition $null$ and the value $f_1(n)$ in the opposite case.

Like in elementary modifiers we have: $\pi_1^i, \ldots, \pi_n^i \in T_{\Sigma''}(x_1, \ldots, x_q, y_1 \ldots y_p)_{s_j}$, where $(x_1, \ldots, x_q)$ are the parameters of the modifier being defined, and R_i is a Σ'' term built over $\pi_1^i, \ldots, \pi_n^i$. The form of the conditions ϕ_i depends on the underlying data type specification language. The terms in the conditions ϕ_i, like the right hand side arguments R^i, belong to $T_{\Sigma''}(\pi_1^i, \ldots, \pi_n^i)$.

The main reason for the introduction of conditional elementary modifiers is the possibility of using in the conditions some variables in addition to the parameters of the modifier being defined. These variables are universally quantified like variables in patterns.

Example
$$Mod(x) = \forall n \text{ cases}$$
$$null(ac_1(n)) = x \text{ then } ac_2(n) := f_1(n) \mid$$
$$null(ac_1(n)) = not(x) \text{ then } ac_2(n) := f_2(n)$$
end cases

In this example, the variable n, unlike the parameter x, is universally quantified and, therefore, the modification is performed for a given x (given by the invocation of the modifier Mod) and for all n.

4.4 Composed Update Expressions

Several forms of update expression composition are proposed.

- Conditional updates of the following form:
  begin ϕ_1 **then** $Em_1 \mid \ldots \mid \phi_p$ **then** Em_p **end**
  indicating that an update expression Em_i is chosen if its condition ϕ_i is valid. If several conditions ϕ_i are valid, the update expression with the smallest index is chosen.
  Note: This form of update is different from the conditional elementary modifier in two ways: the Em_i are any update expressions; there are no universally quantified variables.
- $m_1; m_2$ indicating that the execution of m_1 should be followed by that of m_2.
- m_1 **and** m_2 indicating that the order of execution of m_1 and m_2 is unimportant. It is the specifier's responsability to ensure that the same result will be produced in any order of execution. A sufficient but not necessary condition for this is that m_1 (resp. m_2) does not update an elementary access function used or updated by m_2 (resp. m_1).
  This composition is generalized for n update expressions, with the same responsability for the specifier: all permutations must lead to the same result.
- $m_1 \bullet m_2$ indicating that the updates specified by m_1 and m_2 should be applied to the same state. If m_1 and m_2 specify the update of the same access function (their sets of updated elementary access functions are not disjoint), each of them must update it at different points; otherwise, the update m_1 is taken into account. This composition is generalized for n update expressions.

Each of the composition operators **and** and $\bullet$ has its own purpose: the composition by **and** lets some liberty to the implementor. The specifier uses **and** to indicate that the order is unimportant. The composition by $\bullet$ gives the specifier a greater expression facility by removing the need to care for intermediate results or value preserving in the specification. Examples are given in [9].

5 Semantics of Update Expressions

The semantics of an update is a transformation of a $< \Sigma', Ax >$-algebra into another one, respecting the partitioning of $< \Sigma', Ax >$-algebras into $state_A(\Sigma', Ax)$, as mentioned in Section 2.

To give the semantics of different update expressions, we first give the semantics of the basic update expressions, namely *elementary modifiers* and *conditional elementary modifiers*. On the basis of the semantics of these expressions, the semantics of composed update expressions and defined modifiers is then given.

We denote by $\overline{ass}$ the extension to $T_{\Sigma''}(X)$ of assignment ass ($ass : X \to A$, $ass = \{ass_s : X_s \to A_s | s \in S\}$, $\overline{ass} : T_{\Sigma''}(X) \to A$).

We denote by $[\![m]\!]$ the transformation associated with an update expression m. It respects the partitioning of $< \Sigma', Ax >$-algebras into $state_A(\Sigma', Ax)$, i.e.:

$$\forall A \in Alg(\Sigma, Ax), \ [\![m]\!] : state_A(\Sigma', Ax) \to state_A(\Sigma', Ax)$$

For instance, the semantics of **nil** is the simplest one, since no update is produced: $[\![\mathbf{nil}]\!]A' = A'$

5.1 Semantics of Elementary Modifiers

The definition of the semantics of an elementary modifier is
$$[\![\forall(x_1 \ldots x_p)[ac(\pi_1, \ldots, \pi_n) := R]]\!]A' = F(A')$$
where F is the total map on the class of Σ'-algebras which transforms a Σ'-algebra A' into a Σ'-algebra B' by replacing $ac^{A'}$ with $ac^{B'}$ which is defined below.

$\forall v_1, \ldots, v_n \in A'_{s_1}, \ldots A'_{s_n}$,
- if there exists an assignment $ass : \{x_1, \ldots, x_p\} \to A'$, such that
$v_1 = \overline{ass}\pi_1, \ldots, v_n = \overline{ass}\pi_n$ and $v = \overline{ass}R$
 - then $ac^{B'}(v_1, \ldots, v_n) = v$
 - otherwise, $ac^{B'}(v_1, \ldots, v_n) = ac^{A'}(v_1, \ldots, v_n)$.

5.2 Semantics of Conditional Elementary Modifiers

The definition of the semantics of a conditional elementary modifier is:
$[\![\forall y_1, \ldots, y_p$ **cases**
ϕ_1 **then** $ac(\pi_1^1, \ldots, \pi_n^1) := R^1 | \ldots |$
ϕ_m **then** $ac(\pi_1^m, \ldots, \pi_n^m) := R^m$
end cases $]\!]A' = F'(A')$
where F' is the total map on the class of Σ'-algebras transforming a Σ'-algebra A' into a Σ'-algebra B' by replacing $ac^{A'}$ with $ac^{B'}$ in the following way.

$\forall v_1, \ldots, v_n \in A'_{s_1}, \ldots A'_{s_n}$,
- if there is no i such that there is an assignement ass: $\{y_1, \ldots, y_p\} \to A'$ with
  - $v_1 = \overline{ass}\pi_1^i, \ldots, v_n = \overline{ass}\pi_n^i$,
  and
  - ϕ_i is valid for this assignment in $Ext_{\Sigma''}(A')$ with the conventional interpretation of logical connectors,
 - then $ac^{B'}(v_1, \ldots, v_n) = ac^{A'}(v_1, \ldots, v_n)$;
 - otherwise, let I be the set of i satisfying the condition above, $j = min(I)$ and $v = \overline{ass}R^j$, then $ac^{B'}(v_1, \ldots, v_n) = v$

5.3 Semantics of Composed Update Expressions

- Let U be a conditional update of the form:
  begin ϕ_1 **then** $Em_1 | \ldots | \phi_p$ **then** Em_p **end**
  and let I be the set of i, such that $Ext_{\Sigma''}(A') \models \phi_i$. Then:
  - If $I = \emptyset$, then $[\![U]\!]A' = A'$.
  - Otherwise, $[\![U]\!]A' = [\![Em_{min(I)}]\!]A'$.
- $[\![m_1; m_2]\!]A' = [\![m_2]\!]([\![m_1]\!]A')$
- $[\![m_1 \text{ and } m_2]\!]A' = [\![m_2 \text{ and } m_1]\!]A' = [\![m_1; m_2]\!]A' = [\![m_2; m_1]\!]A'$
  This definition is generalized for n arguments. The semantics of m_1 **and** ...
  and m_n is that of all the permutations of $m_1, \ldots m_n$.
- $[\![m_1 \bullet m_2]\!]A' \equiv G(A')$
  where G is a total map transforming a Σ'-algebra A' into a Σ'-algebra B'
  by replacing each $ac^{A'}$ by $ac^{B'}$ as follows.
  Let $[\![m_1]\!]A' = A1$ and $[\![m_2]\!]A' = A2$. Then G transforms A' into a Σ'-algebra
  B' by replacing, for each operation name $ac : s_1, \ldots, s_n \to s$ in $\Sigma_{\epsilon ac}$ and each
  value v_i of sort s_i, $ac^{A'}$ by $ac^{B'}$ in the following way:

  - if $(ac^{A'}(v_1, \ldots, v_n) = ac^{A1}(v_1, \ldots, v_n)) \wedge (ac^{A'}(v_1, \ldots, v_n) = ac^{A2}(v_1, \ldots, v_n))$
    then $ac^{B'}(v_1, \ldots, v_n) = ac^{A'}(v_1, \ldots, v_n)$ (there is no update at this point);
  - if $(ac^{A'}(v_1, \ldots, v_n) \neq ac^{A1}(v_1, \ldots, v_n)) \wedge (ac^{A'}(v_1, \ldots, v_n) = ac^{A2}(v_1, \ldots, v_n))$
    then $ac^{B'}(v_1, \ldots, v_n) = ac^{A1}(v_1, \ldots, v_n)$ (the update comes from $A1$);
  - if $(ac^{A'}(v_1, \ldots, v_n) = ac^{A1}(v_1, \ldots, v_n)) \wedge (ac^{A'}(v_1, \ldots, v_n) \neq ac^{A2}(v_1, \ldots, v_n))$
    then $ac^{B'}(v_1, \ldots, v_n) = ac^{A2}(v_1, \ldots, v_n)$ (the update comes from $A2$);
  - if $(ac^{A'}(v_1, \ldots, v_n) \neq ac^{A1}(v_1, \ldots, v_n)) \wedge (ac^{A'}(v_1, \ldots, v_n) \neq ac^{A2}(v_1, \ldots, v_n))$
    then $ac^{B'}(v_1, \ldots, v_n) = ac^{A1}(v_1, \ldots, v_n)$ (both m_1 and m_2 update the same
    access function at the same point, the first update is taken into account).

This definition is generalized for n arguments.

5.4 Semantics of the Definition and Invocation of Defined Modifiers

Let $mod(x_1, \ldots, x_n) = Em$ be a modifier definition. Then, for any $D(A)$-algebra
A' and ground Σ'' terms $t_1, \ldots, t_n$ of sorts $s_1, \ldots, s_n$ respectively, the map $mod^{D(A)}$
associated with mod in a dynamic system $D(A)$ is defined as:

$$mod^{D(A)}(< A', < t_1^{A'}, \ldots, t_n^{A'} >>) = [\![Em[t_1/x_1, \ldots t_n/x_n]]\!]A',$$

where $Em[t_1/x_1, \ldots t_n/x_n]$ is the update expression obtained by replacing each
x_i in Em by t_i.

Thus the semantics of an invocation $mod(t_1, \ldots, t_n)$ is:

$$[\![mod(t_1, \ldots, t_n)]\!]A' = mod^{D(A)}(< A', < t_1^{A'}, \ldots, t_n^{A'} >>)$$

6 States and Behaviors of the System

We summarize in this section the main definitions related to the notions of state and behavior of a dynamic system.

Let $DS = < (\Sigma, Ax), (\Sigma_{eac}, Ax_{Init}), (\Sigma_{ac}, Ax_{ac}, \Sigma_{mod}, Def_{mod}) >$ be a specification of a dynamic system, and $\Sigma' = \Sigma \cup \Sigma_{eac}$.

System's state. As already mentioned, a state of the system, defined by the specification DS is a Σ'-algebra satisfying the axioms Ax.

Initial states. A subset of the set of states represents the possible initial states of the specified system. It corresponds to an enrichment of the specification $< \Sigma', Ax >$ with Ax_{Init} , thus:

$$state_{Init}(DS) = \{A' \in Alg(\Sigma', Ax >)|A' \models Ax_{Init}\}$$

Behavior of the system. A behavior is a sequence of updates which are produced by the invocations of some defined modifiers. Several sequences of states $(e_0, e_1, e_2, ...)$ correspond to a behavior $(m_0, m_1, m_2, ...)$ depending on the choice of the initial state:

- the initial state e_0 belongs to $state_{Init}(DS)$;
- each e_{i+1} is the result of the application of the modifier m_i to e_i ($e_{i+1} = [\![m]\!]e_i$) .

The semantics of updates as it is defined in the previous section guarantees that if e_0 belongs to a dynamic system $D(A)$, then any e_i also belongs to $D(A)$ (the state changes, but the data types do not change).

This formalism is deterministic for two reasons: the semantics of elementary modifiers and, therefore, of all modifiers ensures that only one state (up to isomorphism) is associated with the application of a modifier to a state; besides the specification of dependent access functions, $< \Sigma_{ac}, Ax_{ac} >$, is sufficiently complete with respect to $< \Sigma \cup \Sigma_{eac}, Ax >$ (cf. Section 3). Thus, only one sequence of states starting with a given initial state is associated with a behavior.

Reachable states. The set of reachable states, $REACH(DS)$ is the set of states which can be obtained by a sequence of updates corresponding to the invocations of some modifiers of Σ_{mod}, starting from an initial state.

Thus, the set $REACH(DS)$ is recursively defined in the following way:

- $state_{Init}(DS) \subset REACH(DS)$
- $\forall m \in \Sigma_{mod}, \forall t_1 \in (T_{\Sigma''})_{s_1} ... t_n \in (T_{\Sigma''})_{s_n}, \forall A' \in REACH(DS)$, $[\![m(t_1, ..., t_n)]\!]A' \in REACH(DS)$.

6.1 Properties and invariants

To prove that a property F is valid in any extended state of a dynamic system $D(A)$, i.e, that:

$$\forall A' \in |D(A)|, Ext_{\Sigma''}(A') \models F,$$

one can use the logic and tools of the underlying algebraic specification language.

An invariant is a property, *Inv*, which must be valid in all reachable states:

$$\forall A' \in REACH(DS), Ext_{\Sigma''}(A') \models Inv$$

Example: $max \geq delay$ is an invariant in the example of Figure 1.

To verify an invariant *Inv*, one can proceed by induction on the reachable states. First, it must be proved that *Inv* holds in the initial states. To do this, it is sufficient to use the logic and tools of the algebraic specification language to prove that *Inv* is a consequence of $Ax \cup Ax_{Init}$. Then it must be proved that the application of each modifier preserves *Inv*.

Currently, there is no formal calculus for the modifiers definitions. Therefore, the demonstration of the following properties must be done on the basis of the definitions of the semantics, i.e on the properties of the elementary modifiers and their compositions given in the previous section:

$$\forall A' \in D(A), \forall mod \in \Sigma_{mod}, \forall t_1 \in (T_{\Sigma''})_{s_1} \ldots t_n \in (T_{\Sigma''})_{s_n}$$
$$Ext_{\Sigma''}(A') \models Inv => Ext_{\Sigma''}(\llbracket mod(t_1 \ldots t_n) \rrbracket A') \models Inv$$

7   Related Works

"Evolving algebras", also called "Abstract State Machines", have been proposed by Gurevich [14] and then intensively used for formal definition of various algorithms and programming language semantics. They are based on the notion of a universal algebraic structure consisting of a set (superuniverse), a number of functions, and a number of relations. Data types (universes) are modeled by unary relations on the superuniverse. Functions can be either static or dynamic. A static function never changes, a change of a dynamic function produces a new algebra. Another means of algebra modification is changing the number of elements in the underlying set (importing new elements).

When writing a specification with the use of a conventional Abstract State Machines, one can write the signature of any function operating with values of one or more universes. One cannot, however, define formally the semantics of a static function as an abstract data type. As a result, one gets a specification where a number of data types and functions are introduced informally (one can make sure of this, looking at the definition of C [15] where almost all static functions and data types are defined in plain words). Besides, there is no notion similar to those of dependent access functions and modifiers with patterns present in our approach.

"Dynamic abstract types" are informally introduced in [6] as a wishable general framework for specification. It is proposed that such a type should consist of an abstract data type and a collection of dynamic operations. Four levels of specification are outlined: value type specification, instant structure specification, dynamic operation specification, and higher-level specification. Access functions and modifiers, as defined here, are just dynamic operations, and the specification technique proposed in our paper can be used for this type of specification.

An idea similar to our state-as-algebra approach is proposed in terms of a new mathematical structure, called "d-oid", by Astesiano and Zucca [1]. A d-oid, like our dynamic system, is a set of instant structures (e.g., algebras) and a set of dynamic operations (transformations of instant structures with a possible result of a definite sort). Here dynamic operations serve as counterparts of our access functions and modifiers. However, the approach in question deals only with models and does not address the issue of specifying the class of such behaviors, which is our focus.

The idea of dynamic types is also investigated in [26]. Although no direct definition of a dynamic abstract type is given in that paper, it has contributed by formal definitions of a static framework and of a dynamic framework over a given static framework. We have used the idea of dynamic operations to define the semantics of our modifiers, and we propose in addition an approach to their formal specification.

Another similar approach is the "Concurrent State Transformation on Abstract Data Types" presented by Grosse-Rode in [12] and recently revised in [13] as "Algebra Transformation Systems". States are modeled as partial algebras that extend a fixed partial algebra considered as a static data type. All functions are given at the same level. Dynamic functions are considered totally undefined in the static data type. A state on a given partial algebra is a free extension of this algebra, specified by a set of function entries. Invariant relations between dynamic operations are given by axioms at the static level. Transitions between states are specified by conditional replacement rules. A replacement rule specifies the function entries that should be added/removed when the condition is valid.

There are some restrictions on the partial equational specifications for the static data types, the admissible partial algebras and states, and the replacement rules in order to have the same structural properties as the algebraic specification logic. A problematic issue is the checks that the replacement rules are compatible with the axioms. This leads to severe restrictions on the use of the formalism. We do not have this problem because the axioms of the data types are clearly isolated, and, moreover, we don't consider the axioms on dependent accesses in the state. In [13] the semantics is revised and a theoretical framework for the composition of these algebra transformation systems is given.

The "Hidden Sorted Algebra" approach [11], where some sorts are distinguished as hidden and some other as visible, treats states as values of hidden sorts. Visible sorts are used to represent values which can be observed in a given state. States are explicitly described in the specification in contrast to our approach.

The above work combined with Meseguer's rewriting logic [19] has served as basis of the dynamic aspects of the CafeOBJ language [4]. There, states and transitions are modeled, respectively, as objects and arrows belonging to the same rewrite model which is a categorical extension of the algebraic structure. Meseguer's rewriting logic is also basis of the specification language Maude [20].

Another approach to the formalization of object behaviors is the concept of "Coalgebra" presented in [21]. Each object state is represented as an element of a special set of a coalgebra, with a notion of equality of object behaviors which is close to the behavioral equivalence defined for hidden sorted algebras [11].

Our framework is different of the three ones above, since we consider states as algebras, not only as elements of an algebra. It avoid the specification of the, often complex, data type corresponding to the state.

Finally, the specification language Troll [16] should be mentioned. Troll is oriented to the specification of objects where a method (event) is specified by means of evaluation rules similar to equations on attributes. Although the semantics of Troll is given rather informally, there is a strong mathematical foundation of its dialect Troll-light [10], with the use of data algebras, attribute algebras and event algebras. A relation constructed on two sets of attribute algebras and a set of event algebra, called *object community*, formalizes transitions from one attribute algebra into another when a particular event algebra takes place.

8 Conclusion

In this paper we have presented a specification method based on the concept of implicit state by giving some syntax and its semantics. This approach is based on the *algebras-as-states* paradigm which has been recently re-explored by several authors. Our proposal aims at combining the advantages of these works with a strong motivation to keep the specifications as abstract and non algorithmic as possible. This is achieved via several means.

Our specifications of dynamic systems are extensions of some algebraic specification of data types which gives a formal and abstract definition of these types. As said above, it is an advantage w.r.t. Abstract State Machines. It is also an advantage w.r.t. approaches such as VDM or Z since data types are defined independently of any predefined library.

The notions of elementary accesses and dependent accesses makes it possible to describe behaviors where an internal memory evolves, without deciding at the specification level what will be stored or computed by the implementation. The notion of dependent access has been designed to provide a convenient means for describing abstractly states where several related values evolve: such accesses can be implemented either by some memory locations or by some functions, depending on efficiency considerations.

The powerful concepts of patterns in modifier definitions and conditional elementary modifiers make it possible to specify global changes of the implicit state in a non algorithmic way. It avoids the use of loops and iterations and provides a black-box way of specifying complex modifications of the state.

The fact that elementary modifiers are hidden ensures encapsulation.

This framework has been validated on several case studies and is easy to learn and use. We plan to use it as a basis for an algebraic specification language of object oriented systems. Such a language should allow the description of systems where several, named, encapsulated, implicit states coexist and communicate, appear and disappear, independently of any specific object oriented programming approach.

Acknowledgement We warmly thank Pierre Dauchy for his numerous and important contributions to AS-IS.

References

1. E. Astesiano and E. Zucca. D-oids: a model for dynamic data types. *Mathematical Structures in Computer Science*, 5(2):257–282, 1995.
2. P. Dauchy. Développement et exploitation d'une spécification algébrique du logiciel embarqué d'un métro. Thèse, Université de Paris-Sud, Orsay, 1992.
3. P. Dauchy and M.-C. Gaudel. Algebraic specifications with implicit state. Rapport interne 887, Laboratoire de Recherche en Informatique, February 1994.
4. R. Diaconescu and K. Futatsugi. *CafeOBJ Report*, volume 6 of *AMAST series in Computing*. World Scientific Publishing Co. Pte. Ltd, 1998.
5. H. Ehrig and B. Mahr. *Fundamentals of algebraic specification, Equations and Initial Semantics*, volume 6 of *EATCS Monographs on Theoretical Computer science*. Springer-Verlag, 1985.
6. H. Ehrig and F. Orejas. Dynamic abstract data types : An informal proposal. In *Bull. of EATCS*, volume 53, pages 162–169, 1994.
7. M.-C. Gaudel. *Algebraic Specifications*, chapter 22. Software Engineer's Reference Book, McDermid, J., ed. Butterworths, 1991.
8. M.-C. Gaudel, P. Dauchy, and C. Khoury. A formal specification of the steam-boiler control problem by algebraic specifications with implicit state. In *Formal Methods for Industrial Applications, Specifying and Programming the Steam Boiler Control*, volume 1165 of *LNCS*, 1996.
9. M.-C. Gaudel, C. Khoury, and A. Zamulin. Dynamic systems with implicit state. Rapport interne 1172, Laboratoire de Recherche en Informatique, May 1998.
10. M. Gogolla and R. Herzig. An algebraic semantics for the object specification language TROLL-light. In *Recent Trends in Data Type Specifications*, volume 906 of *LNCS*, pages 290–306, 1995.
11. J. Goguen and R. Diaconescu. Towards an algebraic semantics for the object paradigm. In *Recent Trends in Data Type Specifications*, volume 785 of *LNCS*, 1994.
12. M. Grosse-Rhode. Concurrent state transformation on abstract data types. In *Recent Trends in Data Type Specification*, volume 1130 of *LNCS*, pages 222–236, 1995.
13. M. Grosse-Rhode. Algebra transformation systems and their composition. In *Fundamental Approaches to Software Engineering*, volume 1382 of *LNCS*, pages 107–122, 1998.
14. Y. Gurevich. *Evolving Algebras 1993: Lipari Guide, In Specification and Validation Methods*, pages 9–36. Oxford University Press, 1995.
15. Y. Gurevich and J. Huggins. The semantics of the C programming language. In *Computer Science Logic*, volume 702 of *LNCS*, pages 274–309, 1993.
16. T. Hartmann, G. Saake, R. Jungclaus, P. Hartel, and J. Kush. Revised version of the modelling language TROLL. Technical Report 03, Technishe Universitaet Braunschweig, Informatik-Berichte, 1994.

17. C.-B. Jones. *Systematic Software Development using VDM*. Prentice Hall International series in computer science, 1989.
18. C. Khoury, M.-C. Gaudel, and P. Dauchy. AS-IS. Rapport interne 1119, Laboratoire de Recherche en Informatique, August 1997.
19. J. Meseguer. Conditional rewriting logic as a unified model of concurrency. *Theoretical Computer Science*, 96(1):73–155, April 1992.
20. J. Meseguer and Winkler. Parallel programming in Maude. In *Research Directions in High-Level Parallel Programming Languages*, volume 574 of *LNCS*, pages 253–293, 1992.
21. H. Reichel. An approach to object semantics based on terminal coalgebras. In *Recent Trends in Data Type Specifications*, volume 906 of *LNCS*, pages 129–152, 1994.
22. J.-M. Spivey. *The Z Notation, A reference manual*. Prentice Hall International series in computer science, 1987.
23. A.-V. Zamulin. Specification of an Oberon compiler by means of a typed gurevich machine. Technical Report 58939450090000701, Institute of Informatics Systems of the Siberian Division of the Russian Academy of Sciences, Novosibirsk, 1996.
24. A.-V. Zamulin. Typed Gurevich Machines. Technical Report 36, Institute of Informatics Systems, Novosibirsk, 1996.
25. A.-V. Zamulin. Typed Gurevich Machines Revisited. In *Joint NCC&ISS Bulletin*, volume 7 of *Comp. Science*, pages 95–121, 1997.
26. E. Zucca. From static to dynamic data-types. In *Mathematical Foundations of Computer Science*, volume 1113 of *LNCS*, pages 579–590, 1996.

Rigorous Development in UML

K. Lano
Dept. of Computing,
Imperial College,
180 Queens Gate, London SW7 2BZ
kcl@doc.ic.ac.uk

A. Evans
Dept. of Computing,
University of York
andye@cs.york.ac.uk

Abstract. The Unified Modelling Language (UML) is becoming the de facto industry standard notation for object-oriented analysis and design. In this paper we propose a development process using UML and other notations which supports formal analysis and verification, so enabling the notation to be used for highly critical systems.

We will illustrate the development process using a small example of a traffic light control system.[1]

1 Introduction

The UML [12] combines and extends elements of previous OO notations such as OMT, Booch and Objectory. In contrast to these methods, its notations are precisely defined using the Object Constraint Language (OCL) and a meta-model to express the allowed forms of diagrams and their properties. In previous papers we have shown how the semantic meaning of some UML diagrams can also be precisely defined [8, 7, 3]. This semantics supports the use of *transformational development*: the refinement of abstract models towards concrete models, using design steps which are known to be correct with respect to the semantics (all properties of the abstract model remain valid in the refined model).

For highly critical applications (systems where the consequence of incorrect functioning may include loss of life or severe financial loss), it is important that the development process used can help detect and eliminate errors. The process should in particular support the *verification* of refined models against abstract models by comparing their semantics.

A number of problems have been recognised with the implicit method for using UML [13], for example:

1. Use cases have been extended from being simply a requirements elicitation tool, to being a notation which (via the **extends** and **uses** dependencies between use cases) can describe quite complex control flow. Premature and inappropriate design can therefore result.

---

[1] This work was partly supported by a grant from the Laboraturio de Methodos Formais of the Departamento de Informatica of Pontificia Universidade Catolica do Rio de Janeiro.

2. Statecharts are a design-oriented notation not ideally suited for abstract behaviour specification, and are used to describe the behaviour of individual objects, instead of system-level modelling.

We attempt to remedy the first problem by not allowing dependencies between use cases, and by using Yourdon-style Data and Control-flow Diagrams (DCFD's) [14] to describe the overall context of data and control flows between the system and the external agents and devices it interacts with. We deal with the second problem by using *operation schemas* which describe in an abstract way the response of the system or an object to an input event or request.

Our proposed process can be summarised as follows:

1. Requirements – modelled using Yourdon context diagrams and/or UML use case diagrams (without dependencies between use cases).

2. Essential Specification – described using UML class diagrams, operation schemas (from Fusion and Octopus), statecharts and sequence diagrams.

3. Design – modelled using UML class diagrams, statecharts, sequence diagrams and collaboration diagrams.

In order to support verification, a number of well-defined relationships between these models can be given:

1. Each input event/message on the system context diagram should have a system response described by an operation schema.

2. The effect described by an operation schema for an event **e** must be established by the completed response sequence to **e** described in design level statecharts, that is, by the transitions specified for **e** and the set of their generated events and transitions.

3. Design level class diagrams should satisfy all the properties asserted in the specification level class diagrams.

4. Sequence diagrams should be consistent with collaboration diagrams: the structure of object inter-calling should be the same.

5. Collaboration diagrams should be consistent with statecharts: messages sent by an object in response to a message **m** should correspond to events generated from transitions for **m** in the statechart of the object.

Of these, 2 and 3 are formal verification steps, because class diagrams, operation schemas and statecharts have precise formal semantics in our formalisation. 1, 4 and 5 are syntactic checks which could be implemented in CASE tools.

2 Semantics and Verification Rules

A mathematical semantic representation of UML models can be given in terms of *theories* in extended first-order set theory as in the semantics presented for Syntropy in [2] and VDM^{++} in [10]. In order to reason about real-time specifications the more general version, Real-time Action Logic (RAL) [10] can be used.

A RAL theory has the form:

theory *Name*

types *local type symbols*

attributes *time-varying data, representing instance or class variables*

actions *actions which may affect the data, such as operations, statechart transitions and methods*

axioms *logical properties and constraints between the theory elements.*

Theories can be used to represent classes, instances, associations and general submodels of a UML model. These models are therefore taken as *specifications*: they describe the features and properties which should be supported by any implementation that satisfies the model. In terms of the semantics, theory **S** satisfies theory **T** if there is an interpretation σ of the symbols of **T** into those of **S** under which every property of **T** holds:

$$\mathbf{S} \vdash \sigma(\varphi)$$

for every theorem φ of **T**. A design model **D** with theory **S** is a correct refinement of abstract model **C** with theory **T** if **S** satisfies **T**.

In addition to standard mathematical notation such as $\mathbb{F}$ for "set of finite sets of", etc, RAL theories can use the following notations:

1. For each classifier or state **X** there is an attribute $\overline{\mathbf{X}} : \mathbb{F}(\mathbf{X})$ denoting the set of existing instances of **X**.

2. If α is an action symbol, and **P** a predicate, then $[\alpha]\mathbf{P}$ is a predicate which means "every execution of α establishes **P** on termination", that is, **P** is a *postcondition* of α.

3. For every action α there are functions $\uparrow(\alpha, \mathbf{i})$, $\downarrow(\alpha, \mathbf{i})$, $\leftarrow(\alpha, \mathbf{i})$ and $\rightarrow(\alpha, \mathbf{i})$ of $\mathbf{i} : \mathbb{N}_1$ which denote the activation, termination, request send and request arrival times, respectively, of the **i**-th invocation of α. These times are ordered as:

$$\leftarrow(\alpha, \mathbf{i}) \leq \rightarrow(\alpha, \mathbf{i}) \leq \uparrow(\alpha, \mathbf{i}) \leq \downarrow(\alpha, \mathbf{i})$$

Also

$$\mathbf{i} \leq \mathbf{j} \Rightarrow \leftarrow(\alpha, \mathbf{i}) \leq \leftarrow(\alpha, \mathbf{j})$$

4. If α and β are actions, then $\alpha \supset \beta$ "α calls β" is defined to mean that

$$\forall \mathbf{i} : \mathbb{N}_1 \cdot \exists \mathbf{j} : \mathbb{N}_1 \cdot \uparrow(\alpha, \mathbf{i}) = \uparrow(\beta, \mathbf{j}) \wedge \downarrow(\alpha, \mathbf{i}) = \downarrow(\beta, \mathbf{j})$$

Either Z or OCL notation could be used for axioms in theories, representing the semantics or constraints of UML models. In [9] we define a translation from OCL into Z.

2.1 Object Models

A UML class **C** is represented as a theory of the form given in Figure 1. Each

```
theory ΓC
types C
attributes C̄ : F(C)
    self : C → C
    att₁ : C → T₁
    ...

actions createC(c : C)    {C̄}
    killC(c : C)    {C̄}
    op₁(c : C, x : X₁) : Y₁
    ...
axioms

        ∀c : C ·
            self(c) = c ∧
            [createC(c)](c ∈ C̄) ∧
            [killC(c)](c ∉ C̄)
```

Fig. 1. Theory of Class C

instance attribute $\mathbf{att_i} : \mathbf{T_i}$ of **C** gains an additional parameter of type **C** in the class theory $\Gamma_\mathbf{C}$ and similarly for operations[2]. Class attributes and actions do not gain the additional **C** parameter as they are independent of any particular instance. We can denote $\mathbf{att(a)}$ for attribute **att** of instance **a** by the standard OO notation **a.att**, and similarly denote actions $\mathbf{act(a, x)}$ by $\mathbf{a.act(x)}$.

Similarly each association **lr** can be interpreted in a theory which contains an attribute $\overline{\mathbf{lr}}$ representing the current extent of the association (the set of pairs in it) and actions **add_link** and **delete_link** to add and remove pairs (links) from this set. Axioms define the cardinality of the association ends and other properties of the association. In particular, if **ab** is an association between classes **A** and **B**, then $\overline{\mathbf{ab}} \subseteq \overline{\mathbf{A}} \times \overline{\mathbf{B}}$, so membership of $\overline{\mathbf{ab}}$ implies existence for elements of a link.

---

[2] The class theory can be generated from a theory of a typical **C** instance by means of an **A**-morphism [2].

3 Software Requirements

The system to be constructed in this case study is a controller for two pairs of
traffic lights at a crossroads (Figure 2). Traffic lights 1 and 3 must always show
the same indication, as must lights 2 and 4. Traffic lights cycle from Green to
Amber to Red on the 'go red' cycle, and Red, Red and Amber, Green, on the
'go green' cycle. There is a delay of 3 seconds in the Red and Amber state, and
5 seconds in the Amber state. The safety requirement is that at least one pair
of traffic lights must be red at any given time.

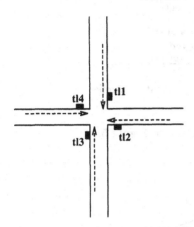

Fig. 2. Traffic Light Layout

The system responds to a signal 'change_direction'. The response should be
to set the currently red signals to green, and the currently green signals to red.
TN is the type $\{1, 2, 3, 4\}$ indexing traffic lights. A Use Case diagram similar to

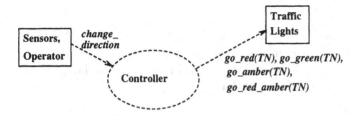

Fig. 3. Context Diagram of Traffic Light Control System

Figure 3 could also be defined, with agents being the signal generator (operator
or sensors) and the traffic light actuators.

4 Essential Specification Level

We could model the system as a collection of two traffic light pairs containing distinct traffic lights **tl1** and **tl3**, and **tl2** and **tl4**. The abstract object model is given in Figure 4. **State** is the enumerated type {**green, amber, red, red_amber**} for the illumination state of an individual traffic light.

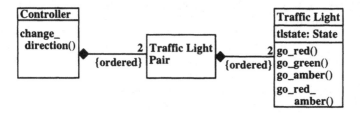

Fig. 4. Abstract Object Model of Traffic Light Controller

The behaviour of individual traffic lights is given in Figure 5.

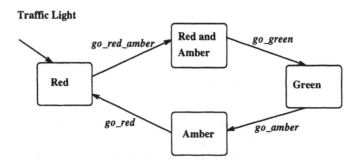

Fig. 5. Statechart of Traffic Light

A sequence diagram would show that the traffic light must be in the **red_amber** state for at least 3 seconds, and in the **amber** state for at least 5 seconds.

The invariant that the light pairs always illuminate the same lamps is expressed as an invariant of **TrafficLightPair**:

TrafficLightPair
self.traffic_light[1].tlstate = self.traffic_light[2].tlstate

where **composite[i]** denotes the **i**-th element in a composite list of objects.

The safety constraint is formalised as:

Controller
self.traffic_light_pair[1].traffic_light[1].tlstate = red or
self.traffic_light_pair[2].traffic_light[1].tlstate = red

We need to show that these invariants are maintained by operation schemas and their implementations. In implementations we may require that the invariants are also maintained at a finer level of granularity than the complete execution of the operation (ie, they are true at certain points during the operation execution) depending on the concurrency policy in force.

The operation schemas express the required effects of the operations listed in the use cases of the system, without any decomposition into methods of individual objects. As we discuss in [11], this style of essential model description is often clearer than the artificial localisation of such specifications used in Syntropy essential models [1].

operation change_direction
reads traffic_light_pair, traffic_light
writes tlstate

precondition

> (tl1.tlstate = green and tl3.tlstate = green and
> tl2.tlstate = red and tl4.tlstate = red) or
> (tl1.tlstate = red and tl3.tlstate = red and
> tl2.tlstate = green and tl4.tlstate = green)

postcondition

> if tl1.tlstate@pre = green
> then
>   tl1.tlstate = red and tl2.tlstate = green and
>   tl3.tlstate = red and tl4.tlstate = green
> else
>   if tl1.tlstate@pre = red
>   then
>   tl1.tlstate = green and tl2.tlstate = red and
>   tl3.tlstate = green and tl4.tlstate = red

tl1, etc are abbreviations for OCL expressions:

> tl1 = traffic_light_pair[1].traffic_light[1]
> tl2 = traffic_light_pair[2].traffic_light[1]
> tl3 = traffic_light_pair[1].traffic_light[2]
> tl4 = traffic_light_pair[2].traffic_light[2]

The notation e@pre denotes the value of e at activation of the operation. If an attribute e does not occur in the **writes** list, then e can be used instead of e@pre since the values of these expressions are then the same.

The precondition excludes the case that **change_direction** occurs if **tl1.tlstate@pre** $\in$ {**amber, red_amber**}, or other combinations other than a 'stable state'.

In this description, there is no detail concerning *how* these changes of state are brought about. This is a concern of later design stages.

5 Design

We enhance the original object model to include additional operations for the **TrafficLightPair** class (Figure 6).

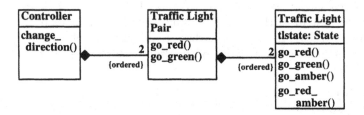

Fig. 6. Refined Object Model of Traffic Light Controller

Statecharts for the controller and traffic light pair classes are given in Figures 7 and 8.

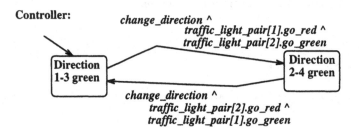

Fig. 7. Statechart of **Controller**

Verification that the reaction achieves the effect specified in the operation schema is direct. We have to check that each transition for **change_direction** in the controller statechart results in a poststate satisfying the postcondition of the operation schema, under the assumption of the guard on the transition (including the properties implied by membership of the source state) and the precondition of the operation schema.

For example, in the case that direction 1-3 is initially green, the transition for **change_direction** in the **Controller** state machine terminates once the transition for **go_red** on the state machine for **traffic_light_pair**[1] and then the transition for **go_green** on the state machine for **traffic_light_pair**[2] terminate. The first of these transitions results in a state where

$$\text{traffic\_light\_pair}[1].\text{traffic\_light}[1].\text{tlstate} = \text{red}$$
$$\text{traffic\_light\_pair}[1].\text{traffic\_light}[2].\text{tlstate} = \text{red}$$
$$\text{traffic\_light\_pair}[2].\text{traffic\_light}[1].\text{tlstate} = \text{red}$$
$$\text{traffic\_light\_pair}[2].\text{traffic\_light}[2].\text{tlstate} = \text{red}$$

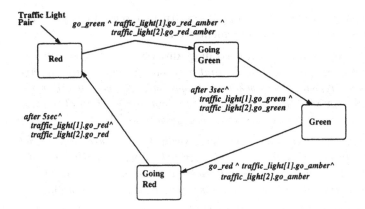

Fig. 8. Statechart of **TrafficLightPair**

and the second in the specified state

traffic_light_pair[1].**traffic_light**[1].tlstate = red
traffic_light_pair[1].**traffic_light**[2].tlstate = red
traffic_light_pair[2].**traffic_light**[1].tlstate = green
traffic_light_pair[2].**traffic_light**[2].tlstate = green

as required. It can also be checked that each transition maintains the safety invariant.

Finally, we need to check that the disjunction of the guards of all the transitions for **change_direction** is logically weaker than the operation schema precondition, which is also the case.

6 The Role of Transformations

In a complex development UML models may have hundreds of classes and associations. Any changes in the structure of this data from the abstract to refined models must be carried out in a way which ensures the correctness of the concrete system with respect to the abstract.

There are three kinds of transformation which have been developed:

1. Enhancement transformations, which simply extend a model with new model elements. For example, adding new classes, invariants, attributes, operations or associations to a class diagram, or introducing state nesting or new transitions to a statechart. Figure 6 represents an enhancement of Figure 4.

2. Reductive transformations, which allow a model expressed in the full UML notation to be reexpressed in a sublanguage of this notation. For example, 'flattening' of nested or concurrent states into equivalent sets of basic states, or replacing association qualifiers by association classes [8].

   These transformations can give a partial semantics of full UML models in terms of a sublanguage of UML [4].

3. Refinement transformations, which support re-writing models in ways which lead from analysis to design and implementation.

The refinement transformations on class diagrams we have verified are: *refining class invariants, rationalising disjoint associations, eliminating many-many associations, relational composition of aggregations, specialising interfaces, strengthening association constraints, relational composition of selector associations* [9, 7], *moving associations into aggregations* [8].

The transformations on statecharts we have verified are: *source and target splitting of transitions, abstracting events, strengthening transition guards, eliminating transitions with false guards, collecting common transitions, restricting source of transitions, introducing sequencing and iteration* [9, 7].

These transformations also include the introduction of *design patterns* [6].

Enhancement transformations are *complete* in the sense that any UML class diagram or statechart can be constructed by iterating such transformations on an initially empty class diagram or statechart. They are also simple to verify, since they result in a logically stronger theory (although possibly an inconsistent theory).

Reductive transformations are complete in the sense that any model in the full notation can be equivalently expressed in the subnotation by applying these transformations. These transformations apply to statecharts without history entry nodes or deferred events, and reduce them to state machines without nested or concurrent states: ie, in which all states are basic.

Refinement transformations are not complete, in that it is possible to devise refinements which are not expressible as a combination of the transformations given above. It should however be the case that these transformations cover a wide range of those used in practice by developers.

Examples of transformations are given in the following sections and in [7, 8].

6.1 Class Models and Transformations

Consider an alternative analysis model of the traffic light control system where the **TrafficLightPair** class is not defined during analysis, so that the controller is directly related to the four separate traffic light objects (Figure 9). For this

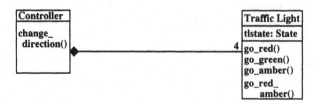

Fig. 9. Initial Class Diagram of Traffic Light System

version the operation schema is the same as that in Section 4 except that **tl1**, etc, abbreviate

tl1 = **traffic_light[1]**
tl2 = **traffic_light[2]**
tl3 = **traffic_light[3]**
tl4 = **traffic_light[4]**

and **traffic_light_pair** is not in the **reads** list. This version of the system can be refined to that presented in Section 4, using the following transformations.

Composing Aggregations Composition associations in UML represent a strong 'part of' relationship between a 'whole' entity and several 'part' entities. Such a relationship should have several properties [12]:

1. One-many or one-one (a whole can have many parts, but a part cannot belong to different wholes at the same time): if whole objects a and a' are related to the same part b, then $a = a'$.

2. Deletion propagating: deleting the whole deletes its parts.

3. Transitive.

4. Irreflexive

If we have a situation as in Figure 10, where two aggregations **ab** and **bc** exist between different classes **A**, **B** and **C**, which have no common objects, then the relational composition **ac = ab; bc** of these two aggregations also satisfies the properties 1 to 4 above if **ab** and **bc** do:

1. If $(a, c), (a', c) \in \mathbf{ac}$, then there are b, b' such that

$$(b, c), (b', c) \in \mathbf{bc} \ \wedge \ (a, b), (a', b') \in \mathbf{ab}$$

But then $b = b'$ by property 1 of **bc**, and so $a = a'$ by property 1 of **ab**.

2. $\mathbf{kill_A}(a) \supset \mathbf{kill_B}(b)$ for each $(a, b) \in \mathbf{ab}$, and $\mathbf{kill_B}(b) \supset \mathbf{kill_C}(c)$ for each $(b, c) \in \mathbf{bc}$, so $\mathbf{kill_A}(a) \supset \mathbf{kill_C}(c)$ for each $(a, c) \in \mathbf{ac}$, as required.

3. **ab** and **bc** are trivially transitive since there can be no pairs $(x, y), (y, z) \in$ **ab**, etc. Likewise **ac** is trivially transitive since **C** is disjoint from **A**.

4. Similarly **ac** is trivially irreflexive.

If there are specific cardinalities $1 : \mathbf{n}$, $1 : \mathbf{m}$ for **ab** and **bc** respectively, then **ac** has cardinality $1 : (\mathbf{n} * \mathbf{m})$.

In the case of the traffic light system, we can use this transformation to deduce that the model of Figure 4 refines the model of Figure 9.

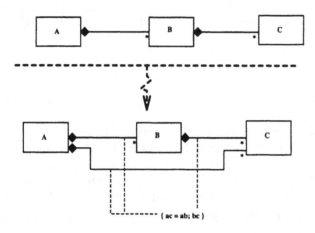

Fig. 10. Transitivity of Composition Aggregations

6.2 Refinement of Operation Schemas to Statecharts

If an operation schema definition for operation e has the form

precondition Case1 or Case2
if Case1@pre
then Post1
else
  if Case2@pre
  then Post2

where **Post2** ⇒ **Case1**, **Post1** ⇒ **Case2** and ¬ (**Case1** ∧ **Case2**), then this is expressible as a binary state machine of the form of Figure 11.

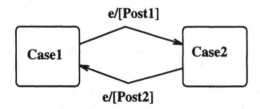

Fig. 11. Implementation of Operation Schema

The statechart of Figure 11 can then be further refined to replace postconditions [**Post**] by suitable sequencing of actions which ensure these postconditions.

In the case of the traffic light control system, we could apply this transformation to the operation schema of Section 6.1 to obtain Figure 12 (**tl1** denotes **traffic_light**[1], etc).

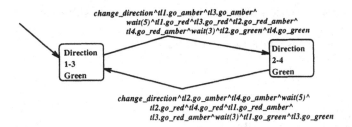

Fig. 12. Abstract Controller Statechart

6.3 State Machine Models and Transformations

Sequential Decomposition Sequential decomposition allows the introduction of procedural control flow into a statechart description of a method. It can be used in the step from a statechart to an activity diagram. Figure 13 shows a typical example. Here, **Int** is a new state, with no other incident transitions. The theory

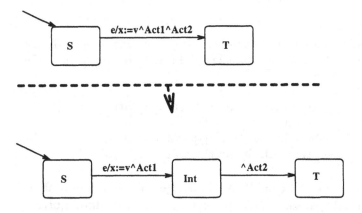

Fig. 13. Sequential Decomposition Example

interpretation is that t_1, the abstract transition for **e** from **S**, is mapped to t_2; t_3 where t_2 is the concrete transition for **e** from **S**, and t_3 is the automatic transition from **Int**.

If the original transition had labelling $e/x := v \frown$ **Act1** $\frown$ **wait(n)** $\frown$ **Act2** where **wait(n)** indicates a delay of at least **n** time units, then the decomposed version has instead the labelling **after n** $\frown$ **Act2** on transition t_3.

Annealing A transformation involving refinement of both class diagrams and state machines is *annealing* [5]. This involves the replacement of a local attribute of a class with a reference to an object, or the addition of an intermediate reference between objects. In terms of dynamic models, a transition in a single statechart is replaced by a succession of two transitions in separate statecharts, one invoked by the other.

Figure 14 shows a typical case with two attributes.

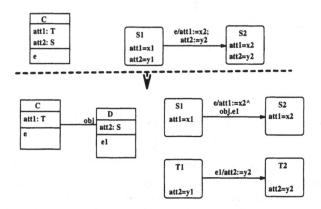

Fig. 14. Annealing

In the traffic light case study, an annealing step from the models given in Section 6.1 and Figure 12 would introduce **TrafficLightPair** objects and define the theory interpretation σ:

$$\text{traffic\_light}[1] \longmapsto \text{traffic\_light\_pair}[1].\text{traffic\_light}[1]$$
$$\text{traffic\_light}[2] \longmapsto \text{traffic\_light\_pair}[2].\text{traffic\_light}[1]$$
$$\text{traffic\_light}[3] \longmapsto \text{traffic\_light\_pair}[1].\text{traffic\_light}[2]$$
$$\text{traffic\_light}[4] \longmapsto \text{traffic\_light\_pair}[2].\text{traffic\_light}[2]$$

This transformation is shown in Figure 15. **Act1** is tl1.go_amber^tl3.go_amber^ wait(5)^tl1.go_red^tl3.go_red, where tl1 = traffic_light[1], tlp1 = traffic_light_pair[1], etc., whilst **Act1'** is Act1 with tl1 = traffic_light[1], tl3 = traffic_light[2].

Combining this with sequential decomposition of the traffic light pair transitions shows that the design of Section 5 refines the version given in Section 6.1.

Conclusions

We have proposed a systematic development process using UML notations. The steps of this process can be verified, in principle, and make use of formally correct transformations on UML models. We are currently working on tool support for such a process, which should enable it to be trialed for use in an industrial context.

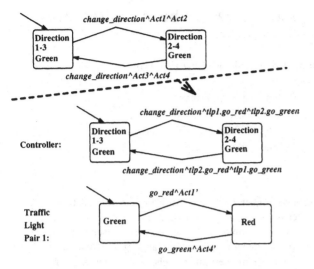

change_direction^Act1^Act2

Direction 1-3 Green

Direction 2-4 Green

change_direction^Act3^Act4

Controller:

change_direction^tlp1.go_red^tlp2.go_green

Direction 1-3 Green

Direction 2-4 Green

change_direction^tlp2.go_red^tlp1.go_green

Traffic Light Pair 1:

go_red^Act1'

Green

Red

go_green^Act4'

Fig. 15. Annealing of Traffic Light System

References

1. S. Cook, J. Daniels, *Designing Object Systems*, Prentice Hall, 1994.
2. J C Bicarregui, K C Lano, T S E Maibaum, *Objects, Associations and Subsystems: a hierarchical approach to encapsulation*, ECOOP 97, LNCS, 1997.
3. A. Evans, R. France, K. Lano, B. Rumpe, *Developing the UML as a formal modelling language*, UML 98 Conference, Mulhouse, France, 19 98.
4. M. Gogolla, M. Richters, *Equivalence Rules for UML Class Diagrams*, UML 98.
5. S. Goldsack, K. Lano, E. Durr, *Invariants as Design Templates in Object-based Systems*, Workshop on Foundations of Component-based Systems, ESEC 97.
6. K. Lano, N. Malik, *Reengineering Legacy Applications using Design Patterns*, STEP '97, IEEE Press, 1997.
7. K. Lano, J. Bicarregui, *Semantics and Transformations for UML Models*, UML 98 Conference, Mulhouse, France, 1998.
8. K. Lano, J. Bicarregui, *Formalising the UML in Structured Temporal Theories*, ECOOP 98 Workshop on Behavioural Semantics, Technical Report TUM-I9813, Technische Universitat Muchen, 1998.
9. K. Lano, J. Bicarregui, *UML Refinement and Abstraction Transformations*, ROOM 2 Workshop, University of Bradford, 1998.
10. K Lano, *Logical Specification of Reactive and Real-Time Systems*, Journal of Logic and Computation, Vol. 8, No. 5, pp 679–711, 1998.
11. K. Lano, R. France, J-M. Bruel, *A Semantic Comparison of Fusion and Syntropy*, to appear in *Object-oriented Systems*, 1998.
12. Rational Software et al, *UML Documentation*, Version 1.1, http://www.rational.com/uml, 1997.
13. A. Simons, I. Graham, *37 Things That Don't Work in Object-Oriented Modelling with UML*, ECOOP 98 Workshop on Behavioural Semantics, Technical Report TUM-I9813, Technische Universitat Muchen, 1998.
14. E. Yourdon, *Modern Structured Analysis*, Prentice-Hall, 1989.

Using Explicit State to Describe Architectures[(*)]

Antónia.Lopes and José.Luiz.Fiadeiro

Department of Informatics
Faculty of Sciences, University of Lisbon,
Campo Grande, 1700 Lisboa, PORTUGAL
{mal,llf}@di.fc.ul.pt

Abstract. In order to achieve higher levels of abstraction in architectural design, we investigate extensions to parallel program design based on the use of explicit state variables to accommodate the action-based discipline of interaction that is typical of architecture description languages. Our study focus on primitives that support non-determinism, choice and fairness in guarded-command based languages, and on refinement principles that are compositional with respect to interconnection.

1   Introduction

Formal approaches for describing software architectures tend to use process-based languages. Typical examples are the architecture description languages WRIGHT [2], based on CSP, Darwin [16], based on the π-calculus, and Rapide [15], based on partially ordered sets of events. The fact that software architectures address the structure of systems in terms of components and interconnection protocols between them suggests the adoption of formalisms in which interaction is event-based. For instance, the ability to specify if a given action of a component is under the control of the component or the environment is paramount for the definition of connector roles – e.g. the fact that, in a client-server architecture, the choice of service is under the control of the client. This form of behaviour has been modelled using external and internal choice operators as, for instance, in WRIGHT [2].

However, such process description languages are notably lacking in abstraction mechanisms. Their primitives are directed to structuring the flow of control in an explicit way and, hence, there are crucial properties of protocols that cannot be captured at a higher level of abstraction. For instance, the description of a pipe-filter architecture with a particular discipline on the pipe (e.g. FIFO), or a client-server architecture with fairness requirements, typically requires a rather involved encoding [2].

In contrast, formalisms that use an explicit notion of state, such as Unity [3], TLA

[(*)] This work was partially supported through contracts PCSH/OGE/1038/95 (MAGO) and 2/2.1/TIT/1662/95 (SARA).

[12] or fair transition systems [17], provide a more flexible way of modelling the behaviour of components in the sense that execution sequences emerge from the interference of actions on the state rather than an explicit prescription of an ordering on the actions. The problem with such approaches is that interaction between components in a system is modelled through a shared state, exactly the dual of what is favoured by architecture description languages. As a result, these approaches do not support the separation between the description of the components of a system and their interaction – interaction has to be implemented in the programs that model the components.

Our purpose in this paper is to show how the two approaches can be reconciled in a parallel program design language that adopts an explicit state but an action-based discipline of interaction. The language that we discuss is an extension of CommUnity [5]. CommUnity was developed precisely as having the same computational model as Unity but a coordination model based on private state and shared actions. However, it lacked mechanisms for addressing some of the key issues that are required by architecture description languages such as the ability to handle non-determinism and choice, and refinement mechanisms that support role instantiation and are compositional with respect to component interconnection.

Section 2 refines this initial motivation by expanding on the issues that we have identified as fundamental for languages based on explicit state to accommodate architectural description. Section 3 presents the extended language and its model-theoretic semantics. This semantics is based on labelled transition systems that differ from what is traditional in reactive system modelling in the way the environment is taken into account. Section 4 is concerned with component interconnection, for which a categorical semantics is adapted from previous papers., e.g. [6]. Section 5 formalises component refinement in terms of morphisms that differ from the ones used to model interconnection. A notion of compositionality is formalised in this setting. These notions are applied in section 6 to architectural connectors.

2 Motivation

We start by illustrating the ideas briefly described in the introduction and motivating some of the proposed extensions to CommUnity.

Shared state vs shared actions. Consider that, in the development of a given system, the need for a component Merge has been identified that receives two streams of data, merges them, and makes the resulting stream available to the environment.

If the interaction between the component and its environment is uniquely based on shared state, then it is not possible to design Merge without assuming a particular interaction protocol. For instance, it is necessary to program the acknowledgment of the reception of each data item in each input channel and make assumptions on the way the environment acknowledges the reception of data items [1].

In contrast, an approach based on shared actions allows us to describe, at the level of each component, only what the component contributes to each action – its local view of the action – without assuming a fixed protocol. This is because the execution of shared actions is under the control both of the component and the environment. This mode of interaction – synchronous communication via shared actions – is very general in the sense that other modes of communication can be programmed over it [9], for instance as architectural connectors. Indeed, protocols themselves can be developed separately as components with which other components synchronise for communicating with one another, thus promoting the separation between the description of the behaviour of the individual components and their interaction.

Internal vs external choice. When designing a component, it is often important to specify, whenever there is more than one shared action that is enabled, whether the choice between them is determined by the component or by the environment. For instance, in the case of a server, the choice between services should not be decided by the server itself but left to its clients. Process description languages support this distinction through separate internal and external choice operators.

In an approach based on explicit state, conditions on the state of the component may be used to define when the component makes each action available. For instance, in object-based languages enforcing "design by contract" [18], pre-conditions define when methods are available for execution in the sense that, if called by its environment, the object ensures their execution with a certain post-condition. This is why refinement of methods does not allow pre-conditions to be strengthened: strengthening the pre-condition of a method would violate the contract established between the object and its environment according to which the object lets the environment choose the method whenever its pre-condition is true. This means that the programmer who is going to implement the server must make sure that the execution of the services will not be blocked when their pre-conditions hold.

However, in program design languages based on guarded-commands, such conditions cannot be captured through the guards of each action. This is because guards are typically used as mechanisms for ensuring safety by blocking the execution of actions. Hence, refinement does not allow them to be weakened. For instance, in the design of the control system of a boiler in a central heating system, the action that releases hot water into the system may be required to be blocked if the temperature of the water raises above a certain threshold determined by the specification of the piping system. A developer may decide to lower this threshold in an implementation because of physical restrictions imposed by internal components of the controller itself.

CommUnity reconciles these two design mechanisms by guarding actions with two conditions: the safety guard that must be true whenever the action is enabled, and the progress guard that, when true, implies that the action is enabled and, hence, available for the environment to choose it. The key issue here is the separation between guards and enabledness of actions. Our proposal makes guards a specification mechanism for enabledness in the sense that they do not fully determine the enabling condition of an action but impose constraints on it.

Underspecification vs Non-determinism. Safety and progress guards establish an interval in which the enabling condition of an action must lie: the safety guard is a lower bound for enabledness, in the sense that it is implied by the enabling condition, and the progress guard is an upper bound in the sense that it implies the enabling condition. As such, the corresponding action may be underspecified in the sense that its enabling condition is not fully determined, and, hence, subject to refinement by reducing this interval, i.e. weakening the progress guard and strengthening the safety guard. Underspecification is an essential mechanism for ensuring that design can be conducted at the required level of abstraction, avoiding implementation decisions to be made in early stages. CommUnity supports other mechanisms for underspecification such as non-deterministic assignments.

Such forms of underspecification model what is sometimes called allowed non-determinism [11] in the sense that they determine a range of possible alternative implementations whose choice cannot be controlled by the environment of the component. In contrast, mechanisms such as progress guards model required non-determinism in the sense that they specify alternative forms of behaviour that must be exhibited by every single implementation, thus allowing the environment to control it. The distinction between these two forms of non-determinism is essential for supporting abstraction and choice in architectural design.

Fairness. The above mentioned extensions to CommUnity, motivated by the need to support architectural description, are concerned with the coordination aspects of architectures, i.e. with the mechanisms that are made available to coordinate the behaviour of the components within a system. In what concerns the computational side of components, i.e. the mechanisms that guarantee that each component behaves, individually, as intended, it is necessary to make available another notion of progress – one that ensures that certain states are eventually reached. Such progress properties – liveness – are typical of "classical" reactive system specifications based on shared state and private actions. Therefore, we extended CommUnity with locally-controlled actions for which the progress guard ensures liveness in all fair computations.

3 Programming the Individual Components

The syntax of CommUnity with the extensions motivated above is as follows:

```
program P is
var output      out(V)
    input       inp(V)
    internal    int(V)
init      I
do        []        g : [B(g), U(g)  →   ||      v: ∈ F(g, v)]
      g∈sh(Γ)                      v∈D(g)
          []     prv g : [B(g), U(g)  →   ||      v: ∈ F(g, v)]
      g∈prv(Γ)                     v∈D(g)
```

where
- V is the set of *variables*. Variables can be declared as *input*, *output* or *internal*. Input variables are read from the environment of the program but cannot be modi-

fied by the program. Output and internal variables are local to the program, i.e., they cannot be modified by the environment. We use *loc(V)* to denote the set of local variables. Output variables can be read by the environment but internal variables cannot. Each variable *v* is typed with a sort *Sort(v)*.

- *Γ* is the set of *action names*; each action name has an associated guarded command (see below). Actions can be declared either as *private* or *shared* (for simplicity, we only declare which actions are private). Private actions represent internal computations and their execution is uniquely under the control of the program. In contrast, shared actions represent interactions between the program and the environment. Hence, their execution is also under the control of the environment. Each action *g* is typed with a set *D(g)* consisting of the local variables that action *g* can change – its write frame. For every local variable *v*, we also denote by *D(v)* the set of actions that can change *v*. The pair *<V,Γ>* is called the signature of the program.
- *I* is a proposition over the set of local variables – the initialisation condition.
- For every action *g∈Γ*, *B(g)* and *U(g)* are propositions over the set of variables – its *guards*. When the safety guard *B(g)* is false, *g* cannot be executed. When the progress guard *U(g)* holds, the program is ready to execute *g*. More precisely, (1) when *g* is a shared action, if *U(g)* holds, the program cannot refuse to execute *g* if the environment requests it, and (2) when *g* is a private action, if *U(g)* holds infinitely often then *g* is taken infinitely often. For simplicity, we write only one proposition when the two guards coincide.
- For every action *g∈Γ* and local variable *v∈D(g)*, *F(g,v)* is a non-deterministic assignment: each time *g* is executed, *v* is assigned one of the values denoted by *F(g,v)*, chosen in a non-deterministic way (when *D(g)=∅*, the only available command is the empty one which we denote by **skip**).

Example 3.1. Consider that, in the context of the development of a given system, the need for two components *Merge* and *Consumer* is identified. The component *Merge* merges two streams of natural numbers and transmits the resulting stream to the environment, guaranteeing that the output is ordered if the input streams are also ordered. The component *Consumer* receives a stream of natural numbers and stores it.

Consider first the component *Consumer*. In order to illustrate the ability of CommUnity to support the high-level description of system behaviour, assume that, at a given level of abstraction, one is just concerned with coordinating the joint behaviour of the components in the system, ignoring for a moment the details of the internal computation performed by *Consumer* (the storing of the data),

```
program Consumer is
var output    cl: bool
    input     i: nat, eof: bool
init          ¬cl
do            rec : [ ¬eof ∧ ¬cl, false → skip ]
    [] prv    close : [ true, eof∧¬cl → cl:=true ]
```

The fact that the internal computation related to the storing of data is being abstracted away is reflected in the fact that the body of action *rec* – modelling the reception of values from the environment – is empty, meaning that it does not change the abstract state, and its progress guard is *false*, meaning that we cannot make precise how the reception is controlled. In section 5, we shall see how refinement mechanisms can be used to extend this program with details on the computational aspects.

The program above is, therefore, primarily concerned with the interface between *Consumer* and its environment. Part of this interface is established via the input channel i along which data are transmitted to *Consumer*. The (shared) action *rec* accounts for the reception of such transmissions. This action is shared between *Consumer* and its environment meaning that both *Consumer* and the environment have to give permission for the action to occur. The safety guard of *rec* requires *Consumer* to refuse a transmission when communication has been closed (see below). However, because the progress guard has been set to *false*, an implementation of *Consumer* can arbitrarily refuse to accept transmissions because there is no upper bound on the enabling condition of *rec*.

The other means of interaction with the environment is concerned with the closure of communication. The component can receive, through the input channel *eof*, a Boolean indicating that transmission along i has ceased. This should trigger a communication closure as indicated in the progress guard of *close*. Fairness then guarantees that the assignment is eventually performed. The assignment sets the output variable *cl* thus signaling to the environment that the component has stopped accepting transmissions. This is often important for coordination purposes, namely for managing the configuration of the system. Notice that *Consumer* can arbitrarily decide to execute *close*. This is because, being a private action, the environment cannot interfere with its execution. The only influence of the environment is to set its progress guard, i.e. to trigger the action. Hence, a specific choice of implementation may dictate conditions under which closure is required beyond the reception of a signal on the input variable *eof*, for instance related to the space made available for storing data. This will be illustrated in section 5.

Consider now the component *Merge*. It can be designed in CommUnity as follows.

```
program Merge is
var output    o: nat, eof: bool
    input     i₁,i₂: nat, eof₁,eof₂: bool
    internal  rd: bool
init          ¬eof∧¬rd
do            rec₁ : [ ¬(eof₁ ∨ rd)∧(eof₂∨i₁≤i₂) → o:=i₁ ‖ rd:=true ]
    []        rec₂ : [ ¬(eof₂ ∨ rd)∧(eof₁∨i₂≤i₁) → o:=i₂ ‖ rd:=true ]
    []        send : [ ¬eof ∧ rd → rd:=false ]
    [] prv    close : [ ¬eof ∧ ¬rd ∧ eof₁ ∧ eof₂ → eof:=true ]
```

The two input streams and the corresponding signal of end of data are received through the input variables i_1, i_2, eof_1 and eof_2. The resulting stream is transmitted through the variable o and the environment is informed of the end of data through the variable *eof*. The reception of a message in the input channel i_k is modelled by the shared action rec_k. The execution of this action is blocked when the end of data has already been signaled in this channel or the other channel presents a lower number to be read. Whenever rec_k is executed, the program copies the message presented in channel i_k to the output variable o and the action *send* becomes ready to be executed. The program waits for the reading of that message to become ready again to receive one more message. Finally, after each channel has signalled that it has ended transmission, the program signals the end of data in the output channel *eof*. Because the closing of the communication does not involve the environment, this is modelled by a private action (the action *close*). Notice that, in this program, the safety and progress guard coincide for every action, meaning that these actions have a unique implementation. ∎

The mathematical model that we adopt for system behaviour is based on labelled transition systems. Because, as discussed in sections 1 and 2, we are interested in capturing the coordination aspects required for software architectures, namely the fact that a component can be guaranteed to make its services available for the environment to choose, the way the environment is taken into account in these models is different from what is traditionally found in the literature. The typical situation in reactive systems [17,12] is to take models that reflect the behaviour of a component in a given environment. That is, a model already exhibts a joint execution of the component and its environment. In our case, a model reflects the behaviour that the component *offers* to its environment. More concretely, the branching structure of transition systems is intended to reflect required non-determinism on the behaviour of the component individually. Internal non-determinism, which accounts for choice between different implementations, is essentially modelled by the existence of more than one such transition system as a model of a program. Openess to the environment is explicitly modelled through a special label $\perp$ that identifies steps performed by the environment.

We assume fixed an algebra $\mathcal{U}$ for the data types used in CommUnity. We denote by V_s, where $s \in S$, the set of variables of sort s. We denote by $Reach(T)$ the set of reachable states of a transition system T.

Definition 3.2. A model for a program signature $<V,\Gamma>$ consists of a labelled transition system $T=<W,\rightarrow,W_0>$ over the set $\Gamma_\perp$ and an S-indexed family of mappings $\mathcal{V}_s:V_s\rightarrow[W\rightarrow\mathcal{U}_s]$ s.t.:

1. The set W_0 of initial states is non-empty;
2. For every $w \in W_0$ and S-indexed family of mappings $\mathcal{R}_s:inp(V_s)\rightarrow\mathcal{U}_s$, there exists $w' \in W_0$ s.t. $w \equiv_{loc(V)} w'$ and $\mathcal{V}_s(i)(w')=\mathcal{R}_s(i)$, for every $i \in inp(V)$ and $s \in S$;
3. For every $w,w' \in Reach(T)$ and $g \in \Gamma_\perp$ s.t. $w \xrightarrow{g} w'$ and for every S-indexed family of mappings $\mathcal{R}_s:inp(V_s)\rightarrow\mathcal{U}_s$, there exists $w'' \in W$ s.t. $w' \equiv_{loc(V)} w''$, $\mathcal{V}_s(i)(w'')=\mathcal{R}_s(i)$, for every $i \in inp(V)$ and $s \in S$, and $w \xrightarrow{g} w''$;
4. For every $w \in Reach(T)$ there exists $w' \in W$ s.t. $w \xrightarrow{\perp} w'$;
5. For every $v \in loc(V), w,w' \in Reach(T)$, and $g \notin D(v)$, if $w \xrightarrow{g} w'$ then $\mathcal{U}(v)(w)=\mathcal{U}(v)(w')$,

where $w \equiv_X w'$ abbreviates $\mathcal{U}(v)(w)=\mathcal{U}(v)(w')$ for every $v \in X$. ∎

A model for a program signature consists of a labelled transition system and a map that interprets the variables as functions that return the value that each variable takes in each state. Conditions 1 to 4 ensure that a model cannot constrain the behaviour of the environment. More concretely, a model is such that (1) its set of initial states is non-empty, (2) it does not constrain the initial values of the input variables nor (3) the values that input variables can have in the other reachable states, and (4) it does not prevent the execution of environment steps. Furthermore, condition 5 requires that the values of the local variables remain unchanged during the actions whose domain do not contain them. In particular, because $\perp \notin D(v)$, local variables are not subject to interference from the environment.

A model of a program is a model for its signature for which the initial states satisfy the initialisation constraint, the assignments are enforced, actions can only occur when their safety guards hold and are made available whenever their progress guards are true.

Definition 3.3. Given a program P and a model M for its signature, $M \models P$ iff:
1. For every $w_0 \in W_0$, $\mathcal{V}, w_0 \models I$;
2. For every $g \in \Gamma$, $v \in D(g)$, $w, w' \in Reach(M)$, if $w \xrightarrow{g} w'$ then $\mathcal{V}(w')(v) \in [\![F(g,v)]\!]^{\mathcal{V}}(w)$;
3. For every $g \in \Gamma$ and $w, w' \in Reach(M)$, if $w \xrightarrow{g} w'$ then $\mathcal{V}, w \models B(g)$;
4. For every $g \in \Gamma$ and $w \in Reach(M)$, if $\mathcal{V}, w \models U(g)$ then there exists $w' \in W$ s.t. $w \xrightarrow{g} w'$. ∎

As mentioned before, a model M such that $M \models P$ must be regarded as a model of the behaviour that the program offers to its environment: it defines a set of potential initial states and a set of potential transitions at each state — the choice between the alternatives that are not locally controlled, such as initialisation and modification of input variables and the execution of shared actions that are enabled, is left to the environment. In this way, S represents the degree of cooperation of the program P with respect to its environment.

The definition above makes clear that, for a program to admit models, it is necessary that, for every action g, the progress guard $U(g)$ implies the safety guard $B(g)$. Furthermore, because the emptiness of $F(g,v)$ for some $v \in D(g)$ also prevents action g to occur, it is also necessary that $U(g)$ implies the non emptiness of $F(g,v)$, for every $v \in D(g)$. Programs satisfying such conditions are called *realisable*.

For capturing the liveness properties of programs, we also have to model the way in which the locally-controlled actions that are infinitely often enabled are scheduled by the operating system. As usual, we shall consider infinite computations and we require strong fairness for private actions. That is, we consider paths in which any locally-controlled action which is infinitely often enabled cannot be neglected indefinitely. As usual, we say that an action is enabled at a state when there is a transition from that state that is labelled with the action.

Definition 3.4. A model of a program P consists of a model M for its signature s.t. $M \models P$, and a function $\Pi: W \rightarrow 2^{Path(M)}$ s.t., for every $w \in Reach(M)$ and $\pi \in \Pi(w)$, π starts at w and, for every $g \in prv(\Gamma)$, if g is enabled infinitely often in π then g is taken infinitely often in π. ∎

Consider again the program *Consumer*. After receiving the signal of end of data, and if the communication has not been closed already, the progress guard of action *close* becomes true. If this signal is stable, then the guard remains true while the action is not taken. Under strong fairness, *close* will eventually be executed.

4 Specifying How Components Interact

Software Architecture is about the modularisation of systems in terms of components and interconnections. Many of our previous papers [e.g., 5,6] have argued in favour of the use of Category Theory as a mathematical framework for expressing such inter-connections following Goguen's work on General Systems Theory [8]. The notion of morphism between programs captures what in the literature on parallel program design is known as superposition. Most of the conditions expressed in the definition below are standard when defining superposition and are more thoroughly discussed in our previous paper [5].

Definition/Proposition 4.1. A program morphism $\sigma:P_1 \to P_2$ consists of a (total) function $\sigma_{var}:V_1 \to V_2$ and a partial mapping $\sigma_{ac}:\Gamma_2 \to \Gamma_1$ s.t.:

1. For every $v \in V_1$, $o \in out(V_1)$, $i \in inp(V_1)$, $h \in int(V_1)$: $Sort_2(\sigma_{var}(v))=Sort_1(v)$, $\sigma_{var}(o) \in out(V_2)$, $\sigma_{var}(i) \in out(V_2) \cup inp(V_2)$ and $\sigma_{var}(h) \in int(V_2)$;

2. For every $g \in sh(\Gamma_2)$ s.t. $\sigma_{ac}(g)$ is defined and $g' \in prv(\Gamma_2)$ s.t. $\sigma_{ac}(g')$ is defined: $\sigma_{ac}(g) \in sh(\Gamma_1)$ and $\sigma_{ac}(g') \in prv(\Gamma_1)$;

3. For every $g \in \Gamma_2$ s.t. $\sigma_{ac}(g)$ is defined and $v \in loc(V_1)$: $\sigma_{var}(D_1(\sigma_{ac}(g)) \subseteq D_2(g)$ and $\sigma_{ac}(D_2(\sigma_{var}(v)) \subseteq D_1(v)$;

4. For every $g \in \Gamma_2$ s.t. $\sigma_{ac}(g)$ is defined and $v \in D_1(\sigma_{ac}(g))$: $\vdash (F_2(g,\sigma_{var}(v)) \subseteq \sigma(F_1(\sigma_{ac}(g),v)))$;

5. $\vdash (I_2 \supset \sigma(I_1))$;

6. For every $g \in \Gamma_2$ s.t. $\sigma_{ac}(g)$ is defined, $\vdash (B_2(g) \supset \sigma(B_1(\sigma_{ac}(g))))$;

7. For every $g \in \Gamma_2$ s.t. $\sigma_{ac}(g)$ is defined, $\vdash (U_2(g) \supset \sigma(U_1(\sigma_{ac}(g))))$.

Programs and program morphisms constitute a category **c-PROG**. ∎

A morphism $\sigma:P_1 \to P_2$ identifies a way in which P_1 is a component of the system P_2. The map σ_{var} identifies, for every variable of the component, the corresponding variable in the system and σ_{ac} identifies the action of the component that is involved in each action of the system, if ever. Condition 1 states that sorts, visibility and locality of variables are preserved. Notice, however, that input variables of P_1 may become output variables of P_2. This is because the result of interconnecting an input variable of P_1 with an output variable of another component of P_2 results in an output variable of P_2. Condition 2 indicates that morphisms respect the type of actions (shared/private). Condition 3 means that the domains of variables are preserved and that an action of the system that does not involve an action of the component cannot change any variable of the component. Conditions 4 and 5 correspond to the preserva-tion of the functionality of the component program: (4) the effects of the actions have to be preserved or made more deterministic and (5) initialisation conditions are pre-served. Conditions 6 and 7 allow safety and progress guards to be strengthened but not weakened. Strengthening the safety guard is typical in superposition and reflects the fact that all the components that participate in the execution of a joint action have to give their permission. On the other hand, it is clear that progress for a joint action can only be guaranteed when all the components involved can locally guarantee so.

System configuration in the categorical framework is expressed via diagrams. Morphisms can be used to establish synchronisation between actions of programs P_1 and P_2 labelling diagram nodes as well as the interconnection of input variables of one component with output variables of the other component.

This kind of interaction can be established in a configuration diagram through inter-connections of the form depicted above, where *channel* is essentially a set of input variables and a set of shared actions. Each action of *channel* acts as a *rendez-vous* point where actions from the components can meet (synchronise). Hence, action names act as interaction names as in IP [7]. Each variable of the channel provides for an input/output communication to be established between the components. See [4] for more details on the nature of channels.

Example 4.2. The diagram below defines a configuration in which *Merge* and *Consumer* synchronise on actions *send* and *rec*, and the input variables *i* and *eof* of *Consumer* are instantiated with the output variables *o* and *eof* of *Merge*, respectively.

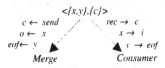

More complex configurations can be described by using other interaction protocols that take the general form

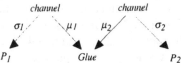

where *Glue* is a program that describes how the activities of both components are co-ordinated in the intended architecture. Such configurations typically arise from the application of architectural connectors to given components of the system, as ex-plained in section 6.

Example 4.3. Consider now the problem of specifying that *Merge* and *Consumer* communicate asynchronously. In this case, we have to interconnect the two programs through a third component modelling a buffer. The buffer coordinates the transmis-sion of messages and informs the *Consumer* when there is no more data to transmit.

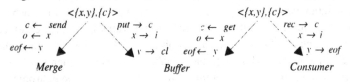

where

```
program Buffer is
var output      o=head(b), eof: bool
    input       i: nat, cl: bool
    internal    b:List(nat), n:nat
init      b=<>∧n=0∧¬eof
do        put : [n<Limit → b:=b^<i> || n:=n+1 ]
[]        get : [¬(n=0) →b:=tail(b) || n:=n-1 ]
[]   prvsig : [ cl∧(n=0) → eof:=true ]
```

The program *Buffer* models a buffer with limited capacify and a FIFO discipline. The private action *sig* is responsible for signaling the end of data to the *Consumer* as soon as the buffer gets empty and *Merge* has already informed, through the channel *cl*, that it will not send anymore data. ∎

Not every diagram expresses a meaningful configuration in the sense that it describes a well configured system. For instance, diagrams in which output variables of different components are connected to one another do not make sense as configurations. Consider that **Var** denotes the forgetful functor from **c-PROG** to **SET** that maps programs to their underlying sets of variables. The class of diagrams that represent correct configurations of interconnected components can be formalised as follows.

Definition 4.4. Given a finite *J*-indexed multi-set of programs $\mathcal{P}$, a configuration diagram of a system with those components is a finite diagram $\iota:I\rightarrow c\text{-}PROG$ s.t.:

1. For every $j\in J$, $j\in |I|$ and $\iota(j)=\mathcal{P}_j$;
2. For every $f:i\rightarrow j$ in I, either ($i=j$ and $f=id_i$) or ($j\in J$ and $i\notin J$ and $\iota(i)$ is a channel);
3. For every $i\in |I|\backslash J$ s.t. $\iota(i)$ is a channel, there exist distinct j,k and morphisms $f:i\rightarrow j$ and $g:i\rightarrow k$ in I;
4. If $\{\mu_i:Var(\iota(i))\rightarrow V: i\in |I|\}$ is a colimit of $\iota;Var$ then, for every $v\in V$, there exists at most one i in I s.t. $\mu_i^{-1}(v)\cap out(V_{\iota(i)})\neq\varnothing$ and, for such i, $\mu_i^{-1}(v)\cap out(V_{\iota(i)})$ is a singleton. ∎

Condition 1 means that every component of a system must be involved in its configuration diagram. Condition 2 states that the elementary interconnections are established through channels. Condition 3 ensures that a configuration diagram does not include channels that are not used. Finally, condition 4 prevents the identification of output variables. The fact that configurations represent systems is proved mathematically by the existence of a colimit for the diagram:

Definition/Proposition 4.5. Given a finite *J*-indexed multi-set of programs $\mathcal{P}$, modelling the components of a system *Sys*, and a configuration diagram ι, describing how these components interact, the program that models *Sys* is the program given by the colimit of ι, which always exists. We denote this program by $\|_\iota\mathcal{P}$. ∎

The colimit of a configuration diagram ι of a system corresponds to the parallel composition of the component programs (the programs that model the components of the system and the glues). Basically, $\|_\iota\mathcal{P}$ is defined as follows:

- the set of input variables of $\|_\iota\mathcal{P}$ consists of the input variables of each component program that are not identified with any output variable of any other component program and the output and internal variables of $\|_\iota\mathcal{P}$ are the (disjoint) union of, respectively, the output and the internal variables of the components;
- the shared actions of $\|_\iota\mathcal{P}$ are the joint actions defined by the synchronisation points and the set of private actions of $\|_\iota\mathcal{P}$ consists of the joint actions that represent the simultaneous execution of private actions of different components;
- the initialisation condition of $\|_\iota\mathcal{P}$ is given by the conjunction of the initialisation conditions of the component programs;
- the actions of $\|_\iota\mathcal{P}$ perform the parallel composition of the assignments of the joint actions and are guarded by the conjunction of the guards of the joint actions.

5   Refinement

A key factor for architectural description is a notion of refinement that can be used to support abstraction. In particular, refinement is necessary when, as illustrated in section 3, one wants to conduct the description of the architecture of a system at the level of the coordination that needs to be established between its components, leaving computational concerns for later stages of design. The notion of refinement can be captured by means of a different class of morphisms between programs.

Definition/Proposition 5.1. A program refinement morphism $\sigma:P_1\rightarrow P_2$ consists of a (total) function $\sigma_{var}:V_1\rightarrow V_2$ and a partial mapping $\sigma_{ac}:\Gamma_2\rightarrow\Gamma_1$ s.t. conditions 1 to 6 of definition 4.1 hold and

7. For every $i\in inp(V_1)$, $\sigma_{var}(i)\in inp(V_2)$ and $\sigma_{var}\downarrow(out(V_1)\cup inp(V_1))$ is injective;
8. For every $g\in sh(\Gamma_1)$, $\sigma^{-1}(g)\neq\varnothing$;
9. For every $g_1\in\Gamma_1$, $\vdash(\sigma(U_1(g_1)))\supset\bigvee_{\sigma_{ac}(g_2)=g_1}U_2(g_2))$.

Programs and refinement morphisms constitute a category **r-PROG**.   ∎

A refinement morphism supports the identification of a way in which a program P_1 is refined by another program P_2. Each variable of P_1 has a corresponding variable in P_2 and each action g of P_1 is implemented by the set of actions $\sigma^{-1}(g)$ in the sense that $\sigma^{-1}(g)$ is a menu of refinements for action g. The actions for which σ_{ac} is left undefined (the new actions) and the variables which are not in $\sigma_{var}(V_1)$ (the new variables) introduce more detail in the description of the program.

Condition 7 ensures that an input variable cannot be made local by refinement (refinement does not alter the border between the system and its environment) and that different variables of the interface cannot be collapsed into a single one. Condition 8 ensures that actions that model interaction between the program and its environment have to be implemented. Condition 9 states that progress guards can be weakened but not strengthened. Indeed, because progress guards represent a requirement on the availability of an action for execution, refinement has to preserve that availability under the conditions established by the progress guard of the abstract program. Naturally, the circumstances under which this availability is guaranteed can be widened, which corresponds to the weakening of the progress guard.

Because condition 6 (see definition 4.1) allows safety guards to be strengthened (which corresponds to the preservation of the safety properties of the abstract program), the "interval" of (allowed) non-determinism defined by the two guards can be reduced by refinement. This is intuitive because refinement, pointing in the direction of implementations, should reduce allowed non-determinism. This is the reason why initialisation conditions can be strengthened and the non-determinism of assignments decreased. Notice that when the two guards coincide there cannot be any further refinement: the enabling condition for the action has been fully determined.

Preservation of required properties (including required non-determinism) and reduction of allowed non-determinism are intrinsic to any notion of refinement, and justify the conditions that we have imposed on morphisms. The morphisms that we used for modelling interconnections do not satisfy these properties. In particular, programs are not necessarily refined by the systems of which they are components,

which is consistent with other notions of refinement and parallel composition, e.g.
CSP [9].

Example 5.2. In order to illustrate refinement consider the following program.

```
program Consumer2 is
var output    cl : bool
    input     i : nat,  eof : bool
    internal  x : nat,  rd : bool,  s : array(nat,N),  k : nat
init          ¬cl∧rd∧k=1
do            rec   : [ ¬eof∧¬cl∧rd∧k<N → x:=i  || rd:=false ]
[] prv        store : [ ¬rd → rd:=true  || s[k]:=x  || k:=k+1 ]
[] prv        close : [ ((eof∧¬cl∧rd)∨k≥N) → cl:=true ]
```

This program refines the program *Consumer* presented in 3.1. The new private action *store* models the storing of the received data in an array. The program is ready to receive a new number only if the previously received number has already been stored and the array is not full. The degree of internal nondeterminism over the action *close* present in the program *Consumer* given in section 3 was eliminated. The program eventually closes the communication if it receives the signal of end of data or reaches a state in which the array is full. ∎

Refinement and interconnection morphisms, though different as justified above, must be related by two important properties for architectural design to be supported. On the one hand, because composite programs are given by colimits and, hence, are defined up to isomorphism, refinement morphisms must be such that programs that are isomorphic with respect to interconnections, refine, and are refined exactly by, the same programs. The morphisms of *r-PROG* satisfy this requirement because isomorphisms in *c-PROG* are also isomorphisms in *r-PROG*.

On the other hand, refinement must be compositional with respect to parallel composition, i.e. it is necessary that a refinement of a composite system can be obtained from arbitrary refinements of its components. This property also holds for the proposed notions of interconnection and refinement. More precisely, given a finite J-indexed multi-set of programs $\mathcal{P}$, a configuration diagram ι of a system with those components, and refinement morphisms $(\eta_j : \mathcal{P}_j \to \mathcal{P}_j')_{j \in J}$, there exists a refinement morphism $\eta : \|_\iota \mathcal{P} \to \|_{\iota'} \mathcal{P}'$, where ι' is the diagram obtained from ι by replacing the subdiagrams of the form

$$channel \xrightarrow{\ \sigma_i\ } P_i \quad \text{by} \quad channel \xrightarrow{\ \sigma_i;\eta_i\ } P'_i$$

where $(\sigma_i;\eta_i)$ denotes the program morphism defined by the composition of the underlying signature morphisms (it is not difficult to show that this construction gives rise to a configuration diagram for $\mathcal{P}'$).

The morphism η is unique if we require the preservation of the design decisions that lead from each $\mathcal{P}_i$ to $\mathcal{P}_i'$, i.e., $\mu_j;\eta=\eta_j;\mu'_j$, for any $j \in J$ where μ_j and μ'_j are the program morphisms which identify $\mathcal{P}_j$ and $\mathcal{P}_j'$, as a component of, respectively, $\|_\iota \mathcal{P}$ and $\|_{\iota'} \mathcal{P}'$.

Let us consider, for instance, a system *Sys* with two components modelled by programs P_1 and P_2 interconnected through a third program as depicted above. The colimit of this diagram is a program P that models *Sys*. By picking up arbitrary refinements of programs P_1 and P_2, we obtain by composition a program P' that refines P and, hence, also models Sys.

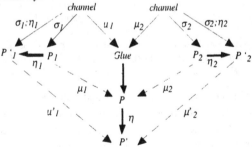

6 Defining and Applying Architectural Connectors

In a previous paper [6], we have shown how architectural connectors in the style of Allen and Garlan [2] can be given a categorical semantics in general, and in the original version of CommUnity in particular.

A connector (type) is defined by an object G – the glue – and a finite set of diagrams of the form depicted above, where each object R models a role of the connector. The roles describe the behaviour required of the components to which the connector can be applied. The glue describes how the activities of these components are coordinated once they instantiate the roles.

Role instantiation was modelled in [6] through the morphisms used for interconnection. However, the correct notion of morphism that models instantiation is the one that corresponds to refinement as argued in [2]. Because refinement is compositional with respect to parallel composition as explained in the previous section, the results developed in [6] are still valid when refinement is used instead of interconnection morphisms to model instantiation. In particular, the meaning of a connector is correctly given by the colimit of its configuration diagram in the sense that the properties inferred at the architectural level are guaranteed to hold in any system that results from the instantiation. Hence, by reasoning about the program resulting from the colimit, we may infer the properties of the underlying protocol.

Example 6.1. As an example, consider the following connector.

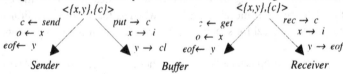

The glue of this connector is the program *Buffer* defined in example 4.4. The connector has two roles – *Sender* and *Receiver* .

program *Sender* **is**
var output $o : nat$, $eof : bool$
    input
    internal $rd : bool$
init $\neg eof \wedge \neg rd$
do $prod :[\neg rd,false \rightarrow o{:}\in nat \,\|rd{:}=true\,]$
  [] $send : [\neg eof \wedge rd ,false \rightarrow rd{:}=false]$
  [] **prv** $close : [\neg eof,false \rightarrow eof{:}=true\,]$

program *Receiver* **is**
var output $cl : bool$
    input $i: nat,\ eof: bool$
    internal
init $\neg cl$
do $rec : [\ \neg eof \wedge \neg cl ,false \rightarrow$ **skip** $\ ]$
  [] **prv** $close : [\neg cl, \neg cl \wedge eof \rightarrow cl{:}=true\ ]$

This connector is usually called a *pipe* [19] and describes the interaction protocol we used in example 4.4. More concretely, it defines asynchronous message passing through a channel with limited capacity that preserves the order of transmission. Furthermore, it defines that the sender has to signal the end of data (through the output variable *eof*) and the receiver is obliged to close the communication as soon as it is informed that there will be no more data. Notice that progress guards are essential to impose this restriction on the behaviour of the receiver and also to leave unspecified when and how many messages the sender (receiver) will send (receive). We chose the least deterministic assignment for the production of messages (denoted by the sort symbol *nat*) in order to avoid committing to a particular discipline of production.

The semantics of the connector is given by the parallel composition of *Sender*, *Receiver* and *Buffer* with the restrictions defined by the configuration diagram. By reasoning about the behaviour of this program it is possible to conclude, for instance, that the correctness of the transmission/reception of data does not depend on the order in which each role processes the data.

The programs *Merge* and *Consumer*, defined in 3.1, refine, respectively, the role *Sender* and *Receiver* (through inclusion morphisms in_1 and in_2) and, hence, the connector *pipe* can be used to interconnect these components.

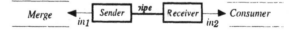

7   Concluding Remarks

This paper was motivated by the need to promote higher levels of abstraction in architectural design while maintaining the separation between the description of component behaviour and the interaction protocols that coordinate their interaction. For this purpose, we investigated extensions to parallel program design based on the use of explicit state variables to accommodate the action-based discipline of interaction that is typical of process-based languages. The idea was to bring together the benefits of the two approaches: the explicit modelling of state facilitates the description of the components of a system in terms of some abstract state whereas the communication features of process languages are ideal for specifying the interaction of the components of a system in a given architecture.

In order to discuss specific proposals and illustrate them over typical examples, our study focused on an extension of the language CommUnity proposed in [5] as an action-based version of Unity. The proposed extension integrates primitives that support non-determinism, choice and fairness, and refinement principles that are compositional with respect to interconnection. The distinction between allowed and required non-determinism motivated another fundamental change to CommUnity. Following Goguen's categorical approach to General Systems Theory [8], we had already proposed in previous papers (e.g. [6]) the adoption of Category Theory for formalising architectural principles and constructions. The work reported in this paper made it clear that separate notions of morphism are necessary for modelling component interconnection during system configuration, and refinement for moving between different levels of abstraction. Similar distinctions were already recognised in [14] for specifications of system behaviourin temporal logic. Work is underway towards the integration of specifications and CommUnity designs in the proposed categorical framework.

A different approach for combining process-based languages and state-based languages is the integration of existing languages, e.g., Z and Lotos [10] or Object-Z and CSP [20]. The advantages of the approach developed herein over such integrations are the following. On the one hand, it is not necessary to consider different specification languages for different aspects of the same system. Instead, CommUnity supports the description of the system at different levels of abstraction. Typically, the initial stages of design are concerned with the architecture of the system (at the coordination level), leaving the detailed description of the functionality of the components for later stages of design. On the other hand, our framework supports the description of connectors as well as their instantiation, at system configuration time, with concrete components for the incremental construction of structured systems, something that is out of the scope of the hybrids mentioned above.

On the contrary, an approach that seems more promising is the extension of existing languages and methods in ways similar to the proposed extension of Community. The relationship between program design based on guarded-commands and specification methods such as B, VDM or Z suggests that the use of private actions and progress guards could be integrated in those methods. The impact of adopting progress guards (for shared actions) on specification languages like B and VDM^{++} was already analysed in [13]. Further work is in progress that investigates the feasibility of these extensions.

References

1. M.Abadi and L.Lamport, "Composing Specifications", *ACM TOPLAS*, 15(1):73-132, 1993.
2. R.Allen and D.Garlan, "A Formal Basis for Architectural Connectors", *ACM TOSEM*, 6(3):213-249,1997.
3. K.Chandy and J.Misra, *Parallel Program Design - A Foundation*, Addison-Wesley 1988.
4. J.L.Fiadeiro and A.Lopes, "Algebraic Semantics of Coordination", in *AMAST'98*, Springer-Verlag, in print.

5. J.L.Fiadeiro and T.Maibaum, "Categorical Semantics of Parallel Program Design", *Science of Computer Programming*, 28:111-138,1997.

6. J.L.Fiadeiro and A.Lopes, "Semantics of Architectural Connectors", in *TAPSOFT'97*, LNCS 1214, Springer-Verlag 1997, 505-519.

7. N.Francez and I.Forman, *Interacting Processes*, Addison-Wesley 1996.

8. J.Goguen, "Categorical Foundations for General Systems Theory", in F.Pichler and R.Trappl (eds) *Advances in Cybernetics and Systems Research*, Transcripta Books 1973, 121-130.

9. C.A.R Hoare, *Communicating Sequential Processes*, Prentice-Hall, 1985.

10. ITU Recommendation X.901-904, *Open Distributed Processing - Ref. Model*, July 1995.

11. R.Kuiper, "Enforcing Nondeterminism via Linear Temporal Logic Specifications using Hiding", in B.Banieqbal, H.Barringer and A.Pnueli (eds), *Temporal Logic in Specification*, LNCS 398, Springer-Verlag 1989, 295-303.

12. L.Lamport, "The Temporal Logic of Actions", *ACM TOPLAS*, 16(3):872-923, 1994.

13. K.Lano, J.Bicarregui, J.L.Fiadeiro and A.Lopes, "Specification of Required Non-determinism", in J.Fitzgerald, C.Jones and P.Lucas (eds), *Formal Methods Europe 1997*, LNCS 1313, 298-317, Springer-Verlag, 1997.

14. A.Lopes and J.L.Fiadeiro,"Preservation and Reflection in Specification", in *AMAST'97*, M.Johnson (ed), LNCS 1349, 380-394, Springer-Verlag, 1997.

15. D.C.Luckham and J.Vera, "An event-based architecture definition language", *IEEE TOSE*, 21(9):717-734,1995.

16. J.Magee and J.Kramer, "Dynamic Structure in Software Architecures", in *4th Symp. on Foundations of Software Engineering*, ACM Press 1996, 3-14.

17. Z.Manna and A.Pnueli, *The Temporal Logic of Reactive and Concurrent Systems*, Springer-Verlag, 1991.

18. B.Meyer, "Applying Design by Contract", *IEEE Computer*, Oct.1992, 40-51.

19. M.Shaw and D.Garlan, *Software Architecture: Perspectives on an Emerging Discipline*, Prentice Hall, 1996.

20. G.Smith, "A Semantic Integration of Object-Z and CSP for the Specification of Concurrent Systems", in J.Fitzgerald, C.Jones and P.Lucas (eds), *Formal Methods Europe 1997*, LNCS 1313, 62-81, Springer-Verlag, 1997.

On the Evolution of Reactive Components
– A Process-Algebraic Approach –

Markus Müller-Olm[1], Bernhard Steffen[1], and Rance Cleaveland[2]

[1] Dept. of Comp. Sci., University of Dortmund, 44221 Dortmund, Germany
{mmo,steffen}@cs.uni-dortmund.de
[2] Dept. of Comp. Sci., SUNY at Stony Brook, Stony Brook, NY 11794-4400, USA
rance@cs.sunysb.edu

Abstract. A common problem in library-based programming is the *downward compatibility* problem: will a program using an existing version of a library continue to function correctly with an upgraded version? As a step toward addressing this problem for libraries of *reactive* components we develop a theory that equips components with *interface languages* characterizing the interaction patterns user applications may engage in with the component. We then show how these languages may be used to build *upgrade specifications* from components and their interface languages. Intuitively, upgrade specifications explicitly describe requirements an (improved) implementation of a component must satisfy and are intended for use by library developers. Under certain reasonable assumptions about the contexts components are to be used in we show that our upgrade specifications are complete in the sense that every correct upgrade of a component is related in a precise manner to its upgrade specification. In particular, these results hold if the language being used to develop contexts is CSP or CCS.

Keywords: action transducer, bisimulation, context, interface language, downward compatibility, process-algebra, refinement.

1 Introduction

Practical software development relies heavily on the use of *libraries* of previously implemented components. By allowing the cost of module development to be amortized over the number of systems that use the modules, libraries contribute to substantially cheaper software. As library components are also subjected to more rigorous validation by virtue of their inclusion in different systems, using them judiciously can also improve the reliability of systems. These obvious benefits have led to a profusion of libraries in a variety of different application areas in programming.

A common problem in library-based programming is the *upgrade* (or *downward compatibility*) problem: given an "improved" version of an existing library, will applications using the existing version of the library continue to function correctly without modification? Users and implementors would clearly wish this

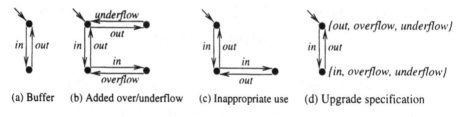

(a) Buffer   (b) Added over/underflow   (c) Inappropriate use   (d) Upgrade specification

Fig. 1. A one-place buffer and its "upgrade".

to be the case, and yet anyone who has maintained a program knows that this rarely holds.

A partial solution in widespread use in the realm of sequential programming relies on the use of component *types* as "interface specifications" (one need only consider the myriad of .h files in existence to see the prevalence of such specifications). Clearly, preservation of types in an upgrade is far too weak to guarantee full downward compatibility, as two procedures may behave quite differently even though they share the same type. If, however, we focus solely on the interaction pattern between components and applications, types indeed provide "full" information: a user need only know the types of parameters and results to interact correctly with a procedure, as a procedure's "interaction pattern" consists of strictly alternating sequences of calls and returns.

The situation for *reactive* components is different. Such components are intended to maintain an ongoing interaction with the system in which they are used, as in control software (e.g. for avionics systems) or user interfaces (e.g. window managers). In this case traditional type information is clearly inadequate, as a component can input and output several times during its execution. Even a component's alphabet of input and output actions, which may be viewed as analogous to type information, says little about allowed interaction patterns, as the next paragraph shows.

As a small but motivating example of the subtle problems arising in upgrades of reactive libraries, consider a library containing an implementation of a one-place buffer as pictured in Fig. 1(a). The programmer's system accesses this buffer via the actions *in* (for input) and *out* (for output), with the buffer initially being empty.

Suppose users complain that a one-place buffer reporting under- and overflows would be far more convenient. In order to address these complaints the maintainer of the library might decide to enhance its functionality by providing the innocuously looking upgrade shown in Fig. 1(b). The question now confronting the programmer and the maintainer is this: can systems constructed using the old buffer component safely use the new implementation of the buffer? As the alphabet of the new component includes that of the old, one would be tempted to say "yes"; however, note that the system in Fig. 1(c) can lead to deadlock when connected with the new component but not with the old. Traditional results of process algebra are also of little use in answering this question, since no reasonable notion of semantic equivalence or refinement would relate the new buffer to the old one. Indeed, in the absence of any information about the context in which the buffer is being used, the only safe answer to this question would be "no".

On the other hand, suppose that the developer of the original buffer module equipped it with the regular *interface language* $(in.out)^*.(in + \varepsilon)$ expressing the (otherwise implicit) assumption that a user could assume a one-place buffer behavior *only if* his system neither tries to store more than one element nor to extract an element from an empty buffer. The system in Fig. 1(c) does not obey this interface language and hence one would not expect to be able to use the buffer upgrade with this system. An upgrade of a module providing additional functionality could have an enlarged interface language in order to allow access to the new capabilities in future systems. The new buffer, e.g., could be equipped with the extended interface language $(in + out + underflow + overflow)^*$. A smaller language might be chosen in order to preserve more potential for future upgrades.

In this paper we study the utility of furnishing reactive components with interface information in the form of such (prefix-closed) interface languages containing the sequences of input and output actions that applications are permitted to exchange with the component. Given such interface information, we define what it means for an upgrade to be correct, and we show that from an interface and a component, one can characterize the correct upgrades of a component via a single labeled-transition-system-like specification. These specifications, which we term *upgrade specifications*, are of particular use to library developers, as they clearly indicate what information in a component must be preserved in order for a component to be downward compatible.

The remainder of the paper develops along the following lines. The next section presents the operational models of components and contexts that we use in our technical development. Section 3 defines the space of upgrade specifications and the next section establishes the main result of this paper, namely, that the correct replacements of a component given a certain interface language can be characterized by a single upgrade specification. The section following then shows that our results hold even for restricted classes of contexts such as the parallel contexts of CCS [9] or CSP [4], and the final section contains our conclusions and directions for future research and discusses related work.

2 Processes and Contexts

Processes. We model processes (components) by labeled transition systems with a designated start state. Formally, a process is a quadruple $P = (S, A, \rightarrow, p_0)$, where S is a set of *states*, A is an *alphabet of actions* that the process might exchange with its environment in a single computation step, $\rightarrow \subseteq S \times A \times S$ is a *transition relation*, and $p_0 \in S$ is the *start state*. We denote the set of processes with action alphabet A by Proc_A and the letters P and Q range over processes.

Given a process P, we write $S_P, A_P, \rightarrow_P$ and p_0 to refer to its state set, alphabet of actions, transition relation, and start state, respectively, and use (possibly decorated versions of) the corresponding lower case letter – p in this case – to range over S_P. P is called *finite-state* if both S_P and A_P are finite. The relationship $(p, a, p') \in \rightarrow$, for which we write $p \xrightarrow{a} p'$ in the following, indicates that in state p, P can evolve to state p' under the observation of a. We generalize the transition relation $\rightarrow$ to words $w \in A^*$ by the usual inductive definition:

$$p \xrightarrow{\varepsilon} p' \text{ iff } p = p' \qquad \text{and} \qquad p \xrightarrow{w \cdot a} p' \text{ iff } \exists p'' : p \xrightarrow{w} p'' \wedge p'' \xrightarrow{a} p' \,,$$

where ε is the empty word, $w \in A^*$, and $a \in A$. The language of a state $p \in S$ is the set $L(p) = \{w \mid \exists p' : p \xrightarrow{w} p'\}$. The language $L(P)$ of process P is the language $L(p_0)$ of its initial state.

A state $p \in S$ is called *reachable* if there is a word $w \in A^*$ such that $p_0 \xrightarrow{w} p$ and a process is called *deterministic* if for any reachable $p \in S$ and $a \in A$ at most one $p' \in S$ exists such that $p \xrightarrow{a} p'$.

Contexts. We adopt the framework of Larsen and Xinxin [7,8] and use *action transducers* as basic operational model of contexts. The idea is to interpret contexts as special transition systems that *consume* actions from the inner *parameter processes* and produce actions for the environment. For the purpose of this paper only unary contexts are needed, i.e. contexts having just one parameter process. Formally, a *context* is a structure $C = (S, A, B, \rightarrow, c_0)$, where S is a set of *context states*, A is the action alphabet of the parameter process, B is the action alphabet of the resulting process, $\rightarrow \subseteq S \times (A \cup \{0\}) \times B \times S$ is the *transduction relation*, and c_0 is the *start state* of the context. Here 0 is assumed to be a distinguished non-action symbol; in particular, $0 \notin A$.

The letter C ranges over contexts and we assume, as for processes, that the constituting parts of a context C can be referenced by S_C, A_C etc. Moreover, c and variables derived from c by decoration range over S_C. The set of contexts for processes with alphabet A is $\mathsf{Ctx}_A = \{C \mid C \text{ is a context and } A_C = A\}$. Note that we allow contexts with different inner and outer alphabet and assume a designated start state in contrast to Larsen and Xinxin in [7,8].

We often use the intuitive notation $c \xrightarrow{b}_a_C c'$ in favor of $(c, a, b, c') \in \rightarrow_C$ and call this a *transduction*. A transduction where $a \neq 0$ is interpreted as follows: if the context is currently in state c it can "consume" an a-labeled transition from the parameter process and evolve to its state c', producing action b in doing so. A transduction with $a = 0$ represents an autonomous step of the context, i.e. a step without an interaction with the parameter process. Formally this intuition is captured by the following definition.

Definition 1 (Context application). *Suppose that C and P are such that $A_C = A_P$. Then $C(P)$ is the process $(S_C \times S_P, B_C, \rightarrow, c_0(p_0))$, where the transition relation $\rightarrow$ is the smallest relation obeying the following two rules:*

$$\frac{p \xrightarrow{a}_P p' \,,\ c \xrightarrow{b}_a_C c'}{c(p) \xrightarrow{b} c'(p')} \qquad\qquad \frac{c \xrightarrow{b}_0_C c'}{c(p) \xrightarrow{b} c'(p)}$$

Here and in the following we use the notation $c(p)$ for pairs $(c, p) \in S_C \times S_P$.

It is well-known that transition systems are a rather fine-grained model of processes. Therefore various equivalences have been studied in the literature that identify processes on the basis of their behavior. In this paper we consider the classic notion of (strong) bisimulation [10, 9].

Definition 2 (Bisimulations). *Suppose P, Q are processes with same action alphabet, i.e. $A_P = A_Q$. A relation $R \subseteq S_P \times S_Q$ is called a* bisimulation *if for all $(p, q) \in R$ the following two conditions hold:*

- *$\forall a, p' : p \xrightarrow{a}_P p' \Rightarrow \exists q' : q \xrightarrow{a}_Q q' \wedge (p', q') \in R$, and*
- *$\forall a, q' : q \xrightarrow{a}_Q q' \Rightarrow \exists p' : p \xrightarrow{a}_P p' \wedge (p', q') \in R$.*

Define $\sim$ to be the union of all bisimulations R. The processes P and Q are called bisimilar, *$P \sim Q$ for short, if $p_0 \sim q_0$.*

It is well-known that $\sim$ is the largest bisimulation on $S_P \times S_Q$. It is also straightforward to prove that any context preserves bisimilarity, i.e. that $P \sim Q$ implies $C(P) \sim C(Q)$.

Interface Languages. The language consisting of all words in A_C^* that a context C potentially exchanges with parameter processes is called its *interface language.* Its formal definition is based on the straightforward inductive extension of the transduction relation $\to_C$ to words:

$$c \xrightarrow{\epsilon}_{\epsilon} c' \text{ iff } c = c' \quad \text{and} \quad c \xrightarrow{w \cdot b}_{v \cdot a} c' \text{ iff } \exists c'' : c \xrightarrow{w}_{v} c'' \wedge c'' \xrightarrow{b}_{a} c' ,$$

where $v \in (A_C \cup \{0\})^*$ and $w \in B_C^*$ are words of equal length and $a \in A_C$, $b \in B_C$. Moreover, the word resulting from removing all occurrences of 0 from a word $v \in A \cup \{0\}$ is denoted by $\hat{v}$. Now, the interface language of C is $\mathsf{IL}(C) = \{\hat{v} \mid \exists w, c : c_0 \xrightarrow{w}_{v}_C c\}$. It is easy to see that $\mathsf{IL}(C)$ is prefix-closed. We say that C *respects* a language $L \subseteq A^*$ if $\mathsf{IL}(C) \subseteq L$.

3 Process Specifications and the Refinement Preorder

We may now formalize the setup indicated in the introduction. An *interface* for a component (=process) P is simply a prefix-closed language $L \subseteq A_P^*$, and describes the protocol agreed upon for using P. Then a new component (=process) Q is a correct upgrade of an old component P that is equipped with interface language L, if it behaves as P in connection with any context that respects L, i.e. if it is drawn from the following set of processes:

$$\mathcal{U}_{P,L} \stackrel{\text{def}}{=} \{Q \in \mathsf{Proc}_A \mid \forall C \in \mathsf{Ctx}_A : \mathsf{IL}(C) \subseteq L \Rightarrow C(P) \sim C(Q)\} .$$

Note that we use strong bisimulation as notion of global behavioral coincidence. $\mathcal{U}_{P,L}$ is thus the set of correct *upgrades of P w.r.t. L*.

As mentioned, interface languages are quite useful for module users, since they provide information they can check their systems against, but less useful to implementors, who would likely prefer a representation that more explicitly states the allowable implementation choices for upgrades. The remainder of this paper is devoted to showing that any set of upgrades can be characterized by a single element in a certain space of simple behavioral *process specifications* that extends the space of processes and is equipped with a behavioral, bisimulation-like refinement preorder.

Definition 3 (Process specifications). *A* process specification *is a pair $\mathcal{P} = (P, \uparrow)$ consisting of a process P and an* undefinedness predicate $\uparrow \subseteq S_P \times A_P$.

In the following we write $p \uparrow a$ in lieu of $(p, a) \in \uparrow$ and call this an a-undefinedness of state p. Moreover, we write $p \downarrow a$ as an abbreviation for $\neg(p \uparrow a)$. The intuitive interpretation of an a-undefinedness of a state p is that a-transitions from state p are completely irrelevant and might thus arbitrarily be removed or added. This intuition is formally captured by the notion of the refinement preorder defined below.

We use calligraphic letters $\mathcal{P}, \mathcal{Q}$ to denote process specifications. The corresponding italic letters P, Q refer to the embodied processes, and we continue to refer to their constituting parts by $S_P, A_P, \ldots, (S_Q, A_Q, \ldots)$ and extend this convention by referring to the undefinedness predicates by $\uparrow_P$ and $\uparrow_Q$.

A process specification $\mathcal{P} = (P, \uparrow)$ is called *total* if no reachable state p has an undefinednesses, i.e. if $p \downarrow a$ for all $a \in A_P$ and reachable $p \in S_P$. Total process specifications correspond to processes, and henceforth we will identify a process P with the corresponding total process specification $(P, \emptyset)$. The definition of the application of contexts to processes extends in a natural way to specifications.

Definition 4 (Application of contexts to specifications). *Suppose $\mathcal{P} = (P, \uparrow_P)$ is a process specification and C is a context such that $A_P = A_C$. $C(\mathcal{P})$ is the process specification $(C(P), \uparrow)$, where the undefinedness predicate $\uparrow$ is the smallest predicate obeying the rule:*

$$\frac{p \uparrow_P a \,, \; c \xrightarrow{\;b\;}_C c'}{c(p) \uparrow b}$$

Note that for a process P, $C((P, \emptyset))$ equals $(C(P), \emptyset)$, the total specification corresponding to $C(P)$.

Definition 5 (Refinement preorder). *Suppose $\mathcal{P} = (P, \uparrow_P)$ and $\mathcal{Q} = (Q, \uparrow_Q)$ are process specifications with the same alphabet $(A_P = A_Q)$. A relation $R \subseteq S_P \times S_Q$ is called a* pre-bisimulation *if for all $(p, q) \in R$ and $a \in A_P$ with $p \downarrow_P a$ the following three conditions hold:*

- $q \downarrow_Q a$,
- $\forall p' : p \xrightarrow{a}_P p' \Rightarrow \exists q' : q \xrightarrow{a}_Q q' \wedge (p', q') \in R$, *and*
- $\forall q' : q \xrightarrow{a}_Q q' \Rightarrow \exists p' : p \xrightarrow{a}_P p' \wedge (p', q') \in R$.

Define $\preceq$ to be the union of all pre-bisimulations R. Given process specifications $\mathcal{P}$ and $\mathcal{Q}$, we write $\mathcal{P} \preceq \mathcal{Q}$ if $p_0 \preceq q_0$. We call $\mathcal{Q}$ a refinement of $\mathcal{P}$ in this case.

Standard arguments establish that $\preceq$ is itself a pre-bisimulation (viz. the largest one) and a preorder (i.e. a reflexive and transitive relation) on process specifications. We call it the *refinement preorder* and denote its kernel $\preceq \cap \succeq$ by $\asymp$. Moreover, it is easy to see that the notions of bisimulation and pre-bisimulation coincide for processes (i.e. total specifications) because processes possess no undefinednesses.

Contexts are monotonic w.r.t. the refinement preorder, i.e. $P \preceq Q$ implies $C(P) \preceq C(Q)$ for process specifications $\mathcal{P}, \mathcal{Q}$ and contexts C with $A_P = A_Q = A_C$. This monotonicity result generalizes the compositionality of contexts w.r.t. strong bisimulation, as $\sim$ and $\preceq$ coincide for total process specifications.

A process specification $\mathcal{P}$ can be interpreted as representing the set $\mathcal{I}(\mathcal{P}) \overset{\text{def}}{=} \{Q \in \text{Proc}_A \mid \mathcal{P} \preceq Q\}$ of all refining processes, its *implementations*. Note that $\mathcal{I}(\mathcal{P})$ contains only the *total* refinements of $\mathcal{P}$, i.e. processes, not (proper) process specifications. Transitivity of $\preceq$ implies that smaller processes have more implementations, i.e., $\mathcal{P} \preceq \mathcal{Q}$ implies $\mathcal{I}(\mathcal{P}) \supseteq \mathcal{I}(\mathcal{Q})$.

4 Characterizing Replacement Sets by Process Specifications

Given a process P and an interface language L, we would like to construct a process specification $\mathcal{S}_{P,L}$, the upgrade specification promised in the introduction. Clearly, we expect that all implementations of $\mathcal{S}_{P,L}$ can replace P in any context C that respects L. This requirement, which we call $\mathcal{S}_{P,L}$'s *soundness* in the following, can be expressed by the following inclusion:

Soundness $\qquad\qquad\qquad\qquad \mathcal{I}(\mathcal{S}_{P,L}) \subseteq \mathcal{U}_{P,L}$.

Preferably, $\mathcal{S}_{P,L}$ should be as small as possible w.r.t. $\preceq$ in order to characterize as many valid replacements for P as possible. Ideally, we would like that it even characterizes *all* valid replacements for P, which can be expressed by

Completeness $\qquad\qquad\qquad\qquad \mathcal{I}(\mathcal{S}_{P,L}) \supseteq \mathcal{U}_{P,L}$.

We call this property $\mathcal{S}_{P,L}$'s *completeness*. We will see that we can indeed construct $\mathcal{S}_{P,L}$ so that it is both sound and complete.

4.1 Construction of Upgrade Specifications

As L is assumed to be prefix-closed, there is a deterministic process, Q, whose language equals L. One possible construction of such a process Q is the following: as states we take languages over A, i.e. $S_Q \subseteq 2^{A^*}$, the alphabet of Q is $A_Q = A$, the transition relation is defined by the rule

$$\frac{\{w \mid a \cdot w \in q\} \neq \emptyset}{q \xrightarrow{a}_Q \{w \mid a \cdot w \in q\}}$$

and the initial state is $q_0 = L$. More precisely, we restrict S_Q to the languages reachable via $\to_Q$-transitions from $q_0 = L$. If L is regular, Q corresponds to the minimal deterministic automaton detecting L and, therefore, it is intuitive to call Q also in general the *minimal deterministic process* for the language L.

The observation underlying the construction of $S_{P,L}$ now is the following: if a component P and a process Q as above run in parallel in a synchronous fashion inside a context C respecting L, then the fact that Q has no a-transition in a certain state means that C cannot consume an a-action in the next step (since it respects L). Therefore, in such a state addition or removal of a-transitions does not change the behavior visible to the environment.

This suggest the following definition: $S_{P,L} = ((S, A, \to, (p_0, q_0)), \uparrow)$, where $S = S_P \times S_Q$ (Q is the minimal deterministic process for L from above) and $\to \subseteq S \times A \times S$ and $\uparrow \subseteq S \times A$ are the smallest relations obeying the rules

$$\frac{p \xrightarrow{a}_P p' , \; q \xrightarrow{a}_Q q'}{(p,q) \xrightarrow{a} (p',q')} \qquad \text{and} \qquad \frac{\neg \exists q' : q \xrightarrow{a}_Q q'}{(p,q) \uparrow a} \; .$$

In place of Q we could use any deterministic process with language L. We refer to the *minimal* deterministic process here only for purpose of unique definition.

As an example, we present in Fig. 1(d) the upgrade specification $S_{P,L}$, where P is the one-place buffer from Fig. 1(a) and $L = (in.out)^*.(in + \varepsilon)$ is its interface language as discussed in the introduction. Note that in this case the minimal deterministic process for L just looks like P itself. Note also that both the original as well as the upgraded buffer from Fig. 1 are refinements of the upgrade specification $S_{P,L}$.

We clearly expect that P implements $S_{P,L}$.

Proposition 6. $S_{P,L} \preceq P$ for all $P \in \text{Proc}_A$ and prefix-closed $L \subseteq A^*$.

An intuitive proof of this proposition is that $S_{P,L}$ can be thought to be constructed from P by the following three transformations, the first and third of which obviously preserve $\asymp$ and the second of which leads to a process that is weaker w.r.t. the refinement preorder $\preceq$:

1. P is unrolled appropriately;
2. a-undefinednesses are added at the states of the unrolled transition system for which further a-evolution is prohibited by L;
3. all a-transitions are removed from states that now contain an a-undefinedness.

4.2 Soundness of Upgrade Specifications

From the intuition underlying the construction of $S_{P,L}$ it is clear that a context C respecting L will never try to exchange an action a with $S_{P,L}$ for which $S_{P,L}$ is undefined. The following lemma intuitively is a consequence of this fact.

Lemma 7. If $\mathsf{IL}(C) \subseteq L$, then $C(S_{P,L})$ is total.

Proof. Suppose $\mathsf{IL}(C) \subseteq L$. We have to show that no reachable state in $C(\mathcal{S}_{P,L})$ has an undefinedness. Let $\mathsf{IL}(c) = \{\hat{v} \mid \exists w, c' : c \xrightarrow{w}_{v}{}_C c'\}$ be the interface language of a state $c \in S_C$.

Suppose that Q is the minimal deterministic process for L used in the construction of $\mathcal{S}_{P,L}$. The states of $C(\mathcal{S}_{P,L})$ have the form $c(p,q)$, where $c \in S_C$, $p \in S_P$, and $q \in S_Q$. Consider the set $G = \{c(p,q) \mid \mathsf{IL}(c) \subseteq L(q)\}$. It is easy to show the following three properties of G:

a) G contains the initial state $c_0(p_0, q_0)$ of $C(\mathcal{S}_{P,L})$.
b) G is closed under transitions of $C(\mathcal{S}_{P,L})$.
c) No state in G has an undefinedness.

These properties suffice to prove the lemma: a) and b) together imply that G contains all reachable states of $C(\mathcal{S}_{P,L})$; c) then yields that no reachable state has an undefinedness. $\qquad \square$

It is now easy to show that a process P can be replaced in a context respecting L by any implementation of $\mathcal{S}_{P,L}$.

Theorem 8 (Single contexts). *Suppose $C \in \mathsf{Ctx}_A$ is a context respecting L and $P, Q \in \mathsf{Proc}_A$ are processes. Then $\mathcal{S}_{P,L} \preceq Q$ implies $C(P) \sim C(Q)$.*

Proof. Suppose $\mathcal{S}_{P,L} \preceq Q$. As contexts are monotonic w.r.t. $\preceq$, we can infer that $C(\mathcal{S}_{P,L}) \preceq C(Q)$. By Lemma 7, $C(\mathcal{S}_{P,L})$ is total. As $\preceq$ and $\sim$ coincide for total processes we thus have $C(\mathcal{S}_{P,L}) \sim C(Q)$. In the same way we can infer $C(\mathcal{S}_{P,L}) \sim C(P)$ because $\mathcal{S}_{P,L} \preceq P$ (Proposition 6). We obtain thus $C(P) \sim C(Q)$ as $\sim$ is an equivalence. $\qquad \square$

The claim of the above theorem might be called 'soundness of $\mathcal{S}_{P,L}$ for single contexts'. As a corollary, we obtain the soundness of $\mathcal{S}_{P,L}$.

Corollary 9 (Soundness). $\mathcal{I}(\mathcal{S}_{P,L}) \subseteq \mathcal{U}_{P,L}$.

Proof. Suppose that $Q \in \mathcal{I}(\mathcal{S}_{P,L})$. By definition of $\mathcal{I}(\mathcal{S}_{P,L})$, $\mathcal{S}_{P,L} \preceq Q$. By Theorem 8 we have for any of the contexts $C \in \mathsf{Ctx}_A$ considered in the definition of $\mathcal{U}_{P,L}$, $C(P) \sim C(Q)$. Thus $Q \in \mathcal{U}_{P,L}$. $\qquad \square$

4.3 Completeness of Upgrade Specifications

The proof of $\mathcal{S}_{P,L}$'s completeness relies on the converse of the implication

$$C(P) \sim C(Q) \Rightarrow \mathcal{S}_{P,L} \preceq Q$$

in Theorem 8 for certain contexts. In general, however, this implication, which expresses 'completeness of $\mathcal{S}_{P,L}$ for single contexts' is invalid in the situation of Theorem 8. Note that completeness of $\mathcal{S}_{P,L}$ only means validity of the weaker implication

$$(\forall C : \mathsf{IL}(C) \subseteq L \Rightarrow C(P) \sim C(Q)) \Rightarrow \mathcal{S}_{P,L} \preceq Q .$$

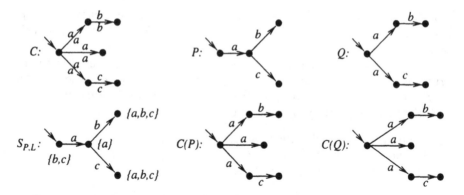

Fig. 2. Incompleteness for non-deterministic context.

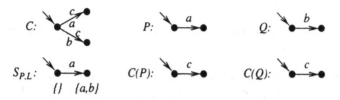

Fig. 3. Incompleteness for non-distinctive context.

The following three phenomena contribute to the incompleteness for single contexts.

Firstly, a context can have different transductions which consume the same action from the parameter process and produce the same action for the environment but lead to different context states. We say then that the context is *non-deterministic*. An example is shown in Fig. 2, where the undefinedness predicate $\uparrow$ of $S_{P,L}$ is shown by annotating the states with the set of actions for which it is undefined. The alphabets in the example of Fig. 2 are $A = B = \{a, b, c\}$ and $L = \mathsf{IL}(C) = \{\varepsilon, a, ab, ac\}$. Clearly, $C(P) \sim C(Q)$ but $S_{P,L} \preceq Q$ does not hold. The problem is that due to the non-determinism of the context the branching structure of a parameter process P need not necessarily be preserved in correct replacements Q for that context. Like bisimulation, however, the refinement preorder $\preceq$ preserves branching.

Secondly, a context can exchange different actions with its parameter process and yet produce the same observable behavior. We say that the context is *not distinctive* in this case. A simple example is given in Fig. 3 where the alphabets are $A = \{a, b\}$, $B = \{c\}$ and L is chosen to be $\mathsf{IL}(C) = \{\varepsilon, a, b\}$. Again $C(P) \sim C(Q)$, although $S_{P,L} \preceq Q$ does not hold. Correct replacements in contexts that are not distinctive cannot (always) completely be described by a process specification because $\preceq$ preserves the identity of actions.

A third, somewhat less severe problem is that C can have a properly smaller interface language than L. A very simple example of this kind is presented in Fig. 4. Here, $A = \{a\}$ and B is arbitrary. We choose $L = A^*$ which certainly is

$$C: \quad\bullet \qquad P: \quad\bullet \qquad Q: \quad\bullet \xrightarrow{a} \bullet \qquad C(P) = C(Q): \quad\bullet \qquad S_{P,L}: \quad\bullet \; \{\}$$

Fig. 4. Incompleteness for context with a strictly smaller interface language.

a superset of $\mathsf{IL}(C) = \emptyset$. Trivially, $C(P) \sim C(Q)$ but $S_{P,L} \preceq Q$ is invalid. The problem is that L requires the preservation of more from the behavior of the parameter process P than necessary for the context C.

Before we proceed, let us define the notion of deterministic and distinctive contexts referred to above.

Definition 10 (Deterministic and distinctive contexts). *A context* $C = (S, A, B, \rightarrow, s)$ *is called* deterministic *if for all* $c, d, d' \in S$, $a \in A \cup \{0\}$, $b, b' \in B$ *the implication*

$$c \xrightarrow[a]{b} d \wedge c \xrightarrow[a]{b'} d' \;\Rightarrow\; b = b' \wedge d = d'$$

is valid and, furthermore, $c \xrightarrow[a]{b} d \wedge c \xrightarrow[0]{b'} d' \;\Rightarrow\; a = 0$.

It is called distinctive *if for all* $c, d, d' \in S$, $a, a' \in A$, $b \in B$ *the following implication holds:*

$$c \xrightarrow[a]{b} d \wedge c \xrightarrow[a']{b} d' \wedge (\exists P, P' \in \mathsf{Proc}_A : d(P) \sim d'(P')) \;\Rightarrow\; a = a' \;.$$

Here we identify the context states d *and* d' *with the contexts* D *and* D' *that possess the same components as* C *except of the start states which are* d *and* d' *respectively.*

Determinacy is intended to capture the idea of unique transduction: the external effect induced by an action a consumed from the parameter process is required to be uniquely determined. Autonomous context steps might in general prohibit to transfer this property of unique transduction required in the first condition for *single* actions to whole consumed *action sequences*. Therefore, the second condition requires in addition that 0-transductions (which are unique by the first condition) do not compete with non-0 transductions.

While determinacy allows the inference of outer behavior from inner behavior, the idea of distinctivity is to allow just the opposite: to infer inner behavior form outer behavior. Let us, for the purpose of explanation, look first at a somewhat simpler notion, *local distinctivity*, that requires the stronger implication

$$c \xrightarrow[a]{b} d \wedge c \xrightarrow[a']{b} d' \;\Rightarrow\; a = a' \;.$$

A locally distinctive context allows to infer from a certain action b observed by the environment immediately the action a of the component process inducing b. The weaker notion of distinctivity does not necessarily allow *immediate* inference of a from the observed action b alone but from b together with the future behavior. Thus detection of a might be delayed but is conceptually possible from the total behavior presented to the environment.

The following lemma shows that the above list of phenomena leading to incompleteness of $S_{P,L}$ for single contexts is comprehensive.

Theorem 11 (Completeness for single contexts). *Suppose $C \in \mathsf{Ctx}_A$ is a context, $L \subseteq A^*$ is a prefix-closed language, and $P, Q \in \mathsf{Proc}_A$ are processes. If C is deterministic and distinctive and $\mathsf{IL}(C) = L$ then $C(P) \sim C(Q)$ implies $S_{P,L} \preceq Q$.*

Proof. Suppose that C is deterministic and distinctive, that $\mathsf{IL}(C) = L$, and that $C(P) \sim C(Q)$. Let R be the minimal deterministic process for L used in the construction of $S_{P,L}$. Given the determinacy and distinctivity of C it is rather straightforward (albeit tedious) to show that the relation

$$S \stackrel{\text{def}}{=} \{((p,r),q) \mid \exists c : \mathsf{IL}(c) = L(r) \text{ and } c(p) \sim c(q)\}$$

is a pre-bisimulation between $S_{P,L}$ and Q. This establishes the claim of the theorem, as $((p_0, r_0), q_0)$, the pair of initial states of $S_{P,L}$ and Q, is contained in R because $\mathsf{IL}(c_0) = \mathsf{IL}(C) = L = L(R) = L(r_0)$ and $C(P) \sim C(Q)$. $\square$

Theorem 11 shows that deterministic distinctive contexts that exhaust the agreed protocol language L (i.e. $\mathsf{IL}(C) = L$) are of particular importance. We call such contexts *witness contexts for L*. That witness contexts always exist is the claim of the following lemma. As a consequence $S_{P,L}$ is complete.

Lemma 12. *There is a witness context for any prefix-closed language L.*

Proof. Suppose given a prefix-closed language $L \subseteq A^*$. Let – as in the construction of $S_{P,L}$ – $Q = (S_Q, A, \rightarrow_Q, q_0)$ be the minimal deterministic process for L. Consider the context $C = (S_Q, A, A, \rightarrow_C, q_0)$, where $\rightarrow_C$ is defined by $c \xrightarrow{b}_C c'$ iff $c \xrightarrow{a}_Q c' \wedge a = b$. It is straightforward to check that C is deterministic and distinctive and that its interface language equals $L(Q) = L$. $\square$

Corollary 13 (Completeness). $\mathcal{U}_{P,L} \subseteq \mathcal{I}(S_{P,L})$ *for any prefix-closed $L \subseteq A^*$.*

Proof. Suppose given $Q \in \mathcal{U}_{P,L}$. By Lemma 12 there is a witness context C for L. As $Q \in \mathcal{U}_{P,L}$ we have $C(P) \sim C(Q)$. By Lemma 11, therefore, $S_{P,L} \preceq Q$, i.e. $Q \in \mathcal{I}(S_{P,L})$. $\square$

5 Restricted Context Classes

The results of the previous section seem to depend on the richness of the space of contexts given by action transducers. While this richness certainly is welcome for soundness considerations – it means that replacement in any reasonable context is correct – it is less clear whether it should also be accepted for completeness considerations: reasonable smaller classes of contexts, which could result e.g. from syntactic restrictions on the way contexts are constructed, might allow more replacements, thereby rendering $S_{P,L}$ incomplete.

Assume that we are interested in a certain context class $K \subseteq \mathsf{Ctx}_A$. Then the set of correct upgrades for a certain process $P \in \mathsf{Proc}_A$ for contexts in K respecting a certain interface language $L \subseteq A^*$ is given by

$$\mathcal{U}_{P,L}^K \stackrel{\text{def}}{=} \{Q \in \mathsf{Proc}_A \mid \forall C \in K : \mathsf{IL}(C) \subseteq L \Rightarrow C(P) \sim C(Q)\} \ .$$

The only difference to the definition of $\mathcal{U}_{P,L}$ is the relativation of the universal quantifier to contexts in K. It is obvious that $\mathcal{U}_{P,L} \subseteq \mathcal{U}_{P,L}^K$ because $K \subseteq \mathsf{Ctx}_A$. Therefore, by Corollary 9, $\mathcal{I}(\mathcal{S}_{P,L}) \subseteq \mathcal{U}_{P,L}^K$, i.e. $\mathcal{S}_{P,L}$ is *sound for K*. The more interesting question is, whether it is also *complete for K*, i.e. whether $\mathcal{I}(\mathcal{S}_{P,L}) \supseteq \mathcal{U}_{P,L}^K$. In order to show completeness, however, it suffices to find a witness context $C \in K$ for L because in this case we can argue as in the proof of Corollary 13. Summarizing we have the following.

Corollary 14. *Suppose $L \subseteq A^*$ is prefix-closed. If K contains a witness context for L, then $\mathcal{S}_{P,L}$ is sound and complete for K, i.e. $\mathcal{I}(\mathcal{S}_{P,L}) = \mathcal{U}_{P,L}^K$.*

In the scenario motivating the considerations of this paper the process library components to be replaced typically run in parallel with the using program. Therefore, parallel contexts are of particular interest. Two prominent views of parallel interaction studied in the realm of process algebra are multiple agreement as in CSP [4] or LOTOS and handshake communication as in CCS [9].

In CSP the parallel composition operator *enforces* synchronization between its components on the common parts of their alphabet. Therefore, in a parallel CSP context of the form $\cdot \parallel Q$ the process Q can control occurence of actions in components placed into such a context. Technically this means that parallel CSP contexts have in general a non-trivial interface language and are thus interesting from the point of view of this paper.

The parallel composition operator of CCS, on the other hand, does not enforce synchronization of the component processes but only *enables* it. In particular, the component processes of a pure parallel composition can proceed independently of each other and, therefore, the interface language of a pure parallel CCS context $\cdot | Q$ (for processes of alphabet A) is just A^*. Thus pure parallel CCS context are of little interest from the point of view of this paper. A more interesting context class, which subsumes parallel contexts, are *standard concurrent contexts* of the form $(\cdot | Q) \setminus M$. Here, the *restriction operator* $\cdot \setminus M$ of CCS is used to enforce synchronization on the action set $M \subseteq \mathsf{Act}$. Standard concurrent contexts are modeled on processes in *standard concurrent form*[1] that are often studied in the realm of CCS (see, e.g., [9]).

In the full version of this paper we recall how to capture the effect of parallel CSP contexts and standard concurrent CCS contexts by action transducers and demonstrate that both context classes contain witness contexts for given interface languages L. Thus, $\mathcal{S}_{P,L}$ is sound and complete for each of these classes.

In the CSP case, witness contexts are rather immediately induced by deterministic processes for the language L in question with a certain care for treating the internal action τ correctly. In contrast the CCS case faces us with a difficulty: standard concurrent contexts straightforwardly constructed from such processes are non-distinctive in general. The reason is the implicit hiding of the

---

[1] A CCS process is said to be in standard concurrent form if it has the form $(P_1[f_1] | \ldots | P_n[f_n]) \setminus M$. For the purpose of this paper Q can be thought to represent the parallel composition $P_2[f_2] | \ldots | P_n[f_n]$ and the relabeling $[f_1]$ can be thought to be subsumed by the component placed into the context.

CCS parallel operator: a synchronization of two complementary actions a and $\bar{a}$ yields just the internal τ-action from which we cannot infer which actions synchronized. (Note that this is different in CSP where actions are not changed on synchronization.) How can we nevertheless construct distinctive contexts? The idea is to enrich the context to output *tracing actions* after each synchronization, from which the actions that synchronized can be inferred. This is akin to including some special output statements into a program for debugging purposes in order to observe the path taken through the program. The resulting context is distinctive in the sense of Definition 10, although it is not locally distinctive. Indeed, this observation was the reason to opt for the more global notion of distinctivity.

6 Conclusion

The motivation for this paper is to initiate a theory of downwards compatibility for reactive components. To this end, we studied the use of interface languages as a means for constraining the applications in which a reactive component is to be used. Such languages describe admissible interaction patterns of applications. As the main technical result we showed how to construct library-developer-oriented upgrade specifications from components equipped with interface languages.

While suggestive, the results in this paper represent only a first step toward an adequate theory of component compatibility. In particular, we deliberately ignored value-passing in order to come to grips with the control-oriented aspects of reactive systems. It would be an interesting topic for future research to extend the framework to a more realistic scenario where, in particular, values are communicated between components and applications and to consider how the results of this paper can be applied and generalized. We anticipate that interface languages would then consist of sequences of actions annotated with types, with one such sequence representing a set of admissible sequences of value exchanges. The consequences of this change remain to be investigated. Another topic to be investigated would involve the consideration of more reasonable notions of global behavioral equivalence, in particular weak bisimulation. Results in [2] suggest that this extension is not problematic, so in this paper we have opted for the simpler, if less realistic, setting of strong bisimulation.

From a more technical point of view, this paper has presented a behavioral refinement preorder on a space of simple process specifications and has shown that the correct replacements of a process in context classes given by prefix-closed interface languages can be characterized by single specifications. This expressiveness result for the space of process specifications draws its inspiration from a similar result for classes of CCS contexts in [2]. That paper proposes a modification in the definition of the CCS *divergence preorder* studied by Walker [11]; the modification enables such a result to hold.

In this paper we simultaneously extended and simplified the underlying formalism of [2] to obtain more general soundness and completeness results, and we showed how they may be applied in the setting of reactive component evolution. Specifically, we considered the more general setting of action transducer contexts proposed by Larsen and Xinxin [7, 8]; we altered the setting of [2] to account for this richer setting; and we showed how components together with "interaction languages" may be transformed into equivalent "partial process" specifications. Moreover, we showed that the complete characterization property of the resulting specifications is stable under reasonable modifications of the type of considered contexts. In particular, we studied, besides the comprehensive class of action transducer contexts, the less extensive classes of parallel CSP contexts and standard concurrent CCS contexts.

The refinement preorder has a bisimulation-like definition and can – for finite-state processes – automatically be checked by adapting known bisimulation-checkers. The finiteness requirement imposed by straightforward automatic support, however, leads also to a restriction to *regular* interface languages, as non-regular languages would give rise to infinite process specifications $S_{P,L}$.

Related to the characterization of correct replacements in contexts is the context decomposition problem studied by Larsen [6, 7]. His work is concerned with characterizing the class of processes Q such that $C(Q)$ sat S holds for a given specification S and context C. Indeed, characterizing the correct replacements of a process P in a *single* context C can be seen as the context decomposition problem, where specifications are given by processes, sat is chosen as the global process equivalence $\sim$ and S as $C(P)$. Context decomposition amounts then to characterizing the processes Q with $C(Q) \sim C(P)$, i.e. the correct replacements of P. The replacement problem in *classes* of contexts, however, that was considered in this paper does not immediately reduce to a context decomposition problem, and our results therefore are fundamentally different from Larsen's.

References

1. J. C. M. Baeten and W. P. Weijland. *Process Algebra*. Cambridge Tracts in Theoretical Computer Science. Cambridge University Press, 1990.
2. R. Cleaveland and B. Steffen. A preorder for partial process specification. In *CONCUR'90*, LNCS 458, 141–151. Springer-Verlag, 1990.
3. M. C. Hennessy. *Algebraic Theory of Processes*. MIT Press, 1988.
4. C. A. R. Hoare. *Communicating Sequential Processes*. Prentice Hall, 1985.
5. C. B. Jones. Tentative steps toward a development method for interfering programs. *ACM TOPLAS*, 5(4):596–619, 1983.
6. K. G. Larsen. *Context-Dependent Bisimulation Between Processes*. PhD thesis, University of Edinburgh, 1986.
7. K. G. Larsen. Ideal specification formalism = expressivity + compositionality + decidability + testablity + ····. In *CONCUR'90*, LNCS 458. Springer-Verlag, 1990.
8. K. G. Larsen and L. Xinxin. Compositionality through an operational semantics of contexts. In *ICALP'90*, LNCS 443, 526–539. Springer-Verlag, 1990.
9. R. Milner. *Communication and Concurrency*. Prentice Hall, 1989.
10. D. M. R. Park. Concurrency and automata on infinite sequences. In LNCS 154, pages 561–572. Springer-Verlag, 1981.
11. D. J. Walker. Bisimulations and divergence. In *LICS'88*, 186–192. IEEE Computer Society, 1988.

Verification of Definite Iteration over Hierarchical Data Structures

V.A. Nepomniaschy

Institute of Informatics Systems
Russian Academy of Sciences, Siberian Division,
6, Lavrentiev ave., Novosibirsk 630090, Russia
e-mail: vnep@iis.nsk.su, fax: (07-383-2)32-34-94

A verification method is proposed for definite iteration over hierarchical data structures The method is based on a replacement operation which expresses the definite iteration effect in a symbolic form and belongs to a specification language. The method includes a proof rule for the iteration without invariants and inductive proof principles for proving verification conditions which contain the replacement operation. As a case study, a parallel replacement operation for arrays is considered in order to simplify the proof of verification conditions. Examples which illustrate the application of the method are considered.

1 Introduction

Formal program verification which means the proof of consistency between programs and their specifications is successfully developed. The axiomatic style of verification is based on the Hoare method [7] which consists of the following stages: constructing pre-, post-conditions and loop invariants; deriving verification conditions with the help of proof rules and proving them. The functional style of verification proposed by Mills and others [1, 9] assumes that each loop is annotated with a function expressing the loop effect. The functions are closely related to loop invariants but differences can be noticed [4]. In the both approaches annotating loops remains a difficult problem especially for programs over complex data structures as arrays, files, trees, pointers. Simplifying verification of such programs is an important problem. Difficulties of verification have been noted both for the functional approach to programs over arrays [10] and for the axiomatic one to programs over pointers [5].

One way to simplify verification of such programs is to impose restrictions to loop forms. Loops can be divided in two groups called definite and indefinite iterations. Typical examples are Pascal for- and while-loops. Definite iteration is iteration over all elements of a list, set, file, array, tree or other data structure. A general form of definite iteration is proposed in [16]. In [2, 6, 8] advantages of for-loops over unordered and linear ordered sets are discussed for the axiomatic approach, and proof rules which take into account the specific character of the for-loops are proposed. In [16] the functional method for verifying definite iteration of the general form is described. However annotating definite iteration remains a difficult problem for programs over complex data structures.

In [12, 13] we proposed a symbolic method of verifying definite iteration of such a form as loops over linear ordered sets which had the statement of assignment to array elements as the loop body. The main idea of the method is to use the symbols of invariants instead of the invariants in verification conditions and a special technique based on the loop properties for proving the verification conditions. In [14] we extended the symbolic method to definite iteration over data structures without restrictions on the loop bodies.

The purpose of this paper is to develop the symbolic method for definite iteration over hierarchical data structures which allow us to represent some cases of while-loops. In Section 2 the notion of hierarchical data structures is defined and useful functions over the structures are introduced. Definite iteration and a replacement operation which represents the effect of the iteration by means of a symbolic form are described in Section 3 along with a proof rule without invariants for the iteration. Inductive proof principles for proving assertions containing the replacement operation are presented in Section 4. A case of study of loop bodies over arrays and a parallel replacement operation which allows to simplify verification conditions proofs are considered in Section 5. Examples which illustrate the application of the symbolic method are given in Section 6. In conclusion, results and perspectives of the symbolic verification method are discussed. Appendix contains proofs of two theorems from Section 5.

2   Data structures

We introduce the following notation. Boolean operations are denoted by symbols $\wedge$ (conjunction), $\vee$ (disjunction), $\rightarrow$ (implication), $\neg$ (negation), $\leftrightarrow$ (equivalence). We suppose that all free variables are bound by universal quantifiers in axioms, theorems and other formulas. Let $\{s_1, s_2, \ldots, s_n\}$ be the multiset (sometimes the set) which consists of elements $s_1, \ldots, s_n$. $s \in T$ denotes the membership of s in the multiset T. Let $T_1 - T_2$ be the difference of multisets T_1 and T_2. For the function $f(x)$ we denote $f^0(x) = x$, $f^i(x) = f(f^{i-1}(x))$ $(i = 1, 2, \ldots)$.

Let us remind the notion of data structures which contain a finite number of elements [16]. Let $memb(S)$ be the multiset of elements of the structure S, and $|\,memb(S)\,|$ be the power of the multiset $memb(S)$. For a structure S the following three operations are defined: $empty(S)$ is a predicate whose value is true if $memb(S)$ is empty and false otherwise; $choo(S)$ is a function which returns an element s of $memb(S)$; $rest(S)$ is a function which returns a structure S' of the same type as S such that $memb(S') = memb(S) - \{choo(S)\}$. The functions $choo(S)$ and $rest(S)$ will be undefined if and only if $empty(S)$. Typical examples of the structures are sets, sequences, lists, strings, arrays, files and trees.

We introduce a number of useful functions related to a structure S in the case of $\neg empty(S)$. We denote $s_i = choo(rest^{i-1}(S))$ for $i = 1, \ldots, n$ provided $\neg empty(rest^{n-1}(S))$ and $empty(rest^n(S))$. So, $memb(S) = \{s_1, s_2, \ldots, s_n\}$. $last(S)$ is a partial function such that $last(S) = s_n$. Let $str(s)$ denote a structure S which contains the only element s.

Let $M = [m_1, \ldots, m_k]$ denote a vector which consists of elements $m_i (1 \le i \le k)$. We will use $pred(M, j)(j = 1, \ldots, k)$ to denote the set $\{m_i \mid 1 \le i < j\}$ if

$j > 1$ and the empty set if $j = 1$. We will consider the vector $M = [m_1, \ldots, m_k]$ as a structure such that $choo(M) = m_1, rest(M) = [m_2, \ldots, m_k]$ (if $k \geq 2$), $empty(rest(M))$ (if $k = 1$). We consider $m \in M$ to be a shorthand for $m \in memb(M)$. Let $con(M_1, M_2)$ be the concatenation operation of vectors M_1 and M_2.

For a structure S we assume that $vec(S) = [s_1, \ldots, s_n]$ provided $\neg empty(S)$, $memb(S) = \{s_1, \ldots, s_n\}$ and $s_i = choo(rest^{i-1}(S))(i = 1, \ldots, n)$. A function $head(S)$ returns a structure such that $vec(head(S)) = [s_1, \ldots, s_{n-1}]$ provided $vec(S) = [s_1, \ldots, s_n]$.

Let us introduce a concatenation operation $con(S_1, S_2)$ for structures S_1 and S_2 by means of a recursive definition. The explicit definition of the operation can be complicated for some structures, for example, trees. The recursive definition as follows: $con(S_1, S_2) = S_2$ if $empty(S_1)$, $choo(con(S_1, S_2)) = choo(S_1)$ and $rest(con(S_1, S_2)) = con(rest(S_1), S_2)$ if $\neg empty(S_1)$. We consider $con(S, s)$, $con(s, S)$, $con(S_1, S_2, S_3)$ to be a shorthand for $con(S, str(s))$, $con(str(s), S)$, $con(con(S_1, S_2), S_3)$ respectively.

The following theorems express some important properties of the concatenation operation for structures.

Th1. $\neg empty(S) \rightarrow con(choo(S), rest(S)) = S$.

Th1 is immediate from the definition of con.

Th2. $con(vec(S_1), vec(S_2)) = vec(con(S_1, S_2))$.

Th3. $\neg empty(S) \rightarrow con(head(S), last(S)) = S$.

Th2 and Th3 are proved with the help of the induction by $| memb(S_1) |$ and $| head(S) |$ respectively.

Let us consider data structures $S_1, \ldots, S_m$. We will use $T(S_1, \ldots, S_m)$ to denote a term constructed from S_i with the help of the functions $choo, last, rest, head, str, con$. Sometimes we will omit all S_i in $T(S_1, \ldots, S_m)$. For a term T which represents a data structure, we will denote the function $| memb(T) |$ as $lng(T)$. The function can be calculated by the following rules: $lng(S_i) = | memb(S_i) |, lng(con(T_1, T_2)) = lng(T_1) + lng(T_2)$ $lng(rest(T)) = lng(head(T)) = lng(T) - 1, lng(str(s)) = 1$.

Let a hierarchical data structure $S = STR(S_1, \ldots, S_m)$ is defined by the functions $choo(S)$ and $rest(S)$ which are constructed with the help of conditional (if-then-else), superposition and Boolean operations from the following components:
- terms which do not contain $S_1, \ldots, S_m$;
- the functions $choo(S_i), rest(S_i), last(S_i)$ and $head(S_i)$ for all $i = 1, \ldots, m$;
- the predicate $empty(S_i)(i = 1, \ldots, m)$;
- terms of the form $STR(T_1, \ldots, T_m)$ such that
$\sum_{i=1}^{m} lng(T_i) < \sum_{i=1}^{m} lng(S_i)$;
- the undefined element ω.

Notice that the undefined value ω of the functions $choo(S)$ and $rest(S)$ means $empty(S)$. The restriction that we impose on terms T_j in the recursive definition of $STR(S_1, \ldots, S_m)$ ensures termination of the definition process.

3 Definite iteration over structures and replacement operation

We recall the notion of definite iteration over structures from [16]. Let us consider the statement

(1) **for** x **in** S **do** $v := body(v, x)$ **end**

where S is the structure, x is the variable called the loop parameter, v is the data vector of the loop body ($x \notin v$), $v := body(v, x)$ represents the loop body computation. We suppose that the loop body uses variables from v(and x), does not change the loop parameter x and iterates over all elements of the structure S. So, the loop body terminates for every $x \in memb(S)$.

Operational semantics of iteration (1) is defined as follows. Let v_0 be the vector of initial values of variables from the vector v. The result of the iteration is $v = v_0$ if $empty(S)$. If $\neg empty(S)$ and $vec(S) = [s_1, \ldots, s_n]$, the loop body iterates sequentially for x defined as $s_1, s_2, \ldots, s_n$.

We associate a function $body(v, x)$ with the right part of the body of iteration (1) such that the body has the same form $v := body(v, x)$. To present the effect of iteration (1), let us define a replacement operation $rep(v, S, body)$ to be a vector v_n such that $v_0 = v$, $n = 0$ provided $empty(S)$, $v_i = body(v_{i-1}, s_i)$ for all $i = 1, \ldots, n$ provided $\neg empty(S)$ and $vec(S) = [s_1, \ldots, s_n]$. It should be noted that in the expression $rep(v, S, body)$ all variables of the term $body$ are considered to be bound in the term. Therefore, substitutions for the occurrences of the variables are not performed in the term $body$.

Important properties of the replacement operation are expressed by the following theorems.

Th4. $rep(v, con(S_1, S_2), body) = rep(rep(v, S_1, body), S_2, body)$.

Th4 is proved with the help of the induction by $|\,memb(S_1)\,|$.

Th5. $\neg empty(S) \rightarrow rep(v, S, body) = body(rep(v, head(S), body), last(S))$.

Th5 follows from Th3 and Th4. Let us denote the iteration (1) by $iter(v, S)$.

Th6. $iter(v, S)$ is equivalent to the multiple assignment $v := rep(v, S, body)$.

Proof. We use the induction by $|\,memb(S)\,|$. If $\neg empty(S)$ then $iter(S)$ is equivalent to the program **begin** $iter(v, head(S))$; $v := body(v, last(S))$ **end**. It remains to use Th5.

To describe a proof rule for the iteration (1), we introduce the following notation. Let P, Q, inv and $prog$ denote a pre-condition, a post-condition, an invariant, and a program fragment, respectively. $\{P\}\ prog\ \{Q\}$ denotes partial correctness of the program $prog$ with respect to the pre-condition P and the post-condition Q. Let $R(y \leftarrow exp)$ (or $R(exp1 \leftarrow exp)$) be a result of substitution of an expression exp for all occurrences of a variable y(or an expression $exp1$) into a formula R. Let $R(vec \leftarrow vexp)$ denotes a result of the synchronous substitution of components of an expression vector $vexp$ for all occurrences of corresponding components of a vector vec into a formula R.

The replacement operation allows us to formulate a proof rule without invariants for iteration (1). Indeed, let us consider the following proof rule.

rl1. $\{P\}\ prog\ \{Q(v \leftarrow rep(v, S, body))\} \vdash$
    $\{P\}\ prog;$ **for** x **in** S **do** $v := body(v, x)$ **end** $\{Q\}$

where the post-condition Q does not depend on the loop parameter x.

Let PROOF denote the standard system of proof rules for usual statements including multiple assignment. The following corollary from Th6 justifies the proof rule rl1.

Corollary 1. The proof rule rl1 is derived in the standard system PROOF.

We will generalize definite iteration (1) allowing for the output from the loop body under a condition. The condition can depend on the loop parameter x but it does not depend on the variables from the data vector v. For this purpose we will define iteration (1) over hierarchical data structures which is equivalent to the generalized one.

Let us consider statement

(2) **for** x **in** S_0 **do if** $cond(x)$ **then** $EXIT$; $v := body(v, x)$ **end**

where S_0 is arbitrary data structure, the condition $cond(x)$ does not depend on the variables from v, $EXIT$ is the statement of termination of the loop.

Let a hierarchical data structure $S = STR(S_0)$ is defined with respect to the structure S_0 and the condition $cond$ as follows.

$(choo(S), rest(S)) = $ **if** $empty(S_0) \vee cond(choo(S_0))$ **then** (ω, ω)
else $(choo(S_0), STR(rest(S_0)))$.

Th7. Generalized iteration (2) is equivalent to iteration (1) with $S = STR(S_0)$.

Proof. We will use the induction by $\mid memb(S_0) \mid = n$. Let us suppose $n > 0$ and the iterations are equivalent if $\mid memb(S_0) \mid < n$. So, $\neg empty(S_0)$. In the case that $\neg cond(choo(S_0))$, iteration (2) is equivalent to program

$v := body(v, choo(S_0))$; **for** x **in** $rest(S_0)$ **do**
if $cond(x)$ **then** $EXIT$; $v := body(v, x)$ **end**.

From $\neg cond(choo(S_0))$, it follows that $\neg empty(S)$ and iteration (1) is equivalent to program

$v := body(v, choo(S_0))$; **for** x **in** $rest(S)$ **do** $v := body(v, x)$ **end**.

It remains to notice that the programs are equivalent because $choo(S) = choo(S_0), rest(S) = STR(rest(S_0)), \mid memb(rest(S_0)) \mid = n - 1$ and the inductive hypothesis is applicable.

4 Induction principles

Verification conditions including the replacement operation are generated by means of the proof rule rl1. To prove the verification conditions, we need a special technique.

Let $prop(STR(S_1, \ldots, S_m))$ denote a property expressed by a first-order logic formula with the only free variables $S_1, \ldots, S_m$. The formula is constructed from function symbols, variables and constants by means of Boolean operations and first-order quantifiers. The function symbols include $memb$, $empty$, vec, $choo$, $rest$, $last$, $head$, str, con. To prove such properties, we present an induction principle.

Induction principle 1. The property $prop(STR(S_1, \ldots, S_m))$ holds for all structures $S_1, \ldots, S_m$ if the following two conditions hold:

1) $empty(S_1) \wedge \ldots \wedge empty(S_m) \rightarrow prop(STR(S_1, \ldots, S_m))$,

2) for all $S_1, \ldots, S_m$ such that $\neg empty(S_i)$ for appropriate $i = 1, \ldots, m$, there exist terms $T_1, \ldots, T_m$ for which $\sum_{i=1}^{m} lng(T_i) < \sum_{i=1}^{m} lng(S_i)$ and $prop(STR(T_1, \ldots, T_m)) \rightarrow prop(STR(S_1, \ldots, S_m))$.

The validity of this principle can be proved with the help of induction by $n = \sum_{i=1}^{m} lng(S_i)$.

Let $prop(rep(v, S, body))$ denote a property expressed by a first-order logic formula with the only free variable S. The formula is constructed from the replacement operation $rep(v, S, body)$, function symbols, variables and constants by means of Boolean operations, first-order quantifiers and substitution of constants for variables from v.

Induction principle 2. The property $prop(rep(v, S, body))$ holds for each structure S if the following two conditions hold:

1) $empty(S) \rightarrow prop(rep(v, S, body))$,

2) for each S such that $\neg empty(S)$ there exists a term $T(S)$ such that $lng(T(S)) < lng(S)$ and $prop(rep(v, T(S), body)) \rightarrow prop(rep(v, S, body))$.

The corollary 2 follows from the induction principle 2 with $T(S) = rest(S)$.

Corollary 2. The property $prop(rep(v, S, body))$ holds for each structure S if the following two conditions hold for each structure S:

1) $empty(S) \rightarrow prop(rep(v, S, body) \leftarrow v)$.

2) $\neg empty(S) \wedge prop(rep(v, rest(S), body)) \rightarrow prop(rep(v, S, body) \leftarrow rep(body(v, choo(S)), rest(S), body))$.

The corollary 3 follows from the induction principle 2 with $T(S) = head(S)$.

Corollary 3. The property $prop(rep(v, S, body))$ holds for each structure S if the following two conditions hold for each structure S:

1) $empty(S) \rightarrow prop(rep(v, S, body) \leftarrow v)$.

2) $\neg empty(S) \wedge prop(rep(v, head(S), body)) \rightarrow prop(rep(v, S, body) \leftarrow body(rep(v, head(S), body), last(S)))$.

5 Case of study: iterations over arrays

At first, we recall the known notion $upd(A, ind, exp)$ which denotes an array resulted from the array A by replacing its element indexed by ind with the value of the expression exp [15]. A notion $upd(A, IND, EXP)$ with $IND = [ind_1, \ldots, ind_m]$ and $EXP = [exp_1, \ldots, exp_m]$ is its generalisation which denotes an array obtained from the array A by the sequential replacement of its ind_j-th element with the value of the expression exp_j for all $j = 1, \ldots, m$. Let Mz denote the projection of a vector M on a variable z.

In the section we assume that the iteration body contains a vector of variables consisted of a variable x, an array A and a vector v of other variables. So, the body of the iteration (1) has the form $(A, v) := body(A, v, x)$. We also assume that $body_A(A, v, x)$ can be represented by $upd(A, IND, EXP)$ for appropriate vectors $IND(x)$ and $EXP(A, v, x)$ where if $A[ind]$ is in $exp_j(A, v, x)$ $(1 \leq j \leq m)$, then ind has the form $r_i(x)(1 \leq i \leq t)$. So, we impose a restriction on IND and EXP such that ind_j and r_i do not depend on variables from v. Notice that the representation of $body_A$ by upd is natural, since such a loop body usually contains the statements of the form $A[ind] := exp$ which can be jointly represented by the statement $A := upd(A, IND, EXP)$.

We will define a parallel replacement operation $\widetilde{rep}(A, v, S, body)$ with respect to the array A as a special case of the replacement operation for which the reasoning technique can be simplifyed. The operation $\widetilde{rep}(A, v, S, body)$ is defined to be a pair (A_n, v_n) such that $A_0 = A, v_0 = v$, $n = 0$ provided $empty(S), A_j = upd(A_{j-1}, IND(s_j), EXP(A, v_{j-1}, s_j)), v_j = body_v(A_{j-1}, v_{j-1}, s_j)$ for all $j = 1, \ldots, n$ provided $\neg empty(S)$ and $vec(S) = [s_1, \ldots, s_n]$. Thus, the definition differs from the replacement operation definition from Section 3 in that EXP included in upd depends on the initial value of the array A.

The parallel replacement operation is correct, if it coincides with the replacement operation. A sufficient condition of its correctness gives the following theorem where $IND(D) = \{ind(s) \mid s \in D, ind \in IND\}$.
Th8. $\widetilde{rep}(A, v, S, body) = rep(A, v, S, body)$, if for every $j = 2, \ldots, n$ and $i = 1, \ldots, t$, $r_i(s_j) \notin IND(pred(vec(S), j))$.

Notice that the condition of the theorem 8 holds for $j = 1$ because $IND(pred(vec(S), 1))$ is the empty set.

We introduce the following notation. A set $IND(S) = \{ind_j(s) \mid s \in memb(S), 1 \le j \le m\}$ is called a replacement domain. The set $IND(S)$ is empty, if $empty(S)$. Let us define a maximal occurrence function $moc(S, k)$. The function $moc(S, k)$ will be undefined for $k \notin IND(S)$. If $k \in IND(S)$, then $moc(S, k) = (i, j)$ where i is a maximal index of the elements of the vector $vec(S) = [s_1, \ldots, s_n]$ such that there exists a number l for which $ind_l(s_i) = k, j$ is the maximal number among such numbers l.

The following theorem gives a procedure for computing the parallel replacement operation with respect to an array A.
Th9. $\widetilde{rep}_A(A, v, S, body)[k] = A[k]$ if $k \notin IND(S)$.
$\widetilde{rep}_A(A, v, S, body)[k] = exp_j(A, \widetilde{rep}_v(A, v, head^{n-i+1}(S), body), s_i)$
if $k \in IND(S), vec(S) = [s_1, \ldots, s_n]$ and $moc(S, k) = (i, j)$.

Notice that $vec(head^{n-i}(S)) = [s_1, \ldots, s_i]$, therefore $\neg empty(head^{n-i}(S))$ and $head^{n-i+1}(S)$ will be defined. Proofs of Theorems Th8 and Th9 are given in Appendix.

Let us consider a special case in which the iteration (1) has the form
(3) **for** x **in** $[e1, e1 + 1, \ldots, e2]$ **do** $A := upd(A, IND(x), EXP(A, x))$ **end**
where $e2 \ge e1$. Then $S = vec(S), n = e2 - e1 + 1, pred(vec(S), j) = \{e1, \ldots, e1 + j - 2\}$ $(j = 2, \ldots, n)$. The following corollaries follow from Th8 and Th9 for the iteration (3).
Corollary 4. $\widetilde{rep}(A, S, upd) = rep(A, S, upd)$ if for every $j = 2, \ldots, n$ and $i = 1, \ldots, t$, $r_i(e1 + j - 1) \notin IND(\{e1, \ldots, e1 + j - 2\})$.
Corollary 5. $\widetilde{rep}(A, S, upd)[k] = A[k]$ if $k \notin IND(S)$.
$\widetilde{rep}(A, S, upd)[k] = exp_j(A, e1 + i - 1)$ if $k \in IND(S)$ and $moc(S, k) = (i, j)$.

6 Examples

Example 1. Copying an ordered file with insertion.

To specify a copying program we introduce the following notation. Let F and G be the files considered as structures; Ω denotes the empty file; $ord(F)$ is a predicate whose value is true if F was sorted in ascending order $\leq$ of elements and false otherwise. We assume that $ord(\Omega)$ and $\omega < y$ for each defined element y and the undefined element ω. $del(F, y)$ is a function which returns a file resulted from the file F by eliminating the first occurrence of the element y. If the element y is not contained in the file F, then $del(F, y) = F$. $hd(F, y)$ is a function which returns a file resulted from the file F by eliminating its tail which begins with the first occurence of the element y. $tl(F, y)$ is a function which returns a file resulted from the file F by eliminating its head which ends with the first occurence of the element y. If the element y is not contained in the file F, then $hd(F, y) = tl(F, y) = F$. $y > F$ is a predicate whose value is true, if $empty(F)$ or $\forall x \in memb(F)$ $y > x$ and false otherwise.

The following annotated program copies the sorted file F to the file G inserting an element w in its proper place.

$\{P\}$ $ins := false; G := \Omega;$ **for** x **in** F **do** $(G, ins) := body(G, ins, x)$ **end**;
if $\neg ins$ **then** $G := con(G, w)$ $\{Q\}$

where ins is a Boolean variable, $body(G, ins, x) =$
if $w \leq x \wedge \neg ins$ **then** $(con(G, w, x), true)$ **else** $(con(G, x), ins)$, $P(F) = ord(F)$,
$Q(F, G) = (del(G, w) = F \wedge ord(G) \wedge w \in memb(G))$.

Two following verification conditions are generated by means of the proof rule rl1 and the standard system **PROOF**. We consider $rep(F)$ to be a shorthand for $rep((\Omega, false), F, body)$.

VC1: $P(F) \wedge \neg rep_{ins}(F) \to Q(F, con(rep_G(F), w))$,
VC2: $P(F) \wedge rep_{ins}(F) \to Q(F, rep_G(F))$.

To prove the verification conditions, we apply the property
$prop(rep(F)) = prop1 \wedge prop2$ where $prop1 = (\neg rep_{ins}(F) \to rep_G(F) = F \wedge w > F)$, $prop2 = (rep_{ins}(F) \to del(rep_G(F), w) = F \wedge w > hd(rep_G(F), w) \wedge w \in memb(rep_G(F)) \wedge w \leq choo(tl(rep_G(F), w)))$. The property $prop1$ specifies the case when the variable ins remains false, w exceeds all elements of the file F, and F is copied to the file G. The property $prop2$ specifies another case when the variable ins becomes true and the file F is copied to the file G with insertion of the element w in its proper place. We apply Corollary 3 in order to prove the property $prop(rep(F))$.

Note that in [16] a mistake has been found in a version of the program with the help of the functional method. Formal verification of the correct program is not described in [16].

Example 2. Merging ordered arrays with cleaning.

Let us consider two ordered arrays A_1 and A_2. The following structure $S = STR(A_1, A_2)$ is constructed by merging of the arrays in an ordered array.

$(choo(S), rest(S)) =$ **if** $\neg empty(A_1) \wedge \neg empty(A_2)$
    then if $choo(A_1) \leq choo(A_2)$ **then** $(choo(A_1), STR(rest(A_1), A_2))$

$$\textbf{else } (choo(A_2), STR(A_1, rest(A_2)))$$
$$\textbf{else if } \neg empty(A_1) \textbf{ then } (choo(A_1), rest(A_1))$$
$$\textbf{else if } \neg empty(A_2) \textbf{ then } (choo(A_2), rest(A_2))$$
$$\textbf{else } (\omega, \omega).$$

The following annotated program merges the ordered arrays A_1 and A_2 in the ordered array A removing repetitive elements.

$\{P\}j := 1; A := \emptyset; \textbf{for } x \textbf{ in } STR(A_1, A_2) \textbf{ do } (A, j) := body(A, j, x) \textbf{ end } \{Q\}$
where $body(A, j, x) = \textbf{if } j > 1 \land x = A[j-1] \textbf{ then } (A, j)$
$\textbf{else } (upd(A, j, x), j+1), \emptyset$ denotes the empty array.

The annotations have the form:

$P(A_1, A_2) = \neg empty(A_1) \land \neg empty(A_2) \land ord(A_1) \land ord(A_2),$
$Q(A, A_1, A_2) = (set(A_1) + set(A_2) = set(A) \land ord(A) \land difel(A))$
where $ord(A)$ is a predicate whose value is true, if A was sorted in ascending order of elements and false otherwise (we assume that $ord(A)$ for $|\ memb(A)\ | \leq 1$); $set(A)$ is a function which returns a set of all elements of A; $+$ is the union operation for sets; $difel(A)$ is a predicate whose value is true, if A does not contain equal adjacent elements and false otherwise.

The following verification condition is generated by means of the proof rule rl1 and the standard system PROOF. We consider $rep(S)$ to be a shorthand for $rep((\emptyset, 1), STR(A_1, A_2), body)$.
$VC : P(A_1, A_2) \rightarrow Q(rep_A(S), A_1, A_2).$

To prove VC, we use the property $prop(S) = (memb(S) = memb(A_1) + memb(A_2) \land (ord(A_1) \land ord(A_2) \rightarrow ord(vec(S))))$ of the structure $S = STR(A_1, A_2)$. To prove the property, we apply the induction principle 1.

The verification condition VC follows from the property $prop(S)$ and the following one $prop(rep(S)) = (set(rep_A(S)) = set(vec(S)) \land difel(rep_A(S)) \land |\ rep_A(S)\ | = rep_j(S) - 1 \land (ord(vec(S)) \rightarrow ord(rep_A(S))))$. We use Corollary 3 in order to prove the property $prop(rep(S))$.

Example 3. The array inversion. The following annotated program presented by the iteration (3) inverts an array $A[1..m]$.
$\{P\} \textbf{ for } k \textbf{ in } S \textbf{ do } (A[k], A[m+1-k]) := (A[m+1-k], A[k]) \textbf{ end } \{Q\}$
where $S = [1, 2, \ldots, trunc(m \setminus 2)]$, $trunc(s)$ is an integer nearest to s, A_0 is an initial value of the array A, $P(A) = m \geq 1 \land A[1..m] = A_0[1..m], Q(A) =$
$\forall i\ (1 \leq i \leq m \rightarrow A[i] = A_0[m+1-i])$. So, $IND = (ind_1, ind_2), ind_1(k) = k, ind_2(k) = m+1-k$, $EXP = (exp_1, exp_2), exp_1(A, k) = A[m+1-k], exp_2(A, k) = A[k]$. Therefore, $exp_1(A, k) = A[r_1(k)], r_1(k) = n+1-k, exp_2(A, k) = A[r_2(k)], r_2(k) = k$.

It follows from $2j \leq m$ that $j < m - j + 2, r_1(j)$ and $r_2(j)$ are not contained in $IND(\{1, \ldots, j-1\})(j = 2, \ldots, trunc(m \setminus 2))$. Therefore, by Corollary 4, $\widetilde{rep}(A, S, body) = rep(A, S, body)$.

The verification condition $P(A) \rightarrow Q(\widetilde{rep}(A, S, body))$ is generated by the proof rule rl1 when the program $prog$ is empty. The correctness proof of the verification condition with the help of Corollary 5 can be realized without induction.

It should be noted that the structure S can be a set $\{1, 2, \ldots, trunc\ (n \setminus 2)\}$

in the program since the result of the parallel replacement operation does not depend on the order of elements of S.

7 Conclusion

The paper presents a symbolic method for verification of definite iteration over hierarchical data structures. The symbolic method differing substantially from the axiomatic and functional methods has some features related with these methods. For definite iteration the symbolic method uses a proof rule which has the form inherent in the axiomatic method, however, without invariants. To justify the proof rule, the axiomatic method is applied. The symbolic method, like the functional one, makes use of a functional representation for the iteration body and for the iteration as the replacement operation.

Let us discuss peculiarities and advantages of the symbolic method. Axiomatization of data structures by means of the concatenation operation con plays an important role in the method. Indeed, useful algebraic properties of the operation con are expressed by Theorems 1, 2, 3. Moreover, the operation con is used to represent a key property of the replacement operation in Theorem 4 and to prove Theorem 5. The symbolic method is based on the replacement operation which allows to eliminate loop invariants in proof rules. Instead of such an invariant, a suitable property of the replacement operation is used in a verification process. As a result, the verification process is substantially simplified because the property, as a rule, is simpler than the invariant. Besides, the induction principle 2 is rather flexible and allows to use different induction strategies as forward, backward and mixed in proving the property. The use of properties of hierarchical data structures simplifies proving verification conditions with the help of the induction principle 1. Theorem 7 allows to represent an important case of while-loops. We have proved a more complicated theorem which generalizes Theorem 7. This theorem is used for verification of programs over pointers. Notice that our paper [14] does not contain hierarchical data structures and the case of study from Section 5.

Advantages of the symbolic method become prominent for programs over complex data structures. For arrays the change of the replacement operation by the parallel one allows us to eliminate or to simplify inductive reasoning. Notice that the parallel replacement operation has been introduced for a special case of arrays in [11] and has been generalized for them in [13]. A variant of the parallel replacement operation has been used for modelling synchronous computations in [3] which are represented by statements equivalent to for-loops over sets with vector assignments as the loop bodies. The statements are expressed by universal quantifiers bounded by sets which are given by Boolean expressions.

The symbolic method of verification is promising for applications. To extend the range of its applications in program verification systems, it is helpful to develop a proof technique which uses the specific features of problem domains. The induction principles developed in framework of the symbolic method can be also useful for the functional method.

References

1. S.K. Basu, J. Misra, Proving loop programs, IEEE Trans. on Software Engineering, Vol. 1, No. 1, 1975, 76–86.
2. S.K. Basu, J. Misra, Some classes of naturally provable programs, Proc. 2nd Int. Conf. on Software Engineering, IEEE Press, 1976, 400–406.
3. K.M.Chandy, J.Misra, Parallel Program Design, Addison-Wesley, 1988.
4. D.D. Dunlop, V.R. Basili, Generalizing specifications for uniformly implemented loops, ACM Trans. on Programming Languages and Systems, Vol. 7, No. 1, 1985, 137–158.
5. P.Fradet, R. Gaugne, D.Le Metayer, Static detection of pointer errors: an axiomatisation and a checking algorithm, Lecture Notes in Computer Sci., Vol. 1058, 1996, 125–140.
6. D.Gries, N.Gehani, Some ideas on data types in high-level languages, Communications of the ACM, Vol. 20, No. 6, 1977, 414–420.
7. C.A.R. Hoare, An axiomatic basis of computer programming, Communications of the ACM, Vol. 12, No. 10, 1969, 576–580.
8. C.A.R. Hoare, A note on the for statement, BIT, Vol. 12, No. 3, 1972, 334–341.
9. R.C. Linger, H.D. Mills. B.I. Witt, Structured Programming: Theory And Practice, Addison-Wesley, 1979.
10. H.D. Mills, Structured programming: retrospect and prospect, IEEE Software, Vol. 3, No. 6, 1986, 58–67.
11. V.A.Nepomniaschy, Proving correctness of linear algebra programs, Programming, No. 4, 1982, 63–72 (in Russian).
12. V.A.Nepomniashy, Loop invariant elimination in program verification, Programming, N3, 1985, 3–13 (in Russian).
13. V.A.Nepomniaschy, On problem-oriented program verification, Programming, N1, 1986, 3–13 (in Russian).
14. V.A.Nepomniaschy, Verification of definite iteration over data structures without invariants, Proc. 12th Intern. Symp. on Computer and Information Sci., Antalya, Turkey, 1997, 608-614.
15. J.C.Reynolds, Reasoning about arrays, Comm. of the ACM, Vol. 22, No. 5, 1979, 290–299.
16. A.M.Stavely, Verifying definite iteration over data structures, IEEE Trans. on Software Engineering, Vol. 21, No. 6, 1995, 506–514.

8 Appendix. Proofs of Theorems Th8 and Th9.

Th8. It is sufficient to prove

(4) $EXP(A_{j-1}, v_{j-1}, s_j) = EXP(A, v_{j-1}, s_j)$ for all $j = 1, \ldots, n$.

Assertion (4) follows from

(5) $A_{j-1}[r_i(s_j)] = A[r_i(s_j)]$ for all $j = 1, \ldots, n$ and $i = 1, \ldots, t$.

Let us consider a generalization of (5) of the form

(6) $A_k[r_i(s_j)] = A[r_i(s_j)]$ for all $j = 1, \ldots, n, i = 1, \ldots, t, k = 0, 1, \ldots, j - 1$.

To prove (6) we will use the induction by k. If $k = 0$, then (6) is true because $A_0 = A$. If $0 < k < j$, then

$A_k[r_i(s_j)] = upd(A_{k-1}, IND(s_k), EXP(A, v_{k-1}, s_k))[r_i(s_j)] = A_{k-1}[r_i(s_j)]$ because $s_k \in pred(vec(S), j), IND(s_k) \subseteq IND(pred(vec(S), j)), r_i(s_j) \notin IND(s_k)$.

It remains to apply the inductive hypothesis $A_{k-1}[r_i(s_j)] = A[r_i(s_j)]$.

Th9. We will use the induction by $\mid memb(S) \mid = n$. If $n = 0$, then $empty(S)$ and $IND(S)$ is the empty set. From this and Ax12, it follows that $k \notin IND(S)$ and Th9. Let us consider the case $n \neq 0$. So, $\neg empty(S)$. By Theorem Th3, $S = con(head(S), last(S))$ and $IND(S) = IND(head(S)) \cup IND(last(S))$. From this it follows that

(7) $\widetilde{rep}_A(A, v, S, body)[k] = upd(\widetilde{rep}_A(A, v, head(S), body), IND(last(S)),$
$EXP(A, \widetilde{rep}_v(A, v, head(S), body), last(S)))[k]$.

Theorem Th9 is proved by the case analysis. Three cases are possible.

1. $k \notin IND(S)$. Then $k \notin IND(last(S))$. From this and (7) it follows that

(8) $\widetilde{rep}_A(A, v, S, body)[k] = \widetilde{rep}_A(A, v, head(S), body)[k]$.

It remains to apply the inductive hypothesis because $\mid memb(head(S)) \mid = n - 1$ and $k \notin IND(head(S))$.

2. $k \in IND(last(S))$. Then there exists j such that $1 \leq j \leq m, ind_j(s_n) = k$, and $\forall l(m \geq l > j \to ind_l(s_n) \neq k)$. From this and (7) it follows the conclusion of Theorem Th9 for $i = n$ of the form $\widetilde{rep}_A(A, v, S, body)[k] = exp_j(A, \widetilde{rep}_v(A, v, head(S), body), s_n)$.

3. $k \in IND(head(S)) \wedge k \notin IND(last(S))$. Then from (7) it follows (8). It should be noted that $moc(S, k) = moc(head(S), k)$, because $k \notin IND(last(S))$. Let us assume $moc(head(S), k) = (i, j)$, where $1 \leq i < n, 1 \leq j \leq m$. It remains to apply the inductive hypothesis of the form $\widetilde{rep}_A(A, v, head(S), body)[k] = exp_j(A, \widetilde{rep}_v(A, v, head^{n-i}(head(S)), body), s_i)$ because $\mid memb(head(S)) \mid = n - 1$. Theorem Th9 follows from this and (8).

Owicki/Gries in Isabelle/HOL

Tobias Nipkow and Leonor Prensa Nieto

Technische Universität München
Institut für Informatik, 80290 München, Germany
http://www.in.tum.de/~{nipkow,prensani}

Abstract. We present a formalization of the Gries/Owicki method for correctness proofs of concurrent imperative programs with shared variables in the theorem prover Isabelle/HOL. Syntax, semantics and proof rules are defined in higher-order logic. The correctness of the proof rules w.r.t. the semantics is proved. The verification of some typical example programs like producer/consumer is presented.

1 Introduction

This paper presents the first formalization in a theorem prover (namely Isabelle/HOL) of the well-known Owicki/Gries method [22] of correctness proofs for shared-variable concurrency. The programming language is a simple WHILE-language with concurrent execution of commands and synchronization via an AWAIT command. We define the operational semantics and the Owicki/Gries proof system and prove the soundness of the latter w.r.t. the former. Our soundness proof is interesting because it does not explicitly mention program locations, as is customary in the literature. Based on the proof rules we develop a verification condition generator (as an Isabelle tactic). Finally we present some typical examples, including the verification of a schematic program where the number of parallel components is a parameter. In particular this example shows that our embedding is more than a glorified verification condition generator: the availability of a full blown theorem prover means we can tackle problems outside the range of automatic methods like model checking.

One can also consider this paper a continuation of the first author's work on formalizing textbooks on programming language semantics [19, 21] because we have closely followed the description of Owicki/Gries in [2]. However, this is only a minor aspect and we are more interested in the practical application of our setup rather than meta-theoretical properties. Therefore we have proved soundness but not completeness of the proof system. Instead, we have concentrated on automating verification condition generation and on matters of surface syntax, which are frequently ignored in similar endeavours.

We are well aware of the non-compositionality of the Owicki/Gries method, and consider this only as a first step towards compositional methods. However, we wanted to start with the most fundamental approach rather than pick one of several competing compositional systems. We believe that a full understanding of the technicalities (from the theorem-proving point of view) involved in formalizing Owicki/Gries is advantageous when tackling compositional proof systems.

2 Related work

The idea of defining the syntax, semantics and proof system of an imperative programming language in a theorem prover goes back at least to Gordon [9], who considered the Hoare-logic of a simple WHILE-language. Stimulated by Gordon's paper, a fair number of concurrency paradigms have been formalized in theorem provers: UNITY is the most frequently chosen framework and has been formalized in the Boyer-Moore prover [8], HOL [1], Coq [11] and LP [4]. A related framework, *action systems*, has also been formalized in HOL [16]. CSP has been treated in HOL [3], Isabelle/HOL [26] and PVS [6]. CCS has been formalized in HOL [18]. TLA has been formalized in HOL [28], LP [7] and Isabelle/HOL [15]. Input/Output Automata have been formalized in Isabelle/HOL [17] and in LP [24]. However, it appears that there has been no work on embedding Hoare-logics for shared-variable parallelism in a theorem prover.

The Owicki/Gries method marks the beginning of a vast body of literature on proof systems for concurrency which we cannot survey here. Further important steps were the compositional system for shared-variable parallelism put forward by Jones [13, 14] (the rely/guarantee method) and the complete version of this system designed by Stølen [25]. For more recent work on the subject see [5].

3 Isabelle/HOL

Isabelle [23, 12] is a generic interactive theorem prover and Isabelle/HOL is its instantiation for higher-order logic, which is very similar to Gordon's HOL system [10]. From now on HOL refers to Isabelle/HOL. For a tutorial introduction see [20]. We do not assume that the reader is already familiar with HOL and summarize the relevant notation below.

The type system is similar to ML, except that function types are denoted by $\Rightarrow$. List notation is also similar to ML (e.g. @ is 'append') except that the 'cons' operation is denoted by # instead of ::. The ith component of list xs is written $xs!i$, and $xs[i:=x]$ denotes xs with the ith component replaced by x.

Set comprehension syntax is $\{e.\ P\}$.

The notation $[A_1;\ldots;A_n] \Longrightarrow A$ represents an implication with assumptions $A_1,\ldots,A_n$ and conclusion A.

To distinguish variables from constants, the latter are shown in sans-serif.

4 The Programming Language

Our programming language is a WHILE-language augmented with shared-variable parallelism ($\|$) and synchronization (AWAIT). We follow [2] in stratifying the language: parallelism must not be nested, i.e. each c_i in $c_1\|\ldots\|c_n$ must be a sequential command. In HOL, there are two ways to encode this stratification: define the type of all programs and a predicate that excludes those programs with nested parallelism, or define the syntax in two layers. We have chosen the latter alternative because it eliminates the well-formedness predicate, thus simplifying statements and proofs about the language. The fact that the language specification becomes longer because a number of constructs appear in both layers is uncritical: although proofs about those constructs have to be duplicated, this duplication is quite mechanical.

4.1 Syntax versus Semantics

How much of the syntax of the programming language do we want to represent in HOL? The choice is between a **deep embedding**, where the (abstract) syntax is represented via an inductive datatype, and a **shallow embedding**, where a term in the language is merely an abbreviation of its semantics. Deep embeddings are required for meta-theoretic reasoning (usually by induction over the syntax), whereas shallow embeddings simplify reasoning about individual programs (because the semantics is directly given) but may rule out certain meta-theoretic arguments. We have chosen a combination of both styles that has become quite established: represent as much as possible by a shallow embedding while still being able to conduct the meta-theoretic proofs you are interested in. Concretely this means that we use a deep embedding for programs themselves, whereas assertions, expressions and even assignments are represented semantically, i.e. as functions on *states*. For the time being we do not say more about the nature of states and merely define the parameterized type abbreviations

(α)`assn` $=$ (α)`set`
(α)`bexp` $=$ (α)`set`

representing both assertions and boolean expressions as sets (of states). The precise representation of states is discussed in §4.3 below. We also define the constant TRUE to be the universal set.

4.2 Component Programs

The core language is a standard sequential WHILE-language augmented with a synchronization construct (AWAIT). We depart from the usual presentation of the language by including assertions directly in the syntax: every construct, apart from sequential composition, is annotated with a precondition, and WHILE is also annotated with an invariant. We emphasize that these assertions are merely annotations and do not change the semantics of the language. Their sole purpose is to record proof outlines which can later be checked for interference freedom. Since we aim at a formalism for designing correct programs, it is only reasonable to include the necessary assertions right from the start. Moreover, it turns out that for proof-theoretic reasons it is very helpful to define the semantics of the language directly on annotated commands.

As discussed above, annotated commands are defined as a datatype with one constructor for each syntactic construct:

```
α ann_com = AnnBasic (α assn) (α ⇒ α)
            | AnnSeq (α ann_com) (α ann_com)
              ("_ ;; _")
            | AnnCond (α assn) (α bexp) (α ann_com) (α ann_com)
              ("_ IF _ THEN _ ELSE _ FI")
            | AnnWhile (α assn) (α bexp) (α assn) (α ann_com)
              ("_ WHILE _ INV _ DO _ OD")
            | AnnAwait (α assn) (α bexp) (α atom_com)
              ("_ AWAIT _ THEN _ END")
```

The optional ("...") annotations describe the obvious concrete syntax. We discuss the different constructs in turn, ignoring their preconditions.

AnnBasic represents a basic atomic state transformation, for example an assignment, a multiple assignment, or even any non-constructive specification. It turns out that it is quite immaterial what the basic commands are. The concrete syntax of assignments is explained in §4.3 below.

AnnSeq is the sequential composition of commands. We use ;; in the concrete syntax to avoid clashes with the predefined ; in Isabelle.

AnnCond is the conditional.

AnnWhile is the loop, annotated with an invariant.

AnnAwait is the synchronization construct. Following [2], its body must be loop-free. Type atom_com of loop-free commands is described in §4.4 below.

The precondition of each annotated command is extracted by the function pre:: $α$ ann_com $⇒ α$ assn. Its definition is obvious and we merely show one clause: pre(c1;;c2) = pre(c1).

The semantics of annotated commands is inductively defined by a set of transition rules between configurations, where a configuration is a pair of a program fragment and a state. A program fragment is either an annotated command, or, if execution has come to an end, the empty program. Adjoining a new element to a type is naturally modeled by the standard datatype

```
(α)option = None | Some α
```

In our case, None represents the empty program. The transition rules are shown in Fig. 1, where $→^*$ is the reflexive transitive closure of $→^1$, and $→_a^*$ is the atomic execution of loop-free commands described in §4.4 below.

4.3 The State and Concrete Syntax

The state during program execution is often modeled as a mapping from variables to values. This is fine in systems with dependent function spaces, but in the case of HOL's simple function spaces it means that all variables must be of the same type. There are two dual ways out of this: a mapping from variables to the disjoint union of all types used in the program, or a tuple of values, one for each variable occurring in the program. Note that in both cases, the state of the

(Some(AnnBasic R f), s) $\to^1$ (None, f s)

(Some(c_0), s) $\to^1$ (None, t) $\implies$
(Some(c_0;;c_1), s) $\to^1$ (Some(c_1), t)

(Some(c_0), s) $\to^1$ (Some(c_2), t) $\implies$
(Some(c_0;;c_1), s) $\to^1$ (Some(c_2;;c_1), t)

$s \in b$ $\implies$ (Some(R IF b THEN c_1 ELSE c_2 FI), s) $\to^1$ (Some(c_1), s)
$s \notin b$ $\implies$ (Some(R IF b THEN c_1 ELSE c_2 FI), s) $\to^1$ (Some(c_2), s)

$s \notin b$ $\implies$ (Some(R WHILE b INV inv DO c OD), s) $\to^1$ (None, s)
$s \in b$ $\implies$ (Some(R WHILE b INV inv DO c OD), s) $\to^1$
                (Some(c;;inv WHILE b INV inv DO c OD), s)

[$s \in b$; (Some c, s) $\to_a^*$ (None, t)] $\implies$
(Some(R AWAIT b THEN c END), s) $\to^1$ (None, t)

Fig. 1. Transition rules for annotated commands

program depends on the variables that occur in it and their types. Hence the state is a parameter of the program type ann_com.

We follow [27] and model states as tuples. For example,

AnnBasic {(x,y). x=y} (λ(x,y). (x+1,y))

is the encoding of the assignment x:=x+1 annotated with the precondition x=y. Fortunately, Isabelle's parser and printer can be extended with user-defined ML functions for translating between a nice external syntax and its internal representation. In the case of assignments, these functions translate between the external $x := e$ and the internal $\lambda(x_1,\ldots,x,\ldots,x_n).(x_1,\ldots,e,\ldots,x_n)$, where $x_1,\ldots,x_n$ is the list of all variables in the program, in some canonical order. Similarly, assertions have the external syntax $\{.P.\}$ (the dots avoid confusion with sets) which is turned into $\{(x_1,\ldots,x_n). P\}$. The translations are quite tricky because abstraction over tuples is not primitive in HOL but is realized by suitable combinations of ordinary abstraction and an uncurrying function of type $(\alpha \Rightarrow \beta \Rightarrow \gamma) \Rightarrow \alpha \times \beta \Rightarrow \gamma$. To build the state space from the external syntax an explicit declaration of the variables is included.

4.4 Atomic Commands

Apt and Olderog [2] require the body of an AWAIT to be loop-free. This subclass of programs is realized in HOL by the type atom_com, which differs from ann_com in two important aspects:

- it contains neither WHILE nor AWAIT,

– it contains no annotations because, as the name indicates, **atom_com** is executed atomically, and hence there is no need to record a proof outline that can be checked for interference freedom.

Yet **atom_com** is sufficiently similar to **ann_com** that we do not show its syntax and operational semantics. Suffice it to say that $\rightarrow^*_a$ is the analogue of $\rightarrow^*$.

4.5 The Parallel Layer

The datatype **par_com** of parallel commands is defined like **ann_com**

```
α par_com = Parallel ((α ann_com option × α assn) list)
          | ParBasic (α ⇒ α)
          | ParSeq (α par_com) (α par_com)        ("_,, _")
          | ParCond (α bexp) (α par_com) (α par_com)
                   ("IF _ THEN _ ELSE _ FI")
          | ParWhile (α bexp) (α assn) (α par_com)
                   ("WHILE _ INV _ DO _ OD")
```

but with some differences:

– Parallel encloses a list of pairs (co, q), where co is an optional sequential command (or None, if the command has terminated), and q a postcondition (remember that the precondition is already part of the annotated co). Strictly speaking it is not necessary to include the postcondition, but it simplifies program verification. There is also some concrete syntax (not shown) of the form COBEGIN c_1 {.q_1.} $\|$ ... $\|$ c_n {.q_n.} COEND.
– The remaining commands are almost like their namesakes in the sequential layer, but with a slightly different concrete syntax, to avoid confusion. The only real difference is the missing precondition annotation. The latter is required to check for interference freedom. But, contrary to the name, there is no parallel execution of parallel commands (only of sequential commands), and hence no interference. AWAIT is superfluous for the same reason.

The operational semantics for **par_com** is a transition relation between pairs of parallel commands and the current state. The execution of the parallel composition of a list of sequential commands Ts proceeds by executing one non-None component of Ts:

[i ∈ Index Ts; Ts!i = (Some c, Q); (Some c, s) $\rightarrow^1$ (ro, t)] $\Longrightarrow$
(Parallel Ts, s) $\rightarrow^1_p$ (Parallel(Ts[i := (ro,Q)]), t)

where Index Ts $\equiv$ {i. i < length Ts}. This is the only rule for Parallel. We omit the rules for the remaining constructs because they are practically identical to the ones in the sequential layer. The only difference is that instead of None as a signal that execution of a parallel command has terminated we use Parallel Ts, where all commands of Ts are None. This is just a trick to avoid the option type. As a result, the first rule for sequential composition looks like this

All_None Ts $\Longrightarrow$ ((Parallel Ts,, c), s) $\rightarrow^1_p$ (c, s)

where All_None Ts checks if the command-components of Ts are all None.

5 Proof Theory

The proof system for partial correctness of parallel programs is introduced in three stages, corresponding to the three layer hierarchy of the programming language. For each layer we show soundness of the proof system based on the soundness of the layer below. For the component layer we diverge most significantly from Apt and Olderog's treatment: having defined the operational semantics on a syntax including assertions, we do not need to formalize a notion of program locations.

Correctness formulas, also called *Hoare triples*, are statements of the form

$$\{P\}\, c\, \{Q\}$$

where c is a program and P and Q are the corresponding *precondition* and *postcondition*. *Partial correctness* means $\{P\}\, c\, \{Q\}$ is true iff every terminating computation of c that starts in a state s satisfying P ends in a state satisfying Q.

5.1 Proof System for Atomic Programs

Following Apt and Olderog, we define a *partial correctness semantics* of an atomic command c by

```
atom_sem c s ≡ {t. (Some c, s) →ₐ* (None, t)}
atom_SEM c S ≡  ⋃  atom_sem c s
              s∈S
```

where s is a state and S a set of states, and validity of a partial correctness formula by

$$(\models_a P\ c\ Q) \equiv (\text{atom\_SEM } c\ P \subseteq Q)$$

where P and Q are sets of states. Note that we employ the concrete assertion syntax $\{.P.\}$ introduced in §4.3 only in the case where P is a specific assertion referring to the variables of a specific program. Generic formulae involving assertions are more directly phrased in terms of variables like P ranging over sets of states.

The rules in the deductive system for atomic commands are the traditional ones. The notation $\vdash_a P\ c\ Q$ stands for provability of a Hoare triple in this system. Soundness of $\vdash_a$ w.r.t. $\models_a$

$$\vdash_a P\ c\ Q \implies\ \models_a P\ c\ Q$$

is proved by rule induction on the derivation of $\vdash_a P\ c\ Q$. Given the following lemmas, all cases are automatically proved:

- atom_SEM is monotonic,
- atom_SEM $(c_1;;c_2)$ S = atom_SEM c_2 (atom_SEM c_1 S),
- atom_SEM (IF b THEN c_1 ELSE c_2 FI) S =
  atom_SEM c_1 (S ∩ b) ∪ atom_SEM c_2 (S ∩ (-b)) .

5.2 Proof System for Component Programs

Proofs for component programs are presented in the form of standard proof outlines, where each command c is preceded by an assertion, pre(c), and apart from these and loop invariants there are no other assertions. For purely sequential programs such a presentation is not necessary, since the weakest precondition can always be derived from the postcondition and loop invariants. However, in the parallel case this is sometimes insufficient to develop a proof; this situation can be remedied by explicitly stating stronger preconditions.

$[\; P \subseteq \{s. \; (f \; s) \subseteq Q\} \;] \Longrightarrow \; \vdash \; (\text{AnnBasic P f}) \; Q$

$[\; \vdash \; c0 \; \text{pre}(c1); \; \vdash \; c1 \; Q \;] \Longrightarrow \; \vdash \; (c0;;c1) \; Q$

$[\; (P \cap b) \subseteq \text{pre}(c1); \; \vdash \; c1 \; Q; \; (P \cap (-b)) \subseteq \text{pre}(c2); \; \vdash \; c2 \; Q \;]$
$\Longrightarrow \; \vdash \; (\text{P IF b THEN c1 ELSE c2 FI}) \; Q$

$[\; P \subseteq \text{inv}; \; (\text{inv} \cap b) \subseteq \text{pre}(c); \; \vdash \; c \; \text{inv}; \; (\text{inv} \cap (-b)) \subseteq Q \;]$
$\Longrightarrow \; \vdash \; (\text{P WHILE b INV inv DO c OD}) \; Q$

$[\; \vdash_a \; (P \cap b) \; c \; Q \;] \Longrightarrow \; \vdash \; (\text{P AWAIT b THEN c END}) \; Q$

$[\; \vdash \; c \; Q; \; Q \subseteq Q' \;] \Longrightarrow \; \vdash \; c \; Q'$

Fig. 2. Proof system for annotated commands

The formation rules for proof outlines are shown in Fig. 2. They look unusual because preconditions are hidden as part of the commands' syntax. Also note that the precondition of each command need not be the weakest one, so we can do without a rule to strengthen the precondition. The following theorem shows that this system is equivalent to the traditional presentation.

Theorem 1 (Equivalence of proof systems) Let $\vdash_{tr} P \; \bar{c} \; Q$ stand for provability of the correctness formula $P \; \bar{c} \; Q$ in the traditional system. By $\bar{c}$ we mean commands without any annotation other than loop invariants. The relation $c \sim \bar{c}$ means that both commands are equal up to annotations (loop invariants must also be equal). Then,

(1) $\vdash_{tr} P \; \bar{c} \; Q \Longrightarrow \exists \; c. \; \vdash \; c \; Q \wedge P \subseteq \text{pre}(c) \wedge c \sim \bar{c}$
(2) $\vdash \; c \; Q \Longrightarrow \exists \; \bar{c}. \; \vdash_{tr} \text{pre}(c) \; \bar{c} \; Q \wedge c \sim \bar{c}$

The proofs are by rule induction on $\vdash_{tr}$ and $\vdash$ respectively.

Proof outlines enjoy the following intuitive property: whenever the control of c in a given computation starting in a state $s \in P$ reaches a point annotated by an assertion, this assertion is true. This is called *strong soundness*.

Theorem 2 (Strong Soundness for Component Programs)
If $\vdash c\ Q$ and $s \in pre(c)$ and (Some c, s) $\rightarrow^*$ (ro, t) then

- if ro = Some r for a command r then $t \in pre(r)$,
- if ro = None then $t \in Q$.

In particular for ro = None we have soundness in the usual way.

The proof is by rule induction on $\rightarrow^*$ with a nested induction on $\rightarrow^1$.

5.3 Proof System for Parallel Programs

Proof of correctness of parallel programs is much more demanding than the sequential case. The problem is that different components can interfere with each other via shared variables. Thus, to conclude that the input/output specification of a list of component programs Ts executed in parallel is simply the intersection (assertions are modeled as sets) of the input/output specification of each component, we need not only study each component program proof independently, but must also guarantee that this proof is not falsified by the execution of any other component. This property, called *interference freedom of proof outlines*, is checked by INTERFREE Ts in the proof rule for parallel composition:

$$[\ \forall i \in Index\ Ts.\ \exists\ c\ Q.\ Ts!i = (Some\ c,\ Q)\ \wedge \vdash c\ Q\ ;$$
$$INTERFREE\ Ts\ ] \implies$$

$$\vdash_P \bigcap_{i \in Index\ Ts} pre(the(com(Ts!i)))\ (Parallel\ Ts)\ \bigcap_{i \in Index\ Ts} post(Ts!i)\ .$$

Remember that each element of Ts is a pair of an optional ann_com and an assn, the postcondition. Function post extracts the postcondition, com extracts the ann_com option, the extracts the command c from Some c (by assumption all commands are wrapped up in Some), and finally pre extracts the precondition.

The remaining proof rules of system $\vdash_P$ are standard and we concentrate on the formalization of INTERFREE, which requires a number of auxiliary concepts:

- An assertion P is invariant under execution of an atomic command r if
  $\models_a (P \cap pre(r))\ r\ P$.
- We say that an atomic command r does not interfere with a standard proof outline $\vdash c\ Q$ iff the following two conditions hold:
  1. $\models_a (Q \cap pre(r))\ r\ Q$,
  2. For any assertion P within c, $\models_a (P \cap pre(r))\ r\ P$.
- Standard proof outlines $\vdash c_1\ Q_1, \ldots, \vdash c_n\ Q_n$ are interference free if no assignment or atomic region of a program c_i interferes with the proof outline $\vdash c_j\ Q_j$ of another program c_j, with $i \neq j$.

So, given two component programs (co,Q) and (co',Q'), showing interference freedom means proving that all assertions in the former are invariant under execution of all basic commands or atomic regions in the latter, and vice versa.

The test in one direction, which does not require the postcondition Q', is realized by function interfree:

```
interfree(co, Q, None) = True
interfree(None, Q, Some a) = ∀(R,r) ∈ atomics a. ⊨ₐ (Q ∩ R) r Q
interfree(Some c, Q, Some a) = ∀(R,r) ∈ atomics a. ⊨ₐ (Q ∩ R) r Q ∧
                               (∀ P ∈ assertions c. ⊨ₐ (P ∩ R) r P)
```

Atomic commands are extracted by the function atomics, which, given an annotated command, returns the set of all pairs (P, r) where r is either the body of an AWAIT-command, or a basic command AnnBasic R f, extracted as Atom-Basic f, and P is the corresponding precondition. The set of all assertions of an annotated command (including loop invariants) is collected by the function assertions.

Function interfree must be applied to all possible combinations of component programs, except for a component program with itself:

```
INTERFREE Ts ≡ ∀ i ∈ Index Ts. ∀ j ∈ Index Ts.
               i≠j ⟶ interfree (com(Ts!i), post(Ts!i), com(Ts!j))
```

With these preparations we can prove soundness of the proof rule for Parallel.

Theorem 3 (Strong Soundness for Parallel Composition)
Let Ts be a list of n component programs so that for each component (c_i, Q_i) the formula ⊢ c_i Q_i holds in the sense of partial correctness, and INTERFREE Ts holds. Suppose that (Parallel Ts, s) $\rightarrow^*_P$ (Parallel Rs, t) for some s ∈ pre(c_i) for i ∈ {1...n}, some list of component programs Rs and some state t. Let Rs_j = (ro_j, Q_j) be the jth component of Rs. Then for j ∈ {1...n},

- if ro_j = Some r_j for a command r_j then t ∈ pre(r_j),
- if ro_j = None then t ∈ Q_j.

In particular if ro_i = None for i ∈ {1...n}, we have that t ∈ Q_i for i ∈ {1...n}.

The proof is by induction on the length of the computation. First we fix j ∈ {1...n}. If the length is positive, we have the following situation:

```
(Parallel Ts, s) →*ₚ (Parallel Rs, b) →¹ₚ (Parallel(Rs[i:=(roᵢ, Qᵢ)]), t)
```

where the last step was performed by the ith component of Rs, (Some 1_i, Q_i), through transition (Some 1_i, b) $\rightarrow^1$ (ro_i, t).

Now two cases arise: i=j and i≠j. The first one is resolved with help of the Strong Soundness of Component Programs Theorem. The second one deserves some more attention.

It is proved by rule induction on the relation $\rightarrow^1$. It turns out that the induction hypothesis is too weak to solve both sequential cases. Therefore we need to prove a stronger lemma whose conclusion contains one more clause than the theorem above, namely INTERFREE Rs. This means that interference freedom is preserved throughout the computation, which is easily proved. Now all cases for i≠j can be solved and the proof is complete.

Soundness of the remaining inference rules for $\vdash_P$ is analogous to the case of atomic programs, with two main differences:

- Because of the lack of None as sign of termination, par_sem is now

  par_sem c s $\equiv$ {t. $\exists$ Ts. (c,s) $\to_P^*$ (Parallel Ts, t) $\wedge$ All_None Ts}

- We also have to consider the rule for while loops, whose proof of soundness relies on the following lemma:

  par_SEM (WHILE b INV inv DO c OD) = $\bigcup_{k=0}^{\infty}$ par_SEM (fwhile b c k)

  fwhile is defined by induction as the following sequence of programs

  fwhile b c 0 = Omega
  fwhile b c (Suc n) = IF b THEN c,,(fwhile b c n) ELSE SKIP FI

  where Omega and SKIP are the abbreviations

  SKIP $\equiv$ ParBasic Id
  Omega $\equiv$ WHILE TRUE INV TRUE DO SKIP OD .

5.4 Verification condition generation

The proof rules of our systems are syntax directed and can be used to generate the necessary verification conditions by using the rules backwards. This process has been encapsulated in an Isabelle tactic. Due to lack of space, we cannot go into details. Suffice it to say that, although the overall structure of the tactic is straightforward, there are some tricky issues involved because the state space is not fixed but depends on the number of variables that occur in the program. Thus we need to prove on the fly special instances of the assignment axiom that are specific to the program under consideration.

6 Examples

We have verified all the relevant examples in [2] and some others taken from the literature. Due to lack of space, we only present the producer/consumer problem (in the first subsection); a second subsection looks at a simple example of a schematic program where the number of components is not fixed.

The examples rely heavily on arrays which are modeled as lists. Thus array access A[i] becomes A!i and array update A[i]:=e becomes A:=A[i:=e].

6.1 Producer/Consumer

This problem models two processes, producer and consumer, that share a common, bounded buffer. The producer puts information into the buffer, the consumer takes it out. Trouble arise when the producer attemps to put a new item in a full buffer or the consumer tries to remove an item from an empty buffer. Following Owicki and Gries we express the problem as a parallel program with shared variables and AWAIT-commands. It copies an array a into an array b

```
{.0 < M₁ ∧ 0 < N ∧ M₁ = M₂.}
COBEGIN
 PROD ∥ CONS
COEND
{.∀ k. k < M₁ ⟶ a!k = b!k.}
```

where N = length buffer, M_1 = length a and M_2 = length b. The precondition imposes that the length of a and b be equal, and a, b and buffer have non-zero length. The full program is shown in Fig. 3.

Both components share the variables in and out, which count the values added to the buffer and the values removed from the buffer, respectively. Thus, the buffer contains in-out values at each moment. Expressions in mod N and out mod N determine the subscript of the buffer element where the next value is to be added or removed.

For readability we use following abbreviations:

```
INIT = 0 < M₁ ∧ 0 < N ∧ M₁ = M₂
I = ∀ k. (out ≤ k ∧ k < in ⟶ a!k = buffer!(k mod N) )
     ∧ out ≤ in ∧ in-out ≤ N
I₁ = I ∧ i ≤ M₁
p₁ = I₁ ∧ i = in
I₂ = I ∧ (∀ k. k < j ⟶ a!k = b!k) ∧ j ≤ M₁
p₂ = I₂ ∧ j = out
```

The command WAIT b END abbreviates r AWAIT b THEN SKIPEND.

The verification of this problem involves proving a total of 88 conditions. Half of them are trivially solved since they refer to triples of the form $(A \cap pre(r))$ r A where the atomic action r does not change the variables in A. The rest are automatically solved by an Isabelle simplification tactic.

6.2 Schematic programs

So far we have only considered programs with a fixed number of parallel components, because that is all the programming language allows. However, we would also like to establish the correctness of program schemas such as

```
COBEGIN A := A[1 := 0] ∥ ... ∥ A := A[n := 0] COEND
```

Although the syntax of the programming language does not cater for "...", HOL does. Using the well-known function map and the construct [i..j] (which represents the list of natural numbers from i to j) we can express the above schematic program in HOL as follows

```
Parallel (map (λ i. {.i < length A.} A := A[i:=0] {.A!i = 0.}) [1..n])
```

```
⊢P vars: in out i j x y buffer b.
{.INIT.}
in:=0,, out:=0,, i:=0,, j:=0,,
COBEGIN
     {.p₁ ∧ INIT.}
     WHILE i < M₁  INV {.p₁ ∧ INIT.}
     DO {.p₁ ∧ i < M₁ ∧ INIT.}
        x:= a!i;;
        {.p₁ ∧ i < M₁ ∧ x = a!i ∧ INIT.}
        WAIT in-out < N END;;
        {.p₁ ∧ i < M₁ ∧ x = a!i ∧ in-out < N ∧ INIT.}
        buffer:= buffer[(in mod N):= x];;
        {.p₁ ∧ i < M₁ ∧ a!i = buffer!(in mod N) ∧ in-out < N ∧ INIT.}
        in:= in+1;;
        {.I₁ ∧ (i+1) = in ∧ i < M₁ ∧ INIT.}
        i:= i+1
     OD
     {.p₁ ∧ i = M₁ ∧ INIT.}
||
     {.p₂ ∧ INIT.}
     WHILE j < M₁  INV {.p₂ ∧ INIT.}
     DO {.p₂ ∧ j < M₁ ∧ INIT.}
        WAIT out < in END;;
        {.p₂ ∧ j < M₁ ∧ out < in ∧ INIT.}
        y:= buffer!(out mod N);;
        {.p₂ ∧ j < M₁ ∧ out < in ∧ y = a!j ∧ INIT.}
        out:= out+1;;
        {.I₂ ∧ (j+1) = out ∧ j < M₁ ∧ y = a!j ∧ INIT.}
        b:= b[j:=y];;
        {.I₂ ∧ (j+1) = out ∧ j < M₁ ∧ a!j = b!j ∧ INIT.}
        j:= j+1
     OD
     {.p₂ ∧ j = M₁ ∧ INIT.}
COEND
{.∀ k. k<M₁ ⟶ a!k = b!k.}
```

Fig. 3. Producer/Consumer Problem

where we have already inserted the necessary annotations to prove

$$⊢_P \ \{.n < \text{length A.}\} \ \text{Parallel}(...) \ \{.∀ \ i. \ 1≤i ∧ i≤n ⟶ A!i = 0.\} \ .$$

Suffice it to say that the proof is fairly straightforward and does not even require induction on **n**, as one may have expected. We do not present the details because they are neither intellectually challenging nor very readable. The problem is that currently both pretty printing and verification condition generation only works for fully instantiated programs but not for schemas. Hence proofs about schematic programs are still more tedious than they could be.

7 Conclusion

We have presented the first formalization and (an improved) soundness proof of the Owicki/Gries method in a general purpose theorem prover. This is another step towards the embedding of realistic imperative programming languages and their verification calculi in a theorem prover. So far we have concentrated on the logical infrastructure and typical examples from the literature. We intend to extend our work in two directions: formalization of a compositional proof system and support for schematic programs as in §6.2. A completeness proof would also be interesting, but this is not our main focus. However, it should be mentioned that our current proof system is incomplete because there is no rule for removing auxiliary variables, an omission that is easy to fix.

The whole development required roughly three quarters of a person year: half a year to produce the first version, and another quarter of a year to polish the theory and document it. Most of the time was consumed by exploring different formalizations. The complete formalization comprises 350 lines of definitions, 1150 lines of proofs and 550 lines of ML code (for the parser and printer translation functions and the tactic explained in §5.4).

Acknowledgment We thank Javier Esparza, David von Oheimb, Cornelia Pusch and Markus Wenzel for the very helpful discussions, and two anonymous referees for their comments.

References

1. F. Andersen, K. Petersen, and J. Pettersson. Program verification using HOL-UNITY. In J. Joyce and C. Seger, editors, *Higher Order Logic Theorem Proving and Its Applications*, volume 780 of *Lect. Notes in Comp. Sci.*, pages 1–15. Springer-Verlag, 1994.
2. K. R. Apt and E.-R. Olderog. *Verification of Sequential and Concurrent Programs.* Springer-Verlag, 1991.
3. A. Camillieri. Mechanizing CSP trace theory in higher order logic. *IEEE Transactions on Software Engineering*, 16:993–1004, 1990.
4. B. Chetali and B. Heyd. Formal verification of concurrent programs in LP and COQ: A comparative analysis. In E. Gunter and A. Felty, editors, *Theorem Proving in Higher Order Logics*, volume 1275 of *Lect. Notes in Comp. Sci.*, pages 69–85. Springer-Verlag, 1997.
5. F. de Boer, U. Hannemann, and W.-P. de Roever. A compositional proof system for shared variable concurrency. In J. Fitzgerald, C. Jones, and P. Lucas, editors, *FME '97: Industrial Applications and Strengthened Foundations of Formal Methods*, volume 1313 of *Lect. Notes in Comp. Sci.*, pages 515–532. Springer-Verlag, 1997.
6. B. Dutertre and S. Schneider. Using a PVS embedding of CSP to verify authentication protocols. In E. Gunter and A. Felty, editors, *Theorem Proving in Higher Order Logics*, volume 1275 of *Lect. Notes in Comp. Sci.*, pages 121–136. Springer-Verlag, 1997.

7. U. Engberg, P. Grønning, and L. Lamport. Mechanical verification of concurrent systems with TLA. In G. v. Bochmann and D. Probst, editors, *Computer-Aided Verification (CAV'92)*, volume 663 of *Lect. Notes in Comp. Sci.*, pages 44–55. Springer-Verlag, 1993.

8. D. Goldschlag. Mechanically verifying concurrent programs with the Boyer-Moore Prover. *IEEE Transactions on Software Engineering*, 16:1005–1022, 1990.

9. M. Gordon. Mechanizing programming logics in higher order logic. In G. Birtwistle and P. Subrahmanyam, editors, *Current Trends in Hardware Verification and Automated Theorem Proving.* Springer-Verlag, 1989.

10. M. Gordon and T. Melham. *Introduction to HOL: a theorem-proving environment for higher order logic.* Cambridge University Press, 1993.

11. B. Heyd and P. Crégut. A modular coding of Unity in Coq. In J. von Wright, J. Grundy, and J. Harrison, editors, *Theorem Proving in Higher Order Logics*, volume 1125 of *Lect. Notes in Comp. Sci.*, pages 251–266. Springer-Verlag, 1996.

12. Isabelle home page. www.cl.cam.ac.uk/Research/HVG/isabelle.html.

13. C. B. Jones. Development methods for computer programs including a notion of interference. Technical Report PRG-25, Programming Research Group, Oxford University Computing Laboratory, 1981.

14. C. B. Jones. Tentative steps toward a development method for interfering programs. *ACM Trans. Programming Languages and Systems*, 5:596–619, 1983.

15. S. Kalvala. A formulation of TLA in isabelle. In E. Schubert, P. Windley, and J. Alves-Foss, editors, *Higher Order Logic Theorem Proving and its Applications*, volume 971 of *Lect. Notes in Comp. Sci.*, pages 214–228. Springer-Verlag, 1995.

16. T. Långbacka and J. von Wright. Refining reactive systems in HOL using action systems. In E. Gunter and A. Felty, editors, *Theorem Proving in Higher Order Logics*, volume 1275 of *Lect. Notes in Comp. Sci.*, pages 183–197. Springer-Verlag, 1997.

17. O. Müller and T. Nipkow. Traces of I/O automata in Isabelle/HOLCF. In M. Bidoit and M. Dauchet, editors, *TAPSOFT'97: Theory and Practice of Software Development*, volume 1214 of *Lect. Notes in Comp. Sci.*, pages 580–594. Springer-Verlag, 1997.

18. M. Nesi. Value-passing CCS in HOL. In J. Joyce and C. Seger, editors, *Higher Order Logic Theorem Proving and Its Applications*, volume 780 of *Lect. Notes in Comp. Sci.*, pages 352–365. Springer-Verlag, 1994.

19. T. Nipkow. Winskel is (almost) right: Towards a mechanized semantics textbook. In V. Chandru and V. Vinay, editors, *Foundations of Software Technology and Theoretical Computer Science*, volume 1180 of *Lect. Notes in Comp. Sci.*, pages 180–192. Springer-Verlag, 1996.

20. T. Nipkow. *Isabelle/HOL. The Tutorial*, 1998. Unpublished Manuscript. Available at www.in.tum.de/~nipkow/pubs/HOL.html.

21. T. Nipkow. Winskel is (almost) right: Towards a mechanized semantics textbook. *Formal Aspects of Computing*, ?, 1998. To appear.

22. S. Owicki and D. Gries. An axiomatic proof technique for parallel programs. *Acta Informatica*, 6:319–340, 1976.

23. L. C. Paulson. *Isabelle: A Generic Theorem Prover*, volume 828 of *Lect. Notes in Comp. Sci.* Springer-Verlag, 1994.

24. J. Søgaard-Andersen, S. Garland, J. Guttag, N. Lynch, and A. Pogosyants. Computer-assisted simulation proofs. In *Fourth Conference on Computer-Aided Verification*, volume 697 of *Lect. Notes in Comp. Sci.*, pages 305–319. Springer-Verlag, 1993.

25. K. Stølen. *Development of Parallel Programs on Shared Data-Structures*. PhD thesis, Computer Science Department, Manchester University, 1990.
26. H. Tej and B. Wolff. A corrected failure-divergence model for CSP in Isabelle/HOL. In J. Fitzgerald, C. Jones, and P. Lucas, editors, *FME '97: Industrial Applications and Strengthened Foundations of Formal Methods*, volume 1313 of *Lect. Notes in Comp. Sci.*, pages 318–337. Springer-Verlag, 1997.
27. J. von Wright, J. Hekanaho, P. Luostarinen, and T. Långbacka. Mechanizing some advanced refinement concepts. *Formal Methods in System Design*, 3:49–81, 1993.
28. J. von Wright and T. Långbacka. Using a theorem prover for reasoning about concurrent algorithms. In G. v. Bochmann and D. Probst, editors, *Computer-Aided Verification (CAV'92)*, volume 663 of *Lect. Notes in Comp. Sci.*, pages 56–68. Springer-Verlag, 1993.

Semantic-Driven Performance Evaluation

EXTENDED ABSTRACT

Chiara Nottegar[1], Corrado Priami,[1] Pierpaolo Degano[2]

[1] Dipartimento Scientifico Tecnologico, Università di Verona
Ca' Vignal 2, Strada Le Grazie 1, I-37134 Verona, Italy – priami@sci.univr.it
[2] Dipartimento di Informatica, Università di Pisa
Corso Italia 40, I-56100 Pisa, Italy – degano@di.unipi.it

Abstract. We propose a structural operational semantics for mobile and distributed agents. From it we derive a stochastic transition system labelled by actions and their costs. These costs reflect the (net) architecture on which agents run. We then map stochastic transition systems to Markov chains, and performance evaluation is carried out using standard tools. The results of our approach are shown to agree with the ones obtained via classical evaluation techniques on a case study involving mobile computation.

1 Introduction

Recently, stochastic process algebras [10,11,2,4,15,17,18] have been proposed as a mean to specify software and to derive general performance measures. Process algebra specifications are built by combining the basic actions, often called prefixes, that a system performs. The occurrence of a prefix is represented by a transition labelled by the associated action. The stochastic variants of process algebras associate probabilistic distributions with prefixes. The transitions are then labelled by a pair $\langle \mu, r \rangle$, where μ represents the action performed and completed in a time drawn from an exponential distribution with parameter r. We easily derive a continuous time Markov chain from a stochastic transition system. The stationary distribution of the chain, if any, is computed through standard numerical tools. Finally, performance analysis is carried out on the basis of stationary distributions. The main limitation of this solution is that the designer of a system must specify its intended behaviour already having in mind all the features of the architecture on which the specification will be implemented. Otherwise there is little hope to associate suitable distributions with prefixes. But the less details are needed at specification time, the better.

Our idea is to retain the advantages of stochastic process algebras without modifying the syntax of the classic process algebras and thus letting specifications be independent of architectural aspects of implementations. The association of probabilistic distributions with prefixes is then a matter of the compiler or the interpreter of the calculus. A compiler necessarily has all the relevant information about the target architecture, so we can re-use it.

The main contribution of the paper is the development of an algebraic representation of systems which is independent of their run-time support. The way in which rates of transitions are computed allows us to take run-time support into account. The neat separation of functional and quantitative information permits to consider different architectures for the same system, and to establish the most adequate in a semiautomatic way.

We are mainly interested in specifying and evaluating distributed applications, possibly involving code migration. To present our proposal in a pure setting, we adopt here the higher order π-calculus $(HO\pi)$ [19]. It is a basic language for mobility in which processes are first class values. Since our technique can be applied to any language with an operational semantics, no real limitation arises from our choice. Our proposal relies on the idea that performance evaluation and other quantitative analysis should start already at the design level. Besides robustness and reliability of the design, these early measures may save efforts. Indeed, if the design meets all behavioural requirements but leads to inefficient implementations, the system must be re-designed. This calls for the integration of behavioural and quantitative analysis of systems in a single methodology.

Our starting point is an enhanced version of operational semantics that gives raise to a hierarchy of specifications of distributed systems increasingly nearer to implementations [8,16]. The definition of the operational semantics follows the SOS style [14], where the activities of a system are represented by transitions deduced according to a set of inference rules driven by the syntax. More precisely, we exploit proved transition systems, a parametric model used in [7.9] to uniformly describe different qualitative aspects of processes. Transitions are labelled by encodings of their proofs. Intuitively, the proof of a transition can be interpreted as the low level routines performed by the run-time support to execute the transition. Then, by inspecting these rich labels we derive the costs of transitions, reflecting the target architecture. In our SOS definition of the operational semantics of $HO\pi$, the cost function is parametric and can be instantiated to reflect different target architectures. In this way, the same definition can describe the behaviour of a system running on different targets.

Many real languages for concurrency, like Facile, PICT, CML, are built on top of a core process calculus like the π-calculus [13] we use here, which can be seen as an intermediate language. Therefore, the compiled code of high level programs can be annotated with information about the physical architecture. along the lines that we propose here.

We end the paper with a case study involving mobile computation. The results given by our approach are shown to agree with those obtained via classical evaluation techniques [1]. This is a very small step towards the applicability of our approach. It is certainly the case that further case studies need to be done in order to refine the technique.

2 Higher Order π-Calculus

In this section we briefly recall the higher order π-calculus $(HO\pi)$ [19], a model of concurrent communicating processes providing the notion of *naming*. Names can represent processes, and thus communications may cause processes to migrate. We slightly enrich its syntax to better express performance analysis.

Definition 1.
Let $\mathcal{N}$ be a countable infinite set of *names* $a, b, \ldots, x, y, \ldots$ and let $\mathcal{S}$ be a countable infinite set of *invisible actions* $\tau_0, \tau_1, \ldots$ with $\mathcal{N} \cap \mathcal{S} = \emptyset$. We also assume a set of *agent identifiers*, each with an arity, ranged over by $A, A_1, \ldots$. Let $\mathcal{P}$ be a countable infinite set of *processes* $P, Q, R, \ldots$ and let $\mathcal{V}$ be a set of *process variables* $X, Y, \ldots$. Let K stand for a process or for a name and let U stand for a process variable or for a name. Thus, we have the following syntax

$$P ::= 0 \mid X \mid \pi.P \mid \sum_{j \in J} P_j \mid P|P \mid (\nu x)P \mid [x = y]P \mid A(U_1, \ldots, U_n)$$

where π may be either $x(U)$ for *input*, or $\overline{x}K$ for *output* (where x is the *subject* and U and K are the *object*) or τ_i for *silent* moves. Also, J in the summation above is a finite index set. Hereafter, the trailing 0 will be omitted.

The prefix π is the first atomic action that the process $\pi.P$ can perform. The input prefix $x(U)$ binds the occurrences of U in the prefixed process P. Intuitively, some name or process U is received along the link named x. The output prefix $\overline{x}K$ does not bind the name or process K which is sent along x. A silent prefix τ_i denotes an action which is invisible to an external observer of the system. We use a set of silent prefixes because different internal actions may have different durations. Summation denotes nondeterministic choice. The process $\sum_{j \in J} P_j$ behaves as one among the P_j. The operator $|$ describes parallel composition of processes. The components of $P_1|P_2$ may act independently; also, an output action of P_1 (resp. P_2) at any output port $\overline{x}$ may synchronize with an input action of P_2 (resp. P_1) at x to create a silent action of the communication. The operator (νx) acts as a static binder for the name x in the process P that it prefixes. In other words, x is a unique name in P which is different from all the external names. The agent $(\nu x)P$ behaves as P except that actions at ports $\overline{x}$ and x are prohibited. However communications along link x of components of P are not prohibited because the resulting action will be a τ. We sometimes write $(\nu x, y)P$ for $(\nu x)(\nu y)P$. Matching $[x = y]P$ is an `if-then` operator: process P is activated if $x = y$. Each agent identifier A has a unique defining equation of the form $A(\tilde{U}) = P$ (hereafter, $\tilde{U}$ denotes $U_1, \ldots, U_n$), where the U_i are all distinct and are the only free names in P.

The operational semantics for the $HO\pi$ is defined in the *SOS* style. The metavariable for the labels of transitions is μ (it is distinct from π, the metavariable for prefixes, though it coincides in three cases). We introduce the set $\mathcal{A}$ of visible actions ranged over by α (i.e. $x(U)$ for input, $\overline{x}K$ for free output, and

$\overline{x}(K)$ for bound output). The bound output is originated by the interplay of output prefix and restriction as shown in Tab. 1.

We define our *enhanced labels*, in the style of [6,3,7]. The label of a transition records the inference rules used during its deduction, besides the action itself. It is then possible to derive different semantic models for $HO\pi$ by extracting new kinds of labels from the enriched ones (in [9] the last two authors studied qualitative aspects of the calculus). We call *proof term* the encoding of the proof in an enhanced label. Finally, we introduce a function ℓ that takes an enhanced label to the corresponding standard action label.

Definition 2. Let $\mathcal{L} = \{\|_0, \|_1\}$ with $\chi \in \mathcal{L}^*$, $\mathcal{O} = \{\sum_{m,h}, =_m, (\nu x), (\tilde{U})\} \ni o$ and let $\vartheta \in (\mathcal{L} \cup \mathcal{O})^*$. Then the set Θ of *enhanced labels* (with metavariable θ) is defined by the following syntax

$$\theta ::= \vartheta\alpha \mid \vartheta\tau_i \mid \vartheta\langle\|_0\vartheta_0\alpha_0, \|_1\vartheta_1\alpha_1\rangle$$

with $\alpha_0 = x(U)$ iff α_1 is either $\overline{x}K$ or $\overline{x}(K)$, and vice versa.
Function ℓ is defined as $\ell(\vartheta\alpha) = \alpha$, $\ell(\vartheta\tau_i) = \ell(\vartheta\langle\|_0\vartheta_0\alpha_0, \|_1\vartheta_1\alpha_1\rangle) = \tau$.

A tag $\sum_{m,h}$ means that a nondeterministic choice has been resolved in favour of the hth component among m summands. Rule Par_0 (Par_1) adds to the label a tag $\|_0$ ($\|_1$) to record that the left (right) component is moving. Restriction is represented in labels to record that a filter has been passed. We record the resolution of a matching through tag $=_m$, where m is the size of the data to be compared. The rules Com_0 and $Close_0$ have in their conclusion a pair instead of a τ to record the components which interacted (and the proof of the relevant transitions). Their symmetric version Com_1 and $Close_1$ are obvious and are omitted. Finally, the invocation of a definition enriches the label of the conclusion of rule Ide with the tag $(\tilde{U})$. We also record in the labels the actual parameters $\tilde{U}$ because their number and size affect the instantiation cost.

Our transition system for $HO\pi$ is in Tab. 1, where an auxiliary transition relation $\xrightarrow{\theta}_I$ is used. The set I contains names that can occur in a communicated process and that are extruded. Rules $Close$ use I to include the receiving process as well in the scope of the extruded names. Rule $Open$ updates the set of these names, that $Close$ empties (note that in rules $Open$ and $Close$ it is $I \subseteq fn(K)$). The actual transitions are generated by rule $HO\pi$ that discards index I. The transitions in the conclusion of each rule stand for all their variants. Recall that a variant of $P \xrightarrow{\theta} Q$ is a transition which only differs in that P and Q have been replaced by processes that are α-equivalent (they only differ in the choice of bound names), and $\ell(\theta)$ has been α-converted, where a name bound in $\ell(\theta)$ includes Q in its scope [13].

Hereafter, we write a transition $P \xrightarrow{\theta} Q$ simply as θ, when unambiguous. We also write $Ts(P_i)$ to denote the set of the transitions enabled in P_i. As usual, we denote transition systems by quadruple $\langle \mathcal{P}, \Theta, \longrightarrow, P \rangle$, where $\mathcal{P}$ is the set of states (processes), Θ is the labelling alphabet, $\longrightarrow$ is the transition relation defined in Tab. 1, and P is the initial state.

$$Act: \quad \pi.P \xrightarrow{\pi}_\emptyset P$$

$$Sum: \quad \frac{P_h \xrightarrow{\theta}_I P'_h}{\sum_{j\in J} P_j \xrightarrow{\sum |J|,h\, \theta}_I P'_h}, \ h\in J \qquad Par_0: \quad \frac{P \xrightarrow{\theta}_I P'}{P|Q \xrightarrow{\|_0 \theta}_I P'|Q}, \ (bn(l(\theta))\cup I)\cap fn(Q)=\emptyset$$

$$Res: \quad \frac{P \xrightarrow{\theta}_I P'}{(\nu x)P \xrightarrow{(\nu x)\theta}_I (\nu x)P'}, \ x\notin n(l(\theta)) \qquad Par_1: \quad \frac{P \xrightarrow{\theta}_I P'}{Q|P \xrightarrow{\|_1 \theta}_I Q|P'}, \ (bn(l(\theta))\cup I)\cap fn(Q)=\emptyset$$

$$Match: \quad \frac{P \xrightarrow{\theta}_I P'}{[x=x]P \xrightarrow{=sise(x)\,\theta}_I P'} \qquad Open: \quad \frac{P \xrightarrow{\vartheta \bar{x} K}_I P'}{(\nu I)P \xrightarrow{\vartheta \bar{x}(K)}_I P'}, \ x\notin I\subseteq fn(K)$$

$$Close_0: \quad \frac{P \xrightarrow{\vartheta \bar{x}(K)}_I P', \ Q \xrightarrow{\vartheta' x(U)}_\emptyset Q'}{P|Q \xrightarrow{(\|_0 \vartheta \bar{x}(K),\|_1 \vartheta' x(U))}_\emptyset (\nu I)(P'|Q'\{K/U\})}, \ fn(K)\cap fn(Q)=\emptyset$$

$$Com_0: \quad \frac{P \xrightarrow{\vartheta \bar{x} K}_\emptyset P', \ Q \xrightarrow{\vartheta' x(U)}_\emptyset Q'}{P|Q \xrightarrow{(\|_0 \vartheta \bar{x} K,\|_1 \vartheta' x(U))}_\emptyset P'|Q'\{K/U\}}$$

$$Ide: \quad \frac{P\{\tilde{K}/\tilde{U}\} \xrightarrow{\theta}_I P'}{A(\tilde{K}) \xrightarrow{(\tilde{K})\theta}_I P'}, \ A(\tilde{U})=P$$

$$HO\pi: \quad \frac{P \xrightarrow{\theta}_I P'}{P \xrightarrow{\theta} P'}$$

Table 1. Proved transition system of the HOπ-calculus.

The standard interleaving semantics is obtained from the proved transition system by relabelling each transition through function ℓ in Def. 2.

3 Stochastic semantics

We first discuss how to assign costs to individual transitions. Then we show how to extract a continuous time Markov chain (CTMC) from a proved transition system. Finally we describe how to evaluate performance measures starting from a CTMC.

3.1 Cost function

We now show how the parameter r of the action $\mu = \ell(\theta)$ from a label θ is derived. The intended meaning of r is that the execution of the action μ is completed in a time drawn from an exponential distribution with parameter r, called the *rate* of the transition. Indeed, this is the interpretation in classical stochastic process algebras, where the designer of a system assign a *fixed* rate to *all* the occurrences of μ. But this is seldom the case in real situations because the actual cost of μ depends on the basic operations that the run-time support of the target architecture performs for firing μ. Typically, the resolution of a choice imposes some operations on the target architecture such as checking the ready list or implementing fairness policies. Therefore, in practice an action fired after a choice costs more than the same action occurring deterministically. The other operations of our calculus reflect analogous routines of the run-time support and delay the execution of an action as well – communications deserve a special treatment, see below. Therefore, we first assign a rate to the transition μ on a dedicated architecture that has only to perform μ. In other words, μ occurs in the empty context. We then model the performance degradation due to the run-time support by introducing a scaling factor for r for any operation of the routine implementing the transition θ. In this way, the new semantics takes into account the target architecture on which a system runs. Also, we automatically derive the distributions of transitions by inspecting the syntactical contexts where the actions which originate them are plugged. In fact, the context in which an action μ occurs in the program represents the operations that the target machine performs for firing μ just because the structural operational semantics of a language specifies its abstract machine. Accordingly, a suitable linearization of the deduction of a transition represents the execution of the corresponding run-time support routines on the target machine. As mentioned above, a proof term θ represents the context in which an action occurs and the proof of the transition it labels. Following this intuition and the discussion above, we assign a cost to each inference rule of the operational semantics via a function denoted by $. In other words, the occurrence of a transition receives a duration time computed according to its deduction.

As a matter of fact, there is no need to fix here function $, and we let it be a parameter to the definition of our model. In this way, it is possible to estimate the performance of different architectures, each with its own cost function.

We propose below a possible definition of $ that considers some features of a somehow idealized architecture like the number of processors of a net or the bandwidth of a channel. Although not very accurate, they permit to derive performance measures that agree with the ones in the literature [1,5]. Other case studies are needed to tune the function $.

We first assign costs to actions in $\mathcal{N} \cup \mathcal{S}$. When applied to a visible action $a \in \mathcal{A}$, our cost function returns the parameter of the exponential distribution which describes the time needed to perform the very basic, low-level operations corresponding to a, independently of the context in which a occurs. Similarly for the invisible actions τ_i that are not communications. We use a function $\$_\mu : \mathcal{N} \cup \mathcal{S} \to \mathbb{R}^+$ defined as

$$\$_\mu(\tau_i) = \lambda_i$$
$$\$_\mu(\overline{x}K) = f_{out}(bw(x), size(K))$$
$$\$_\mu(\overline{x}(K)) = f_{bo}(bw(x), size(K))$$
$$\$_\mu(x(U)) = f_{in}(bw(x), size(U))$$

The real numbers λ_i represent the cost of executing the routine corresponding to the ith internal action τ_i. The functions f_{out}, f_{bo} and f_{in} define the costs of the routines which implement the send and receive primitives. Function f_{bo} differs from f_{out} because y must be a fresh name, so it incorporates a call to a name generator gs (i.e., $f_{bo} = f_{out} + gs$). Besides the implementation cost due to the algorithms of send and receive, the functions above depends on the bandwidth of the communication channel ($bw(x)$) and the size of the objects transmitted.

According to the intuition that contexts slow down the speed of actions, we now determine a slowing factor (in $(0, 1]$) for any construct of the language. The cost of the operators in $\mathcal{L} \cup \mathcal{O}$ is expressed by the function $\$_o : \mathcal{L} \cup \mathcal{O} \to (0, 1]$

$$\$_o(\textstyle\sum_{m,j}) = f_+(m)$$
$$\$_o(||_i) = f_{||}(np), \quad i = 0, 1$$
$$\$_o(=_{size(x)}) = f_=(size(x))$$
$$\$_o((\nu x)) = f_\nu(n(P))$$
$$\$_o((U_1, \ldots, U_m)) = f_{()}(size(U_1), \ldots, size(U_m), np)$$

We have explicitly used a minimal set of parameters affecting the cost of the routines implementing any operator. In particular, the resolution of a choice implementing fairness policies is affected at least by the number of summands. Parallel composition is evaluated according to the number np of processors available. A particular case is $\$_o(||) = 1$ that arises when there is an unbound number of processors. (Recall that we are not yet considering communications.) The cost of matching depends on the size of the data to be compared. The cost of restriction depends at least on the number of names in a process because its resolution needs a search in a table of names. Finally, the activation of a new process via a constant invocation has a cost depending on the size and the number of the actual parameters as well as on the number of processors available.

We now consider synchronizations. To determine their impact on the overall cost function, we follow their deduction. Essentially, the two partners perform independently some low-level operations locally to their environment. These operations (call them *pre-synch*) correspond to the rules applied to fill in the premises of rules Com and $Close$. The application of either of them is recorded by pairing the proof terms corresponding to the pre-synch operations. Note that Com or $Close$ rules can be applied exactly once in a derivation (see Tab. 1). Afterwards, some operations common to both partners are needed to derive the actual transition representing the communication. The cost of these additional operators is derived using $\$_o$.

We compute the slow down factor due to communication as follows. Since it is synchronous and handshaking, we first take the minimum of the costs of the pre-synch operations performed by the participants independently. Thus a communication reflects the speed of its slower partner.

We then use a function $f_{()} : \mathcal{L}^* \times \mathcal{L}^* \to (0, 1]$ to take the distance of the partners into account. For encoding locations, we use here $\chi_0, \chi_1 \in \{||_0, ||_1\}^*$. To see why, consider the binary abstract syntax tree of a process, when the parallel composition | is the only syntactic operator. Then, a sequence χ can be seen as the access path from the root, i.e. from the whole process, to a leaf, i.e. to a sub-process. So, the two arguments of $f_{()}$, together with allocation tables, can be used to determine where the two communicating processes actually reside.

To apply function $f_{()}$, we need an auxiliary function $\underline{\cdot} : (\mathcal{L} \cup \mathcal{O})^* \to \mathcal{L}^*$ that extracts the parallel tags from proof terms, inductively defined as (ϵ is the empty string)

$$\underline{\epsilon} = \epsilon, \quad \underline{||_i \vartheta} = ||_i \underline{\vartheta}, \quad \underline{o\vartheta} = \underline{\vartheta}$$

We can now define the function that maps a proof term θ to a pair $\langle \ell(\theta), \$(\theta) \rangle$, by giving the function $\$$. It is defined inducing on θ and using the auxiliary functions $\$_\mu$ as basis and $\$_o$ and $f_{()}$. The function $\$: \Theta \to \mathbb{R}^+$ is defined as follows

$$\$(\mu) = \$_\mu(\mu)$$
$$\$(o\theta) = \$_o(o)\$(\theta)$$
$$\$(\langle \vartheta_0 a_0, \vartheta_1 a_1 \rangle) = f_{()}(\underline{\vartheta_0}, \underline{\vartheta_1}) \times \min\{\$(\vartheta_0 \alpha_0), \$(\vartheta_1 \alpha_1)\}$$

3.2 Interpretation of costs

The interpretation of a transition $P_0 \xrightarrow{\theta} P_1$ is as follows. The action $\ell(\theta)$ has to wait a delay Δt drawn from the exponential distribution with parameter $\$(\theta)$ before its actual completion. In other words, Δt may be seen as the duration of the transition.

The dynamic behaviour of processes is determined by a *race condition*. All activities enabled attempt to proceed, but only the fastest one succeeds. The fastest activity is different on successive attempts because durations are expressed by random variables. The continuity of probabilistic distributions ensures that the probability of two activities ending simultaneously is zero. Furthermore, exponential distributions enjoy the *memoryless property*. Roughly speaking, the time at which a transition occurs is independent of the time at which the last transition occurred. Thus, the time elapsed by an activity in a state in which another one is the fastest is useless. This means that any time a transition becomes enabled, it restarts its elapsing time as it were the first time that it is enabled.

The race condition replaces nondeterministic choices with probabilistic ones. In fact, we can associate probabilities to transitions as follows. We define the *exit rate* of P (written $r(P)$) as the sum of the rates of all activities that are enabled in P, i.e. $r(P) = \sum_{\theta_i \in Ts(P)} \$(\theta_i)$. The occurrence probability of a transition $P \xrightarrow{\theta} P'$ is the ratio between its rate and the *exit rate* of P, i.e. $\$(\theta)/r(P)$. Consider the process $P = a + (a + b)$. If we define the cost function as

$$\$(a) = 1, \quad \$(b) = 3, \quad \$(+_i) = 1/2$$

the costs of the transitions are

$$\$(+_o a) = 1/2, \quad \$(+_1 +_0 a) = 1/4 \quad \$(+_1 +_1 b) = 3/4.$$

Thus the exit rate of P is $3/2$, and the probability that P fires the transition $+_0 a$ is $1/3$. Following [11], we need the *apparent rate* of an action a in a given process P, $r_a(P)$. It is the sum of the rates of all actions a that are enabled in P, i.e. $r_a(P) = \sum_{\substack{\theta_i \in T_s(P) \\ l(\theta_i)=a}} \$(\theta_i)$. For instance, the apparent rate of a in P is $3/4$. This is the rate captured by an external observer of the system, that can only register actions and their occurrence frequency. Apparent rate allows us to compute *conditional probabilities*, as well. In fact, the probability of a transition $P \xrightarrow{\theta} P'$, with $l(\theta) = a$, given that an action a occurs, is $\$(\theta)/r_a(P)$. For example, the probability of the transition $+_0 a$ in P, given that an a occurs, is $2/3$. Therefore, the rate of a transition is its occurrence probability times its apparent rate. As usual, assume that parallel processes independently decide which actions to fire.

We recall the notion of stochastic process. A family of random variables $\{X(t) \text{ s.t. } t \in T\}$ is a *stochastic process* with index set T. The set T is usually called *time parameter* and t is called *time*. The process is *continuous time* if T is a continuous set. The *state space* of the process is the set of possible values that $X(t)$ can assume. Intuitively, $X(t)$ is the state of the process at time t. Many systems arising in practice have the property that, once in a given state, the past states have no influence on the future. This is called the *memoryless* or *Markov property* and the stochastic processes satisfying it are called *Markov chains*, if their state space is discrete.

The following theorem suggests how to turn a process into a *CTMC*. We restrict ourselves to processes that originate a finite state space and that are closed (i.e they contain no free name). The proof of Theorem 3 is a straightforward adaptation of the one of a similar result for *PEPA* [11]. We first introduce some auxiliary notation.

Given a transition relation $\longrightarrow$, we define $\longrightarrow^*$ as its reflexive and transitive closure, and we let the label of $\longrightarrow^*$, if any, be the string obtained by concatenation of the labels of the sequence of transitions $\longrightarrow$ in the closure. Also, we say that a process P_i is a *derivative* of a process P, if there exists a computation with source P and target P_i (in symbols, $P \xrightarrow{s}^* P_i$). Then, given a process P, we let hereafter $d(P) = \{P_i \mid P \xrightarrow{s}^* P_i\}$ be the set of all derivatives P_i of P. We can now state the theorem.

Theorem 3. *Given a process P, the stochastic process $\{X(t), t \geq 0\}$, where $X(t_i) = P_j$ means that process P at time t_i behaves as process P_j, is a continuous time Markov chain homogeneous in time with state space $d(P)$.*

We now define the instantaneous transition rate of the generator matrix at the level of the proved transition system. Recall that the transitions enabled in a process cannot be disabled by flow of time, i.e. the *CTMC* associated with a process is homogeneous in time. Therefore, the instantaneous transition rate from P_i to P_j is the sum of the rates of the transitions enabled in P_i and leading to P_j. More formally, we have the following proposition.

Proposition 4. *Given* $\langle \mathcal{P}, \Theta, \longrightarrow, P \rangle$, *let* $P_i, P_j \in \mathcal{P}$, *and let* $n = |d(P)|$. *Then, the generator matrix of the corresponding* CTMC *is a square matrix* $\mathbf{Q}$ $n \times n$ *whose elements* $q_{i,j}$ *are defined as*

$$q_{i,j} = \sum_{P_i \xrightarrow{\theta_n} P_j \in Ts(P_i)} \$(\theta_n), \text{ for } i \neq j, \text{ and } q_{i,i} = -\sum_{j \neq i}^{n} q_{i,j}$$

Since the equation in the above proposition defines the instantaneous transition rate from P_i to P_j in terms of the transitions of P_i, and since our semantics is finite branching (our systems are finite state and closed), we can define in *SOS* style the *CTMC* associated with a system. More precisely, we define a stratified transition system whose transition relation $\longrightarrow_M$ is defined in terms of $\longrightarrow$. We let the *CTMC* of a process P_i (written $CTMC(P_i)$) be the minimal transition graph defined by rule

$$CTMC : \frac{P_i \xrightarrow{\theta} P_j}{P_i \xrightarrow{q_{i,j}}_M P_j}$$

where $q_{i,j}$ is defined according to Proposition 4.

3.3 Performance

We give a necessary condition for a process to originate a Markov chain with stationary distribution. Since the chains we consider have a finite state space, we are left to identify transition systems that guarantee the irreducibility of the corresponding Markov chains. If we call *cyclic* a state of a transition system that can be reached by any of its derivatives through a finite sequence of transitions, we have the following theorem.

Theorem 5. *Let* $\langle \mathcal{P}, \Theta, \longrightarrow, P \rangle$ *be a transition system with* P *cyclic. Then, $CTMC(P)$ is irreducible.*

Recall that if $CTMC(P)$ has a stationary distribution Π, it can be computed by solving the matrix equation

$$\Pi \mathbf{Q} = 0 \text{ with } \sum_i \Pi(P_i) = 1 \tag{1}$$

To get performance measures for process P, we associate a *reward* to each action a and we denote it as ρ_a, according to [12,11]. The reward of a process P is the sum of the rewards of the activities it enables, i.e. $\rho(P_i) = \sum_{\theta \in Ts(P_i)} \rho_{\ell(\theta)}$. The total reward of a component P is computed on the basis of an equilibrium distribution Π as

$$R(P) = \sum_{P \longrightarrow P_i} \rho(P_i) \Pi(P_i)$$

In the next section we report an example that shows how rewards are used to carry out performance evaluation.

4   A case study

In this section we use our mathematical framework to compare the relative efficiency of *remote procedure call* (*RPC*) and *remote evaluation* (*RE*) for a network management application presented in [1].

The management of networks based on *IP* uses the *simple network management protocol*. A *network management station* (*NMS*) calls some remote procedure for any server running on the network units which maintain a local data base with information for the maintenance of the network. The procedures above are typically *get* or *set* of values in the data base. This kind of interaction between *NMS* and the server is called *micro-management* and it generates a huge amount of network traffic.

Migration of code can reduce the traffic by sending to the server a piece of code that groups all the calls together. This approach is known as *management by delegation*. To compare our results with those of [1], we use their assumptions (reported below).

We assume that a data block of size X at the ISO/OSI application level generates at the network level an amount of data

$$X' = \alpha(X) + \beta(X)X$$

where $\alpha(X)$ is the cost of the *set-up* phase in a connection oriented protocol, and $\beta(X)$ is the size of the increment due to message encapsulation. For the sake of presentation, we adopt a single *overhead* function η such that

$$X' = \eta(X)X \quad \text{with } \eta(X) = \alpha(X)/X + \beta(X), \ \eta(X) > 1$$

and we write ηX for $\eta(X)X$.

We consider an application that collects data from N network units via Q remote procedure calls to each unit. We also assume that the interactions between *NMS* and any of the units is the same. Thus, we can safely specify the interactions with a single unit. The formal specification in $HO\pi$ is

$$NMS = \overline{a}\,i_1.\,a\,(R).\,\overline{a}\,i_2.\,a\,(R).\ldots.\,\overline{a}\,i_Q.\,a\,(R).\,NMS$$
$$D = a\,(I_k).\,\overline{a}\,r_k.\,D$$
$$Sys^{RPC} = (\nu a)\,(NMS|D)$$

NMS asks i_1 to D and waits for an answer. It repeats this task Q times. The unit D answers a datum r_k to a request i_k from the station. The channel a between *NMS* and D is made private via the operator (νa) in Sys^{RPC}. The corresponding proved transition system is depicted in Fig. 1 (a), where we omit (νa) that prefixes all the labels.

Consider now the solution for code migration based on *remote evaluation* (*RE*). *NMS* sends a piece of code to D which queries *locally* the data base. A single message is needed to send back the Q answers to *NMS*. The specification in $HO\pi$ is

$$NMS = \overline{a}\,G.\,a\,(T).\,NMS \quad D = a\,(X).\,\overline{a}\,Qr.\,D \quad Sys^{RE} = (\nu a)\,(NMS|D)$$

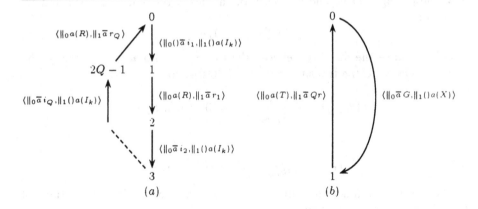

Fig. 1. Proved transition system of Sys^{RPC} (a) and of Sys^{RE} (b). We omitted (νa) that prefixes all the labels.

and the corresponding proved transition system is in Fig. 1 (b). We assume that the agent is killed after the answers are sent back to *NMS*. This allows us to compare the *RPC* and *RE* solutions presented in [1].

According to our framework, we now define the cost function for the two solutions. We assume that requests and answers have average size I and R, respectively. Similarly, the average size of code migration is denoted by C. Let λ be the rate of sending one bit on the channel a; then the rate of sending an object on the same channel is the ratio of λ to the dimension (in bits) of the object. Thus, we have

$$\$(\bar{a}\,i_k) = \frac{\lambda}{\eta_{RPC}\,I}, \quad \$(\bar{a}\,r_k) = \frac{\lambda}{\tilde{\eta}_{RPC}\,R}, \quad \$(\bar{a}\,G) = \frac{\lambda}{\eta_{RE}\,C}, \quad \$(\bar{a}\,Qr) = \frac{\lambda}{\tilde{\eta}_{RE}\,QR}$$

where η_{RPC}, $\tilde{\eta}_{RPC}$, η_{RE} and $\tilde{\eta}_{RE}$ are the overhead of a single answer, a single request, a migration of code and of the Q answers sent back all together. The cost of input on a is related to that of output, but we have to take into account the substitutions of formal parameters with actual ones in the code of the process receiving the message. Thus we divide the cost of output by the number $k \geq 1$.

$$\$(a(x)) = \$(\bar{a}\,x)/k.$$

There is no rise of cost due to the parallel composition because there are two processors: one on the node of the *NMS* and one on that of D, so

$$\$_o(\|_i) = 1.$$

We indicate the rise of cost due to the restriction of the name a, to the invocation of identifiers and to the choice, respectively with

$$\$_o((\nu a)) = 1/n \text{ and } \$_o(()) = 1/p \text{ and } \$_o(+_i) = 1/l.$$

Now, supposing that $\|_0$ and $\|_1$ codify the names of the nodes of *NMS* and D, we assume

$$f_{()}(\|_0, \|_1) = 1/d$$

in order to take the distance between the two nodes into account. Finally, the costs associated to the transitions in the *RPC* case are

$$\$(\theta_{i,i+1}) = \frac{\lambda}{ndkp\eta_{RPC}I}, \quad i = 0, 2, 4, .., 2Q - 2$$

and

$$\$(\theta_{i,i+1}) = \frac{\lambda}{ndk\tilde{\eta}_{RPC}R}, \quad i = 1, 3, 5, .., 2Q - 1.$$

The same cost function $\$$ allows us to associate costs to the transitions of the *RE* specification. We have

$$\$(\theta_{0,1}) = \frac{\lambda}{ndkp\eta_{RE}C}, \quad \$(\theta_{1,0}) = \frac{\lambda}{ndk\tilde{\eta}_{RE}QR}.$$

We now can define the generator matrices $\mathbf{Q}^{RPC}$ and $\mathbf{Q}^{RE}$ of the two specifications according to Proposition 4. Since the initial states of both Sys^{RPC} and Sys^{RE} are cyclic, Theorem 5 ensures that the two systems have stationary distributions Π^{RPC} and Π^{RE}, and we can compute them according to equation (1). We yield,

$$\Pi^{RPC}(2i) = \frac{p\eta_{RPC}I}{Q(p\eta_{RPC}I + \tilde{\eta}_{RPC}R)} \quad \Pi^{RPC}(2i+1) = \frac{\tilde{\eta}_{RPC}R}{Q(p\eta_{RPC}I + \tilde{\eta}_{RPC}R)}$$

with $i = 0, \ldots, Q - 1$, and

$$\Pi^{RE} = \left(\frac{p\eta_{RE}C}{p\eta_{RE}C + \tilde{\eta}_{RE}QR}, \frac{\tilde{\eta}_{RE}QR}{p\eta_{RE}C + \tilde{\eta}_{RE}QR} \right).$$

We end this section by comparing the efficiency of the two specifications. First we compute the throughput of both systems, i.e. the number of completed interactions *NMS-D* per unit time. Since in both systems each activity is visited only once, this throughput will be the same as the throughput of every activity. The throughput for an activity is found by associating a reward equal to the activity rate with each instance of the activity. So we compute the throughput of both systems by associating a reward equal to its rate to the first communication and a null reward to the other communications. Thus,

$$T^{RPC} = \sum_{i=0}^{2Q-1} \rho(i)\Pi^{RPC}(i) = \rho(0)\Pi^{RPC}(0) = \frac{\lambda}{ndkQ(p\eta_{RPC}I + \tilde{\eta}_{RPC}R)}$$

and

$$T^{RE} = \rho(0)\Pi^{RE}(0) + \rho(1)\Pi^{RE}(1) = \frac{\lambda}{ndk(p\eta_{RE}C + \tilde{\eta}_{RE}QR)}.$$

We can state that Sys^{RE} is better than or equivalent to Sys^{RPC} if $T^{RE} \geq T^{RPC}$. More precisely, we want

$$\frac{\lambda}{ndk(p\eta_{RE}C + \tilde{\eta}_{RE}QR)} \geq \frac{\lambda}{ndkQ(p\eta_{RPC}I + \tilde{\eta}_{RPC}R)}$$

hence

$$\eta_{RE}C \leq (Q\tilde{\eta}_{RPC}R - \tilde{\eta}_{RE}QR)/p + Q\eta_{RPC}l$$

Since the overhead η is fixed for any packet of a message, the longer the message, the lower the overhead is. Therefore, we usually have

$$Q\tilde{\eta}_{RPC}R \geq \tilde{\eta}_{RE}QR.$$

The analysis above suggests to use RE when the size of the agent sent is smaller than the sum of all the requests plus the difference of the overhead in the transmission of the answer. We finally note that by letting $p \simeq 1$ (because this cost is not considered in [1]), our results coincide with those in [1].

5   Conclusions and Further Work

The advantage of our approach is that it relies on a formal model which can be used as the kernel of a programming environment. In fact, the $CTMC$'s of the systems can be automatically derived from their transition systems. We only need to manipulate labels of transitions and to merge some arcs. Then, standard numerical packages can be used to derive performance measures. Note that the construction of the proved transition system only amounts to implement an interpreter for the semantic rules. Due to the syntax-directed way in which SOS semantics is defined, the interpreter can be easily written with a functional or logic language.

A calculus like the one we considered here can be the core of a real language (see Facile, PICT, CML, etc.). The compiled code can be annotated to make quantitative analysis. Also, it can be tranformed into syntactically different, yet behaviourally equivalent versions, via the usual equivalence laws (e.g. $P|(Q|R) = (P|Q)|R)$), before beginning to evaluate its performance. In this way, the compiler can help choosing not only the more suited architecture, but also the more adequate syntactic representation. This can be seen as a first step towards a code optimizer for concurrent languages, driven by semantics.

We tested our proposal on an application for network management presented in [1]. Under the same assumptions, our performance results agree with those of [1]. Lack of space prevents us from giving another example, taken from [5], for which again our method gives results in agreement with [5]. This makes us confident that our approach is applicable. Of course, we still need to apply our ideas to real size applications to test whether our method is scalable and to get more experience in the definition of reasonable cost functions.

Acknowledgments. The last author has been partially supported by the CNR Progetto Strategico *Modelli e Metodi per la Matematica e l'Ingegneria and by the MURST Progetto* Tecniche Formali per la Specifica, l'Analisi, la Verifica, la Sintesi e la Trasformazione di Sistemi Software.

References

1. M. Baldi and G.P. Picco. Evaluating the tradeoffs of mobile code design paradigms in network management applications. In *Proceedings of ICSE'98*. ACM Press, 1998.
2. M. Bernardo, L. Donatiello, and R. Gorrieri. A formal approach to the integration of performance aspects in the modelling and analysis of concurrent systems. *Information and Computation*, 144:83–154, 1998.
3. G. Boudol and I. Castellani. A non-interleaving semantics for CCS based on proved transitions. *Fundamenta Informaticae*, XI(4):433–452, 1988.
4. P. Buchholz. On a markovian process algebra. Technical report, Informatik IV, University of Dortmund, 1994.
5. A. Carzaniga, G.P. Picco, and G. Vigna. Designing distributed applications with mobile code paradigms. In *Proceedings of ICSE'97*, pages 23–32. ACM Press, 1997.
6. P. Degano, R. De Nicola, and U. Montanari. Partial ordering derivations for CCS. In *Proceedings of FCT, LNCS 199*, pages 520–533. Springer-Verlag, 1985.
7. P. Degano and C. Priami. Proved trees. In *Proceedings of ICALP'92, LNCS 623*, pages 629–640. Springer-Verlag, 1992.
8. P. Degano and C. Priami. Enhanced operational semantics. *ACM Computing Surveys*, 28(2):352–354, 1996.
9. P. Degano and C. Priami. Non interleaving semantics for mobile processes. *Theoretical Computer Science*, march 1999.
10. N. Götz, U. Herzog, and M. Rettelbach. TIPP- a language for timed processes and performance evaluation. Technical Report 4/92, IMMD VII, University of Erlangen-Nurnberg, 1992.
11. J. Hillston. *A Compositional Approach to Performance Modelling*. PhD thesis. University of Edinburgh, Department of Computer Science, 1994.
12. R. Howard. *Dynamic Probabilistic Systems:Semi-Markov and Decision Systems*, volume II. Wiley, 1971.
13. R. Milner, J. Parrow, and D. Walker. Modal logics for mobile processes. *Theoretical Computer Science*, 114:149–171, 1993.
14. G. Plotkin. A structural approach to operational semantics. Technical Report DAIMI FN-19, Aarhus University, Denmark, 1981.
15. C. Priami. Stochastic π-calculus. *The Computer Journal*, 38(6):578–589, 1995.
16. C. Priami. *Enhanced Operational Semantics for Concurrency*. PhD thesis, Dipartimento di Informatica, Università di Pisa, March 1996. Available as Tech. Rep. TD-08/96.
17. C. Priami. Integrating behavioural and performance analysis with topology information. In *Proceedings of 29th Hawaian International Conference on System Sciences*, volume 1, pages 508–516, Maui, Hawaii, 1996. IEEE.
18. C. Priami. Enabling and general distributions in stochastic process algebras. In *Proceedings of Italian Conference on Theoretical Computer Science*, pages 192–203, Prato, 1998. World Scientific.
19. D. Sangiorgi. *Expressing Mobility in Process Algebras: First-Order and Higher-Order Paradigms*. PhD thesis, University of Edinburgh, 1992.

Implementing Hierarchical Graph-Structures*

Josef Tapken

Faculty of Computer Science, University of Oldenburg,
P.O.Box 2503, 26111 Oldenburg, Germany
Fax: +49 441 798-2965
E-Mail: tapken@informatik.uni-oldenburg.de

Abstract. We present concepts for the implementation of hierarchical
graphs, which can be used as basis for the implementation of tools for
graphical formal description techniques (gFDT) like SDL or statecharts.
Our approach provides a strong modularity of a specification by a loose
coupling between different hierarchy levels and it serves for a rapid development of interactive editors for gFDTs by a special technique of describing hierarchy. Furthermore, this technique allows the reuse of graph
editors in different applications. Our concepts are explained by means
of the graphical design tool MOBY/PLC for a special class of real-time
automata, called PLC-Automata.

1   Introduction

Application of formal methods is necessary in the development of correct distributed systems, e.g. in the area of telecommunication, and particularly for
safety-critical systems like railway-crossings or traffic control.

Very important for the acceptance of formal methods is the availability of
tool support. The description techniques used in the tool should be as simple as
possible in order to minimize the time for a system designer to get familiar with
that tool.

Graphical representations of formal description techniques (FDT) are useful
to increase their acceptance. Examples for practical used FDTs with graphical
representations are statecharts (cf. [8]) or SDL (**S**pecification and **D**escription
Language, see [11]). A commercial design tool for statecharts is e.g. STATEMATE
(cf. [10]) and for SDL the SDT-tool (cf. [18]).

In this paper we present concepts for the development of tools for graphical
FDTs (gFDTs). In doing so we refer to a design tool for PLC-Automata (cf. [3]).
a special class of real-time automata which is tailored towards a certain kind
of hardware called PLC (**P**rogrammable **L**ogic **C**ontrollers). This tool is called
MOBY/PLC (cf. [17], [2]) and is part of the MOBY[1]-workbench which additionally
provides Petri-net based validation methods like simulation and model-checking

---

* This research was partially supported by the Leibniz Programme of the Deutsche
Forschungsgemeinschaft (DFG) under grant No. Ol 98/1-1.
[1] **MO**delling of distri**B**uted s**Y**stems

for SDL-specifications (cf. [6]). In order to show the generality of the concepts we also give a simple SDL-example.

All gFDTs have one problem in common: they loose their readability if the described system becomes very complex. Hence many gFDTs are enriched by several structuring concepts like abstract data types, orthogonality (parallelism) and/or hierarchy (abstraction). In this paper we will concentrate on the handling of hierarchy and exploit the fact that the concept of hierarchy is independent of the special gFDT under consideration. Following this line the object-oriented implementation of a hierarchical gFDT should be based on (derived from) a generic implementation of hierarchical graph structures, instead of extending each implementation of a gFDT by a special hierarchy concept.

In this sense we present the integration of hierarchical graphs into the Moby Class Library (MCL[2]) and show its applicability with respect to the design and implementation of the PLC-tool.

The paper is organized as follows: In section 2 we show an example of PLC-Automata in order to give an idea of the hierarchy concepts used in this class of automata. The core of the paper consists of a formalization and implementation of hierarchical graphs (section 3) and a special technique of describing hierarchy in a system comprising several types of graphs (e.g. like SDL-specifications, which comprise block, process and procedure specifications, section 4). Section 5 gives some hints to related approaches to hierarchical graphs and section 6 summarizes this work and gives some outlook to further work.

2   PLC-Automata

In [3] a new class of real-time automata was introduced which is tailored for modelling the behaviour of PLCs that are often used in practice to solve real-time problems. The automata are provided with a formal semantics in *Duration Calculus* (DC, [1]) to allow formal reasoning about their properties.

PLCs provide two convenient concepts for implementing real-time systems, namely timers and an automatic polling mechanism. The latter concept is realised by the cyclic behaviour of PLCs, whereat each cycle consists of the following phases:

- Poll all input channels and store the read values,
- compute new output values based on the stored input values, and
- update the output channels.

The only phase a programmer has to adapt is the computing phase, whereas the repeated execution of the cycle and the channel handling is managed by the operating system. Via input and output channels a PLC can be connected to sensors and actuators as well as to other PLCs.

---

[2] MCL is a C++-class library which contains the application independent kernel of the MOBY-workbench. Among others, it provides classes for building Motif based interactive graph editors.

Since PLC-Automata are closely related to the behaviour of PLCs, a specification using PLC-Automata consists of a set of parallel automata communicating through channels with each other. Communication is performed implicitly by putting the calculated output values on the output channels, which can be read via an input channel by another automaton. Open systems can be specified by connecting some input and output channels to the interface of the system, which is graphically represented by a set of *ports*.

The parallel composition of the set of automata is called *system view* and is specified in one (or more) *system diagrams*. For the structured description of the system view some ideas of SDL are adopted, especially the notion of blocks and block substructures (cf. [11]). Therefore, a system diagram contains *system nodes* (blocks) which can be specified (refined) by another system diagram or by a description of its behaviour by means of a PLC-Automaton. A PLC-Automaton may also be structured hierarchically by using PLC-Subautomata.

As a running example we adopt the case study described in [3] which handles the gasburner control problem (a case study of the ProCoS-project, cf. [12]) using PLC-Automata. The case study specifies the control unit for a gasburner which gets two Boolean inputs, hr ("heat request") representing the state of a thermostat changed by the user and fl ("flame") indicating the status of a sensor monitoring the flame. The output of the specified system is a Boolean value controlling the gas valve. One real-time requirement for the system is that in every period of 30 seconds gas must not leak for more than 4 seconds.

Fig. 1 shows a screen shot of the system view of the specification. In order to give an idea of the parallel composition of PLC-Automata we divide the automaton described in [3] into two, one for handling the input values and the other one for calculating the output.

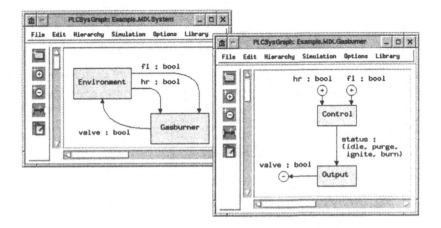

Fig. 1. System view of the gasburner specification

The system view is split into two diagrams. The left diagram shows the environment of the specified system consisting of one not further specified system node Environment, which delivers two input values for the gasburner subsystem (hr and fl) of type bool and receives one output value valve of type bool.

The refinement of the Gasburner node is shown in the right diagram. Thereby the interface of the system node consisting of incoming and outgoing channels is adopted from the left diagram and represented as ports ($\oplus$ and $\ominus$) in the refinement. Furthermore, the refinement contains two system nodes (Control and Output) which are connected by a channel called status. This channel is inscribed with an enumeration type ({idle, purge, ignite, burn}) which contains the output values of the Control system.

The behaviour of the two system components Control and Output is specified by two PLC-Automata (see Fig. 2). The description of the Control-automaton is split into two diagrams in order to show the hierarchy concept for PLC-Automata by using a subautomaton SubControl. (There is no conceptual reason for the seperation.) Each PLC-Automaton contains an interface description consisting of a set of *text symbols* which carry the declaration of input and output variables. (In this paper we do not handle local variables.) These variables have to correspond with channels specified in the upper diagram of the system view.

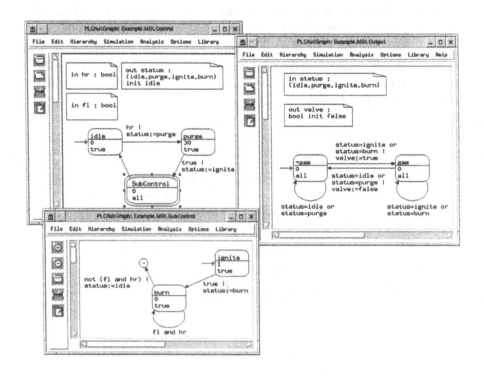

Fig. 2. PLC-Automata of the gasburner specification

A PLC-state is inscribed by its name and a pair (time-value, state-condition). state-condition is a predicate over the input variables and expresses that all inputs which fulfill state-condition should be ignored for time-value time units after entering the state. E.g. state purge of the automaton Control has the state condition true and the time value 30. The transition function is labelled by predicates which are built over all variables of the automaton and by lists of assignments to the output variables.

The operational behaviour of a PLC-Automaton is as follows: The PLC-Automaton checks in every cycle if the actual state is hold longer than time-value or if the state condition evaluates to false under the current binding of the variables, if it does the automaton reacts according to the transition function and all assignments of the transition are executed. (Thereby a transition can be taken if its predicate evaluates to true.) Else the state will be held for another cycle.

Fig. 2 shows that the Control-automaton starts in the state idle and remains there until hr is true. Then the automaton turns to purge and stays there several cycles until 30 seconds are elapsed. After that the initial state (ignite) of the subautomaton SubControl will be activated and held for at least one second. Then the automaton will change to burn and stay there as long as both the flame sensor (fl) and the thermostat (hr) provide the value true. If e.g. the ignition of the gasburner has failed (fl=false) then the subautomaton will be left via its output port and the state idle will be reached. The Output-automaton receives the status from Control and calculates the output value for the gas valve. The valve will be opened (valve:=true) if status is ignite or burn and closed otherwise.

3 Hierarchical Graphs

In this section we present and discuss the data structures (classes) for hierarchical graphs which we implement in MCL.

3.1 Formalization

Hierarchical graph structures like the previously presented diagrams are often described as *compound (directed) graphs* (see e.g. [13]). The definition of hierarchical PLC-Automata (cf. [2]) is also based upon compound graphs. A compound graph $C = (G, T)$ consists of a simple directed graph $G = (V, E_G)$ describing the transition relation and a tree $T = (V, E_T)$ representing a nesting relation between the different nodes. The set of nodes V can be devided into two disjoint subsets, namely the leafs of T, which are called *base nodes*, and the inner nodes of T called *subgraphs*.

Fig. 3 shows the compound graph of the running example neglecting the different types of the graphs (system diagram, PLC-Automaton and PLC-Subautomaton).

Compound graphs are very compact descriptions of hierarchical structures and therefore useful for the definition of the semantics of hierarchical specifications. But they are not tailored to be used directly as base structure for (the

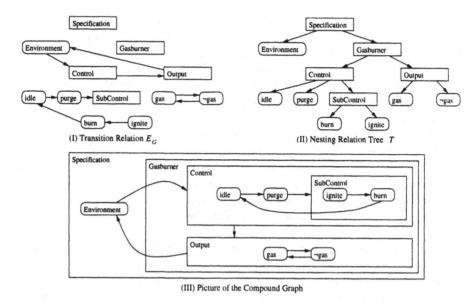

Fig. 3. Compound graph of the gasburner specification

implementation of) a gFDT, because a gFDT has to provide methods for dividing specifications into modules of manageable size in order to allow the user to focus upon certain modules while neglecting others and/or to reuse certain modules in different specifications. In SDL this aim is pursued by the notion of *remote* specifications, i.e. the user separates a part (module) of the specification from its defining context and refers to this part just by using a unique name (*reference*, e.g. see [11]). In compound graphs this compositionality requirement is violated by the fact that they allow inter-level edges, i.e. edges between nodes of different levels.[3]

For the implementation of hierarchy in MCL we use a different structure, called *H-graphs*. *H*-graphs arise from compound graphs by introducing a special class of nodes called *ports*[4] which describe explicitly the interface of a subgraph. Thus inter-level edges are substituted by a list of one-level edges between ordinary nodes and ports. For example the inter-level edge from burn to idle in Fig. 3 is divided into one edge from burn to a newly introduced output port and one from the subgraph SubControl to idle (cf. Fig. 4).

Newly introduced edges connected to a subgraph differ from ordinary edges in the sense that they have exactly one corresponding port inside the subgraph which represents the virtual source (resp. destination) of the edge. The distinction between different types of edges is known from statecharts (cf. [8]) where

---

[3] Two different nodes of a compound graph are in the same level if they have the same predecessor in the nesting relation tree.

[4] Since we consider directed graphs we distinguish input and output ports.

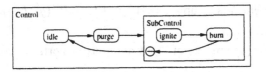

Fig. 4. Part of the previous compound graph

edges are allowed to lead *to* as well as *into* a statechart (resp. *from* and *outof*). But statecharts do not consider ports explicitly, they just allow dangling edges which have no source (or no destination).

The elimination of inter-level edges results in a modular data structure for hierarchical graphs called $\mathcal{H}$-graph. Fig. 5 sketches this structure by means of the gasburner specification. An $\mathcal{H}$-graph contains two types of graphs, namely *interface graphs*, which serve for the description of one compound graph level. and a *design graph*[5] which composes the different levels, i.e. the design graph covers the information of the nesting relation tree.

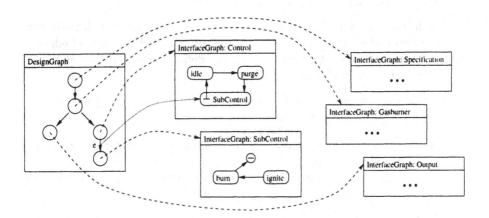

Fig. 5. Data structure of the gasburner specification

The idea of the design graph is that each node represents one interface graph and that each edge represents a refinement of a vertex in the 'source graph' by the 'destination graph'. Therefore, the edge is equipped with an extra link to that vertex being refined.

In the following we formalize the data structure of $\mathcal{H}$-graphs. We first define the class of interface graphs[6].

---

[5] Design graphs arising from compound graphs are actually trees.
[6] We want to allow several edges between two nodes, so we use a different style of a graph definition with source and target functions.

An *interface graph* is a tuple $g = (V(g), P^I(g), P^O(g), E(g), s_g, t_g, \lambda_g)$ with

- $V(g)$ is a set of nodes,
- $P^I(g)$ and $P^O(g)$ are sets of input and output ports (building the interface of g),
- $E(g)$ is a set of edge,
- $s_g : E(g) \longrightarrow V(g) \cup P^I(g)$ and $t_g : E(g) \longrightarrow V(g) \cup P^O(g)$ are functions assigning to each edge the source and target nodes, and
- $\lambda_g : E(g) \longrightarrow \mathcal{P}(\{i, o\})$ is an additional labelling function for edges.

The labelling function determines the status of an edge which can be normal ($\emptyset$), dangling-in (i), dangling-out (o) or dangling-in/out ($\{i, o\}$). Additionally, we postulate that edges do not dangle into (resp. out of) a port, i.e.

- $\forall e \in E(g) \bullet t_g(e) \in P^O(g) \Rightarrow i \notin \lambda_g(e)$, and
- $\forall e \in E(g) \bullet s_g(e) \in P^I(g) \Rightarrow o \notin \lambda_g(e)$.

The interface of a node v in g is described by its dangling edges, thus for $v \in V(g)$ we define

- $D^I(v) = \{e \in E(g) \,|\, t_g(e) = v \wedge i \in \lambda_g(e)\}$, and
- $D^O(v) = \{e \in E(g) \,|\, s_g(e) = v \wedge o \in \lambda_g(e)\}$.

Fig. 5 shows five interface graphs, whereat e.g. the interface graph SubControl contains two nodes (ignite and burn), one output port and two normal edges.

For the composition of interface graphs we define the structure of $\mathcal{H}$-graphs. An $\mathcal{H}$-*graph* is a tuple $H = (d, \mathcal{G}, \rho)$ with

- $d = (V(d), E(d), s_d, t_d)$ is a directed acyclic graph, called *design graph*,
- $\mathcal{G}$ is a set of interface graphs,
- $\rho = (\rho^V, \rho^E)$ is a pair of functions with
  - $\rho^V : V(d) \longrightarrow \mathcal{G}$ is a bijection between the vertices of d and the set of interface graphs, and
  - $\rho^E : E(d) \longrightarrow V$ is a refinement function, with $V = \bigcup_{g \in \mathcal{G}} V(g)$ and the restriction $\rho^E(e) = v \Longrightarrow v \in V(\rho^V(s_d(e)))$.

The bijection ρ^V associates to each vertex in the design graph an interface graph. The edges of the design graph together with the refinement function ρ^E realise the connection between the different hierarchy levels. An edge e in the design graph, e.g. the edge e in Fig. 5, represents the information that the vertex $v = \rho^E(e)$ (SubControl) in graph $\rho^V(s_d(e))$ (Control) is refined by the graph $\rho^V(t_d(e))$ (SubControl).

Since both objects, the vertex v and the refinement $\rho^V(t_d(e))$, provide their own interface description, we have to check their consistency. Thus, we call an $\mathcal{H}$-graph H *consistent* if for all $e \in E(d)$ holds

- $\exists$ bijection $\beta^I : D^I(\rho^E(e)) \longrightarrow P^I(\rho^V(t_d(e)))$, and
- $\exists$ bijection $\beta^O : D^O(\rho^E(e)) \longrightarrow P^O(\rho^V(t_d(e)))$.

For the edge e this requirement holds since the interface graph SubControl has only one output port and the corresponding node has one dangling-out edge.

3.2 Implementation

The implementation of $\mathcal{H}$-graphs is based upon an object oriented implementation of graphs. Both substructures of $\mathcal{H}$-graphs, the interface graph and the design graph, are derived from simple graphs. Real applications like MOBY/PLC are based upon $\mathcal{H}$-graphs simply by deriving concret graphs-like system diagrams from the abstract interface graph.

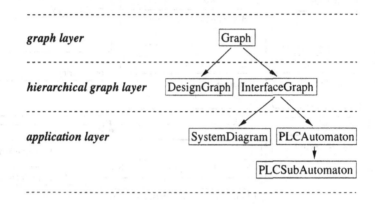

Fig. 6. Layered architecture of MOBY/PLC

This leads to a layered architecture for a concret application which is sketched in Fig. 6. Each box represents a package of classes which build up together the intended data structure.

Fig. 7 shows the main classes of the different packages. Each rounded box describes one class. The name and the superclass is stated in the top line. The members of a class are listed in the lower part of the box.

In MCL a graph is represented by a Graph-object which contains a collection of Vertex-objects. Each vertex stores a reference to its graph and two lists of its incomming and outgoing edges, which are represented by the class Edge. Each edge knows its source and destination.

The data structure of a design graph is build up by the classes DesignGraph, DesignVertex, and DesignEdge, which are derived from the appropiate classes of the graph package. A DesignVertex is enriched by a reference to an InterfaceGraph and a DesignEdge by a reference to a vertex of an interface graph.

Interface graphs distinguish two classes of vertices, namely Ports and refinable vertices (IF_Vertex). A Port carries a flag whether it is an input or an output port. The graph object itself holds a reference to its representing DesignVertex and the edges of an interface graph (IF_Edge) may have two references to ports. These references represent the dangling information of an edge. If there is no reference stored, the edge is a normal one, else a reference links the edge to a port in the refinement graph of the connected vertex.

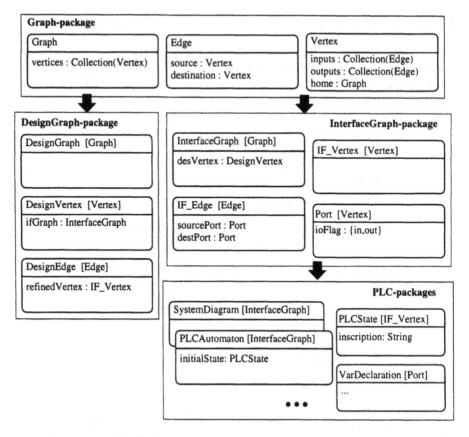

Fig. 7. Main classes of the $\mathcal{H}$-graph data structure in MOBY/PLC

The extensions which are needed for the MOBY/PLC-application are only sketched in Fig. 7. E.g. a PLC-Automaton stores its initial state and the states carry some additional inscriptions. Variables are special ports since they describe the interface of a PLC-Automaton.

3.3 SDL-Example and Discussion of the Approach

In this subsection we discuss the main properties of the presented hierarchy concept and show its application to an SDL-specification.

The data structure for hierarchical specifications which we propose provides the modularity of the specification by a very loose coupling between the different hierarchy levels. Thus each module consisting of one interface graph can be edited independently, in particular several users can simultaneously work on the same specification. Additionally, this concept facilitates the reuse of certain modules in different specifications.

The design graph provides directly an assistance for traversing the whole specification, i.e. in order to edit a leaf of the hierarchy tree the user can access the node in the design graph instead of browsing through the whole specification.

Furthermore, the concept of $\mathcal{H}$-graphs allows us to combine several types of interface graphs in one specification. This feature is necessary e.g. for the running example (see section 2) where we need system diagrams for the description of the system architecture and we need two kinds of automata diagrams for specifying the behaviour of the different components.

It is also useful for a tool which allows to describe distinct parts of one specification in different languages, provided that they have a consistent semantics. This can be relevant for big projects where one part can be adopted from a former project specified in language A (e.g. SDL) and the new part should be specified in language B (e.g. statecharts). One approach to combine semantically several specification languages is elaborated in [7].

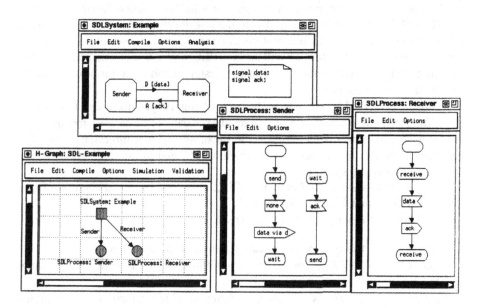

Fig. 8. SDL-specification in MOBY

At the end of this section we give a short SDL-example which shows the applicability of our hierarchy concepts for gFDTs other than PLC-Automata. Fig. 8 shows a screen shot of an SDL-specification in MOBY. It presents a (very) simple communication protocol where the Sender process sends data packages via the channel D to the Receiver and gets the acknowledgement via the channel A. Fig. 8 contains in the lower left corner the design graph with three nodes, which represent the SDL-diagrams on the top and on the right side, namely the block diagram Example and the two process diagrams Sender and Receiver. These types of SDL-diagrams are derived from interface graphs and extended by e.g. channels in block diagrams and several kinds of nodes, like input and output symbols in process diagrams.

4 Descriptions of Generic Hierarchical Graphs

In the previous section we have shown that the concept of $\mathcal{H}$-graphs is suitable to combine several types of interface graphs into one specification. New types can be defined by deriving them from the class of interface graphs. But for the combination of different interface graphs there are some additional informations necessary because not all refinement relations between interface graphs make sense. E.g., in the gasburner specification PLC-states should only be refined into a PLC-Subautomaton and not into a system diagram, whereas a system node could be refined into a system diagram as well as into a PLC-Automaton.

The additional refinement information could be handled by the interface graph itself, but then it is not possible to use one special class of interface graphs in several contexts, e.g. to use system diagrams for the description of system architectures in an SDL-tool as well as in a PLC-tool. On the other hand, if the information is directly implemented in the design graph each application has to define its own design graph.

Thus, it is advisable to use some features of generic programming to describe the refinement capabilities in a hierarchical application.[7] The description of the refinement capabilities is based upon the set of all types of interface graphs GT and the set of all types of nodes VT which are defined in an application. In the PLC-example the graph types
$GT = \{\mathsf{SystemDiagram}, \mathsf{PLCAutomaton}, \mathsf{PLCSubAutomaton}\}$ and the node types
$VT = \{\mathsf{SystemNode}, \mathsf{PLCState}\}$ are used.

A *refinement description* is a tuple $(root, ins, ref)$ with

- $root \in GT$ is the type of the initial graph in a specification,
- $ins : GT \longrightarrow \mathcal{P}(VT)$ is an *insertion function* describing what kind of nodes can be inserted into a graph, and
- $ref : VT \longrightarrow \mathcal{P}(GT)$ is a *refinement function* which determines what refinements are allowed for a node.

For a concrete application the $\mathcal{H}$-graph is instantiated with a special refinement description. In our PLC-example this will be

- $root = \mathsf{SystemDiagram}$,

---

[7] C++ directly supports generic programming by templates, but we avoided the use of templates in MCL in order to enhance portability, because some compilers do not handle templates in combination with extensive inheritance correctly. Instead, we reach the facilities of generic programming by a special class Class which provides runtime class information and allows to create instances of a dynamically determined class.

- $ins(\mathsf{SystemDiagram}) = \{\mathsf{SystemNode}\},$
  $ins(\mathsf{PLCAutomaton}) = \{\mathsf{PLCState}\},$
  $ins(\mathsf{PLCSubAutomaton}) = \{\mathsf{PLCState}\},$ and
- $ref(\mathsf{SystemNode}) = \{\mathsf{SystemDiagram}, \mathsf{PLCAutomaton}\},$
  $ref(\mathsf{PLCState}) = \{\mathsf{PLCSubAutomaton}\}.$

This refinement description states that the specification will start up with a system diagram where only system nodes can be inserted in. A system node can be refined again into a system diagram or into a PLC-Automaton. A PLC-Automaton and a PLC-Subautomaton can only contain PLC-states which on their part can be refined into PLC-Subautomata.

In this refinement description we do not treat ports. There are two ways to handle ports in our concept, first they can be directly associated to an interface graph (no generic description for ports) or they can be treated as a special kind of nodes, then they have to be added to the insertion function.

In MCL the refinement description is used as a parameter for the graphical user interface of a hierarchical editor system, i.e. the buttons and menu entries for creating and refining vertices are automatically generated out of the refinement description. E.g. the contents of the vertical button bars shown in Fig. 1 and 2 are directly dependent on the refinement description of the application. Since the refinement description is evaluated at runtime it is possible to change it during a session by means of a graphical editor.

5 Related Work

In the literature there is a lot of work spread over many different application areas dealing with hierarchical extensions of graph structures. To enumerate all variants of hierarchical graphs and to compare them with our approach would go beyond the scope of this paper. But we want to mention some of the recent publications on this topic.

The definition of compound graphs in [13], which was already discussed in section 3, is application independent and is used for the presentation of graph drawing techniques.

In the context of graph grammars and graph transformations there are several approaches to incorporate hierarchy concepts into graph structures (e.g. [5], [9] and [15]). These approaches mainly focus on dynamic aspects of a system. i.e. on operations on graph structures and not only on the structure itself. The hierarchy is mostly used to build smaller (dynamic) views on the whole system instead of decomposing the system into independent (static) modules. Building dynamic views requires a representation of the whole system as one monolithic data structure.

In [14] a modular extension for graph transformation systems is proposed. The modules, called encapsulated graph objects, are equipped with import and export interfaces comparable to the ports of our interface graphs. In [14] the modules are composed through a separate graph structure, called module system, leading to a fixed hierarchy of two levels. In our approach the (parallel) composition of two interface graphs is described again by an interface graph. This can be iterated to get an arbitrary number of hierarchy levels.

The implementation of $\mathcal{H}$-graphs in C++ and the integration into MCL, a C++-class library for interactive graph editors, was done 'by hand'. But nowadays there exist several tools formally based on graph grammars or graph transformation systems, which support code generation for high level descriptions of graph structures or even the generation of complete (visual) programming environments. [4] contains several descriptions of such tools, e.g. PROGRES, AGG, and DiaGen.

6 Conclusion

In this paper we have shown a flexible concept for implementing hierarchical graphs which is tailored to build a common basis for several implementations of gFDTs.

For the development of a new gFDT-tool the programmer only has to extend the data structure by deriving new classes of interface graphs, nodes and if necessary ports and edges, but (s)he has not to implement the hierarchical relations between these classes, (s)he just defines the refinement description in a graphical editor. In order to change the appearance of the tool the programmer only has to slightly modify the graphical user interface by redefining some methods of the new classes. E.g. (s)he has to add some menu entries to the graph editor or has to overwrite the display methods of a node.

The 'real' functionality of the new tool, like simulation algorithms or compile algorithms to other representations (e.g. from SDL-specifications into Petri nets), can be added to the chosen data structure independently. This can be implemented directly in the new classes or by defining 'service'-classes which operate on the graph structure.

In the MOBY-workbench we successfully applied the concept of $\mathcal{H}$-graphs to implement several graphical design tools. We are currently working on a tool for the validation of SDL-specification, on a hierarchical editor for (Object-)Z-specifications (each basic node contains one Z-schema and the hierarchy is used for structuring the specification), and on the PLC-tool we mentioned in this paper. This tool allows to generate runnable PLC-code out of an automaton specification and is enriched by several validation methods like a simulator for PLC-Automata (cf. [16]), the implementation of specific analysis algorithms for PLC-Automata and a connection to a model checker for timed automata. Furthermore, we are planing to integrate the Z-editor for the description of abstract data types in PLC-Automata.

Acknowledgements

The author thanks H. Fleischhack, E.-R. Olderog, and the other members of the "semantics group" in Oldenburg as well as A. Habel for valuable comments on the subject of this paper.

References

1. Zhou Chaochen, C.A.R. Hoare, and A.P. Ravn. A Calculus of Durations. *Inform. Proc. Letters*, 40/5:269–276, 1991.
2. H. Dierks and J. Tapken. Tool-Supported Hierarchical Design of Distributed Real-Time Systems. In *Euromicro Workshop on Real Time Systems*, pages 222–229. IEEE, 1998.
3. Henning Dierks. PLC-Automata: A New Class of Implementable Real-Time Automata. In *ARTS'97*, LNCS. Springer Verlag, May 1997.
4. H. Ehrig, G. Engels, H.-J. Kreowski, and G. Rozenberg, editors. *Handbook on Graph Grammars: Applications*, volume 2. Singapur: World Scientific, 1999. To appear.
5. G. Engels and A. Schürr. Encapsulated Hierachical Graphs, Graph Types, and Meta Types. In Andrea Corradini and Ugo Montanari, editors, *SEGRAGRA'95. Workshop on Graph Rewriting and Computation*, Electronic Notes in Theoretical Computer Science, pages 75–84, 1995.
6. H. Fleischhack and J. Tapken. An M-Net Semantics for a Real-Time Extension of μSDL. In *FME'97: Industrial Applications and Strengthened Foundations of Formal Methods*, volume 1313 of *LNCS*, pages 162–181. Springer Verlag, 1997.
7. Bernd Grahlmann. Combining Finite Automata, Parallel Programs and SDL Using Petri Nets. In *Proceedings of TACAS'98*, volume 1384 of *LNCS*, pages 102–117. Springer Verlag, 1998.
8. David Harel. On Visual Formalisms. In *Communications of the ACM*, number 5 in 31, pages 514–530, 1988.
9. Michael Himsolt. *Konzeption und Implementierung von Grapheneditoren*. Verlag Shaker, Aachen, 1994. Dissertation.
10. i-Logix. Languages of STATEMATE, January 1991.
11. ITU-T Recommendation Z.100. *Specification and Description Language*. ITU General Secretariat - Sales Section, Geneva, 1992.
12. A.P. Ravn, H. Rischel, and K.M. Hansen. Specifying and Verifying Requirements of Real-Time Systems. *IEEE Transactions on Software Engineering*, 19:41–55, January 1993.
13. Georg Sander. Layout of Compound Directed Graphs. Technical Report A/03/96. FB Informatik, Universität des Saarlandes, 1996.
14. G. Taentzer and A. Schürr. DIEGO, Another Step Towards a Module Concept for Graph Transformation Systems. In *SEGRAGRA'95, Workshop on Graph Rewriting and Computation*, Electronic Notes in Theoretical Computer Science, 1995.
15. Gabriele Taentzer. Hierarchically Distributed Graph Transformation. In J. Cuny. H. Ehrig, G. Engels, and G. Rozenberg, editors, *Graph Grammars and Their Applications to Computer Science*, volume 1073 of *LNCS*, pages 304–320. Springer Verlag, 1996.
16. Josef Tapken. Interactive and Compilative Simulation of PLC-Automata. In W. Hahn and A. Lehmann, editors, *Simulation in Industry, ESS'97*, pages 552 – 556. SCS, 1997.
17. Josef Tapken. MOBY/PLC – A Design Tool for Hierarchical Real-Time Automata. In *Proceedings of FASE'98*, volume 1382 of *LNCS*, pages 326–329. Springer Verlag. 1998.
18. Telelogic AB. SDT – the SDL Design Tool, http://www.telelogic.se/.

A Tool Suite for Multi-paradigm Specification[1]

Lynne Blair[†], Trevor Jones, Gordon Blair

Computing Department, Lancaster University, Bailrigg, Lancaster, LA1 4YR, U.K.
[†]Corresponding author's email: lb@comp.lancs.ac.uk. Fax: +44 (0)1524 593608

Abstract. In this paper, we present a tool suite developed to facilitate the use of a multi-paradigm specification technique. By adopting such a technique, different aspects (or components) of a system can be specified using different formal languages. Using FC2 as our common file format, we can load in different (partial) specifications, compose them and then view the result in textual or graphical format, simulate the composed behaviour, and model check a given logic formula against our (composed) system.

1. Introduction

The tool suite that we present in this paper allows the composition of (partial-) specifications that have been written in a number of different formal paradigms such as process algebra (e.g. LOTOS and CCS), (real-time) temporal logic and (timed) automata. We anticipate that these component specifications will have come from a variety of sources, including other tools such as Autograph and FCTOOLS [4], Eucalyptus [5], Lite [6] and UPPAAL [1]. We thus provide an environment in which our tool can be integrated with others such as these. We have also developed and incorporated a tool to convert temporal logic formulae into automata, so that logic specifications can be composed with other aspects of our system. Used this way, temporal logic is a powerful specification technique and not simply a language for model checking.

2. A Multi-Paradigm Approach

2.1 Why Multi-Paradigm Specification?

Formal specification techniques provide the ability to specify the behaviour of a system in a language that has clear, concise and unambiguous semantics. However, it is well recognised within the formal methods community, and is not at all surprising, that different languages have their own individual strengths and weaknesses. As pointed out in [7], "there will never be a universal FDT (formal description technique) any more than there will never be a universal programming language".

---

[1] FASE'99 - Fundamental Approaches to Software Engineering, Amsterdam, 22-26 March 1999

As systems, and their corresponding specifications, get larger and more complex, it becomes more difficult to find a single formal language that is suitable for specifying the entire system. Instead, our approach allows the best features of several different specification techniques to be exploited. The different specifications can then be brought together using composition rules built on a common semantics.

2.2 Underlying Theory

We use timed labelled transition systems as our common semantics, from which we define timed automata as a higher level semantic model. Then, from each of the different languages mentioned above, we define a mapping onto timed automata. Since we do not have space to present the theory that lies behind our semantics and mappings, we point the interested reader to [3]. Our rules for the composition of different specifications are based on the usual interpretation of (selective) parallel composition; any action in one component specification that occurs in the selected set of synchronising actions must wait to synchronise with a matching action from the other component specification. In contrast, any actions not in the set of synchronising actions may proceed independently. These rules are presented formally in [3].

3. The Composer Tool

3.1 Composition

The user interface to our tool is displayed in figure B.1. As can be seen, input to the tool takes the form of "fc2" files or "aut" files. The FC2 format (see [4]) is used as our common file format. Although we have identified a few problems with this format (see [2]), its use is fairly widespread. Consequently, we can integrate our tool with other tools as mentioned above. For convenience, we also allow the input of "aut" files from Eucalyptus, although we then provide a conversion to FC2.

Composition can either be achieved automatically, through the recognition and matching of syntactically equivalent actions and variables, or it can be done *explicitly*. The latter provides a safer and more flexible composition in which any action (resp. variable) in one automaton can be composed with any action (resp. variable) from another. For example, "send" and "put" may be used in different component specifications for the same action. The inverse may also be true, i.e. different actions (resp. variables) may have (perhaps unintentionally) been given the same name. Explicit composition allows you to distinguish between these.

Note that to carry out further compositions, or perform model checking, a "recomposition" flag should be set at this point (set as default). However, to explore the new automaton in Autograph, the flag must be deselected (see [2] for justification). Clicking "Next" now completes the composition and saves the result to an "fc2" file; a window also appears giving the number of states and transitions in the new automaton. Note that for convenience we also automatically produce another file ("temp.aut") which can easily be loaded into Eucalyptus for quick viewing.

3.2 Simulation

The simulator allows us to step through the system one action at a time by selecting available actions from the user interface (see figure B.2). Once an action has been selected, the simulator progresses to the next state and a new set of possible actions appear. We can also choose to idle in a particular state by incrementing the appropriate variable on the left side of the interface. Note that this may have the effect of disabling certain actions, e.g. when a variable exceeds the bound of a guarded action.

Steps that have been taken through a simulation are recorded in two formats. Firstly, a textual log is provided in the centre of the user interface; this can also be saved to file. Secondly, a graphical trace of (abbreviated) events is displayed beneath the simulator window. Labelled nodes represent the states visited and selected actions are represented by transitions between nodes. The intensity of colour increases with repeated visits to a particular state. During a simulation, we may also end up in one of the special states, labelled TRUE or FALSE. These occur if we have composed an automaton derived from logic formulae, or if we are simulating the results of model checking (see below). Intuitively, TRUE represents a valid path whilst FALSE represents an invalid path. Both of these states are effectively terminal states: once reached, you always stay in this state. However, note that in these states any action is always possible; hence they do not correspond to deadlock. The use of temporal logic as one of our specification techniques, as well as the model checking process, make it useful to visualise such states in our simulator.

3.3 Generating Automata from Temporal Logic

By selecting the "Logic Tool" from the main user interface, the user is able to enter a logic formula (representing part of the system specification) and convert it into an automaton. The user interface to this tool is shown in figure B.3. In this way, the translated formula can be composed with other component specifications. The logic we use is a linear time temporal logic, details of which can be found in [3]. Details of the translation into automata can also be found in this reference. Note however that the current version of the tool only supports an untimed logic, although derivation rules to convert real-time logic into timed automata have been defined. Ongoing work is addressing the issue of urgency/ maximal progress in automata and also exploring the use of a branching time temporal logic framework.

3.4 Model Checking

With model checking, we want to prove that a logic formula is valid with respect to a given system. The process we use to achieve this is to initially construct an automaton for the *negated* formula. This is straightforward through the use of our logic tool (also incorporated into the model checker). We then need to form the *cross product* of the overall system with the negated formula. The rules for this are very similar to those of composition; the difference is that we do not permit the independent progression of automata – if one does an action, they must both do that action. This produces a (possibly empty) automaton. Since we have negated the formula, any path occurring in the resulting automaton shows that the formula is invalid over the given system. These paths can be explored using our simulator. Conversely, if the formula is valid over the system, the resulting automaton will be empty. As with the logic tool described above, we currently only support untimed model checking.

4. Summary

In this paper, we have described a tool suite to provide support for a multi-paradigm specification environment. We achieve this by using timed labelled transition systems as our underlying common semantic model and use timed automata as a realisation of this model. The composition of automata lies at the heart of our tool, which also includes a simulator, a logic tool for the generation of automata from temporal logic and a model checker. The tool has been designed to allow the integration with a number of other tools. Further details on our work can be obtained via the web (see http://www.comp.lancs.ac.uk/computing/users/lb/v-qos.html) or by email.

Acknowledgements

This work was carried out under the V-QoS project with the financial support of EPSRC (GR/L28890), and in collaboration with the University of Kent at Canterbury.

References

1. J. Bengtsson, K. Larsen, F. Larsson, P. Pettersson, W. Yi, C. Weise: "New Generation of UPPAAL", In Proceedings of the International Workshop on Software Tools for Technology Transfer, Aalborg, Denmark, 12-13 July, 1998.
2. L. Blair, T. Jones, "A note on some problems with the FC2 format", web document: http://www.comp.lancs.ac.uk/computing/users/lb/Composer/fc2notes.html, 1998.
3. L. Blair, G.S. Blair, "Composition in Multi-paradigm Specification Techniques", To appear at the 3rd International Workshop on Formal Methods for Open Object-based Distributed Systems (FMOODS'99), 15-18 February, Florence, Italy, 1999.
4. A. Bouali, A. Ressouche, V. Roy, R. de Simone, "The FCTOOLS User Manual (Version 1.0)", April 1996, see http://www.inria.fr/meije/verification/doc.html.
5. H. Garavel, "An Overview of the Eucalyptus Toolbox", Proceedings of the International Workshop on Applied Formal Methods in System Design (Maribor, Slovenia), pp 76-88, June 1996, see http://www.inrialpes.fr/vasy/Publications/Garavel-96.html.
6. Lite: LOTOS Integrated Tool Environment, Tele-Informatics and Open Systems Group, University of Twente, The Netherlands, see http://wwwtios.cs.utwente.nl/lotos/lite/.
7. K.J. Turner (editor), "Formal Description Techniques", Proceedings of the 1st International Conference on Formal Description Techniques (FORTE'88), Elsevier Science, North-Holland, Amsterdam, 1990.

Appendix A: Platform Requirements

The Composer tool has been written in Java™, and can thus be used with all major platforms. In order to integrate our tool with Autograph, Eucalyptus and UPPAAL, we have used a LINUX platform for PCs.

Appendix B: Graphical User Interfaces from the Composer Tool

The following three figures show the graphical user interfaces for the main Composer tool (figure B.1), the simulator (figure B.2) and the logic tool (figure B.3).

Figure B.1

Figure B.2

Figure B.3

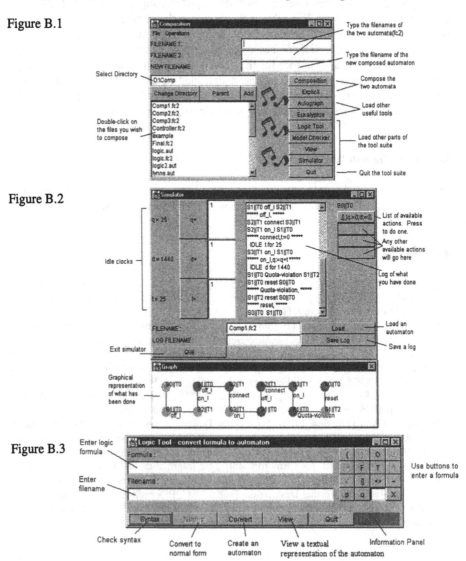

TAS and IsaWin: Tools for Transformational Program Development and Theorem Proving

Christoph Lüth, Haykal Tej, Kolyang, and Bernd Krieg-Brückner*

Bremen Institute of Safe Systems (BISS), FB 3, Universität Bremen
{cxl,ht,kol,bkb}@informatik.uni-bremen.de

Introduction

We will present two tools, TAS and IsaWin, for transformational program development and theorem proving respectively, based on the theorem prover Isabelle [9]. Their distinguishing features are a graphical user interface based on the principle of direct manipulation, and a generic, open system design which allows the development of a family of tools for different formal methods on a sound logical basis with a uniform appearance.

The aim of these tools is to provide a user-friendly framework for formal program development, supported by a powerful theorem prover, and generic over the actual formal method employed. By embedding a formal method into the theorem prover Isabelle, instantiating the generic graphical user interface, and adding customised proof support, we obtain a tool for that formal method which hides the details of the encoding; we call this an *encapsulation* of the formal method.

The Transformation Application System TAS

TAS is a system for formal transformational program development. It hides the details of the encoding of transformational development in Isabelle from the user, leaving him with the main design decisions of transformational program development: which rule to apply, and how to instantiate its parameters. TAS further allows to abstract transformational developments to transformation rules.

Figure 1 shows a screenshot of TAS. In the centre, we see the *notepad* window where icons represent transformation rules, transformational developments and parameter instantiations. The notepad does not contain all known transformations, only those which are explicitly placed there by the user. The user can select from all known transformations by the transformation chooser.

A transformational development can be opened in the *construction area*, where it can be further developed. Transformations are applied by dragging the icons into the construction area from the notepad (or directly from the transformation chooser). The history of the transformational development, and the

---

* This work has been supported by the German Ministry for Education and Research (BMBF) as part of the project UniForM under grant No. FKZ 01 IS 521 B2.

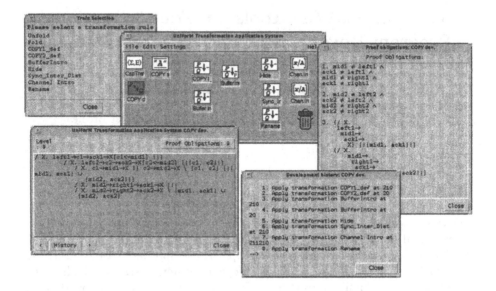

Fig. 1. Transformational Program Development with TAS. Windows, clockwise: transformation chooser, notepad, proof obligations, history and the construction area.

current proof obligations can be displayed in separate windows. Proof obligations are discharged by dragging them into IsaWin, where they turn into ongoing proofs.

IsaWin

IsaWin is a graphical user interface for the theorem prover Isabelle. Here, it is also used to show the proof obligations arising from transformational developments in TAS. It allows access to all of Isabelle's basic functionality, such as forward and backward resolution, simplification, and construction of tactics. It further provides a sophisticated replay mechanism in which external changes are propagated to all objects depending on the changed external objects.

Figure 2 shows a screenshot of IsaWin. We can see the notepad in the upper window, where icons represent theorems, rewriting sets, theories, ongoing proofs and texts. The construction area in the lower window shows an ongoing proof. Theorems and rewriting sets are applied by dragging them into the construction area, where tactical operations such as backward resolution or simplification are triggered, depending on the settings of the tactical buttons on the left of the construction area, and on the type of the object.

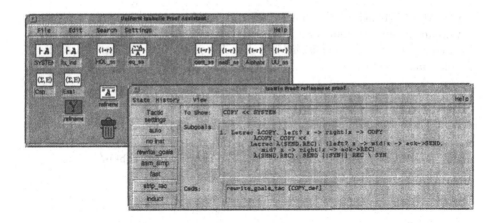

Fig. 2. Theorem Proving with IsaWin.

System Architecture

Both TAS and IsaWin are entirely implemented in Standard ML (SML) as a conservative extension of Isabelle. This approach allows us to take advantage of SML's powerful modularisation mechanisms, and at the same time preserve logical consistency. In particular, we provide a generic graphical user interface GenGUI which is a parameterised module that yields graphical user interfaces by instantiating its parameter. For its implementation we have developed a functional encapsulation of the interface-building library Tcl/Tk into SML, called sml_tk [6]. Consistency is preserved since SML's type system restricts the construction of new theorems. For more details of the system architecture, we refer to [7].

A consequence of this approach is that all tools obtained by instantiating the generic graphical user interface GenGUI have a uniform visual appearance (cf. Fig. 1 and Fig. 2). Their main windows always comprise the notepad and the construction area. The notepad contains icons representing the objects, which can be dragged, moved and dropped onto each other, whereas the construction area allows a more refined manipulation of an object's internals, providing history navigation and replay mechanisms at a generic level.

Moreover, both TAS and IsaWin can be instantiated with any formal method or logic embedded into Isabelle. For TAS, the formal method has to provide a notion of correctness-preserving refinement, such as logical implication in higher-order logic or process refinement in CSP. We will present instantiations with the encapsulations of CSP [10], Z [2,4] and CASL [8].

The UniForM Workbench

TAS and IsaWin have been developed during the UniForM project [3], the aim of which is to integrate different formal methods in a logically consistent way. The

UniForM Workbench [1, 5] embeds TAS and IsaWin into an integrated software development environment, providing servives such as type-safe communication with cooperating tools, persistent and distributed storage, version and configuration management.

Obtaining TAS and IsaWin

In time for the presentation, prototypical versions of TAS and IsaWin will be available from http://www.informatik.uni-bremen.de/~agbkb/.

References

1. E. W. Karlsen. *Tool Integration in a Functional Setting*. PhD thesis, Universität Bremen, 1998.
2. Kolyang, T. Santen, and B. Wolff. A structure preserving encoding of Z in Isabelle/HOL. In J. von Wright, J. Grundy, and J. Harrison, editors, *Theorem Proving in Higher Order Logics — 9th International Conference*, number 1125 in LNCS, pages 283 –298. Springer, 1996.
3. B. Krieg-Brückner. UniForM perspectives for formal methods. In *International Workshop on Current Trends in Formal Methods*, To appear in LNCS. Springer, 1998.
4. C. Lüth, E. W. Karlsen, Kolyang, S. Westmeier, and B. Wolff. Hol-Z in the UniForM-workbench – a case study in tool integration for Z. In J. P. Bowen, A. Fett, and M. G. Hinchey, editors, *ZUM'98: The Z Formal Specification Notation*, volume 1493 of *LNCS*, pages 116–134. Springer, 1998.
5. C. Lüth, E. W. Karlsen, Kolyang, S. Westmeier, and B. Wolff. Tool integration in the UniForM workbench. In *Workshop on Tool Support for System Specification, Development, and Verification*, Advances in Computing Science. Springer, June 1998. To appear.
6. C. Lüth, S. Westmeier, and B. Wolff. sml_tk: Functional programming for graphical user interfaces. Technical Report 7/96, Universität Bremen, 1996. See also the sml_tk home page at http://www.informatik.uni-bremen.de/~cxl/sml_tk/.
7. C. Lüth and B. Wolf. Functional design and implementation of graphical user interfaces for theorem provers. *Journal of Functional Programming*. To appear.
8. T. Mossakowski, Kolyang, and B. Krieg-Brückner. Static semantic analysis and theorem proving for CASL. In *12th Workshop on Algebraic Development Techniques*, number 1376 in LNCS, pages 349– 364. Springer, 1997.
9. L. C. Paulson. *Isabelle - A Generic Theorem Prover*. Number 828 in LNCS. Springer, 1994.
10. H. Tej and B. Wolff. A corrected failure-divergence model for CSP in Isabelle/HOL. In J. Fitzgerald, C. B. Jones, and P. Lucas, editors, *Proceedings of the FME '97 — Industrial Applications and Strengthened Foundations of Formal Methods*, number 1313 in LNCS, pages 318– 337. Springer, 1997.

System Requirements

Hardware:

- Sun Sparc or ULTRA-Sparc; on other systems, availability of Standard ML of New Jersey (Version 109) is a precondition;
- At least 96MB of memory to run, more to compile (only necessary on non-Sparc systems);
- Disk space: 100 MB.

Software:

- Solaris 2.5 or 2.6;
- Tcl/Tk Version 8.0, Netscape Version 4 (can be installed by us if required).

Author Index

Springer
and the
environment

At Springer we firmly believe that an international science publisher has a special obligation to the environment, and our corporate policies consistently reflect this conviction.

We also expect our business partners – paper mills, printers, packaging manufacturers, etc. – to commit themselves to using materials and production processes that do not harm the environment. The paper in this book is made from low- or no-chlorine pulp and is acid free, in conformance with international standards for paper permanency.

Lecture Notes in Computer Science

For information about Vols. 1–1484
please contact your bookseller or Springer-Verlag